CUPCAKES AND COURAGE

✦

Jennifer Brunner

Little Blue Valiant Publishing

Columbus, Ohio

CUPCAKES AND COURAGE

Second Edition
Published by Little Blue Valiant Publishing
35 N. Fourth Street, Suite 200
Columbus, Ohio 43215 USA
www.cupcakesandcourage.com

Brunner, Jennifer, 1957-
Cupcakes and Courage / Jennifer Brunner
ISBN 978-0-9881953-0-1

Cover design by Jennifer Brunner using CreateSpace
Interior design by Jennifer Brunner
Printed in the United States of America by Amazon.com
Distributed by Amazon.com and the author

DEDICATION

This book is dedicated to Rick, Kate, Laura and John with thanks and respect for their sacrifices, support and affection. It is dedicated to each of them with love, for that is what makes courage possible.

Jennifer Brunner

CUPCAKES AND COURAGE

Contents

Jennifer Brunner

ACKNOWLEDGEMENTS

Thanks go to many people in the process of writing and editing this book. When I read Gloria Feldt's book, *No Excuses: Nine Ways Women Can Change How We Think About Power*, I summoned the courage to write it, and I am grateful to her for volunteering to read it and write its introduction and for giving me advice and direction on publishing.

My husband, Rick, suffered my writing this book on what were supposed to be our vacations together over the course of more than a year. He snuck peeks at it while it was underway and encouraged me to keep writing. He pledged his belief in my story and ability to convey it, reviewed and suggested changes in many drafts of the manuscript and reminded me of events to complete the story.

My mother, Barbara Gates, has believed in me always. As a practical mother does, she said to check all of my facts, which I have. Barbara Gould, one of the women mentioned in that same-titled chapter, "Women," and her husband, Bill Motto, have been invaluable sources of encouragement, inspiration, exhortation and critique. She has stood with me with through personal and political thick and thin with extraordinary insight, support and friendship.

Kellye Pinkleton and Ross Goldsmith helped with the practical aspects along the way, with fact-checking and constant enthusiasm. Courtney Kasuboski helped me get the story to the point it could be published and distributed with exceptional skill and aplomb, and Chelsey Kovach helped with proofing and preparation along the way. Jeff Ortega encouraged me to keep telling my story and to do it in my own way. My Aunt, Barbara Jane Patton, agreed to read the book and helped me accurately reflect a history we share.

My thanks to Laura, my daughter, who said the obvious, "Mom, I think you're going to p*!% off some people," and to the one she favors, my sister, Kathy, who said, "Well, Jen, I guess how honest you are depends on just how much you care about p*!%ing them off." Fortunately, or unfortunately, being afraid of doing that has never been a forte of mine in politics.

I thank my sister, Andrea, whom I don't remember ever being without in my life. Together, we had the time of our lives, bringing Gloria Feldt to Columbus to show women and men there her empowering message firsthand. My brother, Dan, introduced me to the unspeakable vagaries of the recent practices of the banking and financial industry that led to its near collapse in 2008. With his help, some prodding from colleague Mike Rankin with a key *Rolling Stone* article on the financial debacle and valuable, initial tutelage from Louis Beck, a conscientious Cincinnati banker, I researched in my U.S. Senate campaign the integrity of a system that has intertwined itself in politics and public policy to all of their—and our—detriment.

Kate and John, Rick's and my other two children, made sacrifices at early ages as campaign staffers in the Secretary of State's race, (and strangely never wanted to be part of a campaign staff again), while Rick dedicated countless hours working as an integral advisor and speaker for all of my campaigns, with Laura cheering us on and recruiting supporters from Boston and New York. I am grateful to them and others in my family for helping me to reach the statewide office that lent itself to these and other untold experiences.

Ohio's United Food and Commercial Workers locals, all of the state's Plumbers and Pipefitters locals and the vast majority of Ohio local unions of International Brotherhood of Electrical Workers, Laborers Local 310 in Cleveland, and many other local unions had the courage to step up in a U.S. Senate primary where the pressure was intense to say and do nothing. They are part of the reason we simply themed our 2010 Senate campaign, "Courage." There were countless campaign workers, volunteers, financial supporters, Facebook friends, Twitter followers and enthusiasts who made successful in its own way a Senate race that my campaign manager

David Dettman called the toughest Senate primary campaign in the country in 2010. It was an amazingly rewarding experience to write about in spite of its outcome.

The Women's Campaign Fund, and specifically, Siobhan "Sam" Bennett, Clare Bresnahan and Julie Daniels (formerly of WCF), have been steadfast supporters of my work in writing this book and when I was a candidate for the United States Senate. Our shared cause of seeing more women elected to office convinces us that government and politics can and will perform better—for all of us—when that happens.

There are countless other friends, coworkers, campaign staff, volunteers, enemies and "frenemies" from politics and life who have helped shape the experiences that are a part of this book. Suffice it to say, I am grateful to each one of them.

✧

INTRODUCTION

By Gloria Feldt

Jennifer Brunner, My American Hero

> *"Many have questioned the efficacy of our [2004] Presidential election in Ohio. I simply questioned its fairness of process."*

> —Jennifer Brunner

My grandparents were all immigrants from tyrant-ruled Eastern Europe during the early decades of the 20th century. They treasured their voting rights as only new citizens can, and they instilled in me their almost sappy love of the American ideals of liberty, justice, and fairness, which you were supposed to get through participating in the democratic process.

Having struggled to get to their promised land, they considered voting their sacred duty. Every election, no matter what. They weren't naïve about politics, nor did they expect their favored candidates to win every time. They just wanted their votes counted honestly and their voices heard fairly.

They would have loved Jennifer Brunner, Ohio's first female Secretary of State. Her passion for fairness in the democratic process shines through every page of her book.

She's a true American hero for cleaning up the state's election system after its 2004 debacle, one that is remembered as one of the most sordid chapters in our nation's history.

Ohio is a perennial battleground state. It has been pivotal to the outcome of every Presidential election in recent history. And since 1944, as Ohio has gone, so has the nation with only one exception, when voters chose Nixon over Kennedy in 1960.

Most elections are won or lost with a mere 2 percent swing. So the consequences of even a scintilla of voter suppression or a few malfunctioning voting machines can turn an entire election and change the course of history. That's why if we want honest elections, we want someone like Brunner with her steady unbiased compass.

Make no mistake: she's a smart lawyer and seasoned political pro, having run for, been elected to, and served in multiple offices, which the book reveals in fascinating detail. But in her forthright memoir, *Cupcakes and Courage,* you see firsthand the qualitative difference between a mere politician and an elected official who is first and foremost a public servant.

Brunner, who was elected Secretary of State in 2008 and served an action-packed four-year term, tells the inspiring story of her life's defining moments, both personal and political. It's a compelling narrative, full of juicy anecdotes that illustrate the power of the individual to make a difference. But unlike the single pink-frosted cupcake on its cover, *Cupcakes* is not an individualistic story—far from it.

Deeply rooted in values of family and social responsibility, this book depicts the journey of a girl who took those values into public service as a woman who audaciously trudged through bi-partisan criticism to protect the rights of the individual voter.

Brunner's unwavering focus on fairness and transparency brought major changes to Ohio's 2008 electoral processes, which in turn helped to restore voter confidence. Her unflinching description of what she did and why after the 2004 Presidential election turned on the shifting sands of Cuyahoga County's voting irregularities[1] deserves to be a political science class staple.

---

[1]

http://whatreallyhappened.com/WRHARTICLES/2004votefraud_ohio .html

Not surprisingly, the masthead of Courage PAC, a political action committee Brunner formed after her unsuccessful 2010 run for U.S. Senate, quotes Thomas Jefferson: "One person with courage is a majority."

Brunner wrote down four goals she wanted to fulfill during her tenure as Secretary of State. What struck me immediately was that each of them is about good governance. All focus on the people of Ohio, on their needs and making democratic governance work for people. How often do you see that?

Unlike so many political leaders whose carefully spun "messaging" aims to obscure rather than amplify the facts, her watchwords are plain and direct: fairness, honest outcomes, and efficient responses to citizen needs. And while many voters today are turned off by candidates who seem to grasp for power and position for its own sake, you just know that Jennifer Brunner is at her core about ideals, not ideology.

She's not without ego. No one could endure the rigors of running for public office, let alone running to win, without a healthy sense of self worth and a strong dose of ambition to make her mark. She's a political animal in the best sense of the term. Someone who knows not just how to make the wheels turn but where the levers are that make them turn most efficiently and effectively. And she has the courage to gun the engine when need be, to move things forward despite the inevitable drag of inertia or self-interested opponents of progress.

She tells her own story with the same kind of meticulousness and honesty that has defined her public service, both in and out of public office.

The cupcakes reflect her solid grounding in the reality of people's lives. Cupcakes speak of simplicity, hominess, community. Her campaign fundraisers involved many neighborhood house parties—"Cupcakes and Coffee" conversations with voters.

The courage emanates from Brunner's core values that drive her intentions and push her to persist in achieving her goals even when others say she can't, or shouldn't risk trying. Her story is the story of every concerned citizen and every voter who wants a say. And it's a rare, detailed explanation of a politician's thinking, her planning, her tactical approaches.

Voting rights—yes, even in my grandparents' rosy view of America—can be as fragile and as fleeting as they are in non-democratic nations around the globe. As a girl growing up in Texas, I heard the rumors of Lyndon Johnson stuffing ballot boxes in Jim Wells County with ballots of dead people.2 We might think those poll taxes, literacy tests, and other Jim Crow laws instituted in the South after the Civil War, and lasting well into the mid-20th Century,3 are well behind us.

But history is repeating itself today in the current wave of voter suppression initiatives sweeping the country. Just as a house that has been cleaned can become a mess again in record time, so the Ohio voting process that Brunner cleaned up—or any state that falls prey to divisive, partisan abuse of power—can be, and in many battleground states, is faced with the risk of corruption and the contortion of the voice and will of its people.

As it has ever been historically, it is often minorities who receive the short end of the voting rights stick. How tragic, considering that this country is the product of minorities, like my patriotic grandparents, at its core.

---

2 http://www.nytimes.com/1990/02/11/us/how-johnson-won-election-he-d-lost.html?pagewanted=all&src=pm
3 http://americanhistory.si.edu/brown/history/1-segregated/white-only-1.html

Even since leaving office, Brunner has held fast to protecting voting rights, starting Fair Elections Ohio, a group that successfully fought back harmful Ohio voter suppression legislation, keeping 2008 voting rules in place for 2012. She has been a strong and steady force that has made Ohio a bright spot in a sea of 2011 and 2012 voter suppression activities across the country.

That's why *Cupcakes and Courage* is such an important book. Through a memoir, it tells a story that, taken to heart, is surely a shake-up for anyone who reads it. The lessons in it are an urgent call to action for the elections this November and beyond. It's a cautionary tale about what happens to democracy when those who can't win honestly manipulate the rules—and how that can be overcome to put a broken democratic process together again.

In 2004, "Cuyahoga County" became a household term, and thus entered the political junkie's lexicon as a metaphor for voter suppression. Grab a cupcake and a cup of coffee and read how one woman with courage can inspire us to prevent the scandalous 2004 election history from happening ever again.

—Gloria Feldt: Author, *No Excuses: 9 Ways Women Can Change How We Think About Power* and co-founder of Take The Lead; former president, Planned Parenthood Federation of America

REFERENCES:

Vote Fraud and 2004 elections:

"Charges of Fraud and Voter Suppression Already Flying" (this one has plenty of brief examples of fraud in multiple states)

http://www.nytimes.com/2004/11/01/politics/campaign/01votin
g.html

On Individual Voter Fraud:

"In 5-Year Effort, Scant Evidence of Voter Fraud"

http://www.nytimes.com/2007/04/12/washington/12fraud.html
?_r=1&pagewanted=all

On Jennifer Brunner's Work After Leaving Office:

Voter ID Laws: Voters' Fate and the Buckeye State
The Washington Spectator, February 10, 2012
Lou DuBose

> "As it turned out, Brunner did more for fair elections in Ohio
> after she was out of office. Barack Obama cannot be reelected
> in 2012 without Ohio's 20 electoral votes. If he is reelected, he
> will owe a debt to Brunner.
>
> In fact, every Democrat working to repeal the "voter reform"
> laws passed by Republican Legislatures since 2007 is indebted
> to Brunner, who ran the first successful campaign outside the
> legal system to overturn a voter-suppression law enacted by a
> state legislature.
>
> Ohio's H.B. 194 imposed drastic restrictions on early voting by
> mail and in person; prohibited voting on Saturday afternoons,
> Sundays, and in the three days before the election; and
> stopped counties from mailing unsolicited absentee-ballot
> applications to voters. Perversely, the bill would have
> prohibited a poll worker from telling a voter that he is in the
> wrong precinct and directing him to the correct one."

Alleged Kennedy Vote Fraud:

"Was Nixon Robbed?"

http://www.slate.com/articles/news_and_politics/history_lesso
n/2000/10/was_nixon_robbed.html

Alleged Lyndon B. Johnson Vote Fraud:

"How Johnson Won Election He'd Lost"

http://www.nytimes.com/1990/02/11/us/how-johnson-won-
election-he-d-lost.html?pagewanted=all&src=pm

Segregation of African-Americans in the US voting system:

"White Only: Jim Crow in America"

http://americanhistory.si.edu/brown/history/1-
segregated/white-only-1.html

RECENT RESOURCES:

This one is recent and crazy--"Former Florida GOP Leader:
Party Openly Discussed Suppressing African-American Vote"

http://www.democracynow.org/2012/8/1/headlines/former_flori
da_gop_leader_party_openly_discussed_suppressing_african_a
merican_vote

"Voter Suppression and Political Polls"

http://campaignstops.blogs.nytimes.com/2012/08/01/voter-
suppression-and-political-polls/

Some recent info on the newly vetoed voter ID law: "Think
Voter ID Laws Couldn't Cost You Your Vote? Think Again."

http://www.huffingtonpost.com/2012/07/25/voter-id-laws-scenarios_n_1699746.html

http://www.nytimes.com/2012/08/18/world/europe/suspense-ahead-of-verdict-for-jailed-russian-punk-band.html?_r=1&nl=afternoonupdate&emc=edit_au_20120820

http://www.huffingtonpost.com/2012/07/25/voter-id-laws-scenarios_n_1699746.html#slide=1269304

http://www.npr.org/2011/07/18/138160440/the-politics-behind-new-voter-id-laws?f=1014&ft=1&sc=tw

"The Ed Show," 8/24/12, MSNBC, with former Ohio Secretary of State Jennifer Brunner and Ohio State Senator Nina Turner

http://www.msnbc.msn.com/id/45755822/ns/msnbc_tv-the_ed_show/#48773214

None dare call it stolen: Ohio, the election, and America's servile press

By Mark Crispin Miller

http://www.harpers.org/archive/2005/08/0080696

✧

PREFACE

The courage of life is often a less dramatic
spectacle than the courage of a final moment, but
it is no less than a magnificent mixture of
triumph and tragedy. People do what they must--
in spite of personal consequences, in spite of
obstacles and dangers and pressures--and that is
the basis of all human morality.

- John F. Kennedy

This quotation from President Kennedy describes what I have observed to be the general character of the people of Ohio. Having served first as a state trial court judge, then as Ohio's Secretary of State and finally as a candidate for the U.S. Senate, I have seen firsthand as I've worked with jurors, witnesses, probation officers and others in the justice system and traveled my state in campaigns and in the duties of statewide office the quiet courage of people in all walks of life when given the chance to be expressed. This is what has made my experiences remarkable. This everyday courage I have seen makes me love my state and country more with each foray into its many communities and facets of daily life. Ohio's diversity is a strong reflection of the lives of Americans in general, and that diversity is one of our nation's real strengths.

Bettina R. Flores said that, "Courage is the atom of change." It is this everyday courage of so many that will allow Ohio—and the country—which are beginning to emerge from some of the worst hardships of memory, to continue to move forward. Aristotle said, "Courage is the first of human qualities because it is the quality which guarantees the others." It is this morality of daily courage in Ohioans and Americans that imbues the vision of the American dream and the hope always for better days. Honoring and respecting that courage allows it to breathe into the fabric of our community resolve for the days ahead.

PROLOGUE

I almost didn't write this book. "I'll never be able to run for office again, if I write anything close to what really happened and how I felt about it," I said.

My pollster in the 2010 U.S. Senate Ohio Democratic primary, Celinda Lake, agreed. She knows what usually happens when truth is spoken to power—power squelches truth, or at least makes sure it never comes out again.

As I began to read Stacy Schiff's recent biography of Cleopatra, *Cleopatra, A Life*, I was struck by that fact that, even though Cleopatra was one of the most powerful rulers in the civilized world during her time, she had never controlled the narrative of her reign. Stacy Schiff is the *first* female author to write Cleopatra's biography, having published it in 2011. Cleopatra reigned from 51 to 31 B.C. She has been referred to throughout history as a "shameless temptress," as using overt sexuality to hold the Egyptian throne, and so on. She offered much more in her time, being the first in many generations to actually learn the Egyptian language (her line of ancestry as a member of the Ptolemy family, who were Greek, acquired the empire after the death of Alexander the Great). Despite her many skills and accomplishments, Cleopatra did not create or preserve the truly human chronicle of her history.

By telling my story, some of the less savory practices in politics may be exposed, but that's the chance anyone takes when they tell their story. Taking that chance may encourage others to speak up, to stand up, and to press for change, which can happen when dissonance is seen as susceptible to harmony. If we can clear the sluggish channels to the root system for power in democracy—campaigns and elections—perhaps more people who simply want to serve can more easily do so.

I ran for office because my passion is fairness. Fairness in a democracy means a system that respects, values, fosters and protects individual rights and equality. Fighting for what is fair has helped me overcome some of my greatest fears, because when you're flying, you must look ahead and not down. Wanting to see fairness in the world propelled me to run first for judge and later for Secretary of State, even though I had sworn off running for office after being the lawyer for political candidates who had left me "not-so-enthused" to become one of them.

That belief and passion (and a healthy dose of hard work) helped me win my first race in a largely conservative county. It later gave me the gumption to leave that office so I could run for a statewide nonjudicial office to serve as Ohio's Secretary of State. I ran because I thought my help was needed.

In 2006, I became the first woman to be elected Secretary of State in Ohio, the nation's seventh largest state, since statehood in 1803. I was the fifth woman in state history to win an executive statewide office in her own right. Once elected, I had twenty-two months to ensure the administration of a clean and smoothly run election. In 2008, Ohio did it. We held a Presidential election vastly different from 2004, one not marred with long lines or Election Day lawsuits, with more than eleven thousand precincts closing on time and returns calmly coming in on a timely basis.

In 2008, Ohio proved to the country that we not only mattered, but that we could make our mark with dignity, despite the squall of partisan storms. Ohio is a microcosm of the rest of the country. As Ohio reaches for a new economy in a new century, the rest of the U.S. can observe and learn from our microcosmic struggles.

Because Ohio is so intrinsically Midwestern, our almost caricature of belief in the individual, that one person can make a difference, is inspirational. To those more jaded souls and regions that believe that what the U.S. has to offer the world is somehow dimming or tarnished, Ohio is not ready to give up, no matter how hard it gets.

Part of Ohio's economic and social strength that helped us lead the nation for years also has led to its need for change. Ohio, as the nation's seventeenth state, boasted traditionally heavy manufacturing and agricultural economies with attendant social and political structures that grew from the male dominated nature of the work. It's not surprising then that no Ohio woman before me ever served as our state's chief elections official. This is in part, I believe, because of the power associated with the position, to appoint and remove election officials among the state's eighty-eight counties and to direct their activities in the most fundamental exercise of power in a democracy—elections and voting. The institutionalized, statutory inclusion of political parties in the process of managing Ohio's elections creates pure, raw, hardscrabble politics that were previously wrestled with from only a male perspective.

No woman before me has ever run for the U.S. Senate from Ohio from the position of already holding statewide office— other women before me held no office or a county office. I knew when I ran for the U.S. Senate in 2010 that it really wasn't about me. My decision to run was about giving a voice to more than fifty percent of the people of my state, women, who have never been represented by anyone like them, someone who knows many of their life experiences, because she has lived them. Sadly, my state still lacks a victory for a woman in even a primary election for U.S. Senate or for the office of governor, but that's not the point of my story.

I didn't win that Senate seat. But I gained a first-person perspective on my state. I am convinced that if we start to tackle changing the political paradigm, many new voices can be added to the dialog, and we will benefit from them in office. Each one of us comes from a unique vantage point, personally, historically and from perspectives such as gender, race, nationality, religious orientation, sexual orientation and gender identity, to name a few. That diversity, honored and taken *together,* forms and informs our social and economic strength.

I have gained a perspective that is different than I would have found in an electoral victory and subsequent entrance into the Senate at this time. The shooting of Congresswoman Gabrielle Giffords is a sobering moment in our history. My mother, as only a mother could, is glad I have made an exit from elective office. I, for one, am glad for the time to finally write about what I've seen. It is something that needs to be shared.

If more who run for office, women and men, would have the courage to simply speak what is in their hearts about why they're running, about what they see in their communities, about how they want to, and can, help—antithetical, bullying, political-machine, money-based politics, the ilk of which actually damages democracy, would wither on its own vines of destruction. The simple desire to serve the public necessarily means inclusion and not division. Because I believe in people, I believe this simple desire will, in the end, win the day. And then, those choosing their governance will have a better idea of whom they are really electing to office and what to expect of them.

When I ran for the U.S. Senate, I said I wanted to change the Democratic paradigm. I still do. But it's not just the Democratic paradigm. The *political* paradigm in general must change so that many Americans who find themselves more and more disillusioned with our nation's political process will not turn away for good.

I believe we can change this, especially as widespread access to telecommunications increases, and the power of the individual—so very American—is further strengthened. With this kind of access to information and direct communication, that one person can make a difference will be reinforced again and again to everyday Americans. Despite the threat of some multi-national interests to discourage and thwart people from coming together for not much more than the latest social networking or marketing scheme, this never-before-seen access to one another is essential for repairing, strengthening and refashioning the character of the American tapestry. We have the tools to inform and strengthen the democracy that is at the core of who we are. We can and must use these tools to help honor and protect each individual voice through the vote.

In a democracy every voice matters. Joining those voices together, we're stronger. America, as never before, can prove that. With the cacophony of forces working to separate us from one another, honoring the individual while calling each of them together can stop the ambivalence that fosters only a few benefitting, often and, tragically, at the expense of many.

Even though we are a venerable democracy, our work begins anew as we traverse through new times, new technologies and new challenges. Today, we have the means to communicate as never before. I remain convinced that the human spirit and the longing for peaceful community cannot be squelched, held down or extinguished and remains to be expressed in new and ever changing ways. It is through this power of people and their better natures that democracy will survive and prevail, because democracy empowers those who honor it. ✧

PART I

✦

BUILDING A STRONG FOUNDATION

Chapter 1

Click!

As we headed toward Dayton in an unmarked State Highway Patrol car driven by a plain-clothes trooper, I looked from the front passenger seat to the back seat as Jeff Ortega clicked off his Blackberry and said, "Well, there's a poll out that runs you against Senator Voinovich."

"How bad is it?" I said. "You're up 42 to 38," he said matter-of-factly, grinning. "Fisher's at 40, and there are others in the low 30's, like Congressman Tim Ryan, running behind Senator Voinovich." I shook my head, incredulous.

It was October of 2008, one month before the U.S. Presidential election in Ohio. In the patrol car along with Jeff and me were our driver, Hugh Fredendall, and my trusted aide, Emily Puffenberger. Jeff had been a reporter for fifteen years before he came to work for me—six years as Statehouse bureau chief for Dix Newspapers, with experience at *The Vindicator* of Youngstown, *The Columbus Dispatch*, *Springfield News-Sun*, the Associated Press wire service and Gongwer News Service.

As Ohio's Secretary of State I faced the daunting challenge of changing Ohio's reputation in Presidential elections as the whole nation watched. At least one state trooper went with me everywhere I went, sometimes two, while a patrol car guarded my house around the clock. By now my family and I had received multiple death threats (for election administration), ginned up by the wild and constant GOP accusations of voter fraud that were helping to sell ads for Fox News and CNN.

Paid Republican radio ads were being run against me—when I wasn't even on the ballot. Along with charges of voter fraud, there were attacks from Greta Van Susteran of national Fox News, Lou Dobbs of CNN and Rush Limbaugh, a reactionary radio personality. There were past and present Republican statewide officials coming together in widely covered press conferences literally standing side-by-side in a photo op for all, in opposition to the policies I had put in place to follow state and federal election law.

There were Sunday morning talk show critiques from the likes of future U.S. Senator Rob Portman as he positioned himself to run for the Senate seat I did not know at the time I would be seeking less than two years later. There were also the usual vitriolic blogging and newspaper headlines, along with a special website showing my head on the body of a buff football player. I was depicted as "wearing the jersey" of the blue team, the Democrats, in supervising Ohio's Presidential election.

By this point, I had won a bipartisan Profile in Courage Award for election work in Ohio's Presidential primary in March 2008. After I received it, I often looked at the shiny platinum silver lantern in its beautiful museum case in my state office. Senator Ted Kennedy and Caroline Kennedy had given the award to me. Shaking my head in times of doubt, of which there were many, I would think to myself, "Well, *someone* thinks I have courage, so I must." And I would keep going.

My staff attorneys and I had already taken bets on how many times we would be sued in the general election season. My wager was 8 times, but it was actually fifteen lawsuits in an eight-week period, including one that went all the way to the U.S. Supreme Court. There we prevailed with a unanimous decision delivered two days after we filed the appeal in mid-October 2008.

I took office as Ohio's fifty-second and first woman Secretary of State knowing that I had just 22 months to turn around a process that had been maligned from Uganda to Kazakhstan and from New York to California. My predecessor in office had been the object of derision, with slings and arrows lobbed at him from around the country and the world, in my opinion usually deservedly, for decisions that were difficult to characterize as anything other than partisan and self-serving. He had overseen the previous Presidential election in 2004, when Ohio's then 20 electoral votes pulled President George W. Bush across the finish line for reelection. Voting conditions were terrible; charges of voter suppression were rampant, and people far and wide did not forget Ohio's 2004 Presidential election. It was my job to restore trust to Ohio elections and in the process return some dignity and respect to my state in the eyes of the nation.

Elections in Ohio are intense. Ohio is a "purple" state that swings periodically from Republican to Democratic and back, reflecting and portending the national mood as one of the nation's microcosms. People like President Barack Obama's campaign manager, David Plouffe, are absolutely fixated on Ohio, and especially on Ohio women in their 50's—like me.

From my experience in Ohio, I find that Republicans are generally convinced that too many people are voting by committing voter fraud, and Democrats are generally sure not enough people are voting, because they're experiencing voter suppression. When you're the arbiter of that, usually everyone is mad at you and you're best to keep your eye (and your actions) on the goal. The result is not the aim, but rather, a smooth election where every eligible voter has the opportunity to vote. That's it, plain and simple.

I was privileged to administer one of the more historic elections in U.S. history in the battleground state of Ohio in the election of Barack Obama. It was a moving experience to preside over Ohio's Electoral College session in which the country elected its first African American president nearly 150 years after President Abraham Lincoln's 1863 Emancipation Proclamation. I was later privileged to be the first woman in Ohio holding statewide office to run for the U.S. Senate.

These experiences taught me a great deal about the character of Ohioans and Americans and about the very nature of democracy. I remain amazed by their character, molded and shaped by and in turn molding and shaping a society that is infused and held together with and at times tormented by democracy, equality and freedom of expression like no other in the known history of humanity.

This is the story from the trenches of elections and politics in a country that is desperately trying to live up to its dreams. This is the story about people and their very traits that make us as a nation both great and at terrible risk of losing our character and heritage in an ever-growing and changing world. It may be the story of one person, but it could be the story of any person who loves their country, their community and their family and cares enough to do something about it. ≈

Chapter 2

Small Town Spirit

Small towns often necessitate that people who live in them do with what they have. In small towns, people make connections that bind them strongly, no matter where they go. The familiarities, coincidences and occurrences of lives in small towns often incubate the faith and courage needed to take risks and to test ideas and fortunes far and wide in a larger world. Small towns tend to help those who are a part of them stay rooted to the values that helped shape their very characters.

Even though the only childhood home I can remember was in the state's capital, Columbus, Ohio, I spent a great deal of time during my childhood in the small town where my parents grew up, South Charleston, Ohio. It prepared me for the hundreds of small towns across Ohio I would see in campaigns. In these towns people tend their small businesses,

Benton Kidwell, my great grandfather, at his gas station in S. Charleston, Ohio, corner of St. Rtes. 42 and 41. Circa 1945

work on farms, raise their children, attend Friday night high school football games, hold bake sales, gossip at the grocery, fight with and support each other and mold their American characters. My parents met and grew up in South Charleston, which is so small that people there still today go to the post office to get their mail. They often exchange news at the local bank, located in the center of town. Until my parents had my younger brother, Dan, and my youngest sister, Kathy, they made the hour drive to that little town, located near Springfield, in Clark County, Ohio, nearly every Sunday for dinner. It was a rural tradition that has largely faded away, except perhaps in families of recent immigrants.

I still remember my mother's Jackie Kennedy-esque hairdo, full of hairspray and coiffed just right, and my tall, lean, lanky dad who had the longest arms in the world if you acted up in the back seat. In the days of my childhood, both parents smoked in the car with all the windows up, and sometimes my mom painted her nails as Dad drove. It's no wonder my sister, Andrea, and I used to bulge our eyes, clutch our throats and feign gagging in the back seat, untethered by seat belts. And it's no wonder we became carsick on an hour's car ride from Columbus to South Charleston and had to take nasty orange Dramamine pills.

When you grow up with the last name of "Junk," which really is my maiden name, it's a given that your life will be at least interesting—and that you're pretty good at spelling four-letter words, since I usually had to say, "My name is Jennifer Junk, J-U-N-K." My Grandmother Junk used to say it was an English name, but it is German, from the Mosel River Valley (a territory that passed back and forth between the Germans and the French numerous times in history). I have looked at pictures of my triple-great grandfather, Clinton Junk, who seemed to be the most procreative relative on that side. His large "Junk" nose (which I've seen repeated about sixty times at one extended family reunion in 1988) definitely made him look like a little Frenchman with a German name.

There were the Swans, my mother's side of the family, proved by Great Uncle Merrill to have descended from the Mayflower, with Diguery Priest (a nonconformist minister) directly linked as my twelfth or thirteenth great grandfather (and some first cousins marrying in the chain of grandparentage). With both sets of parents from a small town, there seemed to be an underlying competition about which side was more respectable.

One thing I know for sure—in this little town, the American dream of prosperity from honest and hard work was alive and well when my parents were growing up. I'm told that my mother's brother, Uncle Skip (named for his dad, Glendon Oscar Swan, Sr.) once called Harvard and Yale to inquire what courses his sons should take in middle school to be able to study there for future medical careers. And that same uncle tried to make it as a walk-on member for the famed Ohio State Buckeyes football team. Even though he didn't make it, he became an expert tool and die maker at International Harvester in Springfield and later framed basement walls in my home when his three grandchildren lived with Rick and me for two and a half years.

My uncle's kind of dream was alive and well in small towns like South Charleston across Ohio and America. But, it took the kind of drive that my mother told me my dad had to make it. My dad had cured his own pigeon-toed-ness by turning his feet out on his early morning paper routes as he walked, folded and threw papers in the light of dawn.

A dream becomes a vision when it is communicated. So my parents communicated that dream to me. They salted it with lessons along the way that grounded me, like, every action has a consequence for which you must be willing to "pay the price." No matter what, win or lose, my parents made sure I always knew they loved me and always would, and that is a lot to send a kid off into the world with.

My mother taught me the practical things about self-confidence. She said to look in the mirror at myself before I left for the day, and if I was satisfied with my appearance, forget about it, knowing I had no worries in that department. She said of the ups and downs with my girlfriends, "Never let them get your goat." My dad emphasized it, and both of my parents demonstrated to me, that if you're honest and you work hard you'll always "get by." I learned that these were critical foundations to successfully navigating any ship of dreams.

This was the only varsity sport a girl could "compete in" at my public high school in 1974

In high school, what simply became known as "Title IX" took effect during my senior year. Finally, girls were allowed to compete in as many sports as boys. For many girls, athletic achievement finally could be in more than cheerleading or intramural softball or volleyball. By this time, my best "sport" had become cheerleading, but despite its limitations, it taught me about leadership.

By my senior year, I had become a bit jaundiced in my attitude about why girls had to play a sideline role, wear short skirts and "spankies" and jump on trampolines doing split jumps in the air. We weren't allowed to ride the bus with the boys on the team, but rather, we had to risk the inexperience of teenage driving ourselves to games. As cheerleaders, we had to dress provocatively in our uniforms, flaunting it on game days in the name of "school spirit" and at games in front of our and other students' parents. No one thought it was odd.

Better yet, our cheerleading advisor was a man who sat in a student desk-chair during practice and read the "Living Bible," a popular version at the time, barely looking up. I suppose he was there to make sure we didn't kill ourselves on the linoleum tile floor of the high school foyer where we practiced, since the boys' basketball team had the gym for practice. Yet, despite his seeming disinterest, he invited the girls on both the varsity and reserve squads to his farm and didn't hesitate to wrestle in the hayloft with them.

Nearly thirty years later when I was judge, I sat on the court's personnel committee to select a new executive director, and was shocked to see my old cheerleading advisor's resume in the pile of applications. "This one looks pretty impressive," said one of the long-time male judges on the committee. Without hesitating I quipped, "Go ahead and interview him if you want to deal with sexual harassment here at the court."

He looked at me quizzically. I said, "He was my cheerleading advisor in high school. Don't ask." And that was that. He never got an interview, and he never knew why. Small town experience teaches that we are part of a community, and how we treat one another in that community has lasting consequences. We pay the price for our actions.

For the first time, during my senior year of high school, there was a girl's track team. I ran the mile like my dad had at Southeastern High School in Clark County, (he set a school record that lasted for years). My dad was my de facto coach, because the female coach assigned to the team hadn't a clue about track. My dad had let me run distance with him during my junior high school years. (One of his scarier adages when I'd complain about how much it hurt was, "Do you want to get better? It's gonna hurt. Keep running.")

So, my first real race was as a mile runner. It meant a lot to me to run track, even though I had to juggle that sport with senior studies, other activities and working part-time at Sears & Roebuck in the nation's first outdoor shopping mall. That shopping mall, Northland Mall, in north Columbus was developed and owned by Cleveland-based developer Dick Jacobs. He later became one of my election law clients in the law firm I started in the corner of my bedroom when my children were 7, 4 and 2. It is the same law firm where I practice law today (in a much more spacious office). My daughter, who was seven at the time I started the practice, now manages it with aplomb. Even a city or a state can be its own small town as time goes on. ≈

Chapter 3

Determination and Persistence

"So who would *you* suggest I date?" asked my bewildered but stubborn and defiant mother to her parents in the mid-1950's. My grandfather, Glendon Oscar Swan, Sr., grandson of a Civil War veteran, Joseph Andrew Swan, did not approve of her boyfriend. He threatened to cut off funding for college if she defied him. My mother, principled, determined and honest to a fault, told her father she would not break it off. After attending two years of college, she was told there was no more money.

Newlyweds, Glendon Oscar Swan, Sr. and Loretta May Allender Swan, 1933, Springfield, Ohio

My grandfather was in management with International Harvester, living on a "gentleman's farm" with my grandmother and their four children. My grandmother, Loretta May Allender Swan, married my grandfather in 1933 when they eloped. They had courted by letter—she from nursing school in Chicago, and he from Springfield, just after he started working in the mailroom at International Harvester, a manufacturer of tractors and other industrial vehicles. In my grandmother's time, nursing students were not permitted to be married.

My mother suspects that my grandfather pressured my grandmother to get married so he wouldn't lose her to a doctor in Chicago. She was beautiful, with olive skin, high cheekbones and rich brown eyes. My grandmother gave in, and they eloped.

Loretta May Allender Swan was also the oldest child in her family. She hid the fact of her marriage for a while and returned to nursing school. But she became so homesick, she dropped out of school and was forever to our estimation the health expert of the family, even without the degree. My grandparents lived on a farm outside of South Charleston during my formative years, and it was my grandmother who taught me how to sew, bake pies and sing a baby's lullaby that today I sing to my granddaughter.

On the not-so-pretty side, my grandparents' elopement was the beginning of a marriage so patriarchally structured that my grandfather told my grandmother that she was not to attend her own mother's funeral (and sadly she didn't), because she was "needed at home." The reality of it was that he had not been favored by her parents after the elopement. The chasm between my grandparents and my grandmother's parents grew to the point that the first time I knew I had a living great-grandfather, Robert Allender, was when I met him at his daughter's (my grandmother's) funeral in 1976. He had lived in nearby Springfield all along. It was scandalous enough that Loretta's parents, Robert Allender and Dorothy Thrasher Allender, had divorced, (she later died in New Mexico), but I would have liked to have known Robert Allender, as I am sure my mother would have, too.

My mother waited until I was 47 years old to tell me things that I had to figure out, like what year my parents really were married. This was part and parcel of the stubborn Scottish constitution of being a Swan—stiff upper lip—don't let on when it's not so good. That's one reason why my grandfather never divorced his second wife, Ruth. He didn't want anyone to read it in the newspaper.

Five generations; clockwise, Barbara Swan Junk (my mother), Glendon Oscar Swan (her father), looking not-so-happy to pose with the women, Leona Rhea Swan (his mother), Leura Trenner Rhea (her mother) and Jennifer Junk Brunner as an infant held by Great, Great Grandma Rhea, Jackson County, Ohio, June 1957

Eighteen months after me came my sister, Andrea. Four years later came Dan, and two years later, Kathy. My parents, along with Andrea (an infant) and I, had moved to the far west side of Columbus from Springfield just after Andrea was born. Later, after Dan was born, we moved to the north side of Columbus, where my mother lived closer to her Aunt Helen, my grandfather's sister.

Kathy was born when we lived there. While she was still a one-year-old, wispy-blonde and wide-eyed baby girl, I brought Kathy to school to share for show-and-tell in my third grade class. She was a stand-in for our dog, Candy, that we had to get rid of because she bit people.

Barbara Swan Junk at age 32; few could rival her beauty, inside or out

My mother has always been quite the beauty. When I described her Jackie Kennedy-esque hairdo, I meant more than that. She has the squared, angular face, high cheekbones, dimples, perfect teeth, beautiful smile and the once dark hair of Jackie. But she also has the olive skin of my grandmother and sparkling green eyes that crinkle to a twinkle when she when she "gets tickled" about something.

My mother was in her 30's during the 1960's, and she was the epitome of the modern beauty of the time. But, before my stay-at-home mother transformed herself into a contemporary "Jackie," she often looked as scary as hell when she wore her brush rollers and batwing glasses in preparation for a gorgeous evening out. This was especially true when she was mad as a hornet at you for dilly-dallying when you were supposed to hurry up and wash your hair so she could put those same prickly rollers in yours.

I finally learned that some of my mom's anger was more at her situation. She was smart, artistic, resourceful and thoughtful yet trapped at home with four young children and no car (we only had one, and my dad was an insurance agent). She didn't have a lot of options. Like many of her contemporaries, my mother was a product of the post-World War II 1950's: when women were done working in the factories and women's college enrollment plunged. At that time, women were provided the "luxuries" of electric vacuum cleaners, washing machines, electric can openers, transistor and electric radios and eventually automatic dishwashers. Men wore white shirts and skinny black ties and bore the brunt of earning the living, and everyone was supposed to be happy with that.

In high school and college, my mother had excelled as a gifted student, orator, linguist, singer, actress and even a decent athlete, and she had exceptional beauty to go with all of that. In her retirement, she has proven to be an amazing artist and painter whose work sells. She was a conscientious mother who studied nutrition and balanced every meal, including breakfast. She made for Andrea and me Little Bo Peep Halloween costumes from sheets of crepe paper, following step-by-step directions she found in a women's magazine when I was in first grade and Andrea in kindergarten.

She read to us from a children's Bible at lunchtime when Andrea and I raced each other home from elementary school to eat lunch and be the first to tell her the latest news from school. I can't remember a time when lunch wasn't ready when we got there, despite her having Dan and Kathy at home as small children. She did this even though my dad most of the time had the one car they owned and was gone from morning to night. Our family was like many others whether they'll admit it or not, with a history of alcoholism passed from generation to generation, with each member not fully understanding or accepting, but trying to hide the nasty fact and act as a "perfect" family should. Being a Swan, my mom was especially good at this, since unfortunately, my father was not immune from this genetic predisposition. He never missed work, just time with his family, as he drank at least a six-pack at night and passed out in front of the TV.

As a product of the 1950's, my mother believed that if she could somehow be a more perfect wife, these problems would go away. In fact, she read an Ann Landers' newspaper advice column early in my parents' marriage where a woman wrote about her husband staying away from home at night. Ann Landers told the woman that she needed to provide a more inviting environment for him to come home to. It did not occur to my mother for many years (and obviously never to Ann Landers) that it wasn't my mother's fault that my father drank and didn't come home until late after work.

My mother would at times become angry and frustrated, and clearly she felt trapped. Her two college yearbooks showed pictures of our gorgeous mom as Greek Week Queen and a member of Chi Omega sorority. Later, her beautiful prom dresses were stuffed into a tall metal can with a lid. Andrea and I wore those dresses until they were in tatters, playing dress up in the basement of our home.

When my grandfather cut off money for college, my mother obtained a teaching certificate for her two years of college, since teachers were needed. She became a teacher in Springfield, married my father, and I was born six months later.

My mother always wanted to finish college. She in fact yearned for it. She took some classes at Ohio State during my junior high years and got straight A's, but she couldn't finish with the demands of a young family, a tight budget and kids of her own about to go to college. When she was getting ready to go back to college at age 69 in Louisiana, Hurricane Katrina hit and destroyed many of the buildings at the college she was planning to attend. She sacrificed for her children to go to college, because it meant so much to her.

L. to R. Barbara Swan Junk, Andrea, Sam Junk, me,
Kathy and Dan, circa 1968

One of my most vivid memories of my mother is of sitting at the kitchen table with her as she told Andrea and me, "Girls, I want you to be able to take care of yourselves and never have to depend on a man for anything." She was emphatic. She meant it. Andrea and I remember it to this day, and she must have made that same exhortation to Kathy.

Andrea went on to start a home business with three small girls, divorced, and moved to a small town to the east of Columbus, Dresden, Ohio, where she had found a job with the Longaberger Basket Company. When the girls had weekend visits with their father, she bought and read books on marketing and management, in part to ease the ache she felt when they were gone. Andrea later went on to become Vice President of Sales at Longaberger, helping it to grow into a billion-dollar enterprise that seemed to grow in tandem with her own self-actualization. She is now an executive with Thirty-One Gifts in Columbus.

Kathy went on to become a senior vice-president of Bank of America, in a position so high, I really couldn't figure out just what she did, except for things like voting the shareholder proxies in Boston when BoA acquired Fleet Bank and supervising TV commercials for the bank that were shot in Los Angeles. All I know is that when she decided to retire at age 43 to be home by choice with her three young children, she had to personally resign to then president, Ken Lewis, about six months before the financial meltdown in 2008. She has since started her own interior design business and continues to live north of Charlotte, North Carolina.

Brother Dan became a lawyer in New York City, managing his large law firm's tobacco litigation and then later moved to his first love of sales, for sophisticated software that facilitates litigation discovery and government inquiry responses. He is an expert in electronic discovery and law relating to document execution in foreclosures. All in all, my mother has 12 grandchildren, three from me, four from Andrea, two from Dan and three from Kathy. My dad lived long enough to know six of them.

As for me, I married Rick, a farm boy from northeastern Ohio who was working on his first of two advanced degrees when I was 21 and he 24. We had our first child, Kate, after almost three years of marriage, and two more within five years after that. Kate, our oldest child, was born during my second year of night law school, four weeks before finals. With her husband and our law partner, Patrick Quinn, she has given Rick and me our first grandchild, Madeline. Maddy is the fifth generation of "oldest child is a girl," starting my grandmother, Loretta, and ending with this new little girl.

That major lesson my mother wanted me to learn—to never have to depend on a man to survive, is one I chose to learn. I am grateful I married someone who was willing to let me learn it because he respected me for my mind and ideas. I have ferociously staked out my independence, and while that is sometimes exasperating, Rick admires me for it. For that, I thank my mom.

Barbara and Sam Junk at dude ranch in Wyoming in the early 1990's

But I also learned from her the exactitude needed for excelling at what you do, compassion for those in need and fighting for what is right by not backing down and never giving up, no matter how hard the fight. My mother did that for her family, sacrificing much in the process without complaint. She turned her anger into resolve for her children and in the process blossomed into the thoughtful and still beautiful woman I know today as an adult.

Whether it was giving my dad a book to read about quitting drinking (which he finally did the last 8 years of his life), calling me after she has known I have been sick to see if I'm feeling better (even in my 40's and 50's) or finally being convinced that Fox News is not the only way to report news, my mother has taught me by example how to stand my ground and fight for what I want. After my father died, I had dreams she would be that woman she planted in me, who never would have to depend on a man. So, I was surprised at how quickly she found my stepdad, John, less than a year after my dad died.

She remarried on a boat named "Persistence" in the middle of Kentucky Lake near Paducah, Kentucky. I gave her away and cried as she looked up at John full of hope. As soon as the minister pronounced them husband and wife, she immediately wanted to know if I was having a hard time because of Dad. "No," I said. "You just look so happy." It took two years, until after she was remarried, for her to be ready to put my dad's ashes in the sea as he had requested.

During her second marriage she and John lived on a boat based in Mandeville, Louisiana, on the north shore of Lake Pontchartrain, above New Orleans, for close to a decade. Together they trained for and made an epic journey across the Gulf of Mexico and up the intra-coastal Atlantic waterway, through the Chesapeake and Hudson Bays, the Great Lakes and down the Mississippi River back to New Orleans. When she was ready to get off the boat, she announced it matter-of-factly. She told John she would wait two years for him to make up his mind, but after that, she would be getting off the boat.

They sold the boat, going into contract just before Hurricane Katrina hit. Their harbormaster, Chris Stucke, made sure it was properly moored and anchored at Beau Chen Marina, where it weathered the storm. (The only boat to break loose was a

¤26

houseboat called, "Ole Basshole.") They closed on the sale of their boat after the hurricane and lived on land near water until she announced her desire to return to Columbus. It was pretty obvious to all of us kids that it would happen. It has. ≈

Chapter 4

Imagination and Drive

Elizabeth Faye Kidwell Junk (center) with sisters Margaret (left) and Mary (right), South Charleston, Ohio, circa 1911

Samuel Lawrence Junk was the second of three children born to Elizabeth Faye Kidwell Junk and Paul Leslie Junk. My Grandmother Junk would have been what my mother called a "career woman" if she had been born in a later generation. She bought and sold antiques— furniture, lamps, glassware, Asian (then called "oriental") art, but most of all, dolls. She could tell you what she paid for a certain rare doll, and even if she didn't have it anymore, she could tell you what she sold it for. She had operated an antique shop from her home and later from her father, Benton Kidwell's, gas station, situated down the street in front of her parents' home. She raised and sold rabbits in wooden hutches built for her by my grandfather in the back yard. He helped her tend a large garden when he was not working as a conductor on the railroad. To me, he mostly mumbled when he talked, and kissing him good-bye as a kid, his whiskers were rough, and he smelled of Old Spice, Mennen's or Aqua Velva aftershave.

Paul Leslie Junk (right) standing in boots with horse, with his siblings in Mt. Sterling, Ohio, circa 1914

When he met Grandma, he was out of school working on laying pipeline for the gas company near the small, rural town of Mt. Sterling, where he grew up. When the pipeline was being laid in South Charleston, he roomed next door to grandma and her parents.

After they married and she would not move to the farm; he found other work. During the depression he would walk to Springfield daily to find work. One time someone coming home to South Charleston stopped and picked him up but made him stand on the running board and hold on the top of the car all the way home to South Charleston. He did it.

Because of his job, he was gone for days at a time. My father, born in 1933, ironically, the year Prohibition was lifted, remembered as a little boy going with his father during those years to charity lines for staples during the Great Depression. My grandfather would tell him to sit and wait inside a corn stalk teepee in the nearby field (the type that looks bucolic in paintings), to stay warm while my grandfather waited in line for eggs and milk to bring home to my grandmother.

Photo taken on the last run of this train in 1946; my grandfather, Paul Leslie Junk standing at back, fifth from right with black cap

There wasn't anything Elizabeth Junk couldn't cook in a pressure cooker or an electric skillet. At this set of grandparents' family dinners, every Junk had developed the fine art of being able to listen to three conversations at once and participate in each intermittently. It was genetically passed on to all of my siblings and me, and Rick and I pitied my poor stepdad, John, when he joined the cacophony of my brother, sisters and me for family dinners—we could rival the best of them from earlier generations.

My Grandfather Junk retired from the railroad at 65; he built a garage and was going to start a lawn mower repair business as a hobby and help his brother, Ken, drive the tractor and plant on the farm in Mt. Sterling. By harvest time he had cancer and only lived five months, mostly bedridden. My grandmother continued her wheeling and dealing in antiques until she started into senility and entered a nursing home. After that, only selling took place, with my dad and his sister, Aunt Barbara Jane, sorting through and putting up the house and its contents for auction.

As the middle child, my dad enjoyed trying on many roles for size with no oldest or youngest child or only-boy expectations placed upon him. One of my father's childhood memories was of holding out a broomstick as an extension of his arm and letting his terrier jump up and grab onto it with its strong jaws. That terrier never let go even as my father swung the broom in a horizontal circular fashion around his head. My dad loved that dog, but he had to give it up when it bit more than broomsticks.

My dad also seemed to have a knack for swinging things in a circular fashion in other settings. He took the rubber band attached to a red rubber ball of what was known as a wooden "Bolo paddle" and swung the ball around the classroom from the end of the rubber band. The ball bounced off of each wall as he swung. When the teacher walked into the room, he let go and quickly seated himself. The ball and rubber band wrapped around her neck.

My father was famous for his sentence construction, but mostly for having a smart mouth. When asked by his English teacher for a simple sentence, he volunteered, "Joe died." In answer to a follow up question requesting a compound sentence, he said, "Joe fell, and Joe died." When the class was asked for a sentence with a subject and predicate, he raised his hand. The teacher eyed him and admonished,

Samuel Lawrence Junk, circa 1951, senior picture from Southeastern High School in Clark County, Ohio

"Sam, if you say Joe died one more time . . ." He said perfunctorily, "Joseph kicked the bucket."

My dad struggled with authority. He was also one of the most competitive people I knew. He wasn't afraid to think big, but he was often his own worst enemy in getting to where he wanted to go, being both fearful and resentful of authority all at once. Studying didn't come easily to him, but he was quick of wit and intelligent. He admired my ability to study, and it took years for me to understand that his declarations that I would become a college professor were not criticism of my abilities to survive in the "real world," but as a statement of admiration for the academic capabilities he felt he lacked.

Once married, my dad had started selling life insurance, progressed to a manager at Prudential in Columbus and eventually started his own independent insurance agency. He studied hard and earned his Certified Life Underwriter (CLU) designation, becoming a member of the Million Dollar Round Table in insurance sales. He became a deacon at the Presbyterian Church where Rick and I were married and Kate was baptized. He was chairman of the elementary school carnival, and the games and carnival rides were beyond compare when he was chairman. He helped with the choir concerts at our junior high school, coached and went to my brother's sports games and was the calmer of my parents in teaching me to drive.

He could rear himself up and puff out his chest to look two inches taller than his six-foot-two-inch frame (a full foot taller than my mother). He often succeeded in scaring new boyfriends and once intimidated a teacher who tried to create a rift between my best girlfriend and me in junior high school. He was my sports coach, my philosopher/teacher and business and general advisor in life. When I chose to work outside the home with young children, he was my example to follow to try and figure out how to meet the needs of my family and of my career and stay sane.

He had traveled all over the U.S. starting at age 10 with his grandparents, my grandmother's parents, Laura and Benton Kidwell, and their oldest daughter, Mary. He was lucky to live less than a block away from his grandparents in South Charleston. Mary planned the trips, and together, they all drove in the 1940's to California, the Grand Canyon and more. He and my mother instilled a love of travel in me, which I have inevitably passed on to my children.

My dad was the one who encouraged me to take that first political job at the Statehouse, and he would have loved to drive the convertible car I rode in the parades during my first two local elections. He would have been amazed as I was (and so would his mother, who campaigned door-to-door for FDR and was a precinct election worker for decades) when I received the John F. Kennedy Profile in Courage Award in Boston in 2008. Instead, my little five-foot-two-inch mother stood proudly alone, beaming when Senator Ted Kennedy asked her to stand in that ceremony and receive her due applause (all of my siblings were there with us). I would imagine, knowing Sam, that somehow he found a way to be there, too.

When I went to college, I read Herman Hesse's book on the Buddha, *Siddhartha,* and told my dad how amazing the book was. He read it, too. In fact, during the last years of his life, he read more about Buddhism and Taoism than any other philosophy or religion and gave each of his four children a copy of the book, *The Mystic Path to Cosmic Power,* by Vernon Howard. The book encapsulates writings and applications of some of the greatest thinkers of all time.

One of my dad's favorite sayings was, "Where there's a will, there's a way." It worked to get me a work permit in one day when I was 16, but it didn't work on his esophageal cancer, which he contracted and died from at age 60. Despite his strong imagination and drive, Buddhist teachings of acceptance allowed him to die with dignity and of course with a sense of humor. Even at the end he was able to describe to us with a smirk the various hallucinations he was experiencing, knowing they weren't real.

Cancer wracked his body so badly that it broke his ribs, but dad would never have stood for a sudden death in a car wreck or from a heart attack. As Rick and hospice and squad workers carried him out of my parents' home on a sheet used as a gurney to get him around the tight hallway corners, my father was still holding up one finger and whispering, "Wait, wait, wait." He lived less than a day after that. As I left him and my mother at hospice that night, it was a strangely beautiful sight to see them in the soft light of the lamp in the peaceful hospice environment on their last night together.

When I was about twelve, my father had taken me to see "how screwed up" some people's priorities were, driving me to the poorer sections of Columbus to see how people lived in dilapidated houses but still had nice cars and big TVs. He was familiar with this from his many years in sales in all kinds of neighborhoods. Despite my dad's quasi-political commentary, all I saw was that someone had to fix up these neighborhoods and help people emerge better. I eventually became a Democrat, even though my parents were mostly Republican. ("Howard" and "Metzenbaum" were dirty words in my household, and Barry Goldwater was a hero.)

My and my siblings' upbringing was an ominous combination of a father who pushed us to see, imagine and go for it and a mother who pushed us to get things done and see it through. In the end, the lesson I most took to heart from my father was the lesson he had learned as his life progressed. He used to say, "If you're honest and work hard, you'll always get by." This ethic was quickly dissipating as the 1960's turned into the 1970's, and the World War II generation was eschewed by the post-Vietnam generation as self-aggrandizing and judgmental. These two key ingredients emphasized by my dad—honesty and hard work— once commonplace and a given in the forties and fifties, would prove to be greater than the sum of their parts for me when applied in tandem in the 1980's and beyond.

My dad would have loved the Internet. He died in 1993, when I was 36, two years before I really started putting the Internet to use to find just the right college for my daughter, Kate. I still call the Internet, "library nirvana." He would have thought the same. It is this engine that is now fueling the imaginations of everyday Americans, keeping ministers and politicians honest and creating new ways to "work hard" as part of how many of us now earn our living.

Despite the challenges for some in keeping abreast of the ever-changing technologies, the Internet and global communications have created an instantaneous and strong way to communicate with people we hardly knew existed. It is our best hope for bringing together the disparate cultures of the world so that we may learn and know that our humanity is our common bond. We honor our parents. We love our children and pets. That doesn't change, no matter the culture. Through this medium we are communicating directly, conveying to one another our hopes, fears, joys and even silliness associated with being human.

Global communication via the Internet and its network "cloud," is so far a protected bastion and vehicle of free speech. It must not be rationed, divided or diminished. The Internet and cellular and broadband telecommunications have already proved to be essential tools for growing the participation in our American democracy, and more recently, for both inciting and nurturing the hope for democracy, equality and peace in other parts of the world.

Ask yourself why despots in second and third world governments, when faced with overthrow, attempt at early stages to cut off telecommunications. This instantaneous and honest form of communication is made for democracy, protecting every person's ability to speak and be heard; it can promote fairness, equality and respect in a civil society. At a more basic level, I am convinced that my dad's air-swinging feats of his childhood with his terrier holding fast to a broomstick would have logged at least a million views on YouTube. ≈

Chapter 5

Partnership

"Wow, this will be a great summer. We have so much in common, but we don't have to get serious," exclaimed Rick Brunner. He was driving me in his Datsun B210 from northeast Columbus to my home with my parents in an area in north Columbus known as Clintonville. It was 1977.

We had just been on our first date—an all day affair that began with driving to Mansfield to Rick's Sigma Nu fraternity brother's wedding at St. Peter's Catholic Church. We had danced to the Eagles, "Best of My Love" at the wedding. I thought he was pretty cool, three years older than me, confident, funny, beautiful face, and I liked the fact he had a beard. Our day ended at Hoover Dam with just him and me. We had stopped back at his place and at my home with my parents so each of us could change. As we left the house, I picked up my guitar to load in the car. We sat along the bank of Hoover Reservoir in Westerville. We both liked music, and we both sang. I pulled out the guitar and sang to him my version of Joe Cocker's, "You Are So Beautiful." He had a rule to never kiss on a first date, but he broke it that day.

Rick and I met each other in the summer of 1977 working at the Central Ohio Area Agency on Aging where the USDA Summer Lunch Program was administered by the Columbus Recreation and Parks Department. He thought I was older than him; I at first spelled his last name with one "n" rather than two. Many would have thought we were an unlikely pair. I grew up in the city in central Ohio; he grew up on a working farm in northeast Ohio. But my roots felt more rural than urban to me. I often traveled to my grandparents' farm in the country and visited my

¤38

other grandparents in the small town of South Charleston. He grew up listening to WMMS, a Cleveland rock and roll radio station that played on the radio in the barn when it was time for milking the cows. He traveled to Cleveland to take bassoon lessons from a member of the Cleveland orchestra and had played keyboards in a rock band at age 14. As a teenager Rick would stay out of school longer than necessary for his orthodontist appointments and stop in to visit his great grandmother Smith (who baked a fresh pie every day) in the city of Alliance. We both valued family and had been taught about honesty and working hard. Our minds engaged and never let go. Everything else followed.

Valley View Farm where Rick grew up, Knox Township, Columbiana County, Ohio

Rick's parents had wanted lots of children. They lost one, Deborah, at birth, three years before Rick was born. His mother miscarried many more times but managed to have Rebekah three years after Rick. When Rick was six and Becky three, his parents took on the challenge of raising two more. Linda and Walt were Rick's mother's first cousins who were sixteen and thirteen and had lost both of their parents. Rick went from becoming the big brother to the middle kid and thought it was the greatest thing in the world that he and Becky had gained a new sister and brother. Linda went to nursing school and eventually married Chuck. Walt went to Vietnam and became a helicopter gunner and later traveled the world repairing large boilers on ships. He married Marcia, his high school sweetheart, a talented nurse.

Ruth (in white satin dress) and Ken Brunner, age 19, 1950

Rick's parents were given insurance money with which to raise Linda and Walt. They never spent it and instead scrimped and carefully watched their money, giving it back to each of them when they married.

When Rick's parents were married in 1950, his mother, Ruth, wore a long sleeved white satin gown trimmed on the sleeves with covered buttons and with a shawl collar. The train was circular. It was, in a word, elegant. An identical one had been made for Linda to wear as a child. Before she had lost her parents, she was the flower girl in Ruth and "Kenny's" wedding. Later, Linda would wear the wedding dress and Becky the flower girl dress. After that, Becky wore the dress and Linda's daughter, Jenny, wore the flower girl dress. The dresses are still boxed and stored today. The tradition ended when Becky had boys.

Tradition plays an important role in Rick's family, and it's one of many things that make his family so special. When Rick and I took on the challenges of caring for my cousin's children for several years, many people looked at us and shook their heads incredulously. These kids were from my family, yet, Rick stepped up to do this as if they were his family. Most people did not understand that "family" in Rick's upbringing meant whoever was there. That was a "tradition" they were willing to share with anyone who was in want or need. Boy scout troops still use the spring-fed farm pond today for camping and campfires. No child has been turned away from the Brunner farm.

Jacob and Eliza Brunner emigrated from Switzerland to Ohio in 1891

Rick's great grandfather, Jacob Brunner, emigrated from Switzerland to Columbiana County, Ohio in 1891, coming through Boston. His wife, Eliza Berger, was said to have had a brother who was a college professor, and that has been cited for Rick's scholarly approach to things, his love of reading and learning, especially history. Jacob and Eliza Berger were from the

Swiss canton of Berne, having lived on a farm on the Swiss mountainside between Frutigen and Adelboden. Rick looks uncannily like Jacob's father, Johannes Brunner. Johannes' son, Jacob, was one of five brothers. In the Swiss tradition, the oldest boy inherited the farm, so three younger brothers, Jacob, John and Samuel, set out for America to see what their chances could be. As immigrants often do, they settled in the same area of Ohio, providing support to one another. Jacob and Eliza had lost a boy and a girl before they made it to Ohio but went on to have seven more boys and three more girls. All made it to adulthood, except Robert, who died at age twelve. Jacob died in the flu epidemic of 1918, as did my mother's great grandfather and at least one of his children.

George and Lera Brunner at their wedding, circa 1929

Jacob Brunner's son, George, was Rick's grandfather. Jacob and Eliza Brunner spoke only German. Rick remembers as a boy hearing yodeling at large family dinners and hearing German spoken among his older relatives. George, born in 1904, did not want any of his children to speak German, and the language was lost. George's sister, the last of Jacob's children, Eliza, named after her mother and known affectionately as "Aunt Lizzie," lived to nearly 90 years old and rode on a motorcycle in her 80's.

Jacob's son, George, married Lera Odessa Fryfogle, Rick's grandmother, after they first met when she was twelve and he was eighteen at the farmhouse that would later be his son's home from age nineteen until the present, in his eighties. Cheese was made on that farm in 1922 when they first met there. Lera had delivered by horse and buggy a part for the cheese-making machine and stood by the fire to get warm. George sat at a table in front of the fire, playing cards with other young men. Later, Lera would care for her mother-in-law, Eliza, who still spoke only German, tending to her needs until she died.

Frutigen Church, Switzerland 1895

The old church in Switzerland as it looked in 1895, four years after Jacob and Eliza Brunner emigrated to the U.S.

Nearly 125 years after Jacob and Eliza Brunner came to Columbiana County, Ohio, Rick and I visited the Canton of Berne, Switzerland, traveling by train to Frutigen and by bus to

Adelboden. In Frutigen we saw the church his great grandparents had attended and on the way to Adelboden the Swiss countryside where they had tended their cattle.

At the church, even though gravesites in Europe are "recycled," the graves that remained from the 1960's bore the same surnames of people from the small rural community among the rolling hills of Columbiana County, where dairy farming still abounds: Schmid (which became Smith), Zurbrugg, Thoeni (which became Denny), Gerber, Fryfogle, and of course, Brunner. Three years later, in Stockholm, Sweden, I found while souvenir shopping, coasters with black and white photographs from around the world of famous places inserted between two plates of glass. When I found one with an 1895 photo of the church at Frutigen—how it would have looked at the time Jacob and Eliza Brunner immigrated to America—I bought three—one for us, one for Rick's parents and one for his sister, Becky. It meant a lot to all of us.

One of the great stories of family lore in the Brunner family is that of Simon Thoeni. He and his wife traveled to America from Switzerland, bringing with them their five children. He had arranged for his money to be sent ahead of time, but it didn't arrive. The family reached New York. They waited, but it still didn't come. In despair and shame Simon Thoeni hung himself, abandoning his wife and children. The money arrived the next day.

His wife, Marguerite, was twenty-seven years old. She was alone with five young children in a strange land. Instead of returning to her family in Switzerland, she traveled to rural Ohio, bought a farm and raised her family in what became a Swiss community. It is said in that community that it was the Zurbruggs who made the first commercial Swiss cheese in America, taking seven-feet wheels of Swiss cheese on buckboards and covered in straw to sell in Pittsburgh. Many in this small farming community repeated that fact with pride as Rick grew up. This was in part because nearly everyone in that community was related through the Zurbruggs.

Rick's mother, Ruth, was a Powell, of Welsh heritage, yet she shares a great-great grandfather with Rick's Dad, again, through the Zurbruggs. Her father, Ken Powell, was a young, moneyed playboy who swept Rick's grandmother, Marie Smith, off her feet when both were in their early twenties. Marie and her identical twin, May, were born in 1902. Together the sisters had quit school and left home at age 14 to work in a factory. They sent their paychecks home to Walter and Alice Smith, their parents, even though they had been told that if they left, they needed not plan on coming back. They became flappers in the early 1920's with pictures to prove it. Later in life, often the twins would appear at functions dressed in the same dress, not even knowing the other had bought it. We observed that losing her sister was harder than losing a husband for Marie Hoover, and these two, even in old age were always hard to tell apart.

Before meeting Ken Powell, Marie had dated Wade Hoover, and May dated and married Earl Sweitzer. Marie's boyfriend, Wade Hoover, was an educated, steady and solid man who cared deeply for her. After Marie met Ken Powell, who had a car and wore snappy suits, she found herself having to break off her relationship with Wade. She was, instead, marrying Ken, who was soon to be the father of Louise, Ruth's older sister.
The night before Marie's wedding to Ken, Wade called her and told her he still loved her. He pleaded with her not to marry Ken Powell, knowing why the marriage was taking place. He told Marie he wanted to marry her, regardless. It must have been difficult for her to hang up that telephone, knowing that the click of the heavy black receiver meant the closure of a very

heavy door to a life she would not have. She did what she believed was her duty.

After years of her having to go to the factory to pick up his paycheck to feed her girls instead of the cash drawer at the local bar, Ken died at age sixty. Wade Hoover had lost his wife, too. Marie and Wade finally married in 1970. They eloped and told their children afterward. She outlived him and always said until she died at age ninety-three that the

Marie Smith Powell and Kenneth Powell,
Alliance, Ohio;
wedding photo, 1926

seven years she had with Wade were the happiest years of her life. Wade Hoover's favorite upholstered platform rocking chair now sits in our home. It's been used to rock many babies.

When Rick and I met, he was twenty-three, and I was twenty. In 1977, dating someone you worked with wasn't out of the ordinary, probably because the question of women in the workplace being on an equal footing with men wasn't even close to being an ideal or a standard in the U.S. When "Rosie the Riveter's" time was in vogue, women worked in factories because they were needed—able-bodied men were for the most part at war for the Allies in World War II. When the war was over, the men came home, and women returned to housework and child care.

But, modern conveniences, television and the world of Madison Avenue advertising confounded the situation for many women, who found it stressful to uphold a mystical model of femininity. It's no coincidence that prescriptions for tranquilizers for women became common during the decade in which Rick and I were born. The façade of this situation, along with similar revolt in other quarters against a white male-dominated system, fomented a righteous feminine uprising that has continued in waves since.

Soon after we met, Rick had asked me on a date twice before I accepted—I really was busy. It was our minds that locked before emotion took hold. He admired and encouraged me to challenge my mind and myself, but most importantly, he made me laugh, and still does. When I watched a movie on the lives of Margaret and Dennis Thatcher, I couldn't help but laugh when Dennis came into a room to speak to Margaret wearing her underwear on his head. It's a sight I have seen before.

I discovered as soon as we met that Rick is brilliant. I've seen him devour thousand-page books in a week, or any book for that matter, in one-third the time it would take other people to read it. He knew history and had read biographies of people from throughout history—especially political figures. As a child, he routinely read the encyclopedia—for fun. In farm life, the chores are endless. He often had to be located to do them, as he would be off by himself outside reading. We both loved music, and it's a big part of our lives.

Soon after we were married and living in Columbus, Rick discovered he could get WMMS radio from Cleveland through television cable. He set a mechanical timer on the stereo for the station to turn on to wake us up, to turn off when we left for work, then to turn back on again just before we arrived home from work and school and off again at midnight. It took some getting used to, having constant music in the background, but now I can do most any task better to music. Both of us sang, he tenor, me second alto.

Rick and me on our wedding day, May 27, 1978; he was 24, and I was 21

We believed in the strength and value of family. We each had never encountered anyone else whom we thought was as smart or worked as hard as the other. When I won the office of Secretary of State and it was my turn to make the victory speech on the stage at our downtown hotel, we held hands walking up to the stage, both of us a bit intrepid about what lay ahead. We were overwhelmed by the outpouring of Democratic enthusiasm in that ballroom of the Capitol Square Hyatt Hotel.

Starting out, even at age twenty, I knew that relationships take work. I had dated plenty but had had less than a handful of serious relationships. I was pragmatic. Why get serious with someone if it was not a good match for the long run? And at that time, a woman with intellect usually had to "dumb down" herself to be accepted by most men. Besides the fact that he actually liked and appreciated my mind, in Rick, I recognized someone who would work as hard at a relationship as I would— a rare find.

During those early days of dating, I told Rick about a paper I had written as part of my Gerontology training at Miami University, about a community day center concept for older adults. He thought it was amazing and bragged about it to other people. I was astonished at no "dumbing down" required with Rick. He not only accepted but encouraged and pushed for both of our academic pursuit, achievement and growth.

Rick had had plenty of serious relationships before me, and they were all named "Sue" but one. I eventually met all of them but the last one. The first Sue was his high school sweetheart. They went to their country high school together. She was shy, a dreamer and bookish, while he was popular and involved in a multitude of activities. He encouraged her to go to college. She did and met someone else. The second Sue he met at (what was then) Mount Union College in Alliance. He was responsible for finding his own way to college with summer jobs, grants and loans. One summer he worked three jobs. This Sue's dad was a doctor. She was a strong advocate for women's equality and later became a doctor, herself. There were many times in our early marriage when I silently thanked her for having pushed him to see a woman in a relationship as an equal partner; I reaped the harvest she had planted. Besides another Sue before me, he dated Carol, whom he encouraged to take a teaching job at an experimental school in North Carolina. She did, and like the first Sue, found someone else.

When we met, neither of us wanted to get serious—he having been burned, and I being cautious. But as John Lennon once said, "Life is what happens to you while you're busy making other plans." Before the end of the summer, Rick said to me, "I want this to continue even after this summer." So did I. We had met June 13, 1977. Less than two months later, in early August 1977, we talked of getting married.

By Labor Day in September 1977, Rick asked me to marry him. I was just a junior in college then. At first I said, "Absolutely not. I won't be married my senior year of college." Wisely, he simply said, "Okay."

"That was it? No arguing with me?" I thought. I paused. "Wait a minute," I said. "Let's talk about this." By the end of the discussion, we agreed to get married after my junior year of college. I could load up on classes and finish at least a semester early, to heck with my senior year. My mother, thinking of her own experiences (as did my father of his only two years of college) was concerned that marriage would end my education. That's the way it was for many of their generation. They told us they would pay for the rest of my college education, even after I was married. I was committed to finishing even without that incentive but not too proud to accept their generosity and be grateful for it.

We didn't have an engagement ring when we decided to marry. I had met Rick while he was a graduate student at The Ohio State University on his summer internship. Now he was about to go to law school at Ohio Northern University in Ada, Ohio. I was still an undergraduate at Miami University in Oxford, Ohio. We were, in two words, poor students.

Marie Hoover, Rick's grandmother, came to the rescue. Rick remembered she had always said to him that when he was ready to marry, she had a diamond for him to give his bride. Rick and I traveled to Alliance to see his Grandma Hoover. We told her we were getting married.

The first time she and I met was at the 100th birthday party of Great Aunt Verdie, her first husband's older sister. Marie Hoover and I both had enjoyed our lengthy conversation there. Afterward, she said matter-of-factly to Rick's mother, "Ruth, you just met your daughter-in-law."

Visiting her at her home, Rick carefully brought up Grandma's earlier promise about the diamond. Her face lit up. Only four feet ten inches tall, she quickly jumped up out of her chair and scurried into the next room. She came back with a diamond ring wrapped in plastic wrap that she had pulled from the soil of one of her potted plants. She was an avid garage sale shopper and often found real "diamonds in the rough." She had warned Rick's mother that if anything happened to her, to look in every nook, cranny and crease of the house to make sure that nothing she had hidden would be lost.

"Here," she said. "Here's the diamond I've been saving for you." It was set in white gold in a simple, round setting and in such a way that it looked twice its size. I unwrapped the plastic and without thinking tried on the ring. It fit—no sizing. I realized too late that I was supposed to let Rick ceremoniously put the ring on my finger. I took it off and let him put it on me. We both smiled.

"Grandma, how much do you want for this ring," Rick said. "Nothin'," she said quickly and then held up her forefinger and said, "Wait. Pay me a dollar, and then you can say you paid for

it." Rick reached in his pocket, found his wallet and handed her a one-dollar bill. That was it. The engagement was official.

When I returned to college at Miami with the ring on my finger, I undertook the ritual of my sorority at the Alpha Chapter of Delta Zeta, called a "candlelight." When a coed was given a fraternity pin or an engagement ring, she secretly told chapter officers, who called for a candlelight. Lights were dimmed, and the sorority sisters formed a circle, humming a song while a single candle was passed from girl to girl. The girl who blew it out had the news to tell—very 1950's, even though it was the late 1970's. But I did it, shocking everyone in my sorority. I was twenty years old and had had no boyfriend when I left for summer vacation.

When my mother went with me to the Lazarus store downtown to select items for Rick's and my wedding registry, the older, blonde-haired woman helping us commented that marriage ceremonies seemed to be coming back into vogue. She said that previously she had not been very busy in the registry department with the era of the 1960's and 1970's. I picked out white stoneware speckled with brown and imprinted with a natural looking wheat design by Stonehenge, called "Winter Wheat." There are still a few pieces of it in use at our law office today.

We were married in the Presbyterian Church at the end of my street in Clintonville in Columbus in May 1978. Rick had finished his first year of law school at Ohio Northern University Law School; he had done well and had applied to transfer to Capital University Law School in Columbus. We had spent many weekends together between the engagement and the big day. I had just a summer's worth of classes left to complete to obtain my undergraduate degree.

Within a week after the wedding and after a short honeymoon to Niagara Falls, I returned to Miami, living in off-campus housing with several other young women, and he returned to the Summer Lunch Program. After a week there, Rick transferred to the Ohio Bureau of Employment Services. My dad called on an army buddy there, Charlie Thompson, who hired Rick for the summer. Rick then entered Capital University Law School full-time, and I worked full-time at the Ohio Statehouse.

When we honeymooned briefly at Niagara Falls, we found a hotel that had waterbeds, even though the walls were enamel painted cinder block. When we checked in with no advance reservations, I announced proudly, "We're on our honeymoon." He told me under his breath, "Don't tell them that. Everyone is here on their honeymoon. They'll take advantage of us." We didn't need for them to make our trip an adventure. I did a pretty good job of that.

At the hotel, I thought the paper bath mat placed in the tub was a shower mat. I heard Rick exclaim from the bathroom, "What the heck?" as he found clumps of paper in the tub when he went in to take his shower. Then, being terribly nearsighted, I washed his contacts down the drain, thinking the contact case was mine and needed washing before I used it.

To make it worse, I had already helped ruin his one pair of glasses. On the way to Niagara Falls we stopped along the highway to help a middle-aged woman change her car's flat tire. Rick lay down at the side of the road to loosen a stubborn bolt and set his glasses on the gravel to see better up close. Not wanting anyone to step on them, I picked up the glasses and placed them on the hood of the woman's car. He finished the job, and we climbed into the Datsun B210 and began to drive away. I was driving.

"Where are my glasses?" he asked. "Uh, oh," I said as I looked in the rearview mirror and saw something shiny sliding off the hood of the woman's car as she pulled out behind us. When we doubled back to retrieve them, the lenses were etched with wide scratches across the front of them. They were not usable. By the time he returned to work after the few short days of our honeymoon, the only corrective vision device he had were his heavy black glasses from his steel mill working days.

Because we started out as friends, we understood that working at a relationship was crucial for any couple. I'm not sure what put him "over the edge" when it came to deciding to marry me, but for me, I had finally found someone whom I knew I loved and trusted and who would work as hard at our relationship as I would. Early stages of love don't often inform choices with rationality. But somehow, somewhere, we knew that it was right and that it could and would work. Over the years, as we looked at other ways our paths could have crossed if we hadn't met at that time (I actually considered going to Mount Union for undergraduate school), we remain convinced we would have met each other one way or another.

As it is with any relationship that stands the test of time, we had no idea how commitment, creativity and capacity for hard work we saw in one another would be essential for the days ahead. That's as I suppose it is for any two kids who start out young and without financial means and build a life together. During our first year of marriage, our joint tax return for 1977 showed a combined gross income of $5800. While some couples keep separate accounts, the thought of two sets of bank fees made it a no brainer to combine all we had into one account and watch every penny. We needed a short-term apartment to start, since Rick didn't know yet whether his transfer to Capital University Law School in Columbus was approved. My dad helped us find a month-to-month lease near where Rick's first apartment had been in northeast Columbus. There we began our life together. We soon met our next-door neighbors who were essentially at the same stage in life we were, Rick and Terri Slee. The four of us have been there for nearly every important event of our married lives, and Terri is the best friend I have next to my Rick.

Rick and I moved nine times in thirty years, staying in the Columbus area, but pushing ourselves each time for a better home that fit our needs at the particular time in our lives. I seldom redecorate; we just move.

We put each other through law school. When he ran out of loans, I worked part-time as a legal writing instructor, applying for the full amount of loans I could get. We shared what we had. I found out I was pregnant with Kate just before his bar exam and insisted we go to Bob Evans restaurant for breakfast to celebrate the Saturday before the exam. He looked like a Zombie; he was so nervous about passing, knowing our first child was on the way. I was already in law school, working full time in the Ohio Senate by that time. Eight months later Kate was born—four weeks before final exams during my second year of
law school. Within three years, when I was working for then Ohio Secretary of State Sherrod Brown, Laura was born, and two years later along came John.

When John was five weeks old, Rick wistfully and then more forcefully began the chant, "A boy needs a dog." Kate was five and Laura was two. Kate, wearing her pink "jelly" plastic shoes and with long brown hair, especially agreed. Curly-haired Laura with her favorite blanket and her thumb in her mouth was fine with it, too. John, who was still being swaddled at five weeks, couldn't have cared less. I had not even returned to work from maternity leave.

L. to R. Rick with puppy named Maggie, Kate, John, Laura and
me, Christmas, 1986

I said, "Rick, he's only five weeks old." Nothing could sway him.
"Maggie," our first dog found *us* as a stray dog someone dropped
off at the farm. She came home in a purple cardboard Pampers
diaper box, her nose barely able to reach the top of the box placed on the floor between the bucket seats of our Chrysler minivan. The veterinarian figured she was three weeks older than John, eight weeks old. She was with us thirteen years, and we've had dogs (and cats) ever since.

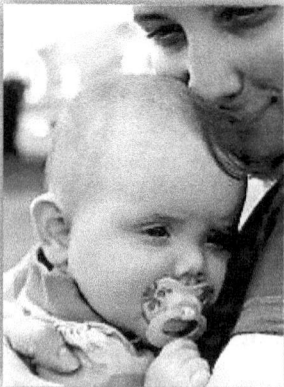

Kate with daughter,
Madeline

Rick and I have built a business together, with me starting it and him growing it. Our children have been our receptionists, our filers, our cleaners, our yard crew and our messengers. It's enabled us to show them what hard work can do and to be with them in doing so. None of them aspired to be lawyers, but that's okay. Kate married her high school sweetheart, Patrick Quinn, who did, and we now practice law with him while she manages the practice with unmatched efficiency and flair.

Laura makes her living singing; here, in a recording studio in New York, NY

Laura, who could memorize the songs from a musical at age four or five after watching a video twice, once created a collage in second grade about what she wanted to be when she grew up. It was a singer on Broadway in New York. She used a feather and glitter to decorate her costume. She earned a scholarship to the Berklee College of Music before she had even applied there, graduating with a music degree in vocal performance in 2006. She is a jazz singer in New York City. John, a gifted athlete and humorist, who is uncannily like my father, is completing his education, engaged to be married and working full-time in a sales position, as my dad did.

John, age 26

A marriage is a union that is a special kind of social and legal partnership between two people. By its nature it cradles, launches and influences rich life experiences, in part because of the commitment it requires. Lives shared in marriage can become greater than the sum of their parts. Marriage begins as a mirror but over time and living becomes a multi-faceted prism, taking in and reflecting wonder and light as no other institution can do. It can and should belong to anyone who wants it.

At the farm; L. to R. Kate, me, Laura, Rick and John, circa 1990

I once read that the kind of love in the most long lasting relationships is the love that is defined as "to cherish." I read it in the newspaper, just like my mom had read Ann Landers' column in the newspaper to try to figure out why my dad did not come home. Fortunately, the column I read turned out to be more reliable.

For good or bad, it's often such brief, chance moments that can affect an entire lifetime, like reading about love being "to cherish" that can ripple to points beyond imagination or estimation. Reading and trying to live what it means "to cherish" has informed me that long lasting love is not the fading spark of "can't eat, can't sleep, can't live without him" kind of love.

Rather, it is the slow, smoldering ember that burns long and deep with affection and tenderness, for someone we treasure and hold dear. It is this kind of love that creates strong relationships and lasting marriages. It allows people to heal after horrific hurts. It allows love to expand and grow, with a circle of love that never ends. It makes telling one another daily, "I love you," a meaningful and edifying act. Cherishing one another, no matter the difficulties or the joy, strengthens the commitment and makes it possible in the first instance. The strength of the union welds a foundation for life and service to others, whether they are offspring, other family members, friends, a business, a community, a country or the world. ≈

Chapter 6

Giving

Many people subscribe to the maxim that life is for learning. Having children is a great gift of learning. Our parents are some of our first teachers, but as adults, the children we bear and care for in our lives become the so-called graduate school. When we become parents or even take on the responsibility of caring for or raising children, we learn more about ourselves—and one another when we share it with a partner. Family upbringings must blend, sometimes with difficulty. We fight about what is right, and children learn how to maneuver through and even manipulate that as part of an intricate dance of family relations. You can watch it at the breakfast table at a restaurant where a family with children dines, no matter where you are in the world. Nuclear and extended family dynamics change dimensions with the addition and development of each child.

L. to R. Kate, John, Rick, Laura and me in South Carolina in November 1995, two years after my dad died; here celebrating my dad's life by the ocean in South Carolina with our extended family

The family is a microcosm of a greater community. Social mores of what is acceptable start in the family. Mastering the art of family relations and development (or at least thinking we have) makes us successful in the greater community of the world.

We know that we have the added responsibility to teach, as our parents taught us. We carry with us the scars from tough lessons learned, agonizing over whether to let a child learn them on his or her own or whether to softly pad the way so the scars aren't so deep. Usually our children tell us in one way or another what will work. In the greater community, our experiences with our children educate us how to be effective with our audience, our target market or our constituency.

The "traditional" family photo; L. to R. Laura, me, John, Rick and Kate in 1987, the year I left the Secretary of State's office (the first time) and entered the private practice of law for a Cleveland firm

The decision of how to "guide" children is analogous to the push and pull of philosophies of government. Are we a paternalistic society? Are we acting like "big brother" (or big sister)? Do we take a laissez faire attitude and say, "let them work it out on their own" and let the markets rule? Or do we set rules and standards, concerned about possible damage without some limits? Many of the issues governments face are already being faced by families every day.

We continue to ask, what is government's purpose in human and social interaction? Is it economic? Is it social? Is it for safety? Is it for allowing "the pursuit of happiness," as mentioned in the Declaration of Independence but not the Constitution? Can government undergird and impart a delicate balance of individual freedom while enhancing noble human characteristics for the greater good of its people?

Governments are not unlike families. When Dad drinks his paycheck or Mom can't work because she's strung out on drugs, the children suffer. The scenario often brings with it violence and pain. When banks and wars take inordinate amounts of the treasury in one way or another, unless more revenue can compensate, debt increases or cuts must be made. Children's education suffers; health care becomes arguably not a right; bridges dangerously await repair, and libraries become costly extravagances, to name a few.

Children teach us much about what we must do to survive, even as we are trying to teach them. My children taught me that I am worthy to be their mother. Every child brings with him or her joys and problems. Knowing that each of my children was somewhere before he or she was born and that each of them chose my husband and me, gave me the strength to try and be the kind of parent they needed me to be. The analogy of "family," and the myriad ways it is defined, have meaning for how we manage the changes we face as nation that is now part of a world that communicates, travels and exchanges resources as never before.

Taking a partner in life, even for a time, is a challenge in that each agrees to hand off some of his or her power to the other. Forceful domination is not a useful part of this schema. When children or new members are added to the already complicated interaction, there is seldom time for prepared or organized choreography, and the resulting improvisation can be thing of great beauty or a tragic disaster.

My father said many times over the years that the third child makes the better parents, because there is one more of them than you. (Imagine what that is like for a single parent. Laura Riggs-Kolman worked for both Rick and me, eventually following me into the Secretary of State's office until she died during my term. Laura was a single mom for years who expected Father's Day gifts as well as Mother's Day gifts from her sons. She was never disappointed.) When the number of children exceeds the number of parents, walking across the street becomes a challenge. There is no longer one child for each parent to hold hands, so two of the children must share one parent. This takes negotiation, depending on the child. There is a constant challenge from children about what is fair, and this sense of fairness is something intrinsic in children that must be heeded and honed through careful and sensitive parenting. Even dogs know what is fair (try giving one a treat and not another).

Rick and I had three children in five years. At about the time I had Kate in 1981, many businesses were figuring out how to craft maternity leave policies. While I was interviewing for a summer internship at a large Columbus law firm during law school and after Kate was born, one of the female partners gave me the "lowdown" on her firm when we exited together to use the ladies room. She said in low tones in the restroom, "Listen, they had to figure out a maternity leave policy for me, because I was the first woman in the law firm to have a baby while I was working here. It hasn't been easy." I didn't get the internship, but this lawyer's restroom confidence was worth the cost of the interview.

L. to R. Laura, Kate and John in 1986

Three years later, after I was a lawyer, I interviewed for an associate position with the same law firm. I was given signs to be hopeful I would land a job as an attorney there and be able to leave the Secretary of State's office for private practice. I soon found out after that interview I was pregnant with John. I made the mistake of telling a mother of one of Kate's school friends about it. This mother's husband also happened to be a partner at this same law firm. I did not get the job. The woman who confided to me in the restroom no longer practices there either.

Children teach you lessons just by their presence (or impending presence). I found out I was pregnant with Laura in 1983, during a several week interview process for a promotion in then Secretary of State Sherrod Brown's office. I faced a dilemma: Did I tell the interview team or not tell them? I chose to tell them. Some thought it a shrewd move that put the known liberal,

Sherrod Brown, "over a barrel." I thought it was the best decision for me, because if they had a problem with that, I didn't want to deal with pressure or expectations that could interfere with both performing the job well and being a good mother to my children. I was awarded the promotion, and we negotiated my maternity leave to our mutual satisfaction.

Two years later, John was born, and maternity leave was by now a more common issue and for which there were policies. I had to take that leave sooner for health reasons in this pregnancy and was afforded three months off, six weeks before he was born and six weeks after.

For those like me who worked outside the home, decisions and challenges relating to childcare were daunting. For many, the more children they have, unless they are upper income, the question of the expense of childcare versus the income earned with a second paycheck becomes almost a toss up. When I was interviewed for a spot on Columbus City Council but not selected, one of the pressing issues I spoke to the screening committee about was the need for affordable quality childcare. I was in the thick of it, knowing that, from day-to-day, my life was delicately balanced as long as my childcare provider and assistant at work remained as stable situations. My "key issue" for city council didn't seem to be a real "grabber" with the mostly male committee members who interviewed me. Kate and Pat still deal with the issues today with our granddaughter, Maddy, while countries like Serbia have been providing it as a government benefit, along with paid maternity leave for years.

In my Senate campaign nearly twenty-five years later I pushed hard on the issue of childcare and other family-related quality of life issues via twelve regional forums on "Women's Issues." We used Maria Shriver's and the Center for American Progress' groundbreaking report on women in the workplace called, "A

Woman's Nation," as a springboard for discussion about issues of childcare, elder care, women's health care issues and workplace flexibility. The forums were successful and were attended by both women and men. The topics emphasized by the various communities' participants showed me the regional differences of the state, often affected by an area's economic and social conditions.

Many large businesses have found that addressing issues such as these creates more productive workers. Others are beginning to understand the value of niche marketing specifically to diverse groups according to their interests, concerns and causes, including LGBT-specific marketing.

Some businesses, such as Deloitte Touche Tohmatsu Limited (Deloitte), rely on research that shows having more women in leadership roles actually increases profitability. Imagine that. Putting women who have learned from managing families and busy households while they pursued careers in positions to manage complex financial and business transactions makes more money for businesses! What I learned from managing my household and business simultaneously prepared me well to be a trial court judge in the busiest trial court of the state (Franklin County, Ohio).

There, male attorneys and even male witnesses marveled at what the job required: keeping a docket moving, taking criminal pleas while giving a civil trial a break and moving seamlessly from task to task regardless of how unrelated. And when it came to managing trials that involved the often sensitive issues connected to families and children, my experiences with children made my work all that much more effective. Motherhood, nothing more, nothing less, prepared me best for managing these tasks.

About a year before Kate was to graduate from high school, I was to face the beginning of the "empty nest" phenomenon (three children in five years means time as a blur during high school years, and then they're gone). I honestly acknowledged to myself that I was not ready for that change as quickly as I knew it would happen. Fate presented me with options to extend it, but at a great price.

In June of 1998, I was hosting a dinner party in my home for a dozen or so people when I received a call from my nearly ninety-year-old Great Uncle Merrill (who at age 89 spent most of his days on the Internet using two computers to research our ancestry and read political events of the day for unsolicited email commentary of which I was often a recipient). He was my grandfather's (Glendon Oscar Swan's) older brother.

"Jennifer?" he said in his high, squeaky voice when I answered the phone. "Glendon has fallen at the retirement home in Springfield and has been taken to the hospital. They didn't find him until 4:00 this afternoon. Did you know you are his power of attorney?" he continued. No, I did not know this. I left that dinner party, still in my sleeveless denim dress and drove to Springfield, where I joined my younger cousin, Kellee. We sat vigil all night outside of intensive care where Grandpa was being treated, talking about our lives and sharing stories of our children and families. My mother was in Tennessee on a boat with my stepdad, and it was difficult to reach her. My nearly eighty-seven-year-old grandfather had been stabilized but was still in intensive care.

The next day, I went to see Grandpa's lawyer, Tom Hackett, in Springfield to try to understand the extent of my responsibilities and what needed to be done to oversee my grandfather's affairs. I had been up most of the night, still in my dress from the dinner party the evening before.

I also kept thinking about some of the things Kellee had made me aware of as we talked through the night. Kellee's brother, Phil, was a single dad with three children, the oldest of whom, Tad, was about nine months older than my son, John. Both were about twelve at the time. Brandee was ten and David was four. Work and being a single dad had been tough for Phil, who had full custody of all three children. He was facing having to move to Columbus for work and live in less than optimum circumstances. He was stressed trying to find a place for three children and navigate getting two of them enrolled in school.

I had met Tad only once at an extended family reunion picnic when he and John were about five years old. There was something about this kid and his endearing grin that stuck in my heart. I was crestfallen to hear Kellee talk about how hard things were for Tad. I knew that once he was past age twelve, it would be difficult to bring him back from teenage influences that could send him on the wrong path.

My grandfather did not get better; I managed his affairs until he died. After his funeral at a family wake at Kellee's farmhouse just outside of South Charleston, I saw that things were not better for Tad, either. I quietly pulled Rick aside and asked what he would think of Tad coming to live with us for a year and going to school with John at Our Lady of Peace Catholic grade school. Considering Rick's upbringing and sense of family, and what he had observed even during the wake, Rick immediately said yes.

I talked to his dad, Phil, and then to Tad. Overcome with more than a good dose of compassion, (and recklessly without checking with Rick or the kids,) I told Phil that if the other kids needed to be with us, that could happen, too. When I asked Tad if he would like to live with us for a year and go to school with John, he was unsure. The better I got to know Tad, the more I understood his keen sense of responsibility he exercised for his younger siblings. That likely contributed to his hesitancy. Kellee prodded Tad to take the chance (she was Tad's favorite aunt). Tad agreed. But first, Phil let the children make a two-week visit to rural North Carolina to see their mother, Carla, whose issues were steady and multiple.

Relations between Phil and Carla were rocky, to put it simply. While the children were there to visit her for two weeks, Carla enrolled Tad and Brandee in school in North Carolina, even though she didn't have custody of them. When Phil told me what had happened, I said, "Well, then, let's go get them." Phil said we could take a "buddy flight" which turned out to be standby (Phil worked for the airlines) to bring the kids back to Ohio. I took an attorney from my firm at the time, Patrick Piccininni, with me, and the three of us went to the Columbus airport at 5:30 in the morning. We learned when we arrived at the airport that the airline had canceled our flight.

Undaunted, I rented a car and drove the three of us to Cleveland to catch a "buddy flight" there. When all was said and done, Rick and I ended up with two children, Tad and Brandee, who came with just the clothes on their backs and their backpacks from school in August 1998. Three months later, four-year-old David joined them after court proceedings in Springfield, where custody originally had been granted to Phil. Phil returned to his job out of state with the airlines, and we planned on regular visits. Now I had lots of children to learn from.

Both parents agreed to our having custody of the three children. These children lived with us for nearly two and half years before they returned to their parents. During this time we juggled and paid for five children in Catholic school and eventually one in college—all while I served as administrative partner of the law firm with both of us working in our own practices.

I used to joke when running for judge in my first campaign in 2000 that campaigning was actually time to myself. I had started the law firm and built it around trying to be flexible for my children. In trying my hand at having my own practice, I had begun our firm's operations from the corner of my bedroom when Kate, Laura and John were seven, four and two. After four years and handing off work to Rick's firm because I had more than enough, Rick left his law firm and joined me.

Once Rick combined his practice with mine, the business grew quickly, and our litigation practice burgeoned. We moved from our house with a staff of five to a small building in Clintonville that we bought from my mom after my dad's death—it had been his independent insurance office. After two years we outgrew and sold that building and moved downtown. The three extra kids came to live with us after we had moved our practice to the downtown office.

I'm not sure how we managed all of this—six kids, a law practice and a household, but the partnership of our marriage created a great framework. Working together made it easier to share the burdens and joys associated with this raucous ride. I had earlier made the conscious decision to limit my "extra-curricular" activities to those directly related to either the children or work. I said to myself, "I only have my children for a limited period of time. With their needs and mine, this is all I can handle and be comfortable." This is not to say that this is right for other women, but it worked for me with my upbringing, values, resources and capabilities.

There would be time later for boards and other community work. That outlook helped to keep me focused. In keeping with this creed, I did pro bono work for the county Democratic Party and became an officer of Laura's French Back-to-Back school program. Rick and I became band booster parents and eventually co-presidents at Watterson Catholic High School where Kate and Laura each served a stint as the band's center snare drummer in their respective times. Twice Rick drove a large, rented truck loaded with all the kids' instruments to Florida when the band played in post-Christmas bowl games there. When we added three more children to our household we hired extra help at home, from 8:00 a.m. to 7:00 p.m. weekdays, splitting each weekday between two people, one for cleaning and the other for helping kids with their homework and driving them to extra-curricular activities.

I had developed a couple of maxims that I still share with other parents today, because it kept things manageable and still allowed the children to excel at what they did. First there was "the rule of two:" no child could be involved in more than two extra-curricular activities outside of school at one time. (So, if there are five children at home, which there were, that means no more than ten extra curricular activities for Mom and Dad to manage.) In addition to the "rule of two" was "the rule of one." It had two parts. If you start something (like ballet classes), you have to finish it. Then, expose yourself to other things, and finally, *pick one thing you love*, are good at and want to pursue—and go for it! With that many children, those simple rules worked beautifully. And for ourselves, Rick and I remembered that with children the days may be long, but the years are short.

Rick and I stressed to all the children the simple philosophy of being honest and working hard, just like our parents had with us. I gave serious thought to having a plaque made to hang on the kitchen wall that would read simply: "Be Honest. Work Hard." Those are the foundational ingredients of success, no matter how you define success.

I was asked by a then Columbus City Councilwoman (later a fantastic director of the Ohio Department of Insurance) Mary Jo

Hudson to join a group of women to start what is now the thriving Women's Fund of Central Ohio. I knew it was a golden opportunity to be on the ground floor of an influential women's organization, just based on who the women were who had been invited to the table. It would have given me closer ties to whom I perceived to be the "movers and shakers" among the women in the Central Ohio community. I very much wanted to participate. The financial commitment, however, was beyond what Rick and I could handle while caring for the extra children.

Thinking back, I could have made a case for special dispensation, but when I stated I could not make the financial commitment because of all the children, no one offered to make allowances, and I did not think of asking for an exception. There is a price to pay for keeping your focus on what you know you can successfully accomplish, but it's worth it in the end. If that situation had occurred today, I would have attempted a "work around" of mutual benefit. What more women of any age ought to remind themselves of is that, regardless of their position or stature, they bring intrinsic value based on who they are and their unique experiences to nearly any situation.

Managing with six children, older siblings helped younger siblings—sometimes too much. Once when midterm grades were due to come home from school, Brandee and John, who had good grades, agreed with Laura and Tad, whose grades needed improvement, not to show us their reports. I finally realized there had been no midterm reports and confronted the children. When I learned the truth, I resolutely started copying famous speeches from the encyclopedia using our single page copier, a vestige from our home office days. "What are you doing?" they asked nervously. "You'll see," I said.
Each of them was given an assignment of copying word-for-word famous speeches from throughout American history. (This had worked well with Kate in earlier years, and she has long

appreciated The Rev. Dr. Martin Luther King, Jr.'s speech, "I Have a Dream.")

Brandee had to copy the Mayflower Compact and Thomas Paine's "Common Sense."

"Make sure you spell all the names right, Brandee. You have a relative in there in the Mayflower Compact," I said. Her eyes were as big as saucers under her blond bangs.

"John, you are to copy John F. Kennedy's Inaugural Speech. Tad, you have FDR's Inaugural Speech, and Laura, you have Martin Luther King, Jr.'s speech," I said. They groaned, took their pencils and started copying. In the end they thought the speeches were interesting, but hated having to copy every word. Conspiracies like this didn't happen again (at least to my knowledge).

Our downtown law office was now operated out of an 1893-vintage Victorian house that had been converted to an office. Our kids were our janitorial staff, (with much supervision from me.) They were paid and had bank accounts for spending money. The boys took a city bus from our home to downtown to do their jobs after school. Once, John saw my white station wagon downtown and hopped off the city bus to try and catch a ride with me the rest of the way to the office. As he would nearly catch up to me, the traffic light would turn green and I'd speed off. He shouted, waved and sprinted, but my time in the car was alone time. With stereo turned up high, I was oblivious to the Laurel and Hardy drama playing out behind me. A great soccer player, John ended up running from the north end of downtown to the southeast end of downtown, more than a mile, in futile spurts that didn't net that ride with Mom.

For the time we had these three special children, we know we helped them see choices that they would not otherwise have seen. We know we helped give them stability and love and give their parents a chance to get back on their feet. These children came to know that many people loved them. Letting them go was one of the hardest things Rick and I have ever experienced. The difficulty of helping our own children cope with that loss, two days before Christmas, 2000, cannot be described adequately with words. Little after that could be characterized as "hard," just as requiring endurance.

L. to R. Kate, David, Laura, Brandee, Tad and John in Washington, D.C. during cherry blossom time, 1999

Rick and I learned much from our second set of children in our lives, but we also learned an unmatched spirit of generosity from our own children that I would be hard-pressed to find in any government office, business, charity or religious institution. Our own three children shared their parents, their friends, their bedrooms, their clothes, their extended family, their

Christmases and the one vacation we could afford to take with six kids. (We traveled in a rented 15-passenger van with a portable TV and VCR strapped with bungee cords to two, stacked milk crates and six sets of ear buds for quiet for the parents.) Our children shared their time learning their lessons in life with Tad, Brandee and David, who in turn shared theirs with Kate, Laura and John.

In sharing as a family, all of these six children taught Rick and me how to be better parents. At one point when things were financially hard, I apologized to our three biological children for making life tougher for them by bringing more children into our home. They protested immediately and said, "Don't say that, Mom. We love them, and we wouldn't have it any other way." Such was the lesson my children taught me in generosity and love. ≈

Chapter 7

Mentors

A most unlikely person was my first political mentor—Donna Hurwitz. It was 1978. Most people would not know who she is, unless they were regulars at the Statehouse in the 1970's. Donna worked in the Statehouse office of Democratic Senator Thomas E. Carney from Girard, Ohio, when I first met her. I was twenty-one years old and married to Rick for just five months. I had graduated from college two months before with a degree in Sociology-Gerontology. I wanted to do more than secretarial work. I had worked in high school and college as my dad's part-time secretary at his insurance office, and I thought with a college degree I was finally ready to do more than I had done before. In reality, I didn't have the experience or education for more. I had previously worked in a typing pool starting at age 16, at Frisch's Restaurant at 19, at Sears Northland during high school and college breaks, in my dad's office on and off over the years and as a program monitor for the USDA summer lunch program in 1977 where I met Rick.

Donna coached me on how to be a state senator's secretary, in this case, Senator Carney. She said, "Jennifer, to be successful at this job you have to think like a Senator. Think about what he would want done and be two steps ahead of him. Think like a Senator," she repeated. She was right, and it's advice I have remembered for every job I've had since, even when I was the boss but needed to train my assistants. (I have told them to think about what it's like to do my job, and then take the initiative.) I know they have been better for it, and so have I. Remembering how it helped me as a young person, even though it's such simple advice, I like to think that Donna's advice lives on through those I've trained with it.

Donna had been engaged to the late state Senator Paul Gillmor, who went on to be the Ohio Senate President and later served in Congress. She broke off her engagement with Paul after falling hopelessly in love with Don King, the president of the Ohio Trucking Association. It was billed as a torrid romance, jilting a senator for a lobbyist. Donna was just following her heart. With Senator Carney as chairman of the Senate Transportation Committee, her new alliance created a conflict for her, so she was leaving, but not before giving me her advice. At one point, when details were coming out about her change of marriage plans, the Columbus Dispatch sensationally referred to her as a "blonde divorcee," as if she were some sort of 1970's amalgam of Marilyn Monroe and Wallis Simpson. Donna was neither—just caring and pragmatic.

Senator Thomas E. Carney, a rotund, white-haired Youngstown area Democrat, a former thirty-year steel worker and former Girard City Council President, was my first political boss. His advice was simple and solid, kind of like him. The first time I had a meeting with him about becoming his secretary, he mumbled through a chaw of tobacco pushing out his cheek, "Jennifer, the first thing in politics is loyalty. You be loyal to me; I'll be loyal to you." When I started law school and had to miss evening committee hearings for night classes, he defended me with other senators whose aides complained that I didn't have to work nights like they did.

After I left his employ (to have Kate during my second year of night law school), every time I changed jobs or was promoted, I visited him as long as he was elected. Each visit, I gave him my card and told him if he ever needed anything he should call me. Later, when I started my own private law practice, I bought homemade baked goods baked by his daughter, Marie, as holiday presents for my clients. I continue to live by that first lesson today, whether it's in politics or life.

Sherrod Brown was a different kind of politician than Senator Carney. Elected to the Ohio House of Representatives at age 21 while still finishing college at Yale University, he was a member of what was known as the "rump caucus" within the House Democratic Caucus. He was joined by cohorts like Tom Sawyer (who later went on to Congress and now is in the state Senate) and Dennis Wojtanowski (who ran Sherrod's first statewide campaign, later became Governor Dick Celeste's first legislative director, then became a powerful lobbyist, and finally, was a senior advisor to Lee Fisher's U.S. Senate primary campaign.)

There was John Begala, who became an assistant director in the Celeste administration at the state Department of Mental Retardation and Developmental Disabilities, but disillusioned with the foibles of his boss, Minnie Fells Johnson, he left. A true policy and political afficionado, he now is the respected executive director of the Center for Policy Solutions in Cleveland, an organization focused on health and social services in the Cleveland area. He also serves as a Senior Fellow and Director of the Urban Center at the Maxine Goodman Levin College of Urban Affairs at Cleveland State University.

There was Dennis Eckart, who also went to Congress, later lobbied, and now practices law and farms. Somewhat less directly, there was David Hartley from Springfield, who now serves as a longtime county commissioner in Clark County, the county of my birth, and who was in my night law school class. There may have been a few more, but these members were the most vocal and caused the southern Ohio Speaker of the House, Vernal G. Riffe, Jr., known as "Vern Riffe," the most headaches. Of all of these members of the rump caucus, Sherrod went the farthest in political office.

The caucus was called "rump," because it was a group of mostly young, liberal, and often "in-your-face," rebels. This rump caucus routinely got under long-time Speaker Vern Riffe's skin (and its members enjoyed it), as "Mr. Speaker" wrestled for discipline within a caucus majority in a House of 99 members. Vern Riffe was old school, meting out punishment in the form of office locations, committee assignments and bills moving out of the powerful House Rules Committee for a House floor vote. The rump caucus was liberal, uncompromising on principle and often with a sense of humor to prove it. Each received their share of old school political punishment.

After working for Senator Carney (who could be raw, but who was always real), Sherrod Brown was like no political boss I had ever heard of or could imagine, and I had seen a myriad of political types in the Ohio Senate. Whereas Senator Carney would throw away mail or refer it to another Senator if it was not from his district, Sherrod Brown had an insatiable curiosity about the people of Ohio and worked to help anyone wherever they were. When my son, John, worked for him in Washington, DC in 2004, he was amazed at the constituent service provided: every letter, telephone call or email was answered within two weeks.

I had often handled constituent tasks for Senator Carney, so John's recitation of this fact impressed me as well. While in law school and working for the Senator, I wrote a paper for a comparative law class, comparing children's rights in what was then the Soviet Union with children's rights in Ohio. (I had completed a year of Russian language studies in high school.) To obtain the research needed for the paper, I had written to the U.S. embassy for information under cover of Senator Carney's letterhead. When he received the information, he was concerned. "Jeez, Jennifer, couldn't you have asked for something about Ireland? For God's sake, they're going to think we're Communists." I apologized but did well on the paper.

A far cry from Senator Carney, Sherrod Brown had actually studied in the U.S.S.R. as a Russian Studies major at Yale. When I joined his staff in the Ohio Secretary of State's office in 1983, I was astounded at his embrace of public service. I quickly learned that if I had an idea that was creative, he became excited about it and let a self-starter like me run with it. He was very bright, and his approach was refreshing. He attracted an exceptionally young and talented staff because of it.

What I couldn't figure out when I worked for him was how he found it intellectually stimulating to spend his time traveling around the state and writing what some of his later staff members would call "love letters" to every person he met, telling

Palm card literature from then state Representative Sherrod Brown's first campaign for Secretary of State, 1982

them it was nice to meet them. (I even remember seeing one of his assistants holding a magnifying glass over a photo to try to read a nametag so that Sherrod could send the person a letter.) I could see no real mental challenge to this, but he did it religiously and has for nearly forty years. He has saved the names and addresses of the people he has met since before computer databases were used for campaigns. He told me in 2008 that he and his staff estimated that over his career he had sent more than 35,000 "love letters." I know plenty of people who have been thrilled to receive them.

Sherrod was not particularly taken with executive office administration. The cadre of young people he brought in as his directors were put under the tutelage of the sage, tough and seasoned Richland County Democratic Party Chairman, Don Kindt. Don brought Sherrod into politics and served as the first of Sherrod's assistant secretaries of state. Each director was given ample opportunities to run with projects from start to finish without being micromanaged. Sometimes we ran right into each other, but that's what Don Kindt was for, and he was good at quelling the discord, often by sheer force of personality.

I learned many lessons watching Sherrod as an office holder, so much that one of the letters I routinely sent as Secretary of State with commissions for gubernatorial appointments was written to Sherrod's brother, Bob, when Governor Ted Strickland appointed him to a board. Soon after I had signed and sent a letter to Bob with his commission and personally handwritten a note at the bottom of the typed letter that he was "perfect for this job," I received an email from Sherrod forwarding Bob's email to him with the words Bob had included in the subject line, "at the feet of the master."

Working for Sherrod Brown as his Legislative Counsel gave me the opportunity to conceive of, write, analyze, lobby, synthesize and present legislation for the Ohio General Assembly like no other job could have. I wrote testimony for legislators who could barely pronounce words such as "distribute" and "distribution." I coached them on their testimony, giving them sample questions and answers for floor speeches. I lined up committee votes, watched them disintegrate in a day and put them back together again in two. Little is more professionally satisfying than sitting in the gallery of the Ohio House of Representatives and watching the sequence of events put into play happen as they are supposed to and quietly know that you have made a difference.

The union-printed business card on tan stock with brown print reflected one of the greatest on-the-job learning experiences anyone could have.

Sherrod let me become knowledgeable in negotiating computer contracts. With the help of Terri O'Brien, the office's first female Information Services director, we lobbied the state controlling board for emergency funding to buy the office's first personal computers as part of a mini-computer text processing system for publishing our own documents. Sherrod eventually designated me to speak on his behalf to the legislature to present the agency's budget, a task he previously had performed personally. He gave me unmatched opportunities, especially when he supported me for a promotion while pregnant with Laura. He was ahead of his time in doing so.

In March 1987, I left the Secretary of State's office early into Sherrod's second administration to enter private law practice. I believed it was time to develop other expertise, thinking no one would hire me for election law. Sherrod occasionally sought advice from me after I left his employ. To my great surprise, there was a burgeoning need for an attorney in Ohio who could provide election law advice and counsel, and my law practice grew to the point that I left the Cleveland law firm I had joined in Columbus and formed my own law firm at the end of 1988. It's the firm I still practice in today.

Bob Taft's win over Sherrod Brown in the 1990 election was Sherrod's first and only election loss. Sherrod Brown's loss in 1990 changed the political course of Ohio for decades. The Ohio Democratic Party lost control of the state apportionment board and has never regained it since it last had the majority (to determine legislative district lines) in 1981. After losing, Sherrod spent two years out of office. He was elected in 1992 to Congress from northeast Ohio. He continued to be reelected until he ran successfully for the U.S. Senate in 2006, the same year I ran for Secretary of State.

Many people (including me) were baffled when he failed to support me in the 2010 U.S. Senate primary. He had previously told me to "go for it" one February Saturday afternoon when I called him to gain his blessing for the run. But then again, he never supported Congresswoman Betty Sutton, despite encouraging her to run. He stayed out of the 2008 Presidential primary in Ohio between then Senators Hillary Clinton and Barack Obama.

Toward the end of the 2010 primary election, Rick and I were chagrined to see that he spoke to a Columbus Dispatch reporter, expressing criticism that I was being "negative" in the Senate primary race and that that would hurt me. He had told others that he had information that Rick and I were making negative statements about my opponent's daughter. It was patently not true, but to Rick's and my disappointment, I did not get a telephone call from him asking me why I would do that; I could have set him straight. He did not call me, and the damage was done. It was later reprinted in the Lima News in western Ohio. Even if you're Secretary of State, it's hard to defend yourself and call out your U.S. Senator for relying on bad information, especially when you don't know the allegations have been made.

Every time I visited Washington and asked for an audience, whether it was in my state elected position or running for U.S. Senate, despite the fact he was an extremely busy U.S. Senator, I received an audience. In the Senate race he continually challenged me about my fundraising. My Senate primary campaign fundraising efforts were successfully being damaged by whispering campaigns that I was going to drop out, that I couldn't raise money and later, by threats and fear tactics from others in my party to keep people from donating to my campaign. Sherrod said to me in the plainest terms, "Jennifer, I believe you have the campaign skills to win this race, but I don't see how you will do this without more money." He was right. Nevertheless, I continued to push for his endorsement saying, "Between Lee and me, which of us will respect you as the senior senator and not try to rush ahead of you when an award of money comes to Ohio?" He would look uncomfortable, and I would put on the "mother guilt" routine that had worked with him in our earlier days of working together, saying, "Wait, wait, don't answer that . . . you don't need to answer!" And we would laugh.

The Sunday before the primary election, his wife, Connie Schultz, a popular, widely read columnist for the Plain Dealer, a Pulitzer Prize winner and ardent feminist, posted on her widely accessed social networking site that "it would be helpful for some Ohio activists to remember that feminists who vote for a guy are not traitors to the cause." Gloria Feldt, author of *No Excuses: Nine Ways Women Can Change the Way We Think About Power,* responded with posts of her own in a spirited and lengthy thread of comments that resulted in discussion between many women and men in the state. Gloria said:

> I agree, Connie, that there is no reason for either women or men to be unkind to others who think or vote differently. But that's not the argument I'm hearing in this exchange. I hear people trashing the idea that women have any responsibility to help other women, whereas I believe we most certainly do.
>
> To be clear with folks like Helen and John: I said that when the male and female candidates are mostly evenly matched, I'll support the woman until we have reached parity. I wouldn't vote for a woman like Palin who is anti-choice and doesn't work to advance women on issues such as Connie mentioned.
>
> That said, I've been researching women's relationship with power for over a year. We've been repeating a pattern since Abigail Adams asked John to remember the ladies and he didn't: The ladies didn't rebel as they had threatened. Women too often say we want rights and equality but we step back from making sure we get them.
>
> Thanks for starting this conversation--it has motivated me to go to an event for Kirsten Gillibrand this evening rather than the concert I'd planned to attend:-)

There was apparently a lot of disagreement going on in Cleveland about the Ohio U.S. Senate primary election. The subject of gender of the candidates was playing heavily into the discussion. It was distressing and disappointing to see how contentious things had become. Supporters in each Democratic camp were sniping at each other, and hard feelings were beginning to form between them.

The anger and anguish from Mary Boyle's close U.S. Senate Democratic primary in 1994 against Joel Hyatt (for what later became Sherrod's U.S. Senate seat) still simmered. Interestingly, in 1994 and also in 2010, Democratic performance plunged terribly in the general election, with the loss of every statewide office. In both cases Mary Boyle and I fought valiantly in the Senate Democratic primary, and women were energized. In both cases we were quietly opposed by the male-dominated establishment within the party structure that "stepped on our air hoses," cutting off needed funding through political maneuvers.

Mary was opposed by a man who had never before held public office. In my case, even though I had won my statewide office handily, running in my own right and with fifty-five percent of the vote in 2006, I was opposed by a man who had previously twice lost races for statewide office, one of them being an ouster from the office of Attorney General (in 1994 when Mary Boyle lost her primary election). As lieutenant governor, Lee Fisher's claim to statewide office was as a member of a joint ticket with Governor Strickland.

I am aware that Sherrod was being bombarded with intense pressure from the leadership of the Democratic Senatorial Campaign Committee (DSCC) to get me out of the race and even for him to endorse Lee Fisher. Lieutenant Governor Fisher certainly appeared to be Washington's favorite, with Harry Reid holding an event for him, Ted Strickland's endorsement and the hiring of so many of that city's consultants. Senator Brown's comments about me being "negative," mirrored an earlier encounter I had had with Senator Bob Menendez of New Jersey, chair of the DSCC in September 2009.

Senator Menendez threatened me in face-to-face meeting, saying that if "either of the candidates in this primary" is being "negative and/or not raising enough money," the DSCC would come into Ohio and work against them. I looked him squarely in the eye, and said, "Senator, if you come to Ohio and work against me, the women of Ohio will never forgive you." He appeared unnerved and said he wasn't "scared" of me.

I immediately countered, "I'm not trying to scare anyone," to which he murmured, "and I know you're not scared of me." I quietly said I was not. He continued, with the statement that being Hispanic made him understand how I felt as a woman (all I could think to myself was that different plumbing is pretty hard to get around). Then he told me I was being negative, stood up and stormed out of the DSCC conference room.

I figured that this guy probably wasn't making my Senator's life very easy with me in the race, and I figured I was right. It's a good idea to not put all your eggs in one basket when it comes to a mentor, because they can sometimes disappoint you, even when they may not want to.

I can't talk about mentors without mentioning Sherrod Brown's first political mentor, who later became mine, too. Don Kindt was the Richland County Democratic chairman in Mansfield, Ohio. Mansfield is about an hour north of Columbus, which is located in the center of Ohio. Ohio has 21 cities with populations of between 50,000 and 500,000 (Columbus is the only city in Ohio greater in municipal population than 500,000, with between 700,000 and 800,000 people).

Cities like Mansfield are considered "micropolitan" areas of Ohio and are often very "purple" in political persuasion, swinging between Democratic and Republican from election to election. When Don Kindt brought longhaired Sherrod Brown dressed in a winter parka to meet Vern Riffe for the first time in the early 1970's, it's said that when Don and Sherrod left, Vern threw his pen across the room in disgust and exclaimed, "Is that the best they can do?"

Don was a wily, battle tested warrior who had an intriguing combination of good ole' boy attitude yet belief in the power of young people as hope for the future. He never ceased to encourage and believe in young people and what they could do. He had a glass eye to replace one shot out in the Korean conflict, and he was always a strong supporter of veterans from that conflict. He had been director of human resources for the Ohio Department of Transportation (ODOT) under Governor Gilligan. It was one of the most political jobs in the state because the department's remote district offices provided some of the best jobs in the hinterlands of the state. He had also been a federal marshal for the U.S. District Court of the Northern District of Ohio, apprehending and bringing in one of the tougher criminals of the time.

When my office was situated next to Don's in the Secretary of State's office, I frequently could hear him loudly ranting about something. More than once I put my ear next to the wall to make sure he wasn't yelling about me. Often, when he stormed into his office, dressed in a perfectly pressed white shirt and black tie, I couldn't tell by his glass eye whether he was looking at me or not. I have since called it "on the job training" to toughen me up for lots of criticism later on after I became an elected official, myself.

Don Kindt had an uncanny way of letting the young directors in Sherrod's office have the room they needed to be creative and accomplish astounding things. Yet, when they tried to eat each other for breakfast, as ambitious political staffers often do, he could almost literally "knock some heads together" and keep them working in tandem. He did this even when Sherrod sometimes stirred the pot (unwittingly or on purpose, as office holders are wont to do). I marveled at Don, hoping that when I was his age (which I am close to now) I could inspire young people as he inspired all of us. Don died peacefully in his sleep in 2012, deserving the rest for many jobs well done.

Congressman Ted Strickland, Fran Alberty, and Judge Jennifer Brunner at Franklin County Democratic Party dinner 2005

Fran Alberty has been another amazing mentor. She was Sherrod's field representative and liaison with the Franklin County (Columbus) Board of Elections. She has been influential among national, state and local political party and labor organizations for decades. She also had been one of the original movers and shakers of the Federated Democratic Women of Ohio (FDWO). FDWO in 1970 recruited and helped elect the first woman to executive statewide office in Ohio, Gertrude Donahey, who became state treasurer. Pete O'Grady was the Ohio Democratic Party chair then. The women involved with FDWO had approached Pete and said they wanted a woman on the ticket. He told them to find him one. They did and saw to it that she was elected. Mary Ellen Withrow was elected state treasurer in 1992. In 2006, I became the third Democratic woman elected to statewide executive office in Ohio. As political consulting veteran, Jerry Austin, once put it, "You're the first Democratic woman elected to statewide [executive] office not to be elected treasurer."

Women in Fran Alberty's heyday were the backbone of political party volunteerism. In 2009, the wife of a former state senator wrote to me, telling me I should not run for the U.S. Senate and that it was "Lee's turn." I wondered how far women had really come. My opponent, Lieutenant Governor Lee Fisher is married to Peggy Zone, who is part of a strong political family in Cleveland. Both her father and her mother served on Cleveland City Council. Her brother, Matt, serves there now. Cleveland's city council is divided into wards where strong political bases are formed and politics are often intense.

The naysayer in my Senate race went on to describe ward activities in the days of Lee Fisher's mother-in-law in a supportive role. She described Mary Zone's work for her husband in the same vein of political support the women of Fran's day supplied. She described people congregating at the Zone house and women fixing pots of pasta for volunteers. When Rick and I read this email, we were incredulous. It was hard to believe someone younger than Fran was chastising me for running, when Fran, now nearly 80, was fully supportive of my candidacy. I can always count on Fran for a straight answer that cuts to the chase. She is not afraid to call it like it is and to step up in support of candidates she sees as the best people to run for office, known or little known. Fran remains on the lookout for Democrats who are smart and savvy and who will do a good job for the people who elect them. When she finds those candidates, she's been there to support them.

Fran still supports the work of the FDWO, exhorting its members to do what it was so effective in, electing women statewide officeholders. FDWO has played an important role in Ohio Democratic Party politics, researching issues for FDWO's endorsed candidates and educating women in the process. It's tougher now for the FDWO to operate as it did in Gertrude Donahey's and Mary Ellen Withrow's day. The social change of more women working outside the home has dwindled the numbers of women able to volunteer their time as they did then. In some of the more rural counties, however, the backbone of the party is the local women's political organization. In those locales, without the "women's group," there would not be much to speak of for local party organization.

Late in the 1980's I met Connie Stonerock who hailed from rural Pickaway County just south of Columbus. She grew into an amazing political strategist and was a consultant for the Ohio House Democratic Campaign Committee (OHDC). Being from a rural part of the state, like Ohio House Speaker Vern Riffe, she had one of the better understandings of the mind of this man who served as Speaker longer than any other Ohioan in the state's history. He was one of the most brilliant and effective politicians the state has ever seen and likely ever will see. I worked on the campaign side of the Ohio House Democratic Caucus' activities, directly for Vern Riffe. It was Connie who helped me process what I observed and learned.

Both Vern Riffe and Ted Strickland hailed from Scioto County. While each worked to give the "homespun" appearance on first meeting, Vern was better at it, which made it easier to underestimate him. This was to Vern's advantage and to his opponent's misfortune. Traditional "liberal" Democrats often despised Vern Riffe, because he used good old-fashioned horse-trading to get things done. That sometimes meant the emergent public policy was less than "pure." To keep order and get things done, punishment was meted out, and loyalty was rewarded.

Ohio House Speaker Vernal G. Riffe, Jr., Ohio's longest serving Speaker of the House of Representatives

Many since have tried to imitate the political style of Vern Riffe, but they've done it badly and simply turned away good people who would have been good partners (or "pahdnas" as Vern would have said). In my work with Speaker Vern Riffe from 1983 as Sherrod Brown's Legislative Counsel in the Secretary of State's office to 1994 as Vern Riffe's attorney and record keeper for the financial affairs of the Ohio House Democratic Committee, I saw Vern Riffe move from politician to statesman. This was most visible during the 1985 savings and loan crisis in Ohio.

Vern, working with Democratic Governor Dick Celeste and Senate President Paul Gillmor, a Republican, quickly quelled a run on the state's savings and loans. They called emergency legislative sessions that lasted long into the night. They gathered the best business and political minds in the state and together put safeguards in place to protect Ohioans from what could have been a major debacle. While thousands of depositors could not access their money for a period of weeks, no depositor lost a dime. Afterward, the investigation of what led to the crisis resulted in the state conviction and imprisonment of financier Marvin Warner, a major Democratic benefactor who had once been ambassador to Switzerland during the Carter Presidential administration.

Even after Sherrod Brown and Tony Celebrezze lost their races for Secretary of State and Governor, respectively, in 1990, and the legislative line drawing process moved to Republican control, Vern Riffe held on to the House majority for another two years. In 1994, he finally lost control of the House, and Joann Davidson became the first and only female Speaker of the Ohio House of Representatives. Even past age 80 Joann Davidson is still sought out nationally and statewide for her experience, balanced judgment and effectiveness as a government and political leader.

In his position as Speaker and leader of his Democratic caucus, Vern Riffe managed both the state and political affairs of the caucus. My job was to assist with legal support for the Democrats' political arm, the Ohio House Democratic Committee (OHDC) and for Vern Riffe's own campaign committee, which often raised more dollars than the OHDC caucus fund. In that capacity, I worked frequently with Connie Stonerock, who was the de facto political director of House Democratic campaign efforts to retain and grow the majority in the Ohio House

She taught me that when Vern called you "honey," it wasn't a good thing. It meant you had done something wrong. I admit I heard it a few times from Mr. Speaker, as he was known. Vern hated getting notices from the IRS, even if they were innocuous or just regular notifications, and he never wanted a caucus bill paid late. He had an apartment in Bexley where all the committee's bills were sent. He opened each bill before I saw it and knew if it was late.

Vern Riffe took many lessons from his father who had been the mayor of New Boston, Ohio. The "Speaker" was an insurance agent with his own independent agency in New Boston, like my dad was in Columbus. Mr. Speaker used to tell me that his father taught him to "always keep control of the money. If you know what's going on with the money, you always know what you need to know." As we moved into the 1994 elections, it was not unusual for me to take my laptop computer to meet him at the OHDC offices, take my instructions from him about what checks needed to be cut and for which candidates, print them out at the Ohio Democratic Party offices nearby and bring them back for him to sign. He saw every invoice that came in and signed every check that went out.

Later, when I started my own law practice and we added partners, I insisted that every check that came in be photocopied and a copy given to each of the partners. It helped us keep everyone honest, and we also knew when a client was paying us out of an account or business we didn't know they had. When I left the firm and this practice slipped, one of the partners started getting checks made to him personally, a practice the rudimentary copies had been designed to prevent. When it was reinstituted, Rick learned of the problem. Vern's advice proved to be solid. In our law firm, each partner sees every check to this day, except now our copies are electronic.

I followed Vern's advice when I took over the Secretary of State's office from Ken Blackwell. Veronica Sherman, my finance director, had staffed the House Finance Committee in Vern's days as Speaker. She understood why, during the first six months of my term, after inheriting an office where documents had been shredded, illegal bonuses had been paid totaling $80,000 just before the previous Secretary left office, and overspending had occurred, I wanted to see every bill before it was paid. This was not a usual practice for an office with a CEO of more than 150 employees. Veronica, Chief of Staff Tom Worley and then Human Resources director Gretchen Green and I met at least every two weeks to review Veronica's spreadsheets of the bills to be paid.

Knowing where the money was going helped me to determine whether it was necessary and what was actually happening in the office. Because the former Secretary had spent nearly two-thirds of the fiscal year's budget in just the first half I was able to make informed decisions on where cuts could be made until the ship was righted with adequate funding the next fiscal year. Vern's advice helped me navigate with greater certainty during those first six months in office.

A year after Ohio Democrats lost control of the state apportionment board, a stupendous loss with the concomitant loss of political funding for being in the minority, the only way the Dems could fight for fair legislative districts in the reapportionment process was through bootstrapping tactics. With Connie's help, I was just the warhorse to aid their efforts. Democrats took out full-page newspaper advertisements against the nonprofit corporation set up by Republicans to accept corporate donations for helping fund their efforts to draw new state legislative lines. The ads ominously cautioned, "Beware!" and pointed out that these corporate donations may violate state law and lead to criminal prosecution because they aided partisan efforts. One Republican attorney stated to Judge Dana Deshler in the litigation that followed that our efforts had been so effective that the GOP fundraising effort was a "ship dead in the water."

We were renegades. On behalf of the Ohio Democratic Party, I filed multiple lawsuits at the direction of Democratic Party Chair Eugene Branstool, a former state senator who authored the state's 1983 public employee collective bargaining law.

Nearly twenty years later, former Senator Branstool's bill was repealed by the legislature with the signature of Governor John Kasich who had been in the Ohio Senate minority when the bill had been adopted. Ultimately, the law was saved from repeal by a powerful labor-backed referendum effort in November 2011 when Ohioans voted to keep the law in place.

During the period of time when Connie schooled me on the ways of the Ohio House and Democratic politics in general, my husband Rick, an accomplished litigation attorney, himself, became my litigation teacher. Between Connie's political tutelage and Rick's legal tutelage, I often felt like a sponge that soaked up lessons, was squeezed and soaked some more, over and over again. But all of these experiences made me smarter and tougher. Connie was a brilliant strategist and never got the credit she deserved for what she did, but she never presumed to be smarter than Vern Riffe. No one was smarter than Vern when it came to the political process.

One of the house races Vern lost in 1994 was that of long-time Columbus legislator Mike Stinziano, a master at constituent services and author of Ohio's landlord-tenant laws that still today provide strong tenants' rights and protections. Even though the race was not looking good for him against Mike's female, Italian-surname challenger, Vern could not turn his back on Mike. He was loyal to his members who had been loyal to him. That's the way it was in politics in those days. Mike's loss was hard for many to take.

In 2007, Mike's son came to work for me as one of my election attorneys in the Secretary of State's office. He left in 2008 to take the job as the director of the Franklin County Board of Elections upon former State Democratic Chair Denny White's retirement. Young Mike now serves in his dad's House seat, after winning handily in 2010. In 2009, after my legislative counsel, Laurel Beatty, was appointed by Governor Strickland to the

Franklin County Common Pleas bench where I had served, the senior Mike Stinziano returned to Ohio from Chicago to take over the legislative work for the office for the rest of my term. You couldn't make that up if you tried. Vern Riffe's influence will be felt in Ohio politics for longer than he could have ever imagined.

Paul Tipps, now an accomplished lobbyist and senior political statesman by all estimations, has one of the most brilliant political minds I know of. A former Montgomery County (Dayton, Ohio) Democratic Party Chairman, he served as Ohio Democratic Party Chairman in 1982 when Democrats swept all statewide offices in a stunning display of political accomplishment. He was a wise chair who let the primary process play out without endorsement. In Sherrod Brown's race for Secretary of State there was a five-person primary. In the race for governor in 1982, there was a three-way primary between Dick Celeste of Cleveland, Bill Brown, Ohio's Attorney General, and former Cincinnati Mayor Jerry Springer. Vern Riffe decided to throw his support to Dick Celeste, helping Celeste win that primary and become Governor in 1982.

In Mary Ellen Withrow's primary race for State Treasurer, there were seven candidates (she was then serving as Marion County Treasurer). Later, after she and State Auditor Tom Ferguson were the only Democrats who survived the 1990 statewide elections, she was named by President Clinton to be U.S. Treasurer. This opened up her seat for then Governor Voinovich to name a Cincinnati Republican to fill it, Ken Blackwell. (More than once I heard people gripe about Mary Ellen Withrow taking the appointment, which would be an unimaginable complaint in the business world. The gripes had more to do with political power than they did with public service.)

Paul, who was also a close confidante of Vern Riffe, has been around the block a hundred times in realms personal, business and political. He understands people. He knows the history. He knows *their* history. He listens, and he learns from everyone he meets. Paul Tipps is one of those individuals involved in politics, much like Don Kindt, who values what young people bring to the process and is willing to give them advice if they are willing to listen. One of the best pieces of advice Paul ever gave me was about Vern Riffe. Frustrated about trying scale the wall of Vern's disgust with Sherrod as one of the star former "rump caucus" members of the House, I confided in Paul I was having trouble getting what I needed from the House for the Secretary of State's office. Paul and I stood on the street in front of the Rhodes State Office Tower. He cautioned patience, saying, "Jennifer, Vern can only be mad at five people at one time. Sooner or later, you'll fall off the list." He was right.

I have thought of and repeated Paul's advice countless times since that on-street, impromptu counseling session. As a leader I've remembered it, knowing that it is not wise to be peeved with too many people at once—it creates too much to remember, and it hinders forward movement. I learned to throw away the emotional baggage I don't need and to see what's left as a problem to deal with that could keep us from our goals. Paul was one of my closest advisors in the U.S. Senate race in 2010, and I'm sure it was painful for him to watch the 15-month torture process that the campaign often seemed to be.

Nonetheless, he encouraged, coached, advised, admonished and supported me like few others have in my political life. I am fortunate to call him a friend, and his legacy in Ohio politics is one to be respected and remembered. ≈

PART II

✦

ENTERING PUBLIC LIFE

Chapter 8

First Campaign

"Why are you running for judge?" asked the panel of volunteer lawyer supporters who were taking me through a mock interview to prepare me for the Columbus Bar Association screening committee. That's the first question every candidate should be able to answer. It's the question that more often than not leaves a candidate speechless or stuttering. This was my first race for office.

Age 7, October 1964, after moving to Glenmont Avenue in Clintonville in north Columbus

I had never planned to run for office, and I had never seen myself as the "candidate type." If someone had seen me in second grade, they would have seen a child afraid to leave the school playground steps after we moved to a new neighborhood and school in 1964. They would have taken me for a shy researcher for life, stuck in the dusty, upper recesses of the State of Ohio Library which for years was housed in the 1930's art deco building that is now the beautifully restored Supreme Court of Ohio.

But my passion was fairness. In my private law practice I had served as a contract hearing officer for the Ohio Department of Natural Resources. Through this experience, I found I loved being the one to instill and ensure fairness in a legal process. I had been former Ohio Attorney General Lee Fisher's legal counsel throughout his lengthy campaign for governor before and during his unsuccessful run in 1998. A prolific fundraiser, he had actually raised more money than former Ohio Secretary of State Bob Taft for the open seat vacated by former Governor George Voinovich. (Governor Voinovich was elected to the U.S. Senate in 1998 when he was term-limited as governor. This was the Senate seat Lee and I would later compete for in the 2010 Senate primary election, he as Lieutenant Governor and me as Secretary of State).

Before 2000, I did not want to *run* for judge. I did not want to run for any office. I just wanted to *be* a judge. But in Ohio, unless an attorney is appointed to a vacancy or to the federal bench, being a judge means running for office.

Clearly, a judicial appointment was not in the cards for me. Lee Fisher, a Democrat, had lost for governor in 1998, and the apportionment board was firmly controlled by the Ohio GOP. With reapportionment every ten years, at age 43, my hope of being appointed by any governor to a judgeship looked like a glimmer on the horizon, so I had to run.

I had been asked previously to run for judge in 1992 by Fran Ryan, former and first woman county chair of the Franklin

Fran Ryan, first woman Franklin
County Democratic Chair; she was
the first to ask me to run for office

County Democratic Party in Columbus. Before that, Fran was a Columbus city councilwoman, briefly a county commissioner, long serving Columbus city clerk and a Carter Administration appointee to the U.S. Department of Labor. Columbus Mayor Michael B. Coleman more recently made her ambassador to the older residents of Columbus. She was, and at age 76 still is a go-getter. After leaving the county Democratic party in her late 60's, she sold cars for George Byers Sons, a local car dealer, and our family bought at least four cars from her.

Most women give the following excuses for why they don't run for public office: they have family concerns; they don't believe they are qualified; or they have not been specifically asked to run. Check off the third issue; Fran asked me to run for judge. I said no for three reasons: I didn't think my family was far enough along for me to run; the children were ten, seven and five. I also wanted to gain more experience as a lawyer before I became a judge. Finally, running against a then sitting judge, Dana Deshler, with the same last name as a once-famous hotel in Columbus, didn't look like a race I could win. I had represented enough candidates and seen enough local campaigns in my law practice to be able to determine what was a winnable race.

I didn't run in 1992, but the thought of running never left my mind. I waited until there was a recent appointee to the bench who had to run as soon as he was appointed. This would make the race as close to an open seat as possible. When I had my target picked, I asked the party chair, Denny White, to breakfast so I could broach the idea with him. When Fran Ryan stepped down as the county chair in 1994, I was among a small group that included Fran Alberty to help Denny become elected chair. I had served as parliamentarian at the party meeting when he was elected and had provided free legal counsel to the party since.

Denny had previously been a Republican, but apparently he decided the Democratic Party was more in line with his thinking. Either way, he was old school, predictable, focused on loyalty, and even better, a common sense street fighter who was as pragmatic as they come. He liked the idea of my running. I knew this seat was my best chance. To run against a new appointee under Ohio election law means that the party simply names one person to oppose the appointee. There is no party primary, but there is a lot of internal jockeying that takes place until the candidate is selected to run.

Denny helped me maneuver through the endorsement process, in great part because I had been a help to the party, and in part because we were friends and both pragmatic. I would be running against a recent appointee, Judge John Bender.

John Bender had been appointed by Governor Taft to replace a long-time Republican judge named Jim O'Grady. My competition in the nomination process was another attorney named Mike O'Grady. It would have been easy for the party to name an "O'Grady" to run for a seat formerly held by an "O'Grady." But it didn't. I had done my homework, and Denny was in my corner. When John Kuliewicz, the chair of the county party judicial screening committee called me to tell me the party had chosen me to run, he said it was "unanimous." I thanked him and said, "That was the screening committee's second vote, right?" (Lawyers don't ever want a judge to be mad at them, so once a judicial nominee is selected by majority vote, they vote a second time and make it unanimous.)

What amazed me at that point was the realization that, now that I was the party's candidate, the judgeship would go to either John Bender or me—that was it. This was so different from other "job interviews" I had experienced. The seat had to be filled, and this would occur on time, on schedule, so that by December, one of us would be elected for the rest of the term until July 2003.

John Bender, having been appointed, was already wearing the robe, but it was a tough position to be in—taking on a new job, hiring staff, assembling a campaign, managing a judicial docket and running for the office—all at the same time and in six months. I did not envy him. Being in private practice with Rick and other attorneys, I had support, time and freedom from the strictures and daily docket of the judicial office. It was a great way to run, especially as a challenger.

John Bender was already a friend. He had served as Bob Taft's chief elections counsel in the Secretary of State's office after Bob Taft defeated Sherrod Brown in 1990. John was appointed to the bench after Bob Taft defeated Lee Fisher in 1998 to become governor. John held previous experience as a municipal judge in Crawford County. Because I had worked with him on behalf of my labor clients on campaign finance rules when he was in the Secretary of State's office, we knew each other well. I called him when I decided to run. "Jennifer," he said, "I'm glad it's you."

Judge John Bender, my
first political opponent
and friend for life

At first I wasn't sure if he thought that
I was a beatable candidate (my name
wasn't "Jennifer O'Grady;" it's
"Brunner," and it took people awhile
to be able to say it like "brew" instead
of "brun")—and this was my first race.
Knowing John as I do now, I believe
he saw the potential for our race to be
amicable. It was. When we attended
candidate nights, we sat together; we
conversed about the campaign and
even the speakers addressing the
attendees before us. Not a negative
word was said between us, and the
local newspaper even wrote an article
on the tenor of our race.

I worked hard in that campaign, getting funds from wherever I
could, holding fourteen fundraising events in six months,
obtaining endorsements and making sure that once I met
someone, they received a letter from me (just like one of my
mentors, Sherrod Brown, did). I learned more about my county
than I thought I could, having lived there most of my life. I
learned it best when I got lost trying to find an event. (I'm
definitely missing the magnetic chip carrier pigeons have that
guides them when they fly.)

In Ohio, judges can't ask for or personally accept money for
their campaigns. They must establish committees to do that for
them. "Where have you been?" queried some lawyers from
whom I sought help. What they meant was, why hadn't I served
on this or that board or bar association committee. I told them
that until now, I had made a conscious (and to myself, I said,
"sane") decision to focus on family and career while the children
were young, but now I was ready to reach out and give back to

my community. Since being a lawyer is a form of public service because of the role lawyers play in society, I wanted to take it a step further and engage in pure public service—as a judge. That made sense to most people.

Even though I didn't really want to run for office to be a judge, as it turned out, I actually liked campaigning. I learned to do what was comfortable for me and what I thought would be comfortable for others. I did not make it a habit of "glad handing" perfect strangers in a crowd until closer to the election when people were actually thinking about the election. For instance, when eating fried chicken at a Catholic school festival, there is little worse than being tapped on the shoulder by a candidate who wants to shake hands after just shaking someone else's greasy hand. Despite my campaign manager's insistence that I do that sort of thing, I wouldn't. I watched one veteran campaigner do that during the time between his father's death and funeral. His father had a highway named after him when he was a state representative, and the candidate was even using his father's thirty-year-old signs. He won handily, but what a price he was paying—or maybe he was pushing himself in honor of his dad. I never knew. All I knew was that I could not have done that.

I won on my own terms. I respected rules in parades, and I reached out to people for their own sake. I heard their stories, learned about their situations, observed their environments and imagined myself serving in the position I was running for and how I could help them. The campaign taught me that it was better to campaign for a job than to be appointed to it. The candidate has time to learn the district, imagine her or himself in the position and actually be better prepared to govern. I was the last person I would have imagined to actually *love* campaigning, but I did and still do.

Early during that first campaign, I had met a Teamsters local union officer at his union hall located behind my law office. I walked in on a conversation he was having with another union official where he was recounting a story about a "doobie." I didn't know until he explained to me that a "doobie" was a marijuana cigarette. I went home and said incredulously to Rick, "Now I know how the Doobie Brothers got their name!" He laughed hysterically. That Teamster member died from a heart attack not long after.

A few months later, I met his widow at the Teamsters picnic at the Columbus Zoo. I expressed my condolences to her (but did not mention the "doobie" lingo I had overheard.) We talked about my responsibilities at home with the extra children living with us, and she remarked, "So, campaigning is actually time to yourself!" She was right, and I used that line as part of my stump speech for the rest of the campaign, getting a chuckle from the audience each time.

One of the hardest things a candidate must do is to "stay on message." Every candidate, especially a new one, is sure that those listening are aware of the seemingly endless repetition of his or her message. In reality, the only ones noticing the repetition are campaign staffers, a few political junkies who go to too many political events, and the other candidates on the circuit. I came to understand that repetition is the key. Voters are bombarded with so much information. It is the multiple and consistent contacts or "touches" from the candidate that impact their memories and prompt them to even recognize the candidate's name, let alone know what he or she stands for. Often, voters simply rely on how they can identify with a candidate or how the candidate made them feel when they listened to him or her speak—if they remember the candidate's name, that is. Hence, there is the need for repetition.

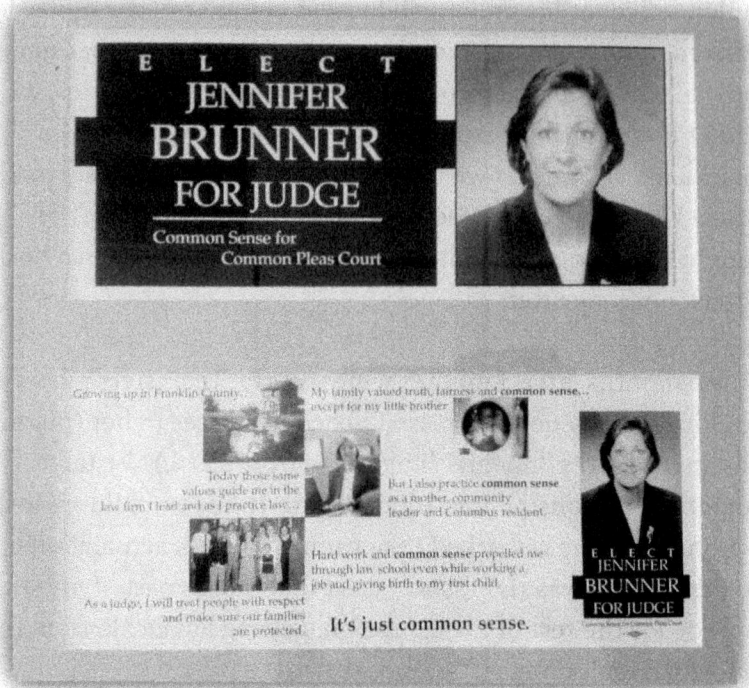

My first campaign literature carried the message, "Common sense for Common Pleas Court," and the literature included shots from my television commercial for consistency of message.

During the campaign, we filmed a television commercial. The process involved a full bevy consisting of a director, a videographer, a makeup artist and a campaign manager, all of whom invaded our home one Saturday morning. They even went through my closet with me for the right clothes to wear in the spot. As part of the shoot, they then traveled to our law office for more shots. It took four hours that day to produce one decent, fifteen-second spot.

In shooting a commercial or news piece, "B-roll" shots serve as filler or background for the spot. The videographer filmed the family strolling through the front yard for B-roll footage.

Everyone was dressed and with makeup. My second daughter, Laura, who was sixteen at the time, looked at me as we strolled for the videographer and smiling sweetly said, "I'll be talking about this in therapy one day, Mom." Fortunately, they did not use that footage, because not even lip reading should show a woman candidate to be a bad mother.

When all was said and done, in that first race in 2000 I raised $75,000 for a six-month campaign, aired our fifteen-second television ad enough times and won the race by a whopping two percentage points. I was sworn in to office December 1, 2000. Governor Taft reappointed John Bender to the bench in 2003. John and I served together until I left the bench September 1, 2005, to run for Secretary of State. We remain close friends today. He has been a source of advice and counsel on matters ranging from my decision to run for Secretary of State to whom I selected to be a part of my team in that office and beyond. I value his friendship and advice. That is the better side of politics. ≈

Chapter 9

Discovering the Meaning of Public Service

I ran for judge because I wanted to do the job, and being a judge is what truly taught me about public service. Judges are subject to limitations on discussing issues, because they must maintain objectivity. My prep team in the campaign helped me devise an acceptable message that I was comfortable delivering: "What is a good judge?" That was my campaign theme. My answer: "A good judge is fair, organized and humble." It was easy to explain why I was organized, with my family situation that included six children and managing a law practice. I could talk about my experience serving as a hearing officer and that I believed strongly in a fair judicial system.

"Humble," was the wildcard people didn't expect. Judges were just scary to most people—in a black robe, sitting high up on a bench and with a gavel to bang people out of order. "Humble" was the last way most people would describe a judge, but it was the clincher. "A good judge is humble. A good judge deals with so many issues that he or she can't possibly know everything. A good judge knows what she doesn't know and isn't afraid to look for the answers." People liked that. They identify with a leader who is like them, isn't afraid to admit that she doesn't know something, but is willing to do the hard work to become better.

Once sworn in and ensconced on that bench, I was amazed at what I didn't know. I was nervous because I was not well versed in criminal procedure or in conducting jury trials. Despite my significant civil trial, administrative law and appellate experience, criminal trials were something I had only tangential knowledge of. I remembered that "humble" part of my campaign speeches and wasn't afraid to ask the attorneys on the cases for help. They liked that. It saved their clients money and time, especially when those clients couldn't make bail. By avoiding mistakes, we could resolve cases sooner and get their clients out of the county jail, even if it meant prison. It meant that I didn't get as high of ratings in the popularity contests of the local "Columbus Monthly" magazine on the question of "knowledge," but that was okay with me. I had one of the lowest reversal rates on appeal in comparison to other judges, and many attorneys told me they were sorry to see me leave the bench when I resigned to run for Secretary of State.

I learned the power of public service in some significant ways while serving as a judge. I had read a "Courts Futures Commission" report issued by the Ohio Supreme Court that set forth a "vision" for what the state's courts should be like in the next twenty-five years. One significant characteristic was that jurors should be permitted to take notes and ask questions. When I told some of my courtroom staff who had been at the courts for years that I planned to do that in my courtroom, I saw some eyes roll. There was no set of comprehensive procedures available for coordinating note taking and asking questions by jurors. I read what rules were available in the Ohio Jury Instructions on jurors taking notes and added to it what seemed fair to everyone involved—jurors, defendants, witnesses, attorneys and the court—including instructions for jurors to ask questions.

I devised a procedure whereby jurors would receive instructions before the trial began about the practice of taking notes and asking questions. Each juror would be given a steno pad and instructed that they did not have to take notes if they did not want to, that the court recognized that some jurors could remember more details by just watching and listening. If jurors had questions, when prompted by the court at the end of a witness' testimony, they could write down their questions, which would be collected by the bailiff. The attorneys and the judge would meet at a "sidebar" to jointly determine which questions could be asked under the rules of evidence. The judge would read the agreed questions to the witness, and the witness would answer to the jury. Counsel would have the opportunity to question the witness as a result of the jury's questions. The jury was told ahead of time that if a question wasn't asked it was because it could not be asked under the rules of evidence and not because it was a bad question.

The least helpful question ever asked was, "Why were the cops hiding in the bushes?" The most insightful question ever asked was, "What is the difference between thrombolytic therapy and a thrombectomy?" Once, in a slip and fall case, the only time the question was asked about what kind of shoes the plaintiff was wearing was when the jury asked it. The attorneys had even constructed a model of the steps on which the plaintiff fell to demonstrate the fall to the jury.

While trials took longer using this practice, no jury verdict in any trial I presided over was overturned by the court of appeals during my tenure as a judge. The practice of jurors asking questions was appealed for criminal trials and affirmed by the appellate court for my district. However, the court of appeals in Cincinnati disapproved of the practice, creating a conflict between judicial districts. The Ohio Supreme Court, the state's highest court, reviewed both cases on their conflict, and the practice was affirmed. Later, after Rick was appointed to the high court's Rules Committee by a Republican justice, he proudly helped write the rules for the entire state based on the practice I had established in my courtroom. One person can make a difference, especially in public service. This was just my first taste of how rewarding it is to pursue your passion and to

First official judicial picture taken in 2001 that hung in the Franklin County courthouse

realize you have helped others in the process.

When I took my seat on the judicial bench in Franklin County, I spent my first day observing the courtroom proceedings of now retired Judge David Johnson as he took pleas and conducted criminal sentencing. He was a kindly man. He took me aside after the judicial session and said to me flatly, "Eighty percent of the crimes we see here are related to drug and alcohol abuse." I found that to be an accurate statement.

"What causes drugs to be so pervasive, especially in the criminal justice system?" I kept asking myself as I managed my own criminal docket.

I attended a session of the Ohio Judicial Conference and learned about co-occurring disorders of mental illness and substance abuse. The Cincinnati Health Foundation had published an extensive report on co-occurring disorders that brought it all home to me. Finally, it was starting to make sense. Thinking of the people in my family whom I had kissed as a little kid and wondered why their breath smelled funny—was it just alcoholism, or was there an underlying chemical imbalance in their brains that was causing them to "self-medicate" using alcohol? And, conversely, when were the symptoms of a drug addiction mimicking a mental illness?

A significantly greater proportion of the population in jails and prisons is drug-addicted or mentally ill or both than in the greater population. Even one of the toughest prosecutors, Doug Stead, and prosecutor-turned-judge Dan Hogan said repeatedly, the courts are not here to treat medical problems. Doug argued for the legalization of drugs. I never agreed with that proposition, because of my own personal family experiences. In my view, making drugs easier to get for people with predispositions to addiction may only worsen the problem without a concomitant increase in treatment services.

My passion for fairness motivated me to try to figure out what I could do as a judge. I wanted to help people caught in the system get out of it and to lower crime for a better quality of life in communities. Quite a few judges detested the "social worker" part of their jobs. A probationer is "yours" when he or she violates his or her terms of probation—a felony court judge decides whether to ship the probationer off to prison or give one last chance. For me, it was a challenge and a responsibility to determine not only what was best for the person in front of me, but what was best for the community, the victims and for the families affected. One of the purposes and principles of felony sentencing in Ohio is to protect the public. There are a lot of ways to do that. Some judges see locking up people as the most effective way to do that, but the reality is that the vast majority of people who go to prison get out. The long-term view necessarily includes (when discretion is permissible) an analysis of all of these factors and more.

Once I had my hands on that Cincinnati Health Foundation Report on co-occurring disorders, I couldn't stop thinking that something needed to be done—and could be done. I talked about it to those who would listen. Finally, at a Christmas party at Judge Alan Travis' home, I met Dr. Sul Ross ("S.R.") Thorward, an amazing psychiatrist then employed at Twin

Valley, the state mental health facility in Columbus. I remember seeing the smile on his face when we talked about making drug and mental health treatment more responsive to probationers. He had found just what he and several of his colleagues had been looking for—a sympathetic judge to help them found a mental health court docket.

I was so passionate about moving forward to do something, I naively applied for a federally funded Byrne criminal justice grant to start a specialized docket at the court, but without conferring with the other judges. My passions had clearly gotten ahead of my other sensibilities. I was promptly hit with a figurative two-by-four in the middle of the forehead for not having obtained the permission of the other judges by a court vote. I deserved it. It was a tough lesson for me to learn when the judges withdrew the grant application I had made on behalf of the court.

But I didn't give up. Eventually David Royer, CEO of the local Alcohol, Drug Abuse and Mental Health (ADAMH) Services Board came to see me and offered his personal help followed by additional help in the form of Julie Rinaldi from his staff. Together, she and I, along with Twin Valley psychiatrist Dr. S.R. Thorward, Twin Valley psychologist Jim Raia, Twin Valley administrator and now Chief Executive Officer, Karen Woods, and municipal court Judge Scott van der Karr, met twice weekly as a steering committee to establish specialized dockets in the courts. We met for breakfast at the Clarmont Restaurant, then a local political eatery close to the courthouse.

Within months we had formed a task force of sixty people from the criminal justice and treatment communities and divided them into six committees to study particular issues that needed to be addressed to form specialized treatment dockets in the municipal and common pleas courts of the county. By this time

I was smarter at dealing with my fellow judges. I asked if I could represent the court on the task force, but I did not tell them I had helped start it. I was given permission but admonished that the court was making no commitments. That was all I needed.

Finally, when one of my fellow judges and former high school classmate, Mike Watson (now a federal judge) served as administrative judge of the court, he said, "Jen, we've decided you can do a drug court, but not a mental health court." I was stunned and speechless at first. My first reaction was to keep pushing for a combined, "SAMI" (substance abuse/mental illness) docket, but I thought better of it and held back. I hesitated for only a second then said, "Okay!" and ran with the drug court concept.

There was so much to do and to do right. In developing this specialized docket, I conferred with Dave Royer, ADAMH's CEO, who gave me some of the best advice in effecting change in government—"the best measure of the success of a program you create is what happens to it when you leave it. If it survives and thrives, your work has been successful. It cannot be dependent on you for its success." To succeed in this way I knew I had to convince many sectors in the court system that this program could and would work. I had to obtain their acceptance and support. In just the court system, alone, this involved the prosecutor's office, the public defender's office, the network of private practice attorneys who were engaged in criminal law, the probation office and the sheriff's office. I needed to get funding, too, and I had to establish relationships and gain commitments from the treatment community, and blend the two. We needed to build in evaluation, so an IT component was needed to be able to collect data as we began operating the program. It seemed like it would be pushing a boulder uphill. It nearly was and proved to be a very tough task.

The Franklin County Common Pleas Court is the second largest court in the state with sixteen judges (now seventeen) in the general division. We handled general cases in our division (no divorces, no juvenile crimes, except for bind-overs to be tried as adults, and no probate—those were handled by other divisions of the court). Franklin County's population was at 1.1 million. The judges had tried to obtain funding for a drug court about 12 years before, but the effort had foundered. Many of the judges believed that a drug court was not needed and that in managing their own dockets, they actually ran their own drug courts. Much education was needed.

Starting a drug court in Franklin County Common Pleas Court taught me the value of what I call, "bringing the stakeholders to the table." When it comes to creating change, it is important to anticipate at the outset who are the people and organizations to be affected by the change in any way, large or small. Offering them the opportunity to be able to participate in crafting that change generally creates a better outcome and more ready acceptance of the change. While it takes more time and patience, change is more likely to occur. When these stakeholders "come to the table" to help make change happen, they add their experience, knowledge and philosophy to the process. As that change is implemented, they become its very ambassadors. It has worked every time for me. It is also known as collaboration, a huge and current (and still more needed) trend in government that carries with it the potential to "un-silo" many government functions, cut costs and improve service. (Considering that "change" was the message in President Barack Obama's 2008 campaign, defining "change" at the outset may also be a good idea to ease some of the inevitable acrimony that occurs in the process of change.)

As for starting a drug court in Franklin County, Ohio, working with a core group composed of Melissa Knopp, Manager of the

Specialized Dockets Section of the Ohio Supreme Court, Joni Moore of the Ohio Department of Alcohol and Drug Addiction Services (ODADAS), my court's Chief Probation Officer Gayle Dittmer, and Julie Rinaldi from the ADAMH board, we constructed several models for the court to consider. With their help, I convened a meeting of nearly twenty individuals from stakeholder organizations whose operations would be affected by the criminal justice side of a drug court. Our core group presented the various models we constructed and gained the larger group's consensus on the best model to use and how it should be modified. I made changes the group had suggested and brought this model before the judges at a special meeting. The county prosecutor, Ron O'Brien, a Republican, attended. He was supportive of our drug court concept.

Just before we were ready to vote on the proposal, after much spirited discussion, I lost a quorum. One of the judges left the meeting. We could not vote. Ron suggested I draft a court order to create the specialized court docket and get enough judges to sign it. None of the judges who were left at the meeting objected. It took me two weeks, but I obtained the signature of every judge on the court. I chased down some in elevators and in the judge's parking lot. For others it was an easy visit to their office. When I presented to the criminal division of the clerk's office this order with all sixteen judges' signatures, the clerk's office was not sure about how to file it. The supervisor, Dorothy, filed it as a special order, and what later became known as the TIES (Treatment is Essential to Success) Program was born with the clicking sound of the electronic file-stamp machine.

After attending extensive training to understand best practices for this new court, I learned that, in some cases, failure to treat underlying mental illness spells failure for some program participants. Some substance abusers are actually self-medicating a mental illness when they abuse drugs. I communicated that to the judges, and I was given the go ahead to include mental health treatment as part of the treatment protocol, virtually what I had been seeking to do all along.

Judge van der Karr was forming a mental health court docket for misdemeanors and I was forming a drug court docket for felonies. Justice Evelyn Stratton of the Supreme Court of Ohio had been pushing for the development of more mental health court specialized dockets throughout the state. She was instrumental in helping me obtain the funding I needed from the Ohio Department of Alcohol and Drug Addiction Services for the drug court. She did this just before she left the country for a return to Thailand where she had been raised as the child of missionaries. I had sent her a last minute "SOS" message that our funding was in jeopardy, emailing it from Nevada, where I was attending classes at the National Judicial College on "How to be a Change Agent in Your Court" (the Ohio Judicial College had graciously volunteered me for this one).

Justice Stratton received my message and sent a stern warning to the person stalling the process at ODADAS. That individual personally walked the authorization over to the local ADAMH board to ensure our court's funding, and the Franklin County drug court became a line item in ODADAS' budget.

Judge van der Karr and I began operation of our specialized dockets a day apart, mine on April 4, 2004, and his on April 5, 2004. These court programs really did change lives. At first, the courtroom deputies from the sheriff's office referred to my TIES Program drug court sessions as "party time," because the sessions were more informal than regular courtroom proceedings. During TIES Program sessions, participants sat at one of the tables in the courtroom reserved for counsel along with the program's probation officer. The exchange occurred directly between the participant and me. Other participants sat in the gallery behind whomever was at counsel table. As the program's judge, I had "staffed" each participant's case ahead of time with a multi-disciplinary team of treatment providers, probation officer, clinical assessor, program coordinator and others. That way, I already knew how the participant was doing in the program before he or she ever opened his or her mouth to answer my question, "So, how did your week go?"

I found that even if I hadn't known, the other participants who sat in the gallery behind the one speaking were all I needed to observe to know when I was being lied to. The other participants would cross their arms and shake their heads when a person began to lie to me. It was important to observe and acknowledge their contributions to the process in being fair and maintaining trust and respect in the program. When people did well, they received applause and rewards such as gift cards, and even European hot chocolate that I had brought back from the hotel on my overseas vacation. If a charity luncheon resulted in extra corporate gift bags being left on chairs, I quietly collected as many as I could carry after the luncheon and handed out their contents during court hearings as incentives to reward success. We used all we could find to help people, and help them we did.

Our first TIES Program Coordinator, Sally Murphy, had an excellent way with participants. She came from a counseling background. She helped boost participants' motivation to stay clean and to succeed. The longer they stayed clean, the better their chances of continuing to stay clean. It was that simple.

Not every person made it, but when they did, I saw with amazement real, palpable transformation—and so did the courtroom sheriff's deputies. By the time I held my last TIES Program hearing before handing off the program to Judge John Connor, there would be weekly up to six sheriff's deputies in the courtroom watching the proceedings as if this was a television reality show. When someone had to be jailed for a dirty drug screen, one deputy in recovery would report to me in the middle of the week about the participant's progress in jail. Transformation occurred beyond that courthouse, too. Family members of some program participants attended courtroom sessions and listened and learned.

Judge van der Karr and I worked with Justice Stratton, Karen Woods and Lieutenant Michael Woody, a retired police officer from Akron, to ask the City of Columbus to form a "CIT" or Crisis Intervention Team within the Columbus Division of Police. This specialized team is specifically trained to deal with the needs of mentally ill citizens accused of committing crimes who would not be doing so but for their mental illnesses. I was pleased to attend the graduation of the first group who received CIT training for the Columbus Division of Police. The training has now extended to the Franklin County Sheriff's office and to other local municipalities' police departments.

It was at about this point, I sat down at my desk in my chambers one afternoon after a drug court session and said to myself, "Brunner, you're in trouble. You like getting things done like this drug court program more than you're going to like listening to testimony about fingerprints for the next twenty years as a judge." My understanding of public service had come full circle—I saw that the people being helped were not just the offenders but also the people who participated in helping them. My role in "getting things done," was serving all of them. I saw that public service wasn't about me; it was about the people I served and how I empowered them, accepting them where I found them. Incredulous, I thought about all the politicians I had known since I first started working in the Ohio Senate at age twenty-one in 1978. I was forty-seven at the time. As a judge, I had been handed extraordinary power. I thought, "If everyone who has this kind of power were motivated to use it to bring people together for the collective good, how much more could we get done and with a lot less difficulty?"

Some young people are attracted to politics and public service because they want to make a difference. Others see excitement and intrigue in the politics often associated with public office. Others just need a job and see it as a way to build the social and political capital to move ahead. Whatever the motivation, it is incumbent on elected leaders to set examples for young people that foster a spirit of public service for the sake of public service. When young people attach themselves to elected officials who simply operate according to "just politics," regardless of their branch of government, their protégés can become tainted for the long term and simply perpetuate the side of politics that most people perceive as "dirty."

Young people who decide to enter public service should be challenged to self-examine their motivation for doing it. They should be encouraged to understand public service is not business, even though business principles can improve its effectiveness. They should be permitted to understand that public service is not a shortcut to wealth built on selling political influence or access. Nor is it a game. Public service is about what people do for people. It requires an examination of morals, duty, sacrifice and skill to determine how to balance the interests of many for greater good. If public servants, elected or not, fail to understand the consequences of how what they do affects people's lives—and take responsibility for it—the vigilance against and resistance to corruption (that is endemic to the core value of public service) is at risk of being lost.

In my first job out of law school, then Secretary of State Sherrod Brown in 1983 asked me why I liked politics when I interviewed for promotion to the Legislative Counsel position in the office. I answered brutally and honestly, "Because it's fun. It's fun to see how people get what they want when they have differing interests." He was disappointed in my answer but hired me anyway. Later he told me he was looking for an answer more grounded in public service, like how Bobby Kennedy had inspired him (he now has RFK's desk in the U.S. Senate).

It took me becoming a judge to fully understand public service. Much like what the scales of justice represent—a balancing of interests, as well as a balanced use of discretion. Being a judge helped me to see not only what the best of intentions could accomplish, but also the havoc that could be wreaked with ill-intentioned actions, whether based in malfeasance, misfeasance or nonfeasance. Whether it was observing other judges, prosecutors or even public defenders, or reviewing the actions of government agencies or the legislature, I learned that the ripple effect of public officials' decisions could affect matters of life and death and shift whole paradigms.

One such graphic example was the case of Chris W. Chris was represented by public defender, Mary Younger, whose judgment I trusted. She referred him to the TIES Program. His offense was burglary, a felony of the fourth degree. The program would not take offenses of violence, unless for extenuating circumstances. After researching it, I learned that burglary charged at the fourth degree felony level was not classified under the law as an offense of violence, even though at first blush many thought it would be.

One evening Chris had broken down the door of an apartment, thinking in a schizophrenic episode that a woman in a van was chasing him. He thought the apartment door was that of the resident manager of the apartment complex; it was simply a resident's. When the police were called, he sat calmly at the curb and waited for their arrival. He was arrested and taken to jail.

When Sally Murphy interviewed him for the TIES Program, she and Chris discussed his situation. Chris wanted to take advantage of the TIES Program. He had been reading about and coming to terms with schizophrenia. He was ready to work on treatment. A common self-medicating drug for schizophrenia is crack cocaine.

According to his dad, Chris' general pattern was to work, earn money, buy drugs, use, crash and start the cycle over again. He was not often in trouble otherwise, and his father, a retired union worker, regularly looked out for him. Chris had landed in jail for his actions ostensibly caused by his disease. He was a good candidate for this new program because of his motivation and because we offered mental health treatment along with drug treatment.

The judge assigned to Chris' case was viewed by some at the court as my nemesis. This judge had openly criticized my decision to let jurors ask questions in criminal cases. He had no compunctions about registering his disagreement with the way I ran my courtroom, even as he would chastise me in front of lawyers and while following me, still in my robe, from the courtroom to my chambers. At one point, this judge took me aside to tell me about my "reputation" with prosecutors in the courthouse. He told me that I was being criticized for sentencing some defendants to probation instead of prison. Interestingly, we both agreed, unlike many other judges in our court, that a misdemeanor plea in felony court should not, alone, be the sole basis for simply slapping on a fine or declaring "time served." We both believed that appropriate supervision could prevent future crime.

At a point in the prosecution process Chris got the word from some police officers that this particular judge was very tough. He was nervous. Chris' judge would not agree to let him enter the TIES Program. Mary Younger came directly to me and asked that I intervene on Chris' behalf. I did and went to my colleague's chambers to try to convince him to let Chris into the program.

First, the judge argued that Chris' alleged crime did not meet the qualifications of the drug court. I set him straight on that; this was not a crime of violence. Then the judge, who had actually supported starting the TIES Program, said to me, "You don't want this in your program." I could have taken it to the mat at that point, but the program was new, and I couldn't afford any disasters as the rest of the court was coming to accept the program. If the program failed, others would lose out. I relented. I shouldn't have. I should have pushed harder. Chris was not referred to the TIES Program.

Chris subsequently convinced his father to bond him out of jail, citing a skin wound that wasn't being treated properly in the jail. After his dad paid the necessary bond, he paid for an extended stay motel for Chris and had a painting job lined up for him. Chris' dad didn't hear from Chris for two days and found him hanging in his motel room after committing suicide.

A couple of months after the funeral, Chris' dad and I met at a restaurant. I learned that Chris had been at my public high school at the same time I attended, but I had not known him then. I wanted Chris' dad to be able to make some sense from Chris' death. I was angry at how the system had failed him. I tried to talk Chris' dad into letting me approach the National Alliance for the Mentally Ill (NAMI) to make a film about Chris' life so others could learn. His dad couldn't bring himself to do that, and this time I had no choice but to relent. No one ever said work in public service always results in happy outcomes. Like people and their lives, we do the best we can, learning from our successes and our failures.

Public service brings many encounters, because it is from beginning to end about helping people. Actions taken in public service can transform a life, a family or a community. Not only does one individual receive benefit or endure harm, but what our public servants do has a ripple effect as Bobby Kennedy described. It ripples beyond the one individual to many, their families, their friends, their co-workers and others in their communities. Every single decision has the potential for multiple and lasting impacts.

After Chris' death, another jailed defendant, a woman whose teenage son was killed in gang violence while she was incarcerated in the county jail, appealed to me by letter to enter the TIES Program. Her boyfriend even came to my courtroom with a letter and sought help. In her letter, she discussed suicide, voicing her fears of the same judge whom she did not know had denied Chris the chance to enter the same program. I took the letter to my colleague and told him for the first time about Chris. He was expectedly defensive, but he listened. He granted her the opportunity to be released from jail to go to her son's funeral, but she was required to pay for the cost of a sheriff deputy's escort. She could not make the payment, and she missed her son's funeral. I never knew what became of her.

Two days before I left the court to run for Secretary of State, this same judge sent me an email acknowledging that we hadn't always seen eye-to-eye on things, but that he admired my passion and told me to keep fighting for "the little guy." I was shocked to receive this and sent an email back thanking him, not knowing much else to say, except to wish him well. I wrote back with tears in my eyes that he would never see, knowing that my attempts had permeated even one of the toughest facades.

An elected official, or any leader for that matter, by virtue of his or her stature, has the ability to bring people together and empower them. Good politics and good public policy should be empowering. A leader focused on public service can inspire, monitor, prod, nudge and exhort people to do things differently, in a new way or not to do something at all. When that leader knows with every fiber of his or her being that something must be done or should not be done, it takes strength and courage to stand firm on that decision and have the intention to see it through. Sometimes it takes compromise, knowing that without it, nothing of value is accomplished. Withering criticisms, actions taken to block progress, threats of retaliation or even physical harm often are lodged against working for the greater good. A well-intentioned and courageous public servant will shoulder on and see the task through, because they are convinced that what they are doing is right. This is why government will never and can never be a clone of business. Their driving forces, even when both are at their best, are entirely different.

As a judge, while leading the effort to create drug and mental health court dockets, I was privileged to experience the dynamic of human potential. When more than sixty people in the community worked together as volunteers on their lunch hours they achieved something no one of them, including me, could ever have imagined achieving alone. "So this," I said to myself, "is what public service is all about. I get it now." There is little else like it. Public service can occur whether leading an army or leading a scout troop to pick up trash along a roadway. It can occur when serving on committee for a charity or serving in elective office. It's about people and helping to make their lives better, in both small and big ways.

Public and community service and the spirit that imbues them are so very American (look at how Americans came together after 9/11). Democracy is empowering. The collective power of many individuals shifts a nation and becomes transformational for its participants. Democracy empowers each to believe that they matter. Even when that empowerment is simply understood as the right to vote, transformation occurs for a life, a family, a workplace, a community, a country or the world. Public service must further these ends. Each person can serve others from wherever she or he is, and we are all better for it. ≈

Chapter 10

Ohio is a Big State

It was July of 2004. I was already serving as a judge, and Rick and I were in Boston for the Democratic National Convention being held there. Judges don't normally go to political conventions, but Rick had delegate status, and Laura was there in college at the Berklee College of Music, studying vocal performance. Traveling to Boston with Rick was a great opportunity to see friends from around the state whom I had not seen in several years, and always, an opportunity I would not pass up to see my beautiful, talented child. Just a month earlier, John had graduated from high school. On the vacation we took him on for his graduation I had sat in the sun, felt the ocean breeze and told myself that I would not make any big life decisions for a year. Rick had already warned me that I should not even think of running for anything more expansive than countywide office until John was out of high school. My intention to do nothing for a year held fast for just one month. It was in Boston at that Democratic National Convention when the world took notice of a young Illinois U.S. Senate candidate named Barack Obama, that I decided to run for Ohio Secretary of State.

I'm not sure how the discussions began, but they ended with Antoinette Wilson, my longtime political consultant who was also attending, talking to Rick and me separately during the convention. We all realized that if I ran for statewide executive office I would have to leave the bench after serving nearly five years. A judge in Ohio cannot run for a nonjudicial office while holding judicial office. Rick and I each separately expressed to Antoinette our concerns about the other's well being if we did that, and each of us doubted the other would go for it. We laughed when we learned that we were looking out for each other, worried that the other wouldn't be comfortable with it. Antoinette was supportive and ready to help, but always her first concern has been about what is best for me. Those kinds of political consultants are rare and very special.

While at the convention I also talked with Denny White, who was now the chair of the Ohio Democratic Party, and he was supportive of it at the time. He hadn't yet considered I would have to leave the bench to make the run. He later backed away from supporting me for the run for that reason, even after I did resign from the bench and announced my candidacy. Finally, months before the primary election filing deadline, he confided in me that I was "running circles" around other candidates and that he was glad I was. He resigned as state party chair in November 2005 to take a position with the Franklin County Board of Elections when it was apparent that Ted Strickland was the likely gubernatorial nominee. This allowed Ted to bring in his own state party chair, Chris Redfern.

Antoinette has been called behind her back by my former Secretary of State staff, the "Ragin' Asian," because of her calm, resolute, but take no prisoners demeanor. She is not afraid to call someone out when it's needed; yet, she has a keen ability to figure out just how far she can go without going over the edge. She is the rainmaker of her political consulting firm, and she makes more money doing corporate consulting than she does political consulting (and suffers a lot less grief), but her passion is political work.

Antoinette Yap Wilson, at 47 years old, is the oldest child of four children of a Filipino-Chinese father who was a respected pediatrician in Perrysburg, Ohio, near Toledo, and a Filipino-Panamanian mother, who is tough as nails and managed her husband's medical practice, as well as nursed him beyond any expected recovery when he suffered a fall on the ice and was virtually given up on by doctors in his later years. The Yap family just lost him in 2010. The family didn't know how respected he was in the community with his years of caring for sick children. The outpouring of support was immense, and there were many Filipino nationals there—so many I felt at my five-foot-seven-inch height like an Amazon woman among them at the funeral.

Antoinette is short, beautiful and dark complexioned, with dark hair and dark eyes. She is always dressed and manicured with taste. She has been a constant source of encouragement for many candidates, especially women. She is famous among women candidates for her lectures on appearance. She had me wearing pearls and lipstick and pantsuits in the race for Secretary of State, especially for our Washington, DC visits. (It was the first time I had ever gone through an entire tube of lipstick when I let Antoinette be the conductor of my fashion train.)

Antoinette married a tall, Bill Clinton-esque-looking husband named Mark Wilson, from West Virginia. Their son, Hunter, is one of the most beautiful and smart boys I have ever encountered. When Hunter played video golf with me, at age 7, he actually helped me get it right, much like the instructor in a driver's education car who puts the brakes on from the passenger side without saying a word. Because of Antoinette's immigrant roots, she maintains close family ties with her extended family and displays boundless energy in getting things done on both the personal and professional fronts without ever seeming to break a sweat.

When Rick, Antoinette and I returned to Columbus from Boston, we met for lunch, dining al fresco at an Indian restaurant, to map out our strategy. Antoinette has always told it to me straight, and she said I would need to raise $2 million dollars to be competitive in a state with eight major and a total of twelve television markets (Cleveland, Columbus, Cincinnati, Akron/Canton, Youngstown, Toledo, Dayton, Steubenville/Wheeling WV, Huntington WV, Mansfield, Zanesville and Lima). It is expensive to run statewide in Ohio, and with more than 8 million registered voters, there is virtually no way a candidate can reach enough of them in a general election without television. If Ohio had statewide broadband coverage (which we don't yet), the amount of money needed would likely change, despite what consultants say. That was an announced goal of the last Democratic governor, but it did not happen. Now that the current Republican governor, John Kasich, is a major proponent of harvesting the rich reserves of natural gas recently identified in Ohio's remote, rural Appalachian areas, the obstacles to do this may finally be set aside.

As discussions in 2004 continued about my running for Ohio Secretary of State, Antoinette took me to see her longtime political confidante, Dennis Lieberman, then the chair of the Montgomery County Democratic Party in Dayton, Ohio. Dennis, a skilled attorney and enterprising county chair, had narrowly lost a battle for chair of the Ohio Democratic Party to Denny White earlier that year. Labor officials like Ron Malone of the Ohio Association of Public School Employees (OAPSE) had been instrumental in changing the winds of favor toward Denny, who lasted until November the following year.

With Dennis Lieberman, Antoinette and I mapped out a plan that I would retire from the judicial bench September 1, 2005 to have enough time to raise the money to win. Democrats were still smarting from the Kerry loss for president the month before. This was even more so in Ohio, because Ohio's twenty electoral votes had put George Bush over the top to win reelection. During the Kerry campaign, a group had grown organically in Ohio with shoots throughout the state called, "Women for Kerry."

It was December 4, 2004, and there were about one hundred women for Kerry who were meeting at the Montgomery County Democratic Party headquarters that evening. (I was somewhat in awe that, at this season of the year, they were not holiday shopping, but rather, viewing a video based on the book by George Lakoff entitled, *Don't Think of an Elephant!: Know Your Values and Frame the Debate--The Essential Guide for Progressives*. The book is about rephrasing Democratic lingo to appeal to a wider audience—I later read the book and found many of its precepts to be true). Dennis put me on the spot and asked me to speak to this group of women right then and there. Being careful not to say I *was* a candidate at that point, since I was still a judge, I spoke of my intention to become one and about the embarrassing way the Ohio Presidential election had been run in 2004 for the nation to see. I received immediate and warm applause.

This was the first test of viability to run for Secretary of State, and it was overwhelmingly successful. I had no time to prepare, and I had to speak from the passion that was my impetus to run—to make things better for people and to improve the standing of my state nationally.

The run for Secretary of State would be for an open seat, because Ken Blackwell was term-limited and planning to run for governor. I figured I had as good a chance as anyone else, and I had been working in that area of the law since 1983, first as Legislative Counsel to Sherrod Brown, as an attorney in private practice, and then serving a brief stint as a member of the Franklin County Board of Elections while Denny White resigned from the board to run for township trustee.

Boards of elections members in Ohio are nominated by the two major political parties (Republican and Democratic) and appointed by the Secretary of State, two from each party. Board members cannot run for political office, because they count the votes. Denny White's (and many others' at times) solution was to resign, find a placeholder appointee who would agree not to stay and who would resign when he had been reelected. This was not exactly the stuff of altruism, but it's what had been done for years. For me, the experience as a board member helped me to better understand the hundreds of elections officials I would be supervising in the future.

By November of 2004, I had already discussed my running for Secretary of State with the president of the Ohio AFL-CIO, Bill Burga, and with the editor/associate publisher of the Columbus Dispatch newspaper, Mike Curtin, a former statehouse reporter and political junkie (now candidate for state representative, himself). I received all but thumbs up at that early stage, and certainly no discouragement. Mike was intrigued at the thought of a judge running for that spot, and with the Dispatch there was no love lost between the paper and the current Ohio Secretary of State, Ken Blackwell.

I started in earnest traveling to Ohio's 88 counties in January of 2005, not as a candidate, but to get to know people in those counties and to discuss with them my intention of running. On December 24, 2004, the Dispatch decided to publish that I was thinking of running for Secretary of State and leaving the bench. The first January meeting of the TIES Program, one of the participants confronted me and said, "Judge, there's something you've not been telling us, and we want to know . . ." So the word was out, and it wasn't easy to tell them what I planned to do.

I had been torn about it, because working with the TIES Program participants was one of the most rewarding things I had ever done. By this time, we had incorporated the *Bridges Out of Poverty* curriculum in our court program, developed by Philip E. DeVol, Ruby K. Payne and Terie Dreussi Smith, using it as a form of relapse prevention. The curriculum was developed originally by Ruby Payne of Aha! Process in a book called *A Framework for Understanding Poverty*. It has been used extensively by educational institutions to understand and address how hidden rules of poverty and middle class affect educational achievement and success. Phil DeVol is from Morrow County, Ohio, and is a former drug counselor. He worked with Terie Dreussi Smith of North Carolina and Ruby Payne to adapt the teachings to work with individuals in social service agencies serving those in poverty. Hence, *Bridges Out of Poverty* was born. I had been exposed to it as a judge, even becoming certified to teach it at the court and to attorneys through the Ohio State Bar Association.

When in Wisconsin Dells, Wisconsin in October 2004, taking a several-day course to become certified to teach this curriculum with my daughter, Kate, who then worked at the Ohio Supreme Court, I was in a tortured state about whether to leave the bench and run for Secretary of State or stay as a judge. While there I worked late into the night in my hotel room revising and improving the TIES Program rule book letting endless hours of CNN political coverage of the Presidential election play on the television in my room. The next day, as I was listening to Phil DeVol talk about the social policy implications of the *Bridges* curriculum, I heard him speak about a "Social Health Index" that could be created to measure social (as opposed to simply economic) well-being.

It was like a light bulb went on in my head when I realized that the Secretary of State, the state's record keeper, could create a social health index for Ohio. Every major western civilized nation has done this, except the U.S. (It had been suggested by Walter Mondale during his 1984 campaign for President.) At the time, five states had each created one. Conceiving of a social health index for Ohio allowed me to see that I could still help my probationers, just from a different vantage point, and I could do this while still helping to clean up Ohio's maligned election process with experience few in Ohio possessed. This realization was the linchpin that allowed me to leave the bench and run for the office without feeling like I was abandoning important work. I wasn't abandoning my TIES Program participants, even though my service to them would be less direct. (Some of them came to my announcement for Secretary of State almost a year later, and it made me proud to have their support.)

In February 2005, I traveled to Akron to meet then Congressman Sherrod Brown in his district office. I had hosted a twenty-year reunion for his Secretary of State staffers in my home two years before, (to which he had brought Connie Schultz for all of us to meet before he married her the next year.) February 2005 was the first time I had talked with him at length in more than a decade. He asked a lot of questions. I sat on the sofa across from his chair and noticed that, even though he was no longer a bachelor, he was still wearing a thin blue sweater that must have been at least fifteen years old. It had a small hole in it over his blue dress shirt. I had to smile; some things never change. As Secretary of State, it was not unusual for him to walk through the Business Services section of the office in his stocking feet and think nothing of it.

Once, his driver, Bob, and I had to pick him up at the airport when he and his first wife were returning from a vacation. He had to go to Cleveland to meet Geraldine Ferraro, Walter Mondale's Vice Presidential running mate. It was Bob and my job to select a suit, shirt and tie to take to him. I was told that people were surprised at how well he was dressed. I was just excited to get to meet the first woman to ever run for Vice President of the United States. Sherrod encouraged me to run for Secretary of State at that meeting and connected me to some key supporters in Akron and Lorain.

Developing support in a campaign is like working through concentric circles. Antoinette had taught me this. You start at the center with whom you know; they tell you others whom you should talk with; and those folks lead you to other people, and so on. It's like that in fundraising, too. A good candidate needs to know himself or herself and be able to trust his or her own judgment. That way, advice given at each layer of the circles can be sorted and sifted, with the best advice identified and intuitively followed in the continuous movement to the outer circles. No matter how much money is said to be required, politics is still and always will be about people. Wealthy candidates who do not take the time to talk with people and do their groundwork, but instead, try to replace it with what money can buy, (including expensive political consultants and fancy "smart apps" for smart phones) seldom win, because they're missing a key ingredient, the power of people. It's uncanny.

I followed Sherrod Brown's advice, and the people he referred me to did not disappoint. They held fundraisers after I declared my candidacy, and they made introductions. Through them I met others who could help me from there. And so it went, as I made my rounds in the concentric circles of the state.

I declared my candidacy the day after I left the bench. Rick's cousin's husband, an information technology entrepreneur, Pawan Murthy, created my website. I had performed his and Kim Brunner's wedding ceremony the month before. I first met her as a six-year-old who, at our wedding stood before me at the reception staring at her cousin's new wife in a wedding gown that must have looked like a princess dress to her. This same child at eight, pointed to my stomach, knowing I was pregnant with Kate, and said simply, "I know about that." When her mother was dying of cancer and Kim was a teen, I took her mother to cancer treatments as she fought to stay alive as long as she could for her two teenage children and Rick's uncle Fred. Rick and I helped with the kids as Midge traveled to DC for experimental trials at the National Institutes of Health. I hired Kim to be there after school for my children and helped her find a job as a page at the Ohio Statehouse for Speaker Vern Riffe. Now, her husband Pawan, was giving me the opportunity to reach those outer concentric circles with a website and an immediate Internet presence that would be so vital to my campaign. It was the circle of family that made it possible for all of us to soar.

With John Kilbane (left), President of Laborers Local 310 in Cleveland at the union hall September 1, 2005, for the launch of my campaign for Secretary of State; this union would later ask me to run for the U.S. Senate; I was happy to oblige

On day one our website was ready to go to accept volunteer signups, take online contributions and to generally give us a well-organized appearance to attract more supporters. I knew from my travels to almost 40 of the 88 counties already (I kept a simple map of Ohio with me and colored in counties—yellow for a visit, orange for a signed-up county volunteer coordinator and green for media coverage) that Ohio's 2004 election debacle was world-renowned. I banked on the Internet to help me garner money and support, especially outside of Ohio. I also knew that being a "down ticket" candidate left me at a fundraising disadvantage, as most money would go to the Governor and U.S. Senate races. I was right on all accounts.

The pre-primary dance for an open seat was an interesting one. The goal was to knock everyone out of the race, hopefully before they got in the race, by a show of political strength to clear the field to avoid a primary. When it comes to the negative things in a primary, much is done silently, in the dark and under the table (and sometimes with a figurative knife). But more is accomplished by plain, old-fashioned hard work.

It took Denny White some time to figure out that I had to resign from the bench to run for Secretary of State. Once he figured that out, he tried to find any candidate he could to run against me to get me to back down, even after I had resigned from the bench (which seemed like trying to close the barn door after the horse left). He drove Franklin County Commissioner Mary Jo Kilroy (who eventually dropped out and ran for Congress) to Auglaize County to speak to the Democrats there. He tried to recruit former Cincinnati Mayor, Charlie Luken. He tried to recruit Peggy Fisher, Lee Fisher's wife. For a while, Brian Flannery from Cleveland was running for Secretary of State, but he dropped out to run for Governor. Lucas County Clerk of Courts Bernie Quilter, son of former Speaker Pro Tem Barney Quilter from Toledo was talking about the race, along with former Cincinnati councilwoman, now State Representative Alicia Reece from Cincinnati. State Representative John Boccieri was planning to run after he had flown Hillary Clinton in his Air Force jet in Iraq and told people she had remarked that he should run for Secretary of State.

With hard work, following my instincts, help from political friends, a robust list of endorsements from Democratic County chairs and a final knockout blow to John Boccieri from Bill Burga, retiring President of the Ohio AFL-CIO that I would be getting the federation's endorsement in the primary, the field was cleared. I was the only nonjudicial statewide candidate not to face even token primary opposition when I filed my petition in February 2006. I had asked then Congressman Ted Strickland, about whom I was ecstatic was running for Governor (because of his bipartisan work with Senator Mike Dewine on funding for mental health in the criminal justice system) to endorse me. Ted would not unless and until John Boccieri got out of the race.

In November 2005, the day before Thanksgiving, Denny White called me when I was at home the day before Thanksgiving to bake pies for my family. Our relationship was strained by this time, since he had worked against me in the primary even after I had given up my judgeship. He told me he was calling to let those closest to him know that he would be resigning as state party chair. Frankly I was shocked to get the call but glad to hear from him. I said okay and wished him good luck, thanking him for calling me, shaking my head and returning to baking my pies. Of course, I called Antoinette, and she was just as amazed that he had called me. When he retired from the Franklin County Board of Elections several years later, I attended and spoke at his going away party at a local restaurant. I think he was as shocked I was there as I was he had called me several years before.

Watching the melee that ensued for the Ohio Democratic Party chair's election in 2005 was an embarrassment. Shouting and at least one sexist slur were called out by participants at the meeting. One man publicly disrespected the party's vice chair, Rhine McLin, a female African American Mayor of Dayton at the time who was trying to conduct the meeting. The man called her "sir," to which she replied that she was not a man, and to which he shouted out that she had a moustache.

Another man, a staunch supporter of Ted Strickland, Joe Rugola, who would take the helm of the Ohio AFL-CIO for four years while Ted served as Governor, shouted at Congresswoman Stephanie Tubbs Jones to "sit down and shut up." A voting process to avoid a paper ballot vote was pushed by a raucous group that insisted voting occur by standing up (kind of like the old town hall voting that took place in early U.S. history so that landowners could make sure their serf-lessees voted as instructed). The intimidation factor was sickeningly evident, and it was not a good start for either Ted Strickland or for Chris Redfern.

Under these maligned circumstances, Chris Redfern became the new chair of the Ohio Democratic Party. While I felt sorry for him having to move into party leadership under those badly managed circumstances, it was one of the worst political spectacles I had ever witnessed.

It was embarrassing to be a Democrat that night. For me, I couldn't decide whether it was worse from the standpoint of having been a judge who was used to maintaining orderly proceedings in a courtroom or a candidate for Secretary of State who would be in charge of elections to ensure they were free from the type of coercion I had just watched.

Things haven't changed in 2012. Chris Redfern was reelected chair with the same denial of paper ballots. Former Ohio AFL-

CIO president, Joe Rugola, ran the meeting and even though paper ballots were available, he denied even the chance to make a motion for them. Ten of the sixty-three or so members in attendance still stood up as was required—again— but this time it was in favor of the challenger, Anthony Giardini, Lorain County Democratic Chair.

In 2006, it took Stephanie Tubbs Jones until the spring of 2006 to endorse Ted Strickland. She controlled significant numbers of Democratic votes in Democrat-rich Cuyahoga County (Cleveland). Watching her endorsement announcement live (I happened to be in Cleveland that day) was tense, with both she and Ted looking uncomfortable. Stephanie, as always, rallied to the occasion and made it look convincing, and Ted smiled nervously. ≈

Chapter 11

A Family Affair

The term, "call time," means time spent on the telephone calling potential donors and asking for money. I had not been permitted to do call time running for judge, since candidates for judge in Ohio can't directly ask for money. In the beginning of my race for Secretary of State, I could not see how I could ask someone I had never met for $1000, but the first time I did and got it, I was astounded. Eventually, I found it easier to ask someone I didn't know for money than someone I knew well. (If I knew them well, I usually knew their financial situation, and if it wasn't good, I felt like I was taking horrible advantage of a friendship.)

There are professional services that maintain online databases of political donors for candidates. The most widely used is now known as "NGP VAN." This stands for "National, Geographic, Political." NGP is based out of Washington, DC. During my first statewide race, we started our fundraising with NGP, but it is not an automatic system (as none are when it comes to entering new data). The campaign must keep the data current, under the old axiom, "Bad data in, bad data out." I went through four fundraising directors, a short subscription to NGP that was inadequately updated as I made the calls, and finally ended up with my daughter, Kate, as my finance director, aided by her predecessor, Pete Lytle, who, upon Kate's taking that role, became my technology director. Pete, with Kate's direction, developed a system that allowed us to keep track of our own donors, add potential and new ones and upload the most recent federal and state campaign reports to keep donor activity up-to-date. Based on the databases of reports we included, we could see donor history with not just my campaign but with whom they had contributed to in Ohio and in federal races around the country. Every time we looked up a potential donor in our system, that donor's history of giving for the last ten years was at our disposal. When a donor's record went on for pages, I had no trouble summoning the courage to ask for money; this person was a professional campaign contributor.

At the same time, I was blessed to have two full-time volunteer researchers, Nate Owen, a college student on summer break, and Kathy Spinelli, an unemployed manager, who took full advantage of the information blooming on the internet in 2006 to learn and find online for us, data about each potential donor, such as who their spouse was, where each worked, telephone numbers for each, and any other interesting information that could be helpful in convincing someone to give to our campaign. They even found potential donors searching this way. I was essentially building my own database of donors to make my call time more productive and to give me opportunities to talk to more than the "usual donors." Besides, it's always tough raising money in a "down ticket" race, with fundraising momentum is subsumed by candidates for governor or senator.

I also knew that, after Ken Blackwell's performance in administering the Presidential election in 2004, there were a lot of out-of-state fundraising opportunities, not because of what someone could get personally from my office, but because people across the country cared about fair elections in Ohio and how it affected the 2008 Presidential election. With President George W. Bush being term-limited in 2008, Ohio, as always, was expected to play an important role in the Presidential race. That proved to be true. When all was said and done, we raised money from people in all 50 states of the U.S. and from Americans in Canada, France, Japan and Mexico. The strength of this support amazed many and demonstrated the power of the Internet.

Our campaign for Secretary of State was an early adopter of a "netroots" strategy, and Pete was already familiar with the netroots community (even though in an earlier life he was a piano player on a Carnival Cruise ship—a later vocation for my daughter, Laura, as a cruise ship show band singer in building her vocal music career). With nudges from Pete along with his technical expertise and with Kate's confidence in what she needed and could do in fundraising (she had already taught herself HTML coding by this time and could upload periodic email appeals from the campaign), we made the Internet a strong engine for raising necessary funds. We needed to air TV ads to reach Ohioans who were not using the Internet. With Ohio's uneven access to broadband, television was and still remains a must. We came close to meeting Antoinette's goal of $2 million for the campaign, raising $1.86 million, and this did not count inkind contributions and a starter loan Rick and I had made to the campaign.

It was during the last six months of the campaign, after Kate took over fundraising, that we raised $1.5 million of that $1.86 million dollar total. Kate was 25 years old at the time and, while managing the finances for the campaign, also finished her college degree at night less than two weeks before Election Day 2006. I can only describe what she did with one word—amazing.

Kate decided to join the campaign and left her safe state job at the Supreme Court of Ohio, after my first manager, Brendon Cull, returned to Cincinnati to take another job. Kate moved to fundraising at first to help Pete keep up with the backend work needed for complete recordkeeping on our donors. Almost immediately, the dollars raised shot up with Kate on fundraising. A good call time manager understands the candidate, selects calls wisely (in relation to campaign events and current events that affect the campaign), and prods the candidate to keep going in what is to a new candidate a harrowing and grinding task. Kate was brilliant at this and born for both business management and marketing (even though she started college on a huge scholarship in music percussion—she now manages the business side of our law firm.)

It's weird looking across the desk at your 25-year-old daughter and meekly asking, can I be done with call time now? I can remember her as a little girl asking if she could be done with her dinner. Now Kate was telling me when I could be done with dialing. She was also telling her 20-year-old brother, John, who was by this time my campaign driver, as she handed him call sheets, "Make sure she makes these calls, whatever you do," with a look that could have slayed dragons.

Our son, John, was 20. He had already worked in Eric Fingerhut's Ohio Senate office at the statehouse during high school as part of an internship, followed by a month stint in Washington, D.C. his senior year of high school in then Congressman Sherrod Brown's office. His freshman year of college, he gained college credit with an internship on the Kerry campaign for president. He loved politics then. (After my subsequent Senate race where he was virtually stalked by whom we believed were Lee Fisher's researchers and then by reporters and bloggers, prodded by what the Cleveland Plain Dealer's Mark Naymik called "Fisher supporters," I doubt he'll ever be an active campaign participant again for anyone.) By August 2006, John decided to take a quarter off of college to be my driver in the campaign. At his age, I had to shut my eyes more than a few times when he drove.

A normal campaign day became leaving the house as early as 6:30 a.m. and returning at 11:30 p.m. or midnight and starting again the next morning. Many would think it would be great for a mother and son or parent and child for that matter to be spending that much time in and out of the car together. The reality of it was that we both had jobs to do, and that familial relationship took a back seat to the exigencies of the campaign until sometimes late at night when I would close my laptop and we'd travel quietly, talking some, but mostly enjoying each other's company before I dozed off exhausted.

John was one of my harshest critics after my speeches, even in my judicial races before this campaign ("You said too many 'ums', Mom;" "you forgot to point this out," and so on.) Often, I could see him standing in the corner in the back of the room, leaning against the wall, arms crossed, one long leg resting over the over, and I could tell by his face what he thought of my speech. I'd hear about it in the car. He watched people's reactions, offered perceptive advice and worked hard for me. And he mixed well with people, even though he'd been somewhat shy as a boy.

September 2006: With son, John, and Georgia Congressman John Lewis; one of my John's favorite photos; he and Kate were moved by Rep. Lewis' story of marching for civil rights in Alabama

Going from being a worker bee in the Kerry campaign to gaining entrée to everything the candidate did was a great experience for John, and he thanked me many times over for it—the TV tapings, the debates, the media interviews—he loved it. He had a great time in the Cleveland parades, especially in Stephanie Tubbs Jones' 11th district parade, where he sweet-talked older (sometimes rather large) women about his mother and how great she was. When I came along soon after, the women very enthusiastically greeted me, saying, "Oh, honey, I already met your sweet son!" He spoke as a surrogate speaker for me when he wasn't driving me.

Meanwhile, Rick was handling a myriad of legal affairs for the campaign and attended each week's campaign meeting run by Kate Anderson, our campaign manager. When I finished my term in the Secretary of State's office, I spent days on end going through endless files from the last ten years of public service. By this time. L.T. Riggs-Kolman, my first campaign scheduler, my treasurer in 2006, my coworker and my friend, had died from pancreatic cancer, a terrible loss for so many of us. As treasurer, she had dutifully kept files of so much that Rick had done during the campaign. I was overwhelmed to see what an integral part of that campaign he had been, quietly making sure legal details were attended to, exhorting people to action when it seemed not enough was being done, and thanking and praising people along the way.

It had baffled me that some in my Senate campaign had insisted that he and my son-in-law Pat Quinn not be involved as our legal counsel in that race, just because they were family. The advisors suggesting it were working only from the standpoint of how Washington thought this would look. They had no idea of how important it was to me that the people I surrounded myself with were people that I could trust implicitly. Regardless of the campaign, Rick had been willing to handle things at home, manage the legal affairs and travel the state for me, speaking on bus tours when I was elsewhere. We talked to people no matter who they were, motorcycle clubs or little old ladies' circles; he make sure we had it covered. At one point, we had three cars on the road simultaneously: John and I in the SUV, Rick in the truck, often with Kellye Pinkleton, our field director, and finally my mom toward the end of the campaign, in a sedan, with someone else driving her. By now my mother lived in Mandeville, Louisiana, with my stepdad, John, and had come to

Ohio to help. Laura wanted to be there, but she was living in Boston at the time, so she attended events with me when she was home and when away was rooting for us from afar. The campaign was truly a family affair.

Laura singing the National Anthem at 2007 swearing in ceremony

One day, late in the Secretary of State campaign, I sat down with Kate and John in the campaign office in the second floor of our 1900 refurbished brick carriage house at the back of our 1893 Victorian law office. "I am the luckiest person in the world to be able to have my family with me in this campaign," I said to them. And I meant it; nothing could have been better. I am still grateful today. When we won, Kate planned the swearing in ceremony and Laura sang, wowing the crowd with the quality of her vocals at the event and as she sung jazz at the party after. People still mention it today.

It tickled me as I traveled throughout Ohio how many extended family members I met and didn't know I had. It seemed like they were coming out of the woodwork. On a trip to Norwalk, Ohio, an elderly gentleman with that familiar French-German approached me and said, "I'll bet you didn't know your dad had a cousin named Ned Junk, did you?" I grinned and said, "Would you be Ned Junk?" Pleased as punch with himself, he said "Yes!" We had our picture taken together. It seems I had met his daughter, Beth, during my first years in the Secretary of State's office when she had been with a firm that supplied temporary helptos bring in the 1984 Presidential election returns. This was in the days before online communication, when boards of elections called in the results, and they were transported to the data entry room in the Secretary of State's office by a bipartisan team and then entered and posted on big screens for reporters standing by in the office.

I also met Flora Rhea at the Rock 'n Roll Hall of Fame in Cleveland at a 600-person convention of the Ohio Association of Public School Employees (OAPSE). OAPSE's attorney, Kristen McKinley, now a feisty and dedicated elected member of the state school board since 2008, graciously hosted me, taking me from table to table. When we arrived at a table of Jackson County union members (Jackson County is in southeast Ohio, part of Appalachia), I was introduced to just "Flora." I said to her that I had relatives from Jackson County, but that I didn't imagine the last name was predominant any more—"Rhea." She exclaimed, "That's my last name!"

Flora had married a son or grandson of one of my great-grandmother's sisters, Aunt Frances. I am the oldest of four children. My mother was the oldest of four, whose father (Glendon Oscar Swan) was second oldest of four, whose mother (Leona Rhea Swan) was the oldest of seven, whose mother, my great-great grandmother, Leura Rhea was our common relative. My great-great Grandma Rhea lived until I was about ten, and I remember her well. Her daughter, Aunt Frances, made peach pie with lard, and it was the absolute best peach pie I have ever had. Flora told me she had Aunt Frances' fried chicken recipe. It was at this event that I was to sing with the guitar-playing Frances Strickland, Ted's wife. After seeing Flora, I had newfound courage I was able to help pass on to Frances, who was terribly nervous to play and sing for this large crowd. We were, after all, on the stage of the Rock 'n Roll Hall of Fame. We both did just fine.

Coming off of the stage, a man I vaguely remembered approached me and said, "Do you remember me?" (That happens a lot to politicians.) I knew that I knew him, but I could not place him. He was the father of a murder victim in one of the toughest criminal trials I presided over when I served on the bench. His son, Ryan Morbitzer, had been gunned down on Eleventh Avenue in the Ohio State Campus area of Columbus in a drive-by shooting on Mother's Day 2002. I had tried both the shooter and the driver in separate trials and with separate juries. Both of them were found guilty.

A judge cannot talk privately to the victims of crimes or their families during the trials of the alleged perpetrator until after the last appeal, except if they are children who need to be adjudged credible to testify. This "no talking" policy is in place, because, if there is a reversal on appeal, and the case needs to be tried again, the judge must remain impartial. This hard-hit family senselessly lost their son on Mother's Day. Ryan's dad and I hugged, with trials and appeals now long behind us. I was grateful for the chance to finally express my condolences and to talk with him about how tough those trials were for everyone. Times like these are the unexpected graces of a campaign.

Later in Jackson County, I met my grandfather, Glendon's, first cousin, Edna, and her husband, Harold. Edna personified the poem, "When I am old I shall wear purple." She had just about everything purple about her attire you could imagine. I was able to publicly recognize them at the event and tell the story about how Glendon and Uncle Merrill as boys would travel by train from Springfield to Jackson County (to a rural area of the county between Beaver and Cove, Ohio) to spend the summer with their grandmother, Leura Rhea. When they returned to Springfield, she would not change the sheets on their beds right away, savoring the imprint of their heads in the pillows for a few days. Families are like that.

But "family" meant more in this campaign. What enabled Kate to leave the management position on the campaign and to move into fundraising was one very special and dedicated person, Kate Anderson. I had known Kate A. from when she served as executive director of Stonewall Columbus and as executive director of the Franklin County Clerk of Courts office for John O'Grady when I served as a judge. Kate A. is an amazing manager. She and her partner, Beth, have been strong supporters of Democratic candidates over the years. I had seen Kate A. at a county party dinner, and she had volunteered to drive me before I had a full-time driver. It was on one of those trips that she volunteered to leave retirement and manage my campaign, full-time—for no pay—as a volunteer. She believed in me, and she believed so strongly in Ohio's importance to the 2008 Presidential election that she was willing to do this. She believed that what happened in Ohio could be the fulcrum for national and world change, affecting who was elected president of the United States of America. Simply put, she believed that the outcome of our race could change the world.

With Patrick Gallaway, left, a gifted communications director and friend

Kate A. is as tough as they come. She was organized, dedicated, thorough, hard working and savvy. I don't think there was anything she couldn't do. Combine that with the kind of conviction she had, and what we had was practically a force of nature. She and Beth, a pediatric physician, were generous, too. And Kate brought more amazing "family" from the LGBT community on board to make the campaign sing.

Patrick Gallaway, previously communications director at Stonewall, left a state job at the Ohio Bureau of Workers Compensation and became the campaign spokesperson and press secretary. Kellye Pinkleton left her position as acting director of Stonewall Columbus to be the campaign's field director. Meanwhile, my Kate was supervising four people in the fundraising department by the end of the campaign.

The Ohio Democratic Party was moving from minor to major status in this campaign in terms of elected statewide officeholders, going from one retiring Supreme Court justice in office to what would be a Governor (Ted Strickland), Lieutenant Governor (Lee Fisher), Attorney General (Marc Dann), Secretary of State (me) and Treasurer (Richard Cordray). That did not mean, however, that a truly "coordinated" campaign was in play in 2006.

Richard Cordray and I combined our field operations to create our own coordinated campaign with the help of Antoinette. Kellye Pinkleton became the "coordinated" field director, with Rich's field director the deputy. Every place my volunteers were, they distributed Rich's literature. Every place Rich's volunteers were, they distributed mine. We even printed specific literature for minority communities with him on one side and me on the other. His opposition was a woman, whom I've since come to know as a friend, Sandra O'Brien, the first woman county auditor from Ashtabula County (far northeast corner of Ohio), who had been shunned by her party after beating outgoing governor Bob Taft's lieutenant governor-turned-state-treasurer in the Republican primary, Jeannette Bradley. Sandy had no money for TV, but she did have a strong ballot name going for her. She put up a good fight.

My opponent, Greg Hartmann, was a transplant from Texas to Cincinnati, and we outed him for that with an email entitled, "Texas Longhorn or Ohio State Buckeye?" toward the end of the campaign. Greg's father was a Houston attorney who had represented Vice President Dick Cheney on the question of his residency in Wyoming when Cheney ran for Vice President with George W. Bush (Vice Presidents cannot be from the same state as presidents, and it was argued Cheney really was living in Texas, even though he claimed Wyoming as his residence). Greg's wife's family owned a large furniture and casket company, and we were sure that he had plenty of access to money for his campaign.

One of my early fundraising directors was nearly apoplectic when Jim Trakas, a former state representative from the Cleveland area dropped out of the Republican primary for Secretary of State, leaving Greg Hartmann unopposed in the primary. I saw it as an opportunity to send an email, touting our strength, entitled, "Another One Bites the Dust." This was a tactic I would need to remember later—when a battle out there can be potentially harmful. I learned not to hunker down or cower, but instead to run to it and fight—knowing that the very action we took could turn it in our favor. Fortunately, with Kate managing fundraising, we kept up with Greg on fundraising, to the point that at one reporting period we surpassed Greg on fundraising and thankfully didn't see major investment in his campaign by family sources.

Not all was a bed of roses in the campaign, and try as hard as I might to act better than most candidates I had represented, I was not immune to thinking I was a genius at campaign strategy. Rick and I came up with the idea of "Send a Sign," where a map of the U.S. was divided geographically by color. We noticed that so many people from around the country had connections in Ohio. When a donor gave money online through our "Send a Sign" program, he or she could designate the town where they wanted it posted. Their yard sign would bear a colored ribbon signifying the part of the country from which it had been donated. When I unveiled this plan at the Chicago summer meeting of the Democratic National Committee, where I was asked to speak on behalf of all state and local candidates, I was handed money immediately from members of the audience and buoyed by its initial success.

But like most attempts to "go viral" this one didn't quite get there. Kellye and Patrick had been polite but silently groaning at this plan because of its administrative difficulty. They were right—but they were kind about it in humoring Rick's and my absolute conviction that this could be a huge moneymaker for the campaign. And Kellye, who can shoulder on through about any kind of adversity with a smile, cheerfully cut ribbons to tie on the signs. Eventually no one talked any more about "Send a Sign," and it died a silent death, to Patrick and Kellye's relief.

When I spoke to the DNC summer convention, I had noticed that there were a lot of bright lights, but I didn't give them a thought. Darcy Burner, running for Congress from the state of Washington, and I had to precede the Rev. Jesse Jackson in speaking. We turned around to speak to him in our "holding pen" of cordoned-off chairs near the stage. I whispered to him, "We're glad we're speaking before you and not after you." He seemed surprised. He gave a great speech.

I went home and spoke at a rally the next day at a shelter house on the west side of Columbus. Someone said to me, "You were great on TV yesterday." I said, "I was? What was I doing?" They had seen me in Chicago, filmed by C-Span. I had wondered why those lights were so bright, and I couldn't see the audience very well. Ignorance is bliss.

By the end of the campaign, we had taken over the entire second floor of our law office carriage house. The second floor included five individual offices and a big open area. Kate A. and I shared an office; Patrick and Kellye shared another; Kate had her own, but I went into her office for call time (she on one side of the desk and me on the other. Erin Duffy, our scheduler, had her own office, needing it for peace and quiet while she handled calls and coordinated efficient scheduling. IT director Pete Lytle and Karen Hamm, who worked on direct mail, were in the fifth office. Volunteers and our two full-time researchers worked in the open area. Volunteers helped us with "opposition" research and with "self" research (to make sure we had answers to all the "dirt" the other side would try to pin on me). We hired consultants for polling (Celinda Lake of Lake Research) and for television advertising (Murphy, Putnam, Schorr from Washington, DC). Antoinette's campaign consulting firm strategically placed our television ads. We won the election with 55 percent of the vote, with Greg Hartmann getting 40 percent and the other two candidates (one Green Party and one independent) together garnering the other 5 percent.

Greg had run several negative ads against me, using cases from my judicial days to characterize me as a "baby-killer" and a "soft-on-crime" judge who let rapists out of prison. We knew these attacks would be coming, because every time Greg's researchers ordered transcripts or public records, the people with whom I'd worked in those jobs would let me know and supply me with the very records that had been requested. There are a lot of benefits to being kind to everyone you work with, besides knowing it's the right thing to do.

In the last two weeks of the campaign, Celinda Lake conducted "rolling tracking" polling. Polling calls were being made each night and were averaged with the previous four nights so that we could gauge how our television advertising seemed to be affecting Ohio voters on a daily basis. Even though there were 35 days of early voting in Ohio in 2006 (some call it "no fault" absentee voting, because no excuse is needed to vote early), it wasn't until 2008 after the Obama campaign strategically used it when I was Secretary of State that Ohio voters were aware of it on a widespread basis.

In 2008 early voting was an important tool to alleviate long lines on Election Day. Celinda had counseled in 2006 that experience thus far had showed that most voters who voted during the first days of early voting were strong in their views and not likely to be swayed by advertising one way or the other. Four years later, during the 2010 campaigns, Ohio voters were subjected to television ad after nauseating television ad during nearly all the 35 days before the gubernatorial and senatorial elections. Apparently, the patterns had changed, or the other mostly Washington consultants hadn't gotten Celinda's memo.

With 35 days of early voting in Ohio, knowing where to target efforts and maximize efficiency with the limited time before the election is not an exact science. In counties like Cuyahoga (Cleveland) where, since 2006, the board of elections has mailed every registered voter an absentee ballot application and early voting had been huge historically, it's still hard to know on a daily basis who has voted and who has not. It was not unusual for a sweet, little old gentleman to pat my hand and say, "Don't worry, honey. I already voted for you." As a candidate I was glad, but as a harried candidate, I couldn't help but think, "Oh, boy, I went to the wrong place today." When I became Secretary of State, we worked with boards of elections to try to obtain early statistics on the incidence of early voting in the counties before

Election Day, but targeting is only a predictor and never a sure bet.

The last weeks of the campaign, the Strickland campaign and the Ohio Democratic Party, with the hard work of Becky Pearsey, organized a statewide bus tour for all of the statewide Democratic candidates—like one big family. I've always believed that, whether campaigning locally, statewide or nationally, it's chance-y at best to try to focus just on particular areas where it would appear there are enough votes to win. Just ask John Kerry, who did so in Ohio in 2004.

The bus tour took us all over Ohio, and the trips were some of the best times in the campaign. I have found time and again that a comprehensive geographic strategy works best. When voters in all areas of the voting district, whether it is a county or a state, get a chance to meet the candidate in person or to see them in local media, victory is more likely, (as long as the candidate is at least likeable and genuine.) Campaigns are really about people; they are the ones who vote.

It's nearly indescribable to see the reactions of Ohioans in remote parts of the state who haven't seen a statewide candidate, let alone a statewide anyone, for years. They are grateful, and their party affiliations matter less at that point. It is moving for the candidates, too.

It's also irritating to see the "trackers" in the audience, who are filming candidates to unnerve them or catch that one gaffe. Remember Senator George Allen and the 'macaque' incident? That is a seedy side of campaigns. Sherrod Brown's press secretary, Joanna Kubler, used her digital camera in 2006 to photograph the trackers and send the photos to all the candidates and their staff, so we could identify them and point them out to our own backers who held up campaign signs in front of their video cameras, or in some cases had a basis to ask them to leave because of their unauthorized presence.

Near the end of the 2006 campaign, Richard Cordray and I stood backstage at a large rally waiting to be introduced. Even though both of us figuratively had been beating our brains out campaigning all over the state (sometimes he went with Rick and me, sitting in the back seat of our SUV while my two dogs panted in the back near him, making the air not-so-sweet), neither of us was ready for it to be over.

It's hard for people to understand when a candidate who really works it, whether that candidate wins or loses, is just happy for the people they've seen, the stories they've heard and the opportunities they've had to see a state that they've grown to love more with each trip into its diverse communities. Ask yourself, "When would you venture to Blakeslee, Ohio, where the town sign says, 'Half a Mile of Smile,' eat a fried bologna sandwich at Sam's Restaurant and find out that the St. Joseph River flows north and not south?" Rick and I treasure this and many other experiences getting to know "Beautiful Ohio." It's not just a cliché; a campaign's rewards are more than just a victory.

But, winning is a whole event in and of itself in which pent up emotions of supporters, family and friends, and yes, you, as the candidate, truly savor the sweet taste of victory. It's also that sense of "shock and awe" that has been described in recent U.S. war efforts. The victory is sweet, but you're not sure what's ahead. (Maybe it's better if you don't really know.)

I want to say that winning is the mother's milk of competition, but a campaign is about more than "competition;" it's the precursor—the test—of an administration that has the potential to get things done for people. Maybe we should think of competition in a female context and envision, as Gloria Feldt in *No Excuses: 9 Ways Women Can Change How We Think About Power,* says that for women leaders, power is often viewed as the "power to" as opposed to the more traditionally male "power over." The sweet taste of victory would be valued as much for its nutrition as for its flavor. Perhaps more women would run for office and raise the U.S.' paltry numbers of elected women in office, if women could see electoral victory as a way to transform their passion into reality.

The best candidates, even when they lose, and they do, make the concession call promptly, when they know that statistically, it's not possible to win, even if significant results are still out. There's little worse than a sore loser. Grace and respect for the process are better followers of a political future than malcontent and disbelief. Grace and respect also make it easier to get over a loss.

L to R: My mother, Barbara Gates; my brother and nephew, Dan and Nathan Junk; daughter Laura, me waving to the crowd, and Rick

Greg Hartmann graciously called me around 9:30 p.m. to congratulate me on winning. He did not know it at the time, but I beat him in his own county, a traditional Republican stronghold. I kept the phone call short, thanking him, but ever the mother in me not forgetting how the nasty commercials he ran against me upset even my grown children. He and his wife had had their fifth child during the campaign. If he attempts a statewide run again, I'm sure someday he'll understand what I mean.

One of the turning points in the campaign was when Greg tried to say in a televised debate in Toledo that I had no management experience. I was ready. I prefaced my comments with the wind-up: "Greg, I don't like to pick fights, but when someone picks a fight with me, I finish it." I looked into the television audience of local chamber of commerce members and saw the eyes of several of the women light up with anticipation. I then ticked off my list of management activities, including my judicial trial docket, the initiation of our county's first adult felony drug court and management of my law firm while managing a busy family at home. I concluded with, "If that's not management experience, Greg, I don't know what is." Some of the audience spontaneously broke into applause, and the televised debate was played repeatedly throughout the state until Election Day 2006.

On election night as the returns came in, my nuclear and extended family and friends surrounded me. I had asked my sisters to be there and bring their daughters with them. My brother and one of his young sons were there, too. I had especially wanted my nieces to see a woman elected to a leadership position and for the first time win the Secretary of State's office in Ohio. My belief was and still is that, we can tell girls and young women they can be whatever they want to be, but the best way for them to know it is to see it. My brother's son, Nathan, who was just six years old at the time and still easy enough to pick up, was photographed with me holding him at that time of victory. It made a difference to this little boy, too. ≈

Chapter 12

Transition

When you campaign for an office, the last thing you think about is, "How will I conduct the transition from the current office holder to me if I win?" There's actually a book about it, and my soon-to-be Chief of Staff, Tom Worley, found it and gave it to me. In the meantime, I had been given some transcripts of information about how Eliot Spitzer ran his transition from New York's Attorney General to Governor, (before his actions made other transitions necessary for him,) but many of the points were the same as in the book Tom gave to me.

But better than a book was the advice of my friend, Tom Hayes, once a director of the famed Cuyahoga County Board of Elections in Cleveland and a "fix-it" guy called on by both Democratic and Republican leaders to clean up messes in various county and state government offices over the years. Tom had been a supporter. A week after the November 2006 election, Tom took me to lunch and said, "Listen, you don't have that big of an office, but you have a big task ahead of you to clean up Ohio elections. Get the best people you can find and leave the dregs of the Democratic job seekers barrel to Strickland. He has enough positions to give them jobs. You need the best people you can get."

Then Tom added, "You'll be competing against Strickland, Cordray, Fisher and Dann for the best people. You'd better get your hiring done as quickly as you can." Mention competition to me, and I'm ready. Tom was right.

Tom Worley was still employed as a mediator for the State Employment Relations Board. He had volunteered to run my transition, taking vacation time from his job to do that. He was clear that he wanted a position in the office, and I didn't have a problem with that. My daughter, Kate, was still on board in the campaign to keep things moving toward closure, and she was a natural fit to keep the transition moving. We had sufficient campaign funds to keep Erin, Patrick and Kellye on board as well, so we had our interviewing team and quickly began the process.

I did not hear from Ken Blackwell, who had lost his gubernatorial election to Ted Strickland and was serving out the remainder of his term as Secretary of State, so I had called him two days after the election. He did not return my call, but his Assistant Secretary of State, Monty Lobb, did. A week after the election, I was invited in to talk with Monty, and Secretary Blackwell's Chief of Staff, Sherri Dembinski. Rick, Tom Worley and I attended the meeting. We were ushered through the Elections Section of the office (by one of the many staff with whom I had worked more than twenty years before when I worked for former Secretary of State Sherrod Brown.)

Entering Monty Lobb's office was somewhat surreal. I was not used to seeing Christian crosses and pictures of Jesus' face (or at least what the artist thought Jesus looked like) in a state office. There was even a cross paperweight that sat atop papers on the heating box that lined the floor-to-ceiling windows of an office with an exceptional view from the fifteenth floor. Ken Blackwell had been the spokesperson for the 2004 campaign for the state constitutional amendment that banned same sex marriage in Ohio. Here was evidence of "God's" support of the less than objective efforts of a sitting Secretary of State who counted the votes for the state issue he advocated. Ironically, by the time I completed my term, my general counsel, Brian Shinn, who is openly gay, occupied that same office while leading our legal team to the finish of my four-year term of office.

This transition had many dimensions. This was a wholesale shift in power from sixteen years of Republican dominance to a new day for Democrats. (The last Democrat to hold this office before me was Sherrod Brown in 1990.) I held a post-election fundraising event in what we thought would be a large enough venue, but it was so packed some people never made it up the second floor to the event.

By this time, we had started interviewing people, and I had been wondering where a former colleague of mine was who was a gifted financial manager. Luckily, Veronica Sherman and her husband, Tom, appeared at the top of the steps at this event. I asked her for her card (she was now Deputy Budget Director for the City of Columbus), and soon after, I contacted her and invited her to interview for the finance director position in the Secretary of State's office. I offered her the job on the spot, and after a day or two of negotiating salary and transition, she accepted. (She remains there today, even with my Republican successor.)

Tom Worley, who was a state government veteran, and I recruited people from existing jobs for the positions of human resources director, finance director, general counsel and information technology director. These positions in any organization are the vital building blocks for a smooth running organization, because they generally exist to serve other functions of the business or agency. It pays to have the best people possible in these positions. It's like learning arithmetic: you have to get your adding and subtracting and multiplication tables correct before you can take on the story problems. You cannot afford mistakes in such basic operations of an office, and my job as Secretary of State would be to rebuild public trust in Ohio elections. When that is your charge, there is no room for error in these basic and essential office functions.

At the first meeting with the Blackwell staff in Monty Lobb's office, we were told that a complete transition manual was being compiled. This was more than I had dreamed of, since I was pretty certain those in Secretary Ken Blackwell's office had not been oblivious to my campaign criticisms of the office and how I said during my campaign I would reform it.

Because of my work in starting a judicial drug court and seeing the results of public service, running as a reformer candidate was a fit. Kathleen Sebelius, who was then Governor of Kansas (now President Obama's Secretary of Health and Human Services) in 2006 had held a private meeting with Rich Cordray and me during the campaign. She had made a special point with me to ensure I had information from the Barbara Lee Foundation that was specific to women candidates (the Barbara Lee Foundation is working to see the election of the first woman president). I learned from that information (much of it based on polling by Celinda Lake) that many women candidates run strong as reform candidates. That was a natural fit for me; it was why I was running in the first place.

With the blessing of Ted Strickland, Ken Blackwell's opponent, I made it a point to whack away at what I disagreed with during the remainder of Ken Blackwell's eight-year tenure. It also meant that I did not have to mention my opponent's name, and many people thought my opponent *was* Ken Blackwell. Most seasoned candidates know that throwing fireballs at one another about issues and records in office are fair game in a campaign— it's part of the healthy debate of democracy. So I postulated that perhaps this promising glimmer of bipartisan cooperation I was seeing from the Blackwell folks was in the greater interest of Ohioans.

But my speculations were short-lived. As soon as Tom asked for a list of employees, including their classifications and salaries and for the office's budget information, just like that, the spigot of information was shut off with a thud. When I called to follow up, I was told by one of Ken Blackwell's folks that transition would not begin until after he had certified the results of the election, and that would be sometime in December.

This was never going to work. I had just 22 months after taking office to engineer a complete turnaround of Ohio elections and to rebuild not just Ohioans' but the nation's confidence in how we exercised our democratic franchise in Ohio—voting. Besides that, I had to compete with the other Democrats who were elected at the same time as me to get the best people I could. Tom knew several well-placed career public servants in the outgoing Taft administration and was certain he could get the employee and budgetary information through back channels, and he did.

We needed a strategy, however, to interview current employees who were not protected by classified service and who desired to stay to determine whether we would keep or release them. The transition book Tom gave me included a story about one new office holder who had defined goals for office and even posted them throughout the office. That struck a chord with me, as I remembered seeing one of the television commercials in my media consultant's bevy of sample commercials, for Ruth Ann Minner, governor of Delaware, who ran for reelection and ticked off the goals she met during her first term, saying "check" after each one. This all made sense to me, and I thought it would help my employees to know what the new administration was all about.

I crafted four goals for office using my laptop to tap them out one-by-one: 1) to restore trust to Ohio elections, 2) to ensure business filings that are quick, efficient and easy to retrieve, 3) to protect people's private information and 4) to create a social health index for Ohio to measure and promote the well-being and quality of life of Ohioans. These four goals became the basis for communicating with existing Blackwell staff. We could cite these goals to them and offer them the chance to interview for a position in the office with a commitment from them that they would help me achieve these goals if we retained them. These four goals were eventually posted throughout the office and helped me to stay focused as we worked to steady the ship of Ohio elections and bring the practices of the office into compliance with the law. A set was posted in the conference room where I met weekly with my directors, and more than once as discussion veered to tangents of what we could do, I would glance at the four goals and pull discussion back to what we knew we had to do.

Communicating with any Blackwell employees before the ordained time of early December was difficult, though. My website, jenniferbrunner.com, had been blocked by the Secretary of State's office as spam, so none of my first emails to unclassified staff made it through the filter. Someone had not thought of blocking my law firm email, though. I called a long-time employee in the Secretary of State's office whom I had determined I would be keeping and asked him if he had received my email to him. He said he had not. While he was still on the telephone, I sent him an email from my law firm email. Bingo! It went through, and Tom and I were home free to contact all of the unclassified employees in the office for interviews with the transition team.

Our emails were already queued to send, and soon after, the Secretary of State's email system received emails from the Brunner law firm that reached each of its unclassified employees. We offered these employees the chance to interview with the new administration to determine if they were comfortable with our goals and to allow us to determine if they would be a fit for our team. We approached it as a "hiring" process and not as a "firing and rehiring" as was being done by one or more of the other newly elected administrations.

I never knew offering jobs to people was so much fun. A good day for me was making three job offers. A great day was making five job offers, and it didn't matter whether it was to new or existing staff. The reactions made the calls one of the best things I did during that time. We had determined that I would make the calls personally to offer jobs to those who had interviewed with us, in keeping with the old political practice that the boss tells the good news and others get to relay the bad news.

JENNIFER BRUNNER
OHIO SECRETARY OF STATE

180 EAST BROAD STREET, 15TH FLOOR
COLUMBUS, OHIO 43215 USA
TEL: 1-614-466-2655
FAX: 1-614-644-0649
WWW.SOS.STATE.OH.US

This was the logo used on stationery during my four-year term. Outgoing Secretary Ken Blackwell had appointed one of his staff people to work with us during the latter part of transition. It was designed on my computer and emailed to the staff person so that we had printed stationery on our first day. It became a basis for other designs and branding used during our administration.

We pushed hard to get our interviewing and hiring done quickly. Thanks to my Kate's efficiency, we set up three teams of interviewers and interviewed daily during the workweek from 9:00 a.m. to 5:00 p.m. I was a member of one of the interviewing teams like the rest of the transition team. When we had completed our most essential interviews, we pulled our team together in the conference room of our law office on a Saturday, placed giant, lined post-it notes on the walls and doors of the room, distributed resumes and notes and began to label each giant sheet on the wall for the positions available. It was a group session, with people calling out the best candidates and Tom writing the names on the sheets for positions named.

This exercise took team trust. We had to rely on each other's judgment that we shared the same outlook for the kinds of people we needed to get a tough job done. I already had hired Gretchen Green, a thirty-year veteran of state and county government, as my human resources director. Her help was critical.

Gretchen Green was another "recruit" Tom knew from his decades in state government. When I interviewed Gretchen, I thought she was one of the most interesting people I had ever met. Her hair, like Kathleen Sebelius' was authentically white. Gretchen often jokes about being "old" because of it, but when I gave her Eric Clapton's autobiography one Christmas, she loved it. She married for the first time in her 50's to Stan, a widowed, retired Statehouse docent who dresses as Simon Kenton to guide school kids in tours. She even knew how to belly dance. With two masters degrees, one in labor relations and the other in public administration, and nerves of steel, (except for the one ear that turned bright red in her interview with me), I was convinced Gretchen was who I needed to direct human resources for the office.

We clicked right away in the job interview. To make her intense job interview even more dramatic, I took a deep breath, shocked even Tom and offered Gretchen the job on the spot. She accepted it. Later, when Tom left my employ to return to the mediation that he loved, Gretchen became my chief of staff and proved to be very able. She chaired the transition with my successor, a Republican, who retained her as his human resources director. Institutional memory is more than valuable, especially when she comes as a red-eared belly dancer married to a Simon Kenton docent, both of whom love rock and roll.

That Saturday at the law firm conference table, Gretchen and Tom guided the rest of us through the process to hire a top notch team that made it possible to achieve unprecedented success in changing an Ohio election system in a remarkably short period of time. I had named for Assistant Secretary of State, Christopher Nance, a former Cleveland staffer of Congresswoman Stephanie Tubbs Jones, who had closely followed election irregularities investigations in Cleveland from 2004. We named directors of business services, finance, human resources, information systems, voting rights institute, communications, legal and legislative, and an elections administrator, four elections attorneys, two legislative staff, two business services attorneys, and several key support and policy staff, including my own assistant, scheduler and driver. When I offered each of them jobs, no one turned us down.

With the help of our new Elections Director, David Farrell, we hired fourteen field staff and two information systems field staff who lived throughout the state where they were close by to assist Ohio's 88 county boards of elections. All were ready to go by the first day in office. Long before I took office, we rolled out our hires in two waves of press announcements, being the first office holder to do so.

Tom Hayes had been right. My elections director, David Farrell, a talented manager from The Ohio State University and former staffer for Lt. Gov. Lee Fisher when he served as Ohio's attorney general from 1991 through 1995, had been a plum target for both Lee Fisher and new state treasurer Richard Cordray, now the director of President Obama's new Consumer Financial Protection Bureau. David had been pressed hard, especially by Lt. Gov. Fisher to work for him, but his desire was to work with us on reforming Ohio's elections. Ohio and I were the luckier for it.

Before I took office, I held a directors meeting in my law office at that same conference table where we had made our team hiring decisions. During that first directors meeting (in which Rick participated as counsel to the transition, having spent countless hours reviewing existing contracts and lawsuits, of which there were twenty-one pending when I took office), we all looked at each other happily, anxious to get started. We were anchored with the four goals and with great respect for one another, beginning a journey as a strong team along a path that was full of anticipation, hope and excitement.

One of the legal counsel I hired, Erick Gale, was my last legal staff hire. I had been nearly ready to hire someone from Cincinnati whose situation would have been tenuous in making the move to Columbus. Erick's resumé had been handed to me by state Democratic Party Chair Chris Redfern, who never asked me to hire him but simply came to see me and handed me his resumé, stating that this young man's parents were upstanding people in his old Ohio House district and he wanted me to know about him. I called Erick for an interview. He was an associate with a large law firm in Columbus that had offices all over the world. I had co-counseled with this law firm, litigated against it and had had its attorneys in my courtroom when I was a judge.

Clearly, I could not pay Erick the large salary that I knew his law firm did. He was earnest and with a quiet demeanor. His experience was exceptional. I asked him why he wanted to make a move to a job that would pay $50,000 less than what he made then. He said simply, "I want to do something that matters." I offered him the job immediately. Another large law firm associate, Beth LaLiberte, took the pay dive as well. She worked in business services as Chief Corporations Counsel. Beth was a strong liaison with lawyers who were frustrated that much of the legal work in the business services section had been handed off to non-attorneys who were subject to decisions that sometimes hurt attorneys' ability to effectively serve their clients. Beth and her team spent months doing the good legal work necessary to help the office simply comply with the law in its procedures and requirements. She was open to answering staff questions, making the accuracy of their statements to the public more reliable and with the strong leadership of Debbie Batta, held down the "fort" as much of the rest of the office tackled elections.

Debbie, with many strong members of her team, succeeded in returning telephones to staff members' desks and permission to use phone calls and email to contact customers with problem filings. They created a mission statement and an incentive and reward program for their employees, moved the customer service center to the same building as the rest of the office, created expedited filing services, returned an outsourced call center and uniform commercial code service center to the main offices and laid the groundwork for offering business service filings for the first time in our Cleveland office. This led to greater job satisfaction for many employees and improved service to the public.

As it turned out, both Erick and Beth were pivotal members of the legal team in negotiating the complex agreements with voting machine manufacturers and corporate and university contractors that were needed to perform what was in 2007 the most extensive voting machine study in the country. Ohio and I were truly blessed. It is this kind of dedication that makes me believe in the future of democracy in our civilized world. It is the quiet, steady but resolute actions of people who say, "I want to do something that matters," that will ensure the survival of democracy. They exist in offices from the U.S. Department of Justice to the clerks at election boards who keep working to make sure every possible detail has been attended to, no matter how late in the day it is or how many meals they miss with their families. Regardless of the party in power, they understand that their duty is to all; they are to be left unhindered to follow the law, wherever it takes them, in the purest sense of public service. They deserve our honor and respect.

In 2008 it was uncovered that attorneys for the U.S. Department of Justice in the second Bush administration were deterred from or even fired for pursuing voter fraud in the form of voter suppression. When the political shenanigans were exposed, there was a sense of vindication felt quietly among many lawyers and judges throughout the country. There will always be the "screamers" and "bullhorn-toting" protestors who mysteriously show up with pre-printed signs with snappy slogans to "fight" for democratic endeavors. They have a rightful place in a free-speaking society. But democracy's ultimate defense will always arise from those who respect and treasure the rule of law and who say to themselves, "How can I not?" They embody the quiet tenacity of sacrifice that ultimately fosters, preserves and protects democracy so it may thrive. They act upon the power of their convictions, knowing that the epitome of democracy is that the power of one is the true impact in a democratic paradigm. ≈

PART III

✦

DEMOCRACY, OHIO-STYLE

Chapter 13

First Day in Office

Formal swearing in ceremony at Bureau of Workers Compensation auditorium in January 2007; oath given by Common Pleas Judge A.J. Wagner of Dayton, a fellow member of my first judicial training class; Rick holding the Bible I studied during my college years

As the time neared for us to take over in the Secretary of State's office, our relationship with the Blackwell administration became even more testy. There was no transition manual as promised. Friendly staff had told us that shredding was going on throughout the day, and in my first visit to the office I had observed an oversized trash can overflowing with shredded paper in a room where the door was left open. I remember thinking, "Hmmm, I don't think that's normal shredding. That's a lot of paper. This will be interesting." When we took over the office, there were only two shredders to be found in the entire three floors of the office. We postulated that shredders had been rented and the evidence of their existence shredded along with countless other documents that would have aided institutional memory.

As it turned out, the Blackwell administration wanted us to keep the employees we had determined we would be letting go for at least a day into our new administration. We indicated we would not. Our punishment was not being able to step foot in the office until my term began. It was so extreme that Secretary Blackwell's Assistant Secretary of State, Monty Lobb, met my Assistant Secretary of State Christopher Nance and new Chief of Staff Tom Worley at 12:01 a.m. the first day of my term to hand them keys to the office. Chris had called me just after midnight and joked that the outgoing Assistant Secretary of State had carried him over the threshold.

I did not retain Ken Blackwell's staff for the extra days he had insisted. Gretchen and Tom, state government veterans, had explained to me the liabilities and expenses that would have created. Both my and former Secretary Blackwell's staff showed up on the first day. Gretchen and Tom provided letters to those who would not be retained, managing a controlled chaotic exodus of disgruntled Blackwell staff, while they whisked in somewhat bewildered but anxious Brunner staff who looked for and found the offices to which they had been assigned (we had at least been provided a diagram of offices). And that is how the first day in office began.

In January 2007, before the first day of the new Democratic administrations, The Ohio State Buckeyes were in the BCS College National Football Championship in Phoenix, Arizona. All the new statewide office holders had been invited to attend the game as official university representatives. Being a veteran in Ohio politics, I knew that this would be a good opportunity to meet many of the Republican legislators with whom I would be working on legislation needed to improve Ohio's elections. Since I had already held my first director's meeting with a strong team in place before I took office, Rick and I attended the BCS game, doing what only an office holder could do—try to forge bipartisan alliances to help my team move forward. I was the only state office holder who went and proud to be designated a university representative for the nation's largest university. I went to nearly every game after. Finally, after growing up in Columbus, the home of the Buckeyes, I became a true Buckeye fan.

L. to R. Lynda and David Farrell and me; David served as Director of Elections from 2007-2011, the entire term; my mother dated his uncle in high school; they live in Pitchin, Ohio with their two boys near what was my grandparents' farm

I had been sworn in before I left Ohio by Judge John Bender, my first political opponent and now my great friend, in the courtroom that had been both his and mine. I took another oath of office just after midnight that first official day of office. Rick, being an attorney, could administer the oath. On a porch outside our hotel in Phoenix, with my new elections director, David Farrell and his wife, Lynda, looking on, I took that oath again, just to be sure. A formal, public swearing in was set for my first week after taking office.

While I would still be in Arizona for the first day in office, I knew my team had things under control after our first directors meeting before that day. What I hadn't expected was a call from Governor Strickland's office, asking me to send back a bill that had been sent to the Secretary of State's office without former Governor Taft's signature. Governor Strickland's legal team had learned from consumer protection attorneys in Akron that this bill gutted consumer rights to sue for violations of the state's consumer sales practices act. This first day in office was the tenth and last day to veto the bill—if Governor Strickland could get it back, and he intended to veto it.

In between the shrimp table and the omelet table at the pre-BCS championship game brunch, called the "Buckeye Bash," I received a call from my staff about the new governor's request.

"Can we do this?" asked Brian Shinn, deputy general counsel.

I quickly exited the tent to better hear him over the Buckeye Battle Cry being played by the band. I remember sitting on a rounded metal stump as an impromptu chair next to a telephone pole, trying to get as far away from the noisy generator outside the tent as I could, which wasn't much quieter than OSU's marching band, known as "The Best Damn Band in the Land (TBDBITL)."

Fortunately, I had retained on my legal staff Gretchen Quinn, a Republican attorney hired in the Taft administration when the former governor served as Secretary of State from 1991 until he was elected governor in 1998. I had to make my first policy decision right there outside the big tent to the tune of the Buckeye Battle Cry. I asked the questions to which I needed answers and then agreed it could be done. But I cautioned, "Everything you do must be documented. Do not give the bill back to the Governor unless he submits a letter requesting it. When you send it back, do so with a letter explaining what you are doing. We will be sued over this."

It took at least one more call from staff as I listened intently bent over with one finger over the ear not attached to the phone, to their reading of the letter out loud to me. I asked for a word here or there to be changed and finally approved the language of our letter tendering back the bill to the governor's office. That moment forged a strong alliance between Brian Shinn, an out gay man from West Virginia, and Gretchen Quinn, a devout trainer of terrier show dogs, who became strong members of my legal team. Brian eventually took over as leader of this team when Eleanor Speelman returned to the Ohio Supreme Court to help new Chief Justice Eric Brown in a smooth transition, after her former boss,' Chief Justice Tom Moyer, unexpected death while still in office.

After helping my staff execute our first policy decision, I boarded the bus to the BCS championship game, politely saying hello to State Senator Steve Stivers (now Congressman Stivers) who had been a sponsor of the bill and whom I'm sure left Ohio thinking the bill was as good as done, and GOP Chair Bob Bennett. I smiled to myself about what I knew had just happened, knowing they would be mortified if they knew. I hummed the Buckeye Battle Cry to myself and was glad I had learned as a judge how to hold a good poker face.

The Republicans in the legislature were outraged. I was sued (the first of dozens of new lawsuits), and we ultimately lost before an all Republican, seven-member Ohio Supreme Court. I took the rap for the governor, knowing that those chances were good when I gave the bill back. The high court found I had abused my discretion. That decision was the first among many that some claimed maneuvered a political outcome in spite of the law. That first day was a portent of many things to come. ≈

Chapter 14

Cuyahoga County

Within weeks of taking office, the annual elections officials' conference was held in Columbus. More than 600 of Ohio's elections officials had descended on the state's capital, curious about what this new Secretary of State would bring to their worlds. All of them are county employees whose elections operations are funded by county government, but with operations requirements set by state and federal law. The state versus local tension is built into the system. The Secretary of State, by state law, mandates implementation of state and federal law. However, she generally does not have the ability to provide the funding needed for the local boards to do as required. The local boards of elections can adopt policies in publicly held meetings by majority vote, and they are encouraged to do so, but this often creates conflict between state and local oversight. Some lament that a lack of uniform practices creates inequality; however, in a state with the diversity of Ohio, some flexibility is needed to minister to the vastly varying needs between remote rural areas with their traditions (including one county polling place which was located at a farmhouse with homemade soup offered to voters) and crowded urban areas with multiple precincts in one polling location, (with concierge poll workers to direct voters to the correct precincts).

The powers of the Secretary of State encompass elements of the powers of all three branches of government—executive, judicial and legislative. The secretary administers laws as a member of the executive branch, but she breaks tie votes at boards of elections, issuing a decision on her vote, much like a judicial decision. There are four board members on every board of elections, two of each major political party, creating many tie votes in areas where partisan clashes arise from personalities, mistrust and heel-digging. Finally, the secretary issues directives much like legislation for carrying out elections. These directives carry the force of law for the state's boards, and they are optimally designed to provide ways to allow for quick pivots with technology or other changes and to smooth the differences between the various boards' practices. I saw them as an effective way to attempt to provide uniformity of procedural and substantive rights to voters.

When I campaigned for the office, I used to say that an umpire can't wear the jersey of one of the teams. Much like the referee in a championship game, the position of Secretary of State in Ohio is a powerful one, more so than many people had previously realized prior to Ken Blackwell. More than once I thought to myself, "No wonder a woman hasn't been elected to this position until now."

To do the job in even a nonpartisan fashion, the Secretary has to have a thorough understanding of legislative, local and state party politics to understand the motivations of the many players with conflicting interests and to "incentive-ize" them to work in such a way as to promote progress for the sake of ensuring voters the best possible voting experiences. For me, it figuratively took skills ranging from hand-to-hand combat to high-level brigadier general strategy to move the battle forward through the thickets and swamps of partisan scheming, nonprofit and academic criticism, some voting rights activists' accusations and exhortations, media speculations of partisan intrigue and everyday human resources and funding issues that affect the administration of the largest citizen-run enterprise that culminates in a thirteen-hour "retail-type" operation called voting in Ohio.

Cuyahoga County is Ohio's most populous county with more than one million voters. While it is just one of Ohio's 88 counties, the success or failure of its election administration largely colors how the country and the world view the state's performance as a whole, especially during Presidential elections. Ohio has for generations been a battleground state—a swing state—in Presidential elections. To change Ohio voters' and the nation's perceptions of Ohio elections, especially after the 2004 Presidential election, systemic changes in Cuyahoga County were needed, and 2007 not only presented that but practically forced it.

Three of Cuyahoga County's four election board members were in Columbus attending the 2007 election officials' conference (known as the OAEO Conference, a moniker for the "Ohio Association of Elections Officials") in January 2007. During the conference I received news that a trial of two of the board's top staffers for crimes constituting election fraud that had been going on resulted in their conviction. The trial had to do with a recount of the 2004 Presidential election sought by the Green Party. When I learned of the verdict, I asked two of the board's members if they had placed these staffers on administrative leave. Their answer was a question: "Do you think we need to do that?" I replied quietly, "Yes, that would be a good idea." It was done that day.

One of the members of the Cuyahoga County Board was the then chair of the Ohio Republican Party, Bob Bennett. Even though Chairman Bennett grew up and had a home in Columbus, he made Cleveland his voting residence (based on a house he owned on Lake Erie) and therefore was eligible to serve on the board of elections of the state's largest county. After the OAEO Conference, he and I had had lunch at his favorite luncheon spot in Columbus, Lindey's Restaurant in German Village. We hit it off well. We exchanged cell phone numbers, and we later had occasion to call each other on various political and election-related issues. I was concerned, however, that in his position as one of two of the state's most prominent partisan leaders, he was able to exert such strong and direct influence on a process that needed balance at its policy making core.

I have often been asked whether nonpartisan or bipartisan is better. Partisan means to the advantage of one political party. Bipartisan means two political parties are being taken into account. Nonpartisan means that no political party is advantaged. Nonpartisan is clearly advantageous from the standpoint of election administration than bipartisan, largely because in a bipartisan situation, the two parties can make deals that do not necessarily benefit the electorate as a whole. Often, the media lauds a bipartisan agreement, because its members believe that nonpartisan, while a worthwhile goal, is not attainable. Because the media feeds best on controversy (and often seasoned reporters have "seen it all") the media often hypothecates that nonpartisan motivation is extinct. In the case of the Cuyahoga County Board of Elections, it probably was.

In Cuyahoga County, each board member was assigned an office and an administrative assistant for a part-time job that paid $25,000 annually but carried with it the coveted benefits of state health insurance and retirement credit in the Public Employees Retirement System. Unfortunately, because of the bipartisan nature of Ohio's election system imbued in state law for decades, there are two camps of employees in most boards of elections, based on the two major political parties. (I later learned that in Summit County this was so pronounced that for each job description, there was a Republican and a Democrat hired for the same job, whether or not two people were needed for the tasks to be performed, just to keep it even—and expensive.)

The local political parties control who gets a job at the board. A job at the board of elections historically has been either a reward for political service or a place to provide a soft landing for someone to whom political chits were owed but no office holder would have them. This has changed in the last few years with requirements for specific qualifications and the advent of computer-based ballot layout and vote processing. The fact hat election administration has become more complicated has had the effect of forcing out some who preferred to retire than retool.

In Franklin County, the state's second largest county in Ohio, an elected, Democratic judge colleague of mine was ultimately ousted from the bench after being ganged up on in a thorough "kitchen sink" disciplinary complaint made by at least eight of her judicial colleagues, all Republicans. Stripped of even her law license because of the proceedings, she was quietly placed by the party in a job at the Franklin County Board of Elections to give her the final few years she needed to earn a pension. She has rarely been seen or heard from again. One party looks away as the other party needs to often unceremoniously take care of one of its own, knowing the political reality that it may need to be in the same position soon. This is one way "bipartisan" works in Ohio, and probably elsewhere as well.

In Cuyahoga County at that time, each employee at the board owed his or her job to some political figure in the county, usually one of the members of the board or a political figure who had (or at one time had) clout with one of the members. The board member positions, themselves, are coveted, and according to one of my early mentors, Don Kindt, from Sherrod Brown's first Secretary of State administration, any county chair who could not engineer a seat on the board was not much of a county chair.

In Cuyahoga County, the tradition was that two seats went to county chairs (Republican and Democratic) and at least one of the other two seats were designated to be a representative of labor or of the African American Congressperson in the federally mandated "majority minority" district created in the Cleveland area. At that time this was the powerful and effective Congresswoman Stephanie Tubbs Jones. The county Democratic chair at the time, Jimmy Dimora, was also serving as a county commissioner. Since the commissioners funded the board, he could not hold both public posts, so the two Democratic seats were held by the head of the Cleveland building trades unions and by an African American lawyer who was close to Congresswoman Tubbs Jones.

The law prescribes that the political parties are the entities that nominate members of the state's boards of elections. When they fail to do so, it is the Secretary of State who must make the choice. The result more often than not is that both the Democratic and Republican county chairs sit on county boards of elections together. This has been seen through politically rose colored glasses as arguably the "best" system in the nation. Supporters argue that its perceived, built-in checks and balances between the two major political parties keeps the system "honest." Laws, directives and policies in Ohio election governance reflect this check-and-balance, party-pitting structure in many ways.

There must be equal numbers of poll workers of each major political party at a polling place (the presiding judge is of the party that won the precinct in the last gubernatorial election). There must be two locks on the door to the room at the board containing the ballots, with a key to just one held by a member of each political party. There must be bipartisan teams to transport ballots from the polling place to the board of elections. This bipartisan transport rule was a practice instituted during my administration, despite complaints and grumbling from county officials who had managed to do everything from taking home voting machines the weekends before elections, known as "sleepovers," to transporting paper ballots in the trunk or back seat of a car driven by one election worker to the board of elections. One famous story from Jefferson County has it that in years past a tired election worker stopped at his mother's house on his way to the board of elections to deliver voted ballots. They remained in the trunk of his car, but he fell asleep at his mother's home, holding up the count for the entire county until he and the ballots could be located.

I carefully watched as events unfolded in the early months of 2007 at the Cuyahoga Board of Elections. The president of the OAEO was the deputy director of the Cuyahoga County Board. At my first meeting with the state's election officials that January 2007, she publicly told me that my ideas for improving Ohio elections just wouldn't work. Soon after, as the criminal trials of two of her top deputies went from bad to worse, from conviction of felonies to sentencing, the board summarily dismissed her and the director of the Cuyahoga County board. When these two top deputies at the board were each sentenced to 18 months in prison for their roles in the 2004 recount, I sat in my state office and mused to myself, "Someone needs to do something about this. This is terrible." Then the realization dropped like a cartoon andiron landing on the street with a crash. "I guess that someone is me," I said, bracing myself.

I knew I had statutory power to remove board of elections members, as well as board directors and deputy directors. The director and deputy director were already gone. "All of them have to go to be accountable to the public for what has happened," I thought. It wasn't that I agreed with the judge's decision on sentencing in Cuyahoga County, but it was the law, and it was reality—and I believed it must have had an effect on the confidence of the community. I took a deep breath and began to think about the process. My job was to clean this up. I had no choice.

The first person I talked with about it was Chris Nance, my Assistant Secretary of State. He not only had worked for Congresswoman Stephanie Tubbs Jones, he had grown up in Shaker Heights, a well-known Cleveland suburb of the county. "Chris," I said, "I need to remove all four members of the Cuyahoga County Board of Elections." I had winced when I said it, thinking he would tell me I was creating more political controversy than I could handle in the hotbed of Cleveland politics. I expected him to say that this would only make the situation worse. I was shocked at his reaction. Chris started with a slow grin and said, "Whoa. Yes, it needs to be done." I was incredulous. "You mean you think it's a good idea?" I asked. "Absolutely!" he said. "Someone's needed to do this for a long time." I had just cleared the first hurdle.

While working for Congresswoman Tubbs Jones, Chris Nance had observed many proceedings of the Cuyahoga County Board of Elections. His former boss, the Congresswoman, had petitioned on the floor of Congress that the vote of Ohio not be certified after the 2004 Presidential election because of the many irregularities documented in, for example, the John Conyers report after that election. Chris knew that Cuyahoga's problems were systemic and that this action presented a viable path to change.

I began telling my other directors, who, in hindsight, I'm sure were bracing themselves for what they could only imagine lay ahead. I could see among their faces mixed emotions of fear, anticipation and respect for a process that would be somewhat like going into a rodeo ring for a long, wild ride.

We began to make plans. State law allowed me to remove a board member for "neglect of duty, malfeasance, misfeasance, or nonfeasance in office, [or] for any willful violation of Title XXXV of the Revised Code." Essentially, if a board member evidenced a willful failure to follow state law I had the power to remove them. But first, court decisions required that I hold a hearing before removing any board member. Thinking pragmatically, I decided to first ask each board member to resign to avoid having to hold hearings and create a public mess. I also thought it was the polite and adult thing to do. Moreover, when I asked each to resign, I also would made it clear that if they did not resign, I would remove them.

Knowing human nature and understanding politics, especially in Cleveland, I determined that a Sunday evening would be the best time to reach board members and also others whom I needed to notify to show the requisite political courtesy. A Sunday evening, I reasoned, would leave the fewest opportunities for any of the four board members to call one another ahead of time or to alert another to duck my calls, since I couldn't simultaneously call all four of them at once to deliver my message.

As it turned out, the calculation to call on a Sunday evening was dead on. The previous week, with Chris Nance's help, we obtained cell numbers of all four board members and then compiled a list of whom I would need to call after calling the four board members. By the evening of Sunday, March 18, 2007, various members of my staff and I had tracked down cell and home telephone numbers for everyone we believed we needed to call. We agreed to meet at 6:30 p.m. at the office for me to make the calls from there.

Tom Worley placed a poster-sized "post-it" note on one of the many exit doors in my office. I was told that Ken Blackwell used this particular door to make quick getaways when he needed to leave unnoticed. The poster had twenty-six names on it, including the names of the four board members. Then Tom took small yellow post-it notes, each numbered 1 through 26. Collectively, we determined which names on the poster were to be assigned which number in calling priority, with Tom affixing the numbers and moving them around as we changed our minds and finally settled on the order of the calls I would make.

By 7:45 p.m., I was ready to make the calls. I took a deep breath and "dove in" to accomplish a task that was going to be anything but fun. First, I called Bob Bennett. I reached him on his cell phone immediately. He was surprised to hear from me. Tom had given me a suggested script on how to convey 1) that a change was needed at the Cuyahoga County Board with the sentencing to prison of two of the board's top staff people, 2) that the dismissal of the director and deputy director was not sufficient to assure the public of the board's smooth future operation, and 3) that I was asking for the resignation of all four board members as a result. I indicated that this was not personal, but that it was needed to ensure public confidence. Finally, I gave them a deadline by which to resign, saying that if they did not, I would undertake proceedings to remove them. Bob Bennett simply said, "You don't want to do this." I told him that my decision had been made, that it was final and exited the conversation. I proceeded to call the other Republican member next to ensure I reached her before he did, followed by calls to the two Democratic members.

Then I called Governor Strickland, Speaker of the Ohio House Jon Husted, President of the Ohio Senate Bill Harris, Congresswoman Stephanie Tubbs Jones, U.S. Senator Sherrod Brown and many others whom I believed should be made aware of what I had done before they read, heard or saw news of it in the media. A press release was prepared for early release the next day. When Brent Larkin of the *Cleveland Plain Dealer* spoke with me the next morning, the first question he jokingly asked me was if I was going to fire him.

That Sunday night I completed twenty-six calls in record time, an hour and fifteen minutes, reaching all four board members on the first try, before they heard the news from anyone but me. I reached the governor, the speaker of the house and the president of the senate, each on the first try. I was able to talk with Congresswoman Tubbs Jones and a host of others. For those whom I couldn't reach, I was able to leave a message so that they were aware I had given them the courtesy of trying.

The next day, Jimmy Dimora, chair of the Cuyahoga County Democratic Party called me, noticeably peeved. He chastised me for not letting him know ahead of time, saying he was getting grief for what I did, but had to tell the complainers that he didn't know about it ahead of time. I told him that was the very reason I did not call him until after I had talked with the four board members; then he could say he would have tried to stop me, but he didn't have the chance. I explained simply that I had given him plausible deniability. There wasn't much more he could say.

The media advisory read as follows:

"Columbus, OH - March 19, 2007 - Pledging to restore trust to elections in Ohio amidst the myriad of challenges facing the Cuyahoga County Board of Elections, the state's chief election officer, Ohio Secretary of State Jennifer Brunner, has asked for the resignation of the four-member board, two Democrats and two Republicans, effective the close of business March 21, 2007.

'Cuyahoga County has historically faced challenges with its board of elections, but we are at a time when these challenges are so great that extraordinary measures are needed to improve the election process in the state's most populous county,' said Brunner.

The Director and Deputy Director positions in the office are currently vacant, with an interim director serving until these positions are filled. The third in charge position is vacant due to a criminal conviction in January. A search committee from the community is interviewing candidates for the top two positions.

'I want the search committee's efforts to be met by a board that is poised to move forward with a fresh approach to ensuring access, accountability, security and convenience in making elections work in Cuyahoga County,' said Brunner.

Brunner made calls to the four board members Sunday evening, asking them to resign no later than close of business on Wednesday. Secretary Brunner recognized these individuals for their service and commitment to the citizens of Cuyahoga County. She contacted the chairmen of the Republican and Democratic parties in Cuyahoga County to inform them of her action. Should members resign or be removed from office, the local political party would need to recommend replacements. The Secretary of State appoints members of boards of elections after reviewing recommendations made by county political parties, with two from each party serving on a board of elections.

'With maximum 18-month prison sentences being handed down to two Cuyahoga County election workers last week for their roles in the 2004 Presidential recount, the tremendous problems that surfaced in the May 2006 primary that delayed even the unofficial vote count for 5 days, and the uncertain future of this board as another Presidential election looms on the near horizon, it is incumbent on me as Secretary of State to provide the direction needed to get this troubled board on track. The voters of Cuyahoga County deserve it, the citizens of Ohio expect it, and the rest of the nation will be watching,' said Brunner."

* * *

These actions reverberated among the news outlets not just in Ohio but nationally, including the Washington Post and the New York Times. I did not expect this, as it seemed to me to be just a local, Ohio issue—removing four county board of elections members—but two months into office, it was becoming clear that any effort in trying to improve elections in Ohio was often national and sometimes international news. Early on, before we even held a press conference in the office (which did not occur for close to three months), our actions were widely covered in the news. Many former and current statehouse reporters remembered my old boss, Sherrod Brown, and his days in the Secretary of State's office, some even telling me that they used to ask him to stop sending out so many press releases or they would quit writing stories about him. I often thought, the old Sherrod I had known would have been ecstatic for the media coverage I wasn't even trying to get.

One-by-one each of the four board of elections members decided to resign: first the Democratic attorney member, then the second Republican member, then the labor member, after some intense discussions, and finally, we were left with one holdout—Bob Bennett, the Ohio GOP Chair. The first newspaper editorial cartoon ever featuring a drawing of me was in the Toledo Blade, where Dave Shutt, a former press secretary for Sherrod Brown when Senator Brown was Secretary of State, was now the editor. I have the original in my office, even with color added by cartoonist Kirk Walters. It's an odd experience to see how a cartoonist sees you, making a caricature of you and emphasizing features, good and bad, that you would prefer be minimized than accentuated. The cartoon features what looks like a SWAT officer pointing to a dialog bubble of someone off screen saying, "You'll never take me alive!" The SWAT officer tells the cartoon image of me, "Bob Bennett's barricaded himself in the Cuyahoga County Board of Elections office," while the cartoon image of the Secretary of State bears a somewhat perplexed look.

Bob Bennett did not go quietly. He made it very clear I would have to remove him and that he would fight every step of the way. By this point, Marc Dann, Attorney General at the time, had already refused me special counsel to manage the twenty-one lawsuits against the office that were still pending when Ken Blackwell left office (the vast majority of them concerned elections). What Marc didn't seem to comprehend was that personnel were needed to manage these twenty-one lawsuits left to me—to monitor their progress, to confer with the assigned assistant attorneys general and to keep me informed and briefed when decisions were needed during the life of the litigation.

I had increased the number of office legal staff to do the remedial and preparatory work needed to prepare for 2008—educating and training board personnel, preparing directives, assisting with a voting machine study I had promised during my campaign to conduct, advising boards of elections and answering questions from the public and legislature on a day-to-day basis. To keep track of and manage lingering and troublesome past litigation was a backward, not a forward activity. And I had to keep moving forward. I often said to my legal staff when I was exhorting them to excellence that there are no "do overs" in elections—we only get one shot to get it right. And a smooth 2008 Presidential election was a long shot, but it could be done.

Marc Dann and I had discussed my request for special counsel to handle past litigation when we met one-on-one in his office. He flatly said to me that he would not provide me with special counsel to represent me in these pending matters. He said his office would handle them. I told him that it was his job to advise me on legal matters but not to manage my office or to handle the political and policy decisions I had been elected to make. I told him that I didn't have the legal staff to both manage past litigation and prepare for future elections. He didn't budge. Then I looked him squarely in the eye and said, "You can't stop me from hiring my own counsel to take over the management of these cases in my office, and that's what I'm going to do." Marc stammered momentarily and acquiesced, saying, "Well, you're right. I can't."

I hired a Republican attorney with extensive federal court experience to manage the litigation to relieve the burden for my staff and to assist me in determining when and whether to fight or settle cases. By the time I left office four years later, just one of the original twenty-one matters of litigation remained unresolved, and it was one involving the integrity of the 2004 Presidential election.

My experience as a judge and as an attorney who filed and tried election cases prepared me well for the secretary of state's office. However, it sometimes made me a more difficult client. I often requested proactive instead of reactive litigation to help us ensure smooth election administration and better public accountability.

One such example was when Diebold and its subsidiary, Premier Election Solutions (formerly Diebold), sued Cuyahoga County and my office, on the advice of its counsel, in a preemptive move to resolve the Cuyahoga County Board's claims against it concerning Diebold's touchscreen voting system. It appeared that the lawsuit, brought by Diebold and its related companies, had been brought to control the venue of litigation so as not to be "hometowned" in a Cuyahoga County court. The suit was brought in Franklin County, where I had served as a judge for nearly five years. I was ecstatic to be sued. I found out on Rick's and my 30th anniversary trip in Stockholm, Sweden. We literally "high fived" when we found out by email around 11:00 p.m. Stockholm time. My response was to immediately ask the attorney general, by this time, former Ohio State University Law School Dean Nancy Rogers, for a countersuit to be filed against Diebold on my behalf for problems that were also occurring in other counties.

In 2008, the boards of elections (beginning in Butler County near Cincinnati) had discovered and turned over to the Secretary of State's office significant operational deficiencies they experienced in tabulating votes of the Diebold system used by more than half the counties in the state. Specifically, they had discovered, and we later confirmed, that the process of uploading votes from voting machine memory cards to the tabulation server resulted in dropped votes during tabulation. With some verification procedures, we were able to document this and to count all votes, but no voting system should have performed in this fashion. Ultimately, we settled that matter in 2010, and we negotiated terms that allowed boards of elections around the state to receive deep discounts in needed upgrades and maintenance of their voting systems, after Diebold had corrected the problems with system upgrades. Had we not been proactive, Ohio voters and election officials would have lost the chance for more improved voting system capabilities that addressed some of the vulnerabilities we discovered in our 2007 voting machine study. Cuyahoga County ended up settling separately, based on its size and divergent claims and came out well in the settlement.

But back in 2007, when it came to removing Cuyahoga County's entire board of elections the question of the Diebold voting system was secondary to that of the board, itself. When I moved forward to remove the entire board, Marc Dann's first assistant attorney general, Tom Winters, whom I had known for years since his days with former Ohio House Speaker Vern Riffe, called me and said, "Jen, are you sure you know what you're doing here?" I answered in the affirmative. He spoke of the political risks, to which I said I would handle the politics; I needed the attorney general to assist me as my lawyer.

Several days later I was informed by Eleanor Speelman, my general counsel, that the attorney general's office was very busy. It could not provide counsel to represent us in filing a complaint to remove Bob Bennett from the Cuyahoga County board for at least two weeks; at least a month would be needed. This was unacceptable, as the May 2007 primary election was just weeks away. I insisted on special counsel and this time was permitted to have it and to choose my own. I chose a Republican, John W. Ferron, who was a good litigator, very thorough and who had the guts to do what was necessary to prove a case. That it was high profile, controversial and political did not phase him. I had to choose a hearing officer. I chose Bill Owen, first assistant prosecutor for then Delaware County Prosecutor, David Yost, a Republican. David Yost became Ohio's state auditor in 2011. Bill had appeared in my courtroom when I was a judge and had proved to be professional, thorough and fair. Eleanor provided a stable and seamless interface with this outside legal team.

Eleanor Speelman was another of Tom and my recruits to the team during the transition. We had asked her to head the office's legal team as general counsel. She brought with her considerable experience, having served as the chief clerk to who was at that time the nation's longest serving chief justice, Thomas J. Moyer. Chief Justice Moyer was a Republican, appointed by former Governor James Rhodes. Eleanor was an unapologetic Democrat. She had served the Chief for twelve years.

Eleanor is a rock. She ran the stairs in the building at lunch time, taking the elevator down fifteen floors and running back up them several times each day. No one could write faster, more directly and with more verve. Her research was indefatigable and spot on. She reviewed litigation pleadings drafted by the Attorney General on my behalf and made them more incisive, more direct and more responsive, and she did so, with tact and alacrity, earning great respect from other lawyers throughout state government.

Certification of the 2008 general election results; clockwise starting at center, Assistant Attorney General Rich Coglianese, Gretchen Quinn, Brian Shinn, Eleanor Speelman, Antoinette Wilson, me, David Farrell and Attorney General Nancy Rogers

Eleanor and I also shared an interesting past. Before she began her tenure with the Chief, she had worked as an independent contractor for me during the early years of my law practice, when I worked from my home in the northeastern part of the county and she from her home in the far southwestern part of the county. Years before, I had once driven to her home to bring work to her and met her three children, two boys and a girl, nearly the same ages as my two girls and a boy.

When Eleanor began her tenure as general counsel for me, she was unfamiliar with election law *per se.* I assured her that she was still perfect for the job. No one, except Gretchen Quinn, on my elections legal staff held this specialized experience, except for me. I knew I would have to be "hands on" in the beginning, fulfilling the role of chief elections counsel until the rest of the attorneys could get "up to speed." They did this rapidly. Because of Eleanor's and my roles with the office's legal team at the time, preparing for the battle with Bob Bennett and for a wholesale change at the Cuyahoga County Board of Elections took us back to our days of collaboration in private practice. Together, we pored over the complaint and other documents that had to be filed to begin the process of Mr. Bennett's ouster.

One night, as we were working late into the evening to prepare the complaint for filing the next day, I walked the steps a floor down to her office and sat across from her at her desk. Together, in the dim light of her office, we put the finishing touches on the complaint to be filed the next day. I looked up from my papers and, grinning, said, "Eleanor, think back to fifteen years ago when we were both working out of our houses on legal projects together with our kids running around—and look at us now." We laughed, shook our heads and kept on working until we finished what had to be filed the next day.

Our complaint against Bob Bennett was served. He responded by suing me in the Franklin County Common Pleas Court, asking the court to stop the proceeding. It had been a media frenzy up to this point, as Mr. Bennett refused to resign and began corresponding with staff at the board of elections. I had summarily suspended him on April 3, 2007, to keep him from interfering with board operations, placed the board on administrative oversight and began personally conducting weekly calls, along with key elections staff in my office. We wanted to provide as much support as we could to Jane Platten, the board's interim director, who stood very alone in this time of administrative transformation and in preparing for the May election. Bennett's suspension letter informed him that the suspension was indefinite in duration and would terminate upon the later of his removal or the final resolution of any litigation contesting his removal.

By this time, Attorney General Dann decided he would represent me personally. We had released this information the day before in a media release:

Columbus, OH - March 30, 2007 - The state's chief election officer, Ohio Secretary of State Jennifer Brunner, announced today that Franklin County Common Pleas Court Judge Patrick Sheeran will hear Cuyahoga County Board of Elections member Robert Bennett's motion to temporarily restrain Brunner from moving forward with a removal hearing in Cleveland against him. Bennett is the only remaining member of the Cuyahoga County Board of Elections after Brunner sought the entire board's resignation and received three out of four.

Judge Sheeran who was out of town when the motion was filed yesterday will hear the matter on Monday, April 2, 2007 at 1:30 p.m. in his chambers in courtroom 6B, 369 S. High St., Columbus, OH 43215.

Ohio Attorney General Marc Dann will personally appear and represent Brunner at the hearing. Bennett is represented by legal counsel from Cincinnati and Columbus initially hired by Cuyahoga County Prosecutor Bill Mason at Bennett's request for the board removal hearing.

Bennett's attorneys filed suit yesterday in Franklin County Common Pleas Court to enjoin the Secretary of State from proceeding with an April 2 removal hearing against Bennett and to declare the law allowing for his removal unconstitutional. By agreement of the parties the April 2nd removal hearing has been postponed until April 9.

Hearing officer William Owen, the first assistant prosecuting attorney of Delaware County, is scheduled to conduct the hearing on Brunner's removal complaint against Bennett on Monday, April 9 at 9:00 a.m. at Euclid City Hall Council Chambers, 585 E. 222nd St., Euclid in Cuyahoga County."

Judge Sheeran (who now manages the TIES Program I had started at the Franklin County Common Pleas Court in 2004) recused. Other judges determined they did not feel comfortable handling the case because of our past relationship as judicial colleagues. Finally, Judge John Connor said he would take the case.

When we appeared before Judge Connor, it was a strange experience for me to be sitting at one of the parties' counsel tables in the courtroom as the defendant, instead of at the bench, and even more so with the attorney general of Ohio personally representing me. Less than two years earlier, I had conducted my last session of the TIES program in Judge

Connor's courtroom as we transitioned the program to him from me. I had been the one wearing the robe then.

Bob Bennett was not in attendance at court, and neither was his counsel, Stan Chesley, who had made his mark representing the plaintiffs in the famed 1977 Beverly Hills Supper Club fire class action litigation, in Southgate, adjacent to Cincinnati. Stan had recovered $50 million through trial and settlement for the families of 165 people who were killed and many more injured, from more than 1000 defendants. Chesley's law firm is billed as the oldest law firm in Cincinnati. For the hearing before Judge Connor, the law firm had sent a young associate, Christopher Stock, to argue the temporary restraining order motion to keep me from removing Mr. Bennett.

Judge Connor methodically went through the four elements that had to be proved to the court's satisfaction in order for a temporary order to be issued. Mr. Stock was not successful, and his client was denied the order. Outside the courtroom, Attorney General Dann and I were barraged by blinding lights for television cameras and by newspaper, television and radio reporters with microphones and tape recorders thrust in our faces as we exited.

Eventually, enough long-time politicos convinced Mr. Bennett to give up the ghost of his board membership. He did so on April 11, 2007, less than one month before the May 8, 2007 primary election in Cuyahoga County. He made his move in exchange for my dropping the matter against him for removal. He resigned as a board member and dismissed his action. Chris Nance handled the signed resignation like it was the Magna Carta. I filed it away after Chris gingerly handed it to me, knowing my work had just begun.

Jimmy Dimora had already given me the authority to fill the two Democratic vacancies on the Cuyahoga County Board of Elections. He said that he did not have time in the statutory fifteen days to convene a Democratic party county central committee meeting to make the required nominations. In the absence of local party action to nominate a board member for a vacancy on the board, the secretary of state by law may select the board member(s) for the vacancy.

This was a gift to me and to Cuyahoga County. My staff and I agreed it would be best to advertise and interview for the board member positions in keeping with my first directive that focused on qualifications of directors and deputy directors of boards of elections. This directive had been issued in part to preempt the Cuyahoga County Board of Elections from filling the vacancies of director and deputy director with politically motivated candidates. I simply wanted people who would do a good job.

After advertising the positions for the two Democratic appointments to the board on my website and in the local media, staff in my office conducted telephone interviews for the two positions, winnowing dozens of candidates to six. Chris Nance and I traveled to Cleveland, using space provide by the Cleveland Foundation to conduct the interviews. Ultimately, I selected the two Democratic board members. I appointed Eben O. "Sandy" McNair, IV, a hard-scrabble Scottish-descent labor attorney who volunteered to his law firm to take a 20% pay cut from the firm while giving his board salary to the firm. He knew there would be much time and effort needed in helping the board to positively rebuild itself. Such dedication and integrity are rare. Sandy was listed among "The Best Lawyers in America in 2006," and holds degrees from St. Lawrence University, the University of Chicago and Cornell University. He is a tireless advocate for his clients and their members and has served his community as a board of elections member in an exemplary fashion.

I conferred late at night with Congresswoman Tubbs Jones about her recommendations for qualified and acceptable candidates to apply for the other position. We both wanted to ensure diversity on the board. Inajo Davis Chappelle, an attorney and partner at Ulmer and Berne, applied with a wealth of board experience and a corporate and business law background. She had represented the Cleveland school district and been former board chair of Boys & Girls Clubs of Cleveland as well as holds degrees from Yale and Columbia Universities. Other extremely qualified candidates made the final cut and impressed Chris Nance and me with their sincere dedication and passion to make a difference in their community. Despite Cleveland's troubles and the reports that may have portrayed it as a troubled community, I never cease to be amazed at the talent, creativity and dedication of so many individuals who steadily work to make Cleveland and greater Cuyahoga County an amazing, culturally rich and thoroughly livable community.

Our media release of April 23, 2007 was a testament to my belief in this developing, new board, as I stated:

> "'I met personally with six finalists for the two board positions last week in Cleveland. I am impressed with the new generation of leadership who have stepped up to serve their community,' said Brunner. 'Inajo Chappell and Sandy McNair represent some of the best the greater Cleveland community has to offer to restore confidence in Cuyahoga County's election process. They are committed to the highest quality of public service and ready to put the time and effort to the task,' added Brunner.

'I am optimistic about the future of the Cuyahoga Board and have a great deal of confidence in the three newly appointed Board members,' added Brunner. Former Cuyahoga County Common Pleas Court Judge Jeff Hastings, a Republican, was the first board member appointed last week.

The appointment of the Republican board members was made according to the statutory framework. The county Republican party nominated former Judge Hastings and sent his name to me for the actual appointment. Before the Cuyahoga County Republican County Central Committee nominated him, he set up a meeting with me in Columbus, and we talked of his intentions to be on the board. I was enthusiastic about his potential nomination and encouraged it. Hastings' experience included stints as senior deputy attorney general in Attorney General Jim Petro's Cleveland office, as a common pleas court judge and as executive director of the Cuyahoga County Republican Party. He holds degrees from Ashland University, Baldwin-Wallace College and the Cleveland-Marshall College of Law. I knew he was well liked by many members of the bar in Cuyahoga County as well. Things moved forward quietly and swiftly after our meeting.

The second Republican appointment could not be made until Bob Bennett resigned. When he did, I received a not unexpected call from Rob Frost, the county Republican chair. Seeing his name come up on my cell phone, I immediately thought that the call would be about his appointment. Rob simply asked if he could meet with me in Columbus, to which I assented.

I was correct in my prediction. We met in my office, and he quietly spoke of his interest in the last open board position. I said I was not surprised and that I thought, based on what I knew of his prior bi-partisan international election observation work and legal background, he would make a good board member. Rob Frost had served as assistant chief legal counsel to former Ohio Auditor Jim Petro and as a city councilman in the Cleveland suburb of Rocky River. He holds degrees from Emory University and Case Western Reserve University. After our meeting, Rob Frost returned to Cuyahoga County and shortly thereafter, his central committee nominated him for the post. I promptly appointed him.

By the May 8, 2007 primary election, the board was reconstituted with four new members. I personally attended the first meeting, on primary Election Day in Cleveland and administered the oath of office to all four board members at the start of the meeting. Jeff Hastings served as chair and ran the meetings in a timely and respectful manner as would be expected of a former judge. I had appointed four attorneys to the board, and the analysis of the issues benefited from their expertise and training.

First meeting of the reconstituted Cuyahoga County Board of Elections, May 5, 2008; L. to R. member Inajo Davis Chappelle, Secretary of State Jennifer Brunner, chair Jeff Hastings and member Sandy McNair (adapted from Cleveland Plain Dealer photo)

The Cuyahoga County Board of Elections' first task was to select a director and deputy director. The board did this with little guidance from me, since the directive on required qualifications was already in place. They chose Jane Platten, who had served ably as interim director during a tumultuous time at the board and Patrick McDonald, a former staff member for Bob Taft when he served as secretary of state in the 1990's. Jane and Pat worked together in an outstanding fashion and were on every weekly call with our office, along with two board members, alternating between weeks. The weekly calls benefitted me as much as them, since this board's challenges were magnified by its sheer number of voters.

Listening to their concerns and proposed solutions helped me better manage and supervise all of the boards in the state. While the Cuyahoga County board's participants appreciated (usually) the personal attention they received from their Secretary of State, I am forever grateful to their participation and willingness to accept our help in their transformation process and thereby to share its effects and benefits with the rest of the state. As the Cuyahoga County board's operations drastically improved, so did the nation's perception of Ohio. ≈

Chapter 15

EVEREST

On the campaign trail for Secretary of State, I heard question after question from people I talked with about the reliability of the state's new voting systems, especially the electronic, touch screen voting systems. I promised what I dubbed a "top-to-bottom" review of Ohio's voting systems if elected. I was able to fulfill that promise in Project EVEREST, a "top-to-bottom review of Ohio's voting systems" that was called by a University of Massachusetts TechReport "the most comprehensive to date" in the nation.

Congress adopted the Help America Vote Act, known as "HAVA," in 2002. Despite the fact that every two years there had been a federal election, it took the precipitous 2000 Presidential election for Congress to come to enough of a consensus that voting procedures and systems that remained primarily locally controlled needed an overhaul. HAVA provided more than $3 billion dollars to move the states to mandated voting systems with an aim to provide greater standardization and quality control of the election process, especially in federal elections. The U.S. Election Assistance Commission was created to administer federal funding to help move states and territories from what were known as "punch card" and mechanical lever voting systems to computer-based systems, whose servers both created ballot layout and tabulated the results of their counts.

This recent evolvement of Ohio's voting systems was described in the EVEREST report as follows:

> With the advent of HAVA, voting machine manufacturers whose new systems met the

applicable federal standards and whose equipment was approved for use in Ohio by the state's Board of Voting Machine Examiners, submitted bids for consideration to the Ohio secretary of state. The secretary of state, in turn, worked with each county's board of elections (BOE) to purchase an approved system — either a direct recording electronic (DRE) or an optical scan system manufactured by Diebold (now Premier Elections Solutions), Hart InterCivic, or Election Systems and Software (ES&S) – that best-suited each particular county.

In May 2004, the General Assembly enacted Substitute House Bill 262, which required all DRE voting machines to provide a voter verified paper audit trail (VVPAT). The approved systems, with VVPAT, were subjected to an Independent Verification and Validation (IV&V) test and a security assessment . . . Approximately half of Ohio's 88 counties used their new voting systems in the November 2005 general election; the other half used their new systems for the first time in the May 2006 primary election.

Before HAVA, nearly 75% of Ohio's 88 counties used the punch card system. Punch card voting systems involved buff-colored, generic, rectangular cards with multiple, numbered, perforated, miniature rectangles that, when "punched" with a stylus or sharp, pointed instrument, (even a ball point pen) created holes in the card. Like the old Cobol or Fortran computer program cards of the 1960's and 1970's, these cards were then read by an automated counter device to detect and record which holes had been punched. One card represented a voter's votes at an election. The small rectangles of cardstock released with each "punch" through the card were called "chads." The 2006 film

Bobby dubbed the term "chad" an acronym that stood for "Card Hole Aggregate Debris." Regardless of whether this is really the origin of the term, as Ohio's 52nd Secretary of State, I am the proud owner of a clear glass Christmas ornament filled with chads, given to me by a Tuscarawas County election official. When I hang it on my tree, I can only smile.

For more than thirty years, voting system technology was fairly static, so an initial investment in a punch card or lever system was a decent investment that lasted for some years without needing replacement. A three-member board of local county commissioners governs each of Ohio's local boards of elections' budgets. The longevity of the punch card and clunky, mechanical lever systems allowed counties to enjoy a fairly peaceful coexistence with state and federal requirements, as long as those requirements remained fairly static.

Before HAVA, some electronic technology had been adopted and put into use. For instance, in Franklin County in Columbus, Ohio, the gray metal lever machines on wheels that gave voters the satisfaction of a loud clunk and opening of the heretofore-closed privacy curtains had been replaced by a more rudimentary electronic voting machine. Franklin County's early electronic voting system involved what looked like a giant "board" full of red blinking lights under a plastic cover that contained ballot names and issues. That plastic cover was fitted over mechanical buttons. Each blinking light represented a ballot position. Once a voter voted for the required number of candidates for an office, the red light(s) for the office held steady. When all the blinking lights were static, the full ballot had been voted, and it was time to press the oblong button at the bottom of the board to cast the voter's ballot. Ballot issues were hard to read. They are required to be placed at the end of the ballot and on this system were often at the far right, lower corner of this giant ballot. Their placement often made an uninformed voter's vote on an issue little more than a "crapshoot," especially in low lighting in school gymnasiums, and this was even more so if the voter was older.

The catalyst for the perceived need for sweeping Congressional change of the nation's voting systems came about with the invention and use in Florida of the famed "butterfly ballot" in the year 2000. This type of ballot, designed to be used with a punch card, is reported to have been designed by an elected elections supervisor in Palm Beach County, Florida, Theresa LePore. On the butterfly ballot, the names of Presidential candidates were listed on opposing pages, along the centerfold between the pages. The punch card was aligned under the ballot, but voters were often confused about which candidate's name actually lined up with which punch hole. According to LaPore, she designed the ballot this way to make the type bigger, so the ballot would be easier to read by Palm Beach County seniors. Unfortunately, ballot designs are often affected by local funding considerations as well. A page less on a ballot means less postage to mail an absentee ballot—to the voter and by the voter in returning it.

Many believe the butterfly ballot cost Al Gore the presidency in 2000. I believe poor administrative election procedures and erroneous legal and political calculations before, during and after the election cost him and the country a fair and accurate election. The lack of a consistent policy in the State of Florida to deal with ballot marking anomalies such as "double bubbles" is reported by Roy G. Saltman in *The History and Politics of Voting Technology*.

According to Saltman, the "double bubble" phenomenon accounted for enough lost votes for Vice-president Al Gore to lose the majority of popular votes he needed in Florida to gain Florida's 20 electoral votes, instead putting then Texas Governor

George W. Bush over the finish line for the needed number of electoral votes. Gore and his legal team's choice to seek recounts in only some counties and not all was, in hindsight, a tragic mistake. It also resulted in a loss of credibility in the minds of many. To some it looked like Gore and his team were "cherry picking" which counties would be most advantageous to recount to give him a win.

The better part of valor would have been for both candidates to simply push for a recount of the entire state and "let the chips fall where they may." Instead, intimidation, bullying, one-upmanship, false accusations and innuendo led to a befuddled and reckless process that leaves us, as a nation, still embarrassed today. Many were left with a diminished view of our judicial system's highest court, which ultimately decided the question of who became U.S. President in 2000. Hoards of lawyers and rambling legal treatment of the parsed processes of this election were the subject of conflicting state and federal jurisdictional battles and a media microscope magnified by 24-hour reporting. The parsing of the votes in 2000 in Florida was, unfortunately, just one springboard of Americans' distrust of their government. This was suborned only temporarily with 9/11 and came back with a vengeance upon the disclosure that there were no weapons of mass destruction in Iraq and that natural disasters like Hurricane Katrina could not summon a swift and cogent response from our federal government.

Al Gore's narrow margin of loss made the 2000 Presidential election one of the closest ever in U.S. history. The process and the results themselves threw the entire 2000 U.S. Presidential election into a chaotic, partisan scramble that failed to resolve misapplied and unevenly applied rules that denied some voters the ability to speak through their votes. It was an election that mattered, and one so close that literally every vote mattered. Every hanging, pregnant, bulging or dangling chad was a question subject to local political sway after examination under a magnifying sheet held above an election judge's head beneath the overhead fluorescent light. What a way for the rest of the world to see the nation's oldest democracy in action.

At the time, I had just been elected a state trial court judge and interestingly took a post-election November 2000 trip with Rick to Key West, Florida. Each day, sitting by the pool, I read the Miami Herald for the blow-by-blow description of this nasty and trying post-election process, feeling like I almost knew the pivotal election officials whose lives and families were being spotlighted as the recount and legal maneuvers dragged on. I had just finished 13 years of primarily election law private practice. But, having a judicial duty ahead of me, it was no longer my place to be involved or to comment, unless the matter was brought before me in court. So I simply read in amazement about what looked to me like a spectacle turned debacle.

The tangled mess in Florida was ultimately resolved by an undesirably and previously uncharacteristically partisan U.S. Supreme Court decision. Saltman, who had been a computer scientist from 1969 to 1996 with the National Institute of Standards and Technology (NIST; formerly National Bureau of Standards), reported that the policy on determining voter intent for double bubble votes on optical scan paper ballots was inconsistent from county to county in Florida, such that, had there been consistent, statewide standards for determining voter intent, just for double bubbles, the result would have been a win for Al Gore, without any other legal maneuvering.

What is a double bubble? Explained in simple terms, a voter fills in an oval on an optical scan ballot (like a college standardized test answer sheet) to record his or her candidate of choice for, for example, President of the United States. With ballot rotation on many ballots (moving the names to different positions on ballots in different voting precincts), or the lack of ballot rotation, the line and oval for a write-in candidate may be located just below the voter's selection. (A write-in candidate is a candidate whose name is not pre-printed on the ballot.)

When a voter has filled in an oval to vote for his or her candidate of choice and then also fills in an oval next to and writes in the same candidate's name in the write-in space, a "double bubble" occurs (much like printing a name underneath a signature). Even though the voter actually voted for just one candidate, two ovals were filled, and that result is read by a machine as two votes, or an "overvote." In a traditional overvote situation (such as voting for three candidates for school board instead of two), it is impossible for an election official to determine which names a voter actually voted for in an "overvote" situation. That is not the case, however, with the double bubble. In the double-bubble situation, voters in effect, "over-emphasize" their vote. When an optical scanner senses two votes for an office where only one vote is permitted, it does not count the vote for that office, because there are too many.

In states like Ohio, there is law that requires boards of elections to determine voter intent on ballots where there are discrepancies or problems. If and when voter intent can be determined, the "overvote" results in an official determination by the local board of elections of what was the voter's intent. In a true "double bubble" circumstance, the voter's vote must be counted. This process did not occur in an orderly fashion or with consistency in Florida in 2000. It did in Ohio in 2008 and continued to do so throughout my administration until my successor, a Republican, discontinued the practice.

In 2008 many election officials chafed under the requirement that double bubbles be identified and processed, because in many cases, this had to be done by hand. But, in 2008, with scores of elections for offices large and small throughout Ohio, more than a handful of candidate elections throughout the state were decided by less than 1000 votes.

Ironically, the vagaries of the 2000 and 2004 Presidential elections, heavily reliant on punch card technology, have been confused by many as having been caused by the computerized technology of touch screen electronic voting. In the minds of many, the lines blur between the punch card voting before 2006 and touchscreen voting from 2006 forward. Regardless, voting machine technology remains substandard to what we use everyday in banking and for travel.

The name EVEREST was a brainchild moniker of a staffer named David Klein, who worked extensively on the study, especially on documentation of the results. The name, EVEREST, stood for "Evaluation and Validation of Election Related Equipment, Standards and Testing." Harnessing the help we needed to perform this study and keeping it on track many times made me think that finishing this project ever, let alone on time, was like climbing Mt. Everest.

Project EVEREST's purpose was to review each type of certified voting systems in Ohio, (systems also used throughout the U.S.). Four major tasks were accomplished in testing each voting system: security assessment, configuration management, performance testing, and operational controls. In lay terms, we wanted to see if the machines could be tampered with or "hacked" if they were being used properly by the state's boards of elections, if they performed with integrity and if the correct operational controls were in place to ensure their integrity.

Accordingly, we designed the study to accomplish what I called "parallel, independent testing" by corporate and academic scientists, which allowed different parties to test Ohio's (and the nation's) voting systems using multiple methods. I knew I was taking a risk that each type of testing entity (corporate versus academic) could reach different conclusions, but science is science, and they came to the same conclusions independently—Ohio's voting systems needed to be "modified to eliminate as many known risks to voting integrity as possible while keeping voting accessible to Ohio's voters," according to the Executive Summary of the report of Project EVEREST.

The overall conclusion made in Project EVEREST was this:

> The findings of the various scientists engaged by Project EVEREST are disturbing. These findings do not lend themselves to sustained or increased confidence in Ohio's voting systems. The findings appearing in the reports necessitate that Ohio's voting process be modified to eliminate as many known risks to voting integrity as possible while keeping voting accessible to Ohio's voters. These changes must be thoughtfully planned with the assistance of the Ohio General Assembly, Governor Strickland and Ohio's election officials. As they are implemented, these changes must be made widely known to the public to facilitate orderly and cost efficient implementation.

> As Ohio's voting system is restructured, all equipment and any related software, along with software updates, must be documented in a central registry to ensure that the state's Board of Voting Machine Examiners has certified all equipment and software in use. Preparation, use and storage of equipment before, during and after an Election Day must be supported by uniform guidelines, procedures and training supplied by a

combination of legislation and secretary of state directives.

It has been said that elections belong to the people. Excessive dependence on any voting machine company to operate the state's elections, when that company's voting system is subject to trade secret or propriety information claims, results in a loss of transparency that should exist to assure election officials and the public that a fair and accurate process has been implemented for democratic self-governance. The information utilized by the scientists in this study included reviews of all three systems' software source codes and related documentation, a thorough orientation to the operation and use of the machines, other system documentation and a review of previous reports of risk assessment of similar voting systems performed by other states and institutions. The information available to the scientists who performed the assessments of this study is some of the most comprehensive information available to date for any such study. This was not accomplished without the assistance and cooperation of the voting machine companies whose equipment and software were studied.

Negotiating concurrent confidentiality agreements that were needed for the study to proceed, first with the voting system manufacturers and then with the companies and universities and their researchers, was one of the most challenging tasks my staff and I faced in this massive undertaking. Differing interests and a lack of trust between the business and academic groups created inevitable conflict, and time was not on our side, with a March 2008 primary election looming. Our study involved a review of each system's source code. Existing voting machine contracts provided the Secretary of State contractual access to these escrowed "brain architecture schemas" known as source codes. But getting timely access to them for each voting system was another story. I knew that being denied this critical access was just a temporary restraining order away in a lawsuit filed by jittery manufacturers, seeking to protect their investments and reputations. I didn't have the luxury of time for litigation with the pivotal 2008 general Presidential election less than one year from the projected completion of the study, so we negotiated . . . and negotiated. We were careful not to let negotiations extend to the point we would have lost leverage because of the ever-shrinking window of time needed to complete this massive project. It was a delicate balance to work with the manufacturers, yet get what we needed to perform the study.

The office's team of lawyers for the negotiations included Eleanor Speelman, our general counsel, along with Erick Gale, formerly of the Jones Day law firm, and Beth LaLiberte, previously with one of Columbus' largest law firms. These three lawyers were diligent, conscientious, professional and resolute in dealing directly with opposing counsel. Eleanor also handled the interfacing with office staff and me. Together, along with many others, they accomplished much. At rough spots, I would be brought in to negotiate and to directly authorize changes to agreements to keep the process moving and meet needed state government procurement requirements and deadlines.

The procurement process to hire the corporate and university contractors for the study was daunting. Unbid state contracts over $50,000 must be approved in advance by the State Controlling Board, a rare entity that came into being during the tenure of the longest serving Ohio House Speaker Vern Riffe. The operation of the State Controlling Board tips the balance of power to the legislature, weakening the autonomy of the executive branch, and it has historically received mixed reviews for its existence and operation. The Board is headed by one executive administration official, the President of the Controlling Board, usually an employee of the Governor's Office of Budget and Management. The Board's existence calls for greater political oversight by the legislature and subjects major state purchases to extensive public scrutiny, especially when the request is controversial, such as purchasing a hotel from a wealthy political contributor to turn into a college dormitory. But the process slows down state purchasing because of the lead-time needed to submit a request, get it on the agenda and have it heard and approved. I was very familiar with this process, having personally appeared before the Controlling Board during my days of service with U.S. Senator Sherrod Brown when he was 49th secretary of state (and again as a new secretary of state for funding to cover a fiscal deficit left to me by my predecessor). The schedule of the Controlling Board was also a major factor in our planning for EVEREST and its completion and release.

We issued RFPs (requests for proposals) for contractors for the study and received a number of responses. We knew initially that we wanted to hire corporate scientific testers, knowing they had high credibility with election officials and voting machine companies. We knew, however, that university researchers had greater credibility with voting rights advocates and other academics. The question was how to include them.

As often in life, the constraints we faced to get the study off the ground were the sand that helped fashion the pearl. Because Controlling Board approval was needed for each contract and because each contract was a separate negotiation in at least three directions, involving the manufacturer and one or both members of the other "camp" (corporate or academic), we were forced to construct a study involving parallel, independent and simultaneous testing between the corporate and academic scientists and compare their results. (I shuddered at the time in what would happen if they had differed significantly.)

The issue of structuring the legal relationships between the researching parties was complex and sensitive. We had been able to easily negotiate the contract with Systest, already a proven testing company for voting machines, and the manufacturers were comfortable with Systest. We had seen the work of the academic testers in the California study that preceded ours. From that study, we knew some of the pitfalls to avoid with academic research teams. Chris Nance had secured a lead researcher for the academic team, Patrick McDaniel from the University of Pennsylvania. He arranged for a pivotal meeting with Patrick in the Cleveland area in the summer of 2007. We met in a public school classroom in Shaker Heights, where Chris had gone to school as a boy.

We discussed timetables and resources. We negotiated with Patrick the length of time it would take to complete the study. We counted backward from the primary election, as most involved in elections learn to do. It was clear that the time it would take to negotiate contracts and get them approved by the State Controlling Board would leave us little time to complete the study before the end of the year. I had remembered seeing contracts go to the State Controlling Board with subcontractors and learned from Veronica Sherman that subcontracts did not need the board's specific approval. I asked Patrick if he and his team (including researchers from Penn State and University of California) were willing to be subcontractors to Systest. The academic researchers' work would be limited to security testing and compared with that of Microsolved, a premier security testing firm based in Columbus that performed extensive testing on gambling equipment at casinos in the Caribbean. Both Patrick and Systest agreed to the arrangement, allowing us to proceed with Controlling Board approval while we were still negotiating the particulars of the contracts between Systest and the academic researchers.

The Controlling Board process was fraught with politics, with local election officials quietly lobbying against us with legislators, many of whom were only too happy to object to what we were doing. In this process, the media was a boon to approval. We had kept the media well apprised of Project EVEREST's progress, which was painstakingly but necessarily slow. No legislator dared vocally or visibly be against testing voting systems to prove Ohio elections were fair or to improve public trust in their integrity. It took two separate State Controlling Board meetings, each two weeks apart, for the needed approval. I appeared personally, backed by our corporate and scientific researchers and attorneys on my staff. At those meetings I observed the perplexed faces of the media at the questions peppered by Controlling Board members at me and that seemed in little need of answering.

My successor in office, Jon Husted, then Speaker of the Ohio House, worked to get me to delay the first hearing. I would not accede to the request and let the first hearing proceed without approval, giving the media time to soak in the enormity of the project and to report what was happening. Allowing myself to get a bit bruised and battered in the public process actually helped garner the understanding of the media and improved our chances of approval at the next hearing. We achieved approval, still needing to return to the bargaining table to cement final details with the researchers as subcontractors.

Chris Nance and I had tried to involve Cleveland State University in the project, because we wanted an Ohio university involved. Candice Hoke, a law professor at Cleveland State's Marshall College of Law had participated in the similar, earlier study in California while she operated a HAVA-funded, student-staffed Center for Election Integrity at the law school. She was a frequent advocate for voting reform in Cuyahoga County and a leader of local Cuyahoga County post-election audits. She served as a member of our office's Voting Rights Institute Advisory Council.

As we developed the research protocol and scope of work with the academic team, Candice was an initial participant. Unfortunately, her approach became too difficult to keep the "herd" of researchers moving forward, so we simply asked her for a proposed scope of work on behalf of the university. We were not able to obtain from her a proposal we found workable. I eventually called the president of the university, then, Michael Schwartz, and apologized to him that we were unable to include Cleveland State. The university stood to gain nearly $300,000 in grant funding from the project. It was unfortunate, but the deadlines needed to be met. Elections don't wait.

In negotiating the fees to be paid to the testing organizations, especially the universities, I discovered what a university "administrative fee" is when Penn State University informed us that it charged a 45% administrative fee for the award of any amount of "grant funding" for research. Hence, a $100,000 award only netted $55,000 of supported research, even though the researchers believed that $100,000 of research was merited. I personally negotiated with top university officials to attempt to reduce this fee but was told it never happened. What I found amazing was that the researchers were so anxious to participate, they didn't threaten to walk away when I had reached my dollar limit. The amounts quoted for research by the universities involved were capped when I finally said, frustrated by the fluctuating costs, "This is how much each gets to do the work, based on our budget for the project." If they objected, no one told me, and no one opted out of the project.

The most difficult part of the negotiations was resolving the differences that arose from and between the various parties of interest regarding confidentiality. Voting machine manufacturers wanted to protect their "trade secrets." Corporate scientific researchers had no problems with this, and these were the easiest contracts to negotiate, with our staff finding more problems in the confidentiality contracts for us as public officials than the corporate scientists did for their functions and operations. It was the addition of the university researchers that created the most friction. Researchers want to publish. Even if they're paid for the research, there is academic reputation that is enhanced by publishing the results of their research, and in academia, research is valued for its own sake. But voting machine manufacturers feared that the researchers, many themselves engineers, would take what they learned about the voting machines and start their own, competing companies or reveal in their research and writing information that a competitor could use. Renegotiations had to occur on the confidentiality agreements already set to allow academic, scientific research to take place in the study. Our job was to harmonize confidentiality agreements between the competing interests of manufacturers, the public disclosure required by our office, and the interests of both corporate testers and academic researchers. We were almost there when, negotiating with Penn State, it nearly fell apart.

I experienced firsthand that a public university's involvement in contract negotiations is anything but an experience with "eggheads." Rather, it can be more a "hard-scrabble," tough, negotiated business deal because of the conflicting interests, personalities and vantage points of all the players. My firsthand experience included a classic good cop/bad cop encounter.

Chris Nance had advised me that an impasse had been reached with Penn State. He and Eleanor gave me the telephone number of the university's "good cop," who was mildly shocked I personally called him but whom I found easy to cut to the chase with and reach agreements in principle. We did so late into one weeknight. I followed up with an outline the next day. We were hopeful for resolution. Then, unexpectedly, he called me to tell me that he would be leaving the negotiations and said with a laugh that the next guy I would be dealing with was more of a bean counter and could be tough.

Penn State's "good cop" had been trying to get us what we needed for a fair price, and at fair terms, especially when it came to the delicate negotiations on confidentiality that would still meet our agreements with the voting machine manufacturers. His description of his replacement turned out to be mild at best. Penn State supplanted him with an individual who could be described as a combination pit bull and sloth and who was quick to defend the university's position. He was immovable as we tried to push him to another point of view for a mutually beneficial resolution.

Faced with what seemed like a negotiator with at least two heads, we all came very close to blowing up the agreement with Penn State, which would have created an undesirable and questionable imbalance in the entire project. I sat at the conference table with my legal team before the tri-legged, gray, flying-saucer-like speakerphone in the large conference room outside my office. That gray thing blankly stared back at me as various voices squawked through the tiny holes in the convex, curved disc. The more exasperated I became, the lower and quieter my voice became, a vestige from the control I had learned from my days as a judge. I could see my staff's eyes getting bigger and watched them shift in their seats with each lowering of the decibel of my voice. The Penn State team had me boxed in on the terms they wanted. I couldn't blow the whole project on this one facet. I knew it. I had no choice except to accept what I could not change, hard as I tried get the university officials to bend.

I finally acquiesced, grimaced and said in a quiet and measured tone, "I'm done." I pushed slowly away from the table, quietly raising myself to a full stand. Staff looked at me apprehensively. I turned and walked out, holding myself like a woman of old leaving the fountain with full urn of water on her head and looking straight ahead. I was about to carry water for Penn State, not its researchers, that neither I nor the State of Ohio had any business carrying. But I had to weigh moving forward with standing on principle, knowing I was on a piece of ice that could easily melt away and leave the project sinking.

The purpose of bringing me in at that juncture had been to help hammer out final language. As the procurer of the study and the administrator of its consequences, my staff and I knew that each contractual delay meant the same delay to the research for the study, which at some point would affect it efficacy. We also knew that the more compressed the time period was, the more people were needed to reach the same level of quality, increasing the cost. Cost was always a factor. Even though the funding for the study was from federal funding, it was still taxpayer money, even if it was not state money. Penn State's terms had added difficulty to our already hefty challenge.

Exasperated, but not wanting to show anything but calm, I left the conference room full of my staff and the squawking gray three-legged flying saucer; I tread quietly into my office, saying nothing, and walked down the short hallway to my office bathroom. Once in that "sanctuary" that I had decorated with calming Asian décor and a watercolor painting of a bluebird that says, "The bluebird carries the sky on its back," I gave the tall, heavy, cherry-stained wooden door a furious slam. I reopened the door and thrust it a second time, this time even harder. I never said a word. The two loud, thuddy crashes did not go unnoticed. Debbie Batta, director of Business Services, later told me that she and her staff halfway across the floor of our high-rise building had heard several strange sounds, wondering about the source. It was just as well they thought there was a fire drill in the offing than to know that the Penn State Nittany Lions had just scored a touchback.

Later that afternoon, I picked up the phone and called the president of Penn State, Graham Spanier, telling him that in my then twenty-four years of being a lawyer and a judge I had never witnessed such unprincipled negotiating as had just occurred in negotiating the role of Penn State University in Ohio's Project EVEREST. His response was the audio equivalent to a deer in the headlights. He was sorry to hear of it, but there was no promise to look into it or to engage in any follow up after that. Suffice it to say, I was ecstatic when The Ohio State University Buckeyes beat the Penn State Nittany Lions that fall. Three years later, Graham Spanier would be tragically stripped of his presidency by Penn State's board of trustees, and ultimately himself charged for failure to have adequately dealt with a child-sex scandal that had been reported to university superiors and that, when revealed, rocked college sports and shocked the conscience of the nation.

When faced with completing the Executive Summary for EVEREST the night before we were scheduled to announce our findings, I reluctantly skipped the state plumbers and pipefitters Christmas dinner party and sat in my family room at home with my feet propped up on an ottoman while I drafted the report's executive summary on my laptop until 2:00 a.m. In initially negotiating our agreements with the voting machine companies, I had anticipated this day—that the report would be finished and the companies would want to read it in advance of its release. I knew this was another pivotal point, like the release of the source code, when we could be stopped cold by a temporary restraining order that would tragically prevent the public from knowing the results of what they had paid for and had a right to know. I had agreed to the advance review by the companies because I believed this was necessary as a means to obtain their cooperation. They were providing us the source codes to which we were entitled and all necessary equipment and documentation needed for the study to have the necessary credibility and integrity. As part of our agreement, representatives of the manufacturers had even conducted training sessions to help our researchers know how the voting systems were to be set up and operated. This turned out to be important to preventing delay in the research process. For the manufacturers, it ensured that all tests on the machines were under proper conditions of use. It also prevented the voting machine companies from siding with numerous defensive local election officials after the study was released who claimed that the machines were not tested in "real life" situations.

While working with the lawyers in my office on the drafting of the contract language that allowed voting machine manufacturers a prior review, I had personally worked on carefully crafted portions of the language. Under the contract terms I was required to permit the voting machine manufacturers three days to review the study's findings before its release. At the same time the language permitted me to release the study's findings before the expiration of the three-day period. It required a careful reading, but it was there, and I knew it was there. My attorneys had questioned me about the language at the time, and I had insisted that it be left as it was with no further modification or discussion. Perhaps the attorneys for the voting machine companies understood what I was doing. Perhaps they didn't. For me, this language was key.

Often, my attorneys consulted with lawyers in the attorney general's office assigned to litigate our cases. During my administration, Secretary of State attorneys routinely conferred with assistant attorneys general because of their knowledge of past court interpretations of federal and state laws in actual courtroom battles about voting rights in Ohio. We generally accepted our assistant attorney generals' advice about our activities so that we could be more easily defended if a lawsuit was brought against us. After paying out hundreds of thousands of dollars to clean up lawsuits from the Blackwell era, we knew this also saved taxpayer money. My attorneys had conferred with the attorney general's office on this particular contract provision as the day drew nearer to release the study's findings.

The attorney general's office was ready with advice, but this time, the advice came personally to me from the highest level in the office, from Marc Dann, himself. At his request, our staff made arrangements to meet at the Starbucks coffee shop on Lane Avenue in Upper Arlington, a quiet, wealthy residential area, not in the hustle and bustle of downtown. There, it was unlikely there would be questioning eyes of the political swirl often found downtown. Marc urged me not to release the report on the day I wanted to, telling me that I should wait the entire three days the voting machine manufacturers were given under the agreement. I told him flatly I would wait one day after it was released to them and then make the report public. I told him the contract, when read carefully, allowed me to do that. He tried first to say that the contract did not permit me to do that. That argument didn't work.

As cooperative as the manufacturers had been, I also knew that extremely negative findings could result in cold and calculated business decisions to protect good will and other assets with a court order to prevent me from releasing the study's findings. The manufacturers' concerns were not public concerns, but public concerns were why I had conducted the study. The attorney general's concerns were for protecting me under a contract. In this case, I didn't care if my actions made it harder to do that. My paramount concern was to make the study's findings public as the first step in deconstructing the problems of 2004 and understanding the architecture we had in place so as to do 2008 right. This study was Ohio's redemption for the debacle of 2004; it had to see the light of day. I owed it to Ohio's voters, and I owed it to the country.

Finally, he said, "But, Jennifer, you're going to get sued for releasing this report before three days."

"But I may get sued anyway to stop me from releasing it if I wait," I countered. "The contract says I can release it after I provide it to them. It's clear, and they approved the language this way," I told him.

"But that isn't the understanding the voting machine companies had," he said.

"It doesn't matter what they understood. It's what's in the contract, " I countered.

I seem to recall some arguments he made about bad faith. I felt a little guilty, but it was the kind of guilt a prisoner feels when he's jumping over the last fence of the prison yard before freedom. I acknowledged to myself that releasing the report in less than three days may not have been in line with the previously amicable tenor of our work with the manufacturers, but in business deals, amicability can be fleeting anyway. With Marc, I stood my ground. "I'll take that risk, even if it means I'm sued." I said.

I knew that once the public and media had the findings of this report, no lawsuit could stop the chain of events that would inevitably be set into action—and which needed to happen—to understand just what had been thrust upon all of us—voters, administrators and voting machine manufacturers alike, with the new voting systems required by the Help America Vote Act of 2002.

Marc continued as my jaw set even more firmly. "I strongly recommend you don't do this," he said looking me right in the eye with a benevolent half smile. "I understand the risks, Marc," I said, "but I'm doing it." And that was it.

Marc got up to leave. I took another sip of my now cold coffee and threw it out. I was shivering by this time and watched him walk out.

Once again, like my actions in Cuyahoga County, I felt more nervous and alone, but I was convinced that this was the right thing to do. I was determined that nothing should deter the findings of this expansive study from going forward. He was not happy with me when he and his staff left in his black oversized state SUV, a Chevy Suburban that once bore orange and yellow flame decals on the side with the words, "Sunshine Express." He had been ridiculed about it, and the flames were eventually removed. Maybe he had been on the right track after all when it came to the disinfectant of sunshine. When the EVEREST Report met the sunshine of public scrutiny, I know Marc was surprised that I was never sued about it.

At around 2:00 a.m. of the morning we were to release the report, I emailed the Executive Summary from my laptop to Eleanor and others on the team and went to bed. When I got up at 8:00, she had been working on it since 5:00 a.m., had made her edits and emailed it back to me. I put on the finishing touches and emailed it for publication. Our project manager, Mike Krippendorf, from Battelle Memorial Research Institute, was stunned at the swiftness of how quickly the two of us could hammer out the words that would be quoted around the world. Later that day, we made our announcement of the conclusions of our study that sent enough national reverberations for the New York Times to cover the announcement with a front page photo of my staff and me. I've looked at that photo so many times, stuck on my refrigerator at home for months afterward. There I was, snapped gesturing with both hands in front of me and somber young and diverse faces of attorneys and staff who had helped mold a gargantuan web of a problem into clear and cogent lines of communication about the urgent and cooperative action needed to untangle it.

The photo in the NY Times on the releasing of results of the EVEREST Report looked a lot like this: L. to R. attorneys Erick Gale, Beth LaLiberte, Jennifer Brunner, Sylvia Brown

My staff and I knew we would kick up a lot of dust with this report. Patrick Gallaway, my communications director, had said in preparing for the announcement, "Let's set up the press conference with people who worked on the report standing

behind you. It gives you an appearance of strength in numbers."
I knew he was right, knowing how alone I had felt and that we
all needed that strength together. I also knew of the storm to
come.

We had already received pushback about the study's findings
from the carefully selected geographically and bi-partisan
balanced group of twelve Ohio election officials who reviewed
the report even before the manufacturers had. But they were
subject to strict confidentiality before the study's release. This
alerted us to the maelstrom that would be created when we
released the study to the waiting media and the public. These
election officials who had reviewed the study had traveled to
Columbus and spent the spans of at least two days reviewing the
findings. They were sequestered, along with our staff, attorney
general staff and Mike Krippendorf from Battelle at the high
security State of Ohio Computer Center, known as "the SOCC."
(The SOCC was just a concept when I worked for Sherrod Brown
as Secretary of State in the 1980's. It is a quality reality today
that, for much of my administration, also provided a place to
store all the state's punch card and optical scan ballots from the
2004 election while litigation dragged on in that case
throughout my term of office.)

As my team and I were developing the EVEREST Project's study
methodology, I had had the opportunity to discuss it with Mark
Ritchie, Minnesota's Secretary of State, who kept mentioning
that we should take advantage of the resource located right in
Columbus, Battelle Memorial Institute, a world-renowned
scientific research institute. When Chris Nance suggested to me
that we needed a project manager for the study, we issued a
request for proposals and settled on Mike Krippendorf from
Battelle, who proved to be a sensitive, able and talented
manager. Mike's work was pivotal to our success as a valuable
interface between the scientific researchers, our staff and me.

He provided solid guidance, advice and credibility, helping us to buttress our methodology and process with consistency that improved our ability to deal with doubts, questions and criticisms directed our way by elections officials, the legislature or the media. In working with the bipartisan team of elections officials in the final review of the results, Mike had suggested that we devise a questionnaire and protocol for them that focused on study thoroughness and methodology, but not specifically on evaluating the scientific conclusions reached, since the science of the study was beyond their training (on which a few of them at the time begged to differ).

The twelve dedicated election officials worked the weekend with us to not only evaluate but brainstorm a suggested course of action based on the study's findings. Even though many were skeptical, their help was invaluable. One of them, Chuck Miller, was the election official who gave me the Christmas bulb with chads filling it. He made one of the most pragmatic suggestions for greater access to voting in rural areas facing tight budgets—using library bookmobiles as voting places. I thought it was a splendid idea, with some tweaking for accessibility for people with disabilities. (His idea never took hold with the other election officials, but I still haven't given up hope for it.)

A team of Secretary of State staff worked day and night on the final report write-up, with everyone sequestered at the high security SOCC in several rooms with multiple workstations, each facing the wall. I spent hours there myself, personally reviewing the report and its language for thoroughness, logic and consistency. Then came the vetting by the team of in-house and attorney general lawyers and technical staff, going through the report line-by-line, photo-by-photo, diagram-by-diagram, comparing the contents with the requirements of the manufacturer confidentiality agreements that applied to each class of study participants: secretary of state staff, election officials, corporate researchers and university researchers—a colossally tedious but intensely necessary process.

The executive summary was the last piece of the study to be placed in the context of the final report. Patrick Gallaway's communications shop worked furiously with the office's attorneys to get the report ready for publication, to put synthesized packets together for reporters for the press conference and to "flick the switch" to make the report "live" on our website. We shot a quick video of me explaining the report's findings to put on YouTube.

On December 14, 2007, less than a year into office, the Ohio Secretary of State's office was ready to reveal what the most extensive voting machine study to date in the country had to show about the electronic and optical scan voting systems required for use throughout the nation as a result of Congressional reform after the 2000 Presidential election. I faced a bevy of reporters, photographers and television cameras in the large atrium of the Statehouse with my hard-working staff standing behind me. It was an impressive sight. Patrick had been right. We looked and were stronger together. I methodically explained our findings.

Having participated at every stage of the study, I could speak like a teacher, covering the study's major conclusions and giving specific illustrations of the types of tests that showed the flaws and vulnerabilities of the systems that had been thrust upon the states by a combination of a Congress that never wanted a Presidential election decided by a Supreme Court again and the lust of the "market" for the sale of voting machines for low-margin profits at massive volumes. But the inexperience of Congress in the ways of election administration that have been and continue to be primarily and stubbornly local lent itself to hasty testing funded in part by manufacturers that missed things like 1980's versions of software that was augmented and modified in multiple computer languages, causing instability at best and sometimes outright failure to perform.

Added to that were the practices of local governments, some better than others, that were often unprepared to take and account for federal money and make decisions about technology, let alone successfully implement it. Most boards had little to no previous exposure to this new voting technology. Moreover, incomplete funding of HAVA deprived the federal government of an initially strong oversight body in the Election Assistance Commission. It also deprived many states of the means to develop and institute necessary training on procedures associated with the new voting systems. In many cases there had only been enough funding to buy the machines, not even extension cords, and certainly not to develop consistent training on the programming, maintenance and use of the machines.

Congress does not frequently succeed at making wholesale change to federal election laws because of this unwieldy concoction of politics and process at all levels of self-governance. Major pieces of legislation, the Voting Rights Act of the 1960's, the Motor Voter Act of the early 1990's, and the Help America Vote Act of 2002, show that major voting overhauls by Congress are few and far between. This is because of the long-entrenched local nature of election administration and the effectiveness of local resistance to change. Resistance by state and local election officials, combined with previously pervasive federal inexperience, has stymied Congressional reform to the extent many would like to see it. There is the local hue and cry that Congress is clueless about how "we" run our elections. With close margins between the two partisan caucuses of the U.S. Senate, I once heard a secretary of state brag that all he had to do was call his Senator, and that, along with similar action from another secretary of state or two, he could stop any elections bill in the Senate. This is why election and voting reform are so hard but also why there are now thousands of citizens who, thanks to the Internet and Facebook voting rights groups, remain ever vigilant for actions of elected officials that would squelch Americans' rights to free, fair, open and honest elections.

The day we released the results of EVEREST, I observed in many of the faces of the reporters in the audience the gravity of what we had done. This was just the beginning of the torrents of controversy we had unleashed on ourselves—from local election officials, university and law professors, members of the legislature, the Ohio Republican Party, Fox News and more. With the exception of local election officials, most of these critics had never had to directly face a voter whose name did not appear on a voting roll or who couldn't find their polling location. The ACLU was not our friend at the time, as it lambasted our call for central counting of optical scan ballots, because of the risk of "overvotes" not being brought to a voter's attention. The upcoming primary election looked like a bog full of snapping creatures with sharp teeth, long necks and thorny tails in some version of an Indiana Jones adventure movie. Despite the enormity of EVEREST, our climb out of the pit had only just begun. ≈

Chapter 16

Power Outages, Ice Storms, Floods and Bomb Threats

"Gary," I said, "I can't make Sandy McNair get it through his head that I need his vote to change Cuyahoga County from touch screen voting machines to optical scan paper ballots. He won't commit. I think he's trying to prevent lawsuits."

I was talking to Gary Dwyer, former chief of the state building trades unions, a retired ironworker now living in Columbus. I had long-known Eben O. "Sandy" McNair IV, a premier labor attorney in Cleveland. Sandy lived in nearby Strongsville and served as a member of the Cuyahoga County Democratic Central Committee. An avid cyclist, he rides for miles every Saturday morning to blow off steam. He has been married to an amazing and grounded attorney, Janet Kleckner, for decades. She is a magistrate of the Summit County Domestic Relations Court.

Before I was ever elected to any office, often during the 1990's when I represented the Ohio AFL-CIO and many of its federated unions, I had taken calls from Sandy seeking campaign finance advice as he represented the United Food and Commercial Workers (UFCW) Local 880 in Cleveland. Together, we had hashed out many campaign finance scenarios for his union client during those days. Many labor organizations in Cleveland and the surrounding areas depended on Sandy and trusted his, judgment, advice and negotiating skills for the wide variety of legal issues and collective bargaining scenarios they faced.

At a Friday morning breakfast at what was at the time *the* local political establishment restaurant, the Clarmont, I had had been seated at the round table that was open to any and all who choose to sit there. Seated next to me was Gary Dwyer. This was in the early days of my foray into the Secretary of State's race, before I had officially declared my candidacy. Gary had joined the state building trades' attorney, N. Victor Goodman, a well-connected Republican from the Columbus office of the Cleveland law firm of Benesch, Friedlander, Coplan and Aronoff. Gary and I discussed my prospective candidacy. He suggested that I go to Cleveland to spend a day with Sandy McNair and have him introduce me to the leaders of his client labor unions.

Gary made a call to Sandy and then gave me the go-ahead to follow up with Sandy. We finally connected as Rick and I drove from the farm to a county party dinner that was an hour or so away. This was in the early days of building political relationships across the state, when Rick was the only driver I had. During those days Rick compiled and handed out press packets, worked the other side of the room for me and compared notes with me after the events. We had begun to explore and experience our special state together—times we are grateful for and will not forget. During that call in the car, Sandy was hesitant to get involved, because Bryan Flannery, a former state representative from Cleveland, was already in the race for Secretary of State, having run four years earlier. I persuaded Sandy to host me anyway, guaranteeing I would not hold him to a personal endorsement, unless and until he was ready.

He agreed to host me for a day. Sandy and I set a date for me to come to Cleveland. He was warming up to the idea of my candidacy, especially because no one before me had the qualifications of being an elections attorney and a state trial court judge. We finally set up a Monday visit, the day when a large labor luncheon would be taking place in downtown

Cleveland. He and his wife invited me to stay the night at their house in Strongsville. Sandy and Janet had a son in Iraq at the time. They were passionately supportive of his service and intensely proud of him. Later, this same son, Ben, would live with Rick and me for six weeks while he took a new job in Columbus and got on his feet, finding his own place to live. He is a delightful young man.

Sandy took me first to meet Loree Soggs, the new president of the Cleveland building trades. Then we met with John Kilbane and Jim Goggin, leaders of Laborers Local 310 (later, the first union to endorse me and where I held my first announcement in my five-day Secretary of State announcement tour). After that I met with Tom Robertson and Bob Grauvogl, now respectively retired and current presidents of UFCW Local 880. We followed this meeting with introductions to representatives of the AFSCME local, and finally, we met with John Ryan of the North Shore AFL-CIO (now Ohio chief of staff for U.S. Senator Sherrod Brown). Later, we attended the labor luncheon.

As the day moved forward and Sandy listened to what I had to say to his clients, I could tell he was warming up to my candidacy. With each meeting, his introductory pitch of my potential candidacy became more emphatic. It was rewarding and insightful to watch Sandy's enthusiasm grow. Seeing the posters in his office that day of people of color, workers struggling and labor images showed me that this Eben O. McNair IV was not just talk—he lived it. Sandy McNair is dedicated to the cause of the downtrodden, underrepresented, beleaguered and denied-but-due, equality creed. Because he was such a true believer made it even more frustrating trying to get his vote in working to turn the ship of Ohio elections with Cuyahoga County as its rudder. I knew his heart was in the right place. He just did not see the path ahead from my vantage point.

Since the 2000 Presidential election, studies became more prevalent about optical scan paper ballots used in American elections. A special hazard of using optically scanned paper ballots is "overvotes," (which occur in "double-bubble" situations as well) in which voters err in marking their ballots with too many choices for the number of candidates permitted to be elected in a race. If more votes are marked than for the number permitted, unless there is a scanner at the precinct to detect and warn the voter of the "overvote" on the spot, no vote is counted for that race. When the scanner detects an overvote, the voter is warned and can ask for a new ballot.

Accordingly, groups such as the Advancement Project to the American Civil Liberties Union (ACLU) argued strenuously for the need for precinct-based scanners (and against central counting at boards of elections offices, even though all absentee ballots are centrally counted). With overvotes, rejected ballots are examined, with only the overvote not counted, but it often occurs after the unofficial count election night. These groups stressed the need for using these precinct based scanners, especially in underprivileged neighborhoods or neighborhoods with predominantly minority voters, many of which are found in Cuyahoga County. Their position was understandable in a more ideal situation. However, in Cuyahoga County, it was practically triage time.

Sandy McNair had taken his position on the board of elections as an opportunity to give back to his greater community and to protect the rights of every voter in Cuyahoga County, much like he did for the members of the unions he represented. This "true blue" streak in Sandy was accompanied by a doggedness that made him a tough labor negotiator who fought to the bone for his clients. He was often in the midst of labor negotiations when I would reach him by phone, working late into the night, often weary but still feisty.

That pivotal night before the Cuyahoga County Board of Elections' vote on changing voting systems, I faced palpable "obstruction" from someone whom I thought would be a strong ally and who wouldn't need a lot of convincing. I needed his vote to help make it possible for Cuyahoga County's voters to trust their voting system. It had been a debacle of an election in May 2006 when the then new Diebold touchscreen system was first put to use by the board. Results were delayed for a week. After learning of even more operational irregularities for Cuyahoga County with this system, I needed real change. But Sandy was not committing.

In fact, he began negotiating—like a good labor lawyer. "How about having 120 scanners in the precincts so we're at least providing them where they may be most needed?"

"No way," I countered. "There's barely enough time to switch systems and train enough poll workers on setup and operation, let alone have them show voters how to use the scanners in the precincts." For the March 2008 primary election I was looking for the first step of a transition and not a quantum leap.

I had previously thoroughly discussed this issue with Jane Platten, the board's competent, dedicated and pragmatic new director. I would never have moved the board in a direction that Jane did not agree with or could not handle. I had conferred with Jane about what was needed in Cuyahoga County in light of the EVEREST recommendations. My best judgment for transitioning the most populous county in the state to a safer and more reliable and trustworthy system was to make the move to paper ballots in phases. Jane agreed with me and believed it was doable. The plan to move to paper ballots was to begin with centrally scanned ballots in the primary election, implementing precinct-based scanners in the general election after voters and poll workers became familiar first with using and handling the paper ballots. Jane and I never forgot the fact that we were dealing with more than one million voters in Cuyahoga County, and this consideration undergirded every move we made.

Eleanor had thoroughly researched the Help America Vote Act. She informed that centrally scanned paper ballots were an acceptable method of counting ballots and the votes on them as long as the board publicized ways to avoid overvoting. Even though we complied with HAVA, the ACLU was still not satisfied, and neither was Sandy. In full negotiating mode, he held out and said he could not support the move unless at least some precinct-based scanners were used in the primary election.

It was now 9:00 p.m. the evening before the pivotal vote by the Cuyahoga County Board of Elections. I wanted an answer, and Sandy said he could not commit. I started becoming frustrated. I called Jane Platten. "What is his problem?" I asked, exasperated. I talked with Tom Hayes, the board's former director. Then, in real desperation, I called the guy who had influenced Sandy before—Gary Dwyer. Gary jumped on it, called Sandy and then called me back.

"I'll be driving to Cleveland tomorrow. I'll take him to lunch and make sure he understands what he needs to do," said Gary. I circled back with Sandy. After more exasperated exhortations and finally being willing to use no more than 60 scanners (representing roughly one in each municipality of Cuyahoga County as a sort of "pilot"), I beat him down enough that he finally assented. I'm sure some of the words I used to convey my frustration would have chagrined my mother, but they didn't seem to faze a marathon labor negotiator like Sandy. By a little after 11:00 p.m. I had Sandy's agreement to vote with Inajo Davis Chappelle to move to a new voting system.

I circled back with Tom Hayes, and he gave me pivotal advice. "The motions should be in two parts," he said. "The first motion should be to change voting systems. The second motion should be to change to an optical scan paper ballot system."

Tom was a veteran in election administration, and this was good advice, both legally and politically. I took it and composed sample language for the next day's board meeting. What Tom knew and I didn't fathom at the time was that making the two Republicans, whom we expected would oppose the change, vote specifically on whether or not to change, was making them publicly state whether or not they believed in the current voting system's efficacy. We believed they did not. As it turned out, they were furious to be cornered in that way. Rob Frost, the Republican County Chair did more than "pop off" about the new Secretary of State at this public meeting; he threw firebombs as reported in the Plain Dealer later that day. Not even a week after the release of the EVEREST report, I was putting my recommendations to the test in Cuyahoga County, and the Republicans there were unhappy about it. A tie vote resulted along party lines as expected. Channel 5 television news in Cleveland reported:

> CLEVELAND -- The Cuyahoga County Board of Elections has deadlocked on whether to switch to a new voting system for the March primary, leaving the state's chief elections officer to break the 2-2 tie.

> Secretary of State Jennifer Brunner has been pressuring the board to scrap its $21 million touch-screen voting machines for an optical-scan system, following a report she released last week citing security flaws with the current system.

"I anticipate she will takes steps to order a new system," said elections board chairman Jeff Hastings, who voted against switching.

The vote fell along party lines with the two Republican board members voting against the measure and the two Democratic members backing what Brunner, a Democrat, asked the board to do.

The three-hour meeting grew heated before the vote with board member Robert Frost criticizing Brunner for not being present.

"That to me is shirking her responsibility," he said.

The vote came after about an hour of public testimony.

It's unusual for any Secretary of State to attend a board of elections meeting. When I had attended in May of 2007, it was to swear in all four new board members; that was it. Rob Frost's frustration was evident.

Ordinarily, a board of elections has two weeks to supply the Secretary of State with a written report, transcript and arguments to support each side's views when there is a tie vote. The Secretary of State acts as the fifth voting member of every board of elections for the purposes of breaking tie votes. Ordinarily, tie votes are broken with a written decision. With the Presidential primary looming on March 5, more than two weeks for the tie vote to be broken was out of the question. It was December 20, 2007. I used the power I had to direct that the board submit all tie vote materials immediately. I was ready for it, with my lawyers already drafting the tie breaking decision after learning of the meeting's outcome. A week after the EVEREST report had been released, I released a pivotal tie vote decision to further reform the operations of the Cuyahoga County Board of Elections. This again made national news, much to my amazement.

In a related editorial board meeting with the Cleveland Plain Dealer, Brent Larkin, the newspaper's editor, followed me out of the editorial board's conference room, (a room that had no table, only sofas and chairs lining three walls for conversations large and small.) We stood in front of his glass front office cubicle, just next to the ed board room.

"Are you sure you know what you're doing?" he asked me incredulously. "You have a little over sixty days to move this entire county to a new voting system," he exclaimed.

"What choice do I have?" I responded. "This county either uses a voting system that doesn't work for it or I push it to go to a system that I know will work better for a county of this size. Besides," I continued, "I know Jane can get this done." Brent just shook his head, looking down.

Meanwhile, I had to convince the Ohio legislature that to ensure that centrally scanned ballots would work in Cuyahoga County it needed to amend the law to permit the mid-day pickup of ballots. There is a process required for Election Day paper ballot use in the precincts that is called "reconciliation." Before ballots can be transported for counting, the presiding judge for a precinct must sign off that the number of ballots being returned to the board of elections (each ballot is numbered on a stub that is torn off the ballot) is the sum total of the number of ballots sent to the precinct. For reconciliation, the number of voted ballots, unvoted ballots and spoiled ballots must equal the number of ballots originally supplied to the precinct. Performing a reconciliation mid-day had to be done without stopping voting. Mid-day ballot reconciliation and pick-up was not provided for in the law. I was able to obtain it from an all Republican-led legislature, a feat that later in the year would not have been possible as the level of partisan fervor increased as the general Election Day drew nearer.

When I took office, I had held to the belief that, even though I am a Democrat, and Republicans controlled the legislature, there was enough common ground. I believed that both parties would want to work together to ensure reliable election results and a smooth election. The hotter the heat in the election kitchen became, the more that idea went up in smoke. By November 2008, the relationship between the two major political parties on election administration was more like bare-knuckled combat. It never ceased to amaze me that year that in their zeal to confound the reforms I was trying to make, some Republicans were willing to risk everything, even the efficacy of the election process as it would affect their *own* candidates.

I received the reluctant approval of the remaining holdout, the President of the Ohio Senate, Bill Harris, for a one-time use of mid-day ballot pickup, so that Cuyahoga was able to move forward in planning for centrally counted ballots with timely returns at the March primary election. The board of elections rented more than a dozen high-speed scanners, placing them on the second floor of the old Halle's Department Store warehouse about ten minutes away from the board's offices at Euclid and Thirtieth in Cleveland. The warehouse had painted white wooden floors and was, well, a warehouse. Vans rented for ballot pickup could drive right into the warehouse and up a ramp for the ballots to be unloaded directly onto a freight elevator for transport to the second floor to be sorted by precinct and scanned by the high-speed optical scanners. Jane planned for bipartisan teams to be involved at each step, including the transporting of the ballots.

In the 2004 Presidential election the lines in Cuyahoga County had been inordinately long, similar to many precincts in low income and some student-dominated areas of Franklin County that year. The subsequent 2006 implementation of electronic voting machines in Cuyahoga County were little improvement. The new touch screen voting machines were not the giant plastic ballot sheet that covered mechanical buttons like Franklin County had used in 2004. Now, all electronic touch screen machines contained limited information per "page" or "screen" of the machine. A critical factor I considered was that a voter could not glance at the ballot all at once. He or she had to move from screen to screen to screen in order to finally cast his or her ballot. With a paper ballot, or even the old-style electronic ballot sheet over buttons, the entire ballot is in front of the voter, who can peruse it without the manual and time-consuming steps to touch the screen over and over again to get to the end of the ballot and finally cast his or her vote.

From my judicial days, many attorneys thought that it was more convenient for me to view a video of a police interrogation in order to determine whether a motion to suppress evidence was warranted. They did not seem to understand that a video of a drunk or scared suspect in a room by himself for ten minutes before the investigator walked in to begin the interrogation was part of the viewing, even fast-forwarding it. Finding the part of a video that is of greatest interest or relevance is time consuming. That's why most judges would rather see a transcript, which is actually easier to cull through than tediously working an electrical device to try to find the salient points needed for a ruling. The differences between electronic touch screen ballots and paper ballots are analogous to video versus transcript. I knew that lines could move more quickly in populated Cuyahoga County with paper ballots. With a given number of electronic voting machines in a precinct, only a certain number of people can vote within a given period of time. With paper ballots, when there is a glut of voters, overflow tables could be provided. Not only could paper ballots be read and voted faster, more ballots could be supplied to more voters, using extra space, with the only eventual long line being the line to scan ballots on precinct-based scanners. This would eventually be Cuyahoga County's method.

It was important to me to get voters used to the paper ballots before introducing scanners—one step at a time. I believed it would work. Jane believed it would work.

I visited the Cuyahoga County Board of Elections numerous times. Sitting in Jane's office, I viewed with great admiration the giant post-it notes she had placed on the wall with to-do lists and process step outlines. (These giant post-it notes were much like what I had used on the door in my office to determine the order of calls I would make to notify state elected and party officials about my decision to request the resignations of the entire board). It was impressive, and Jane seemed to have boundless energy. We were in synch, once even noting that we had purchased and were wearing the same pair of shoes, mine in black, hers in blue. (Yes, women notice these things.) We could only laugh.

I was still holding weekly telephone calls with the Cuyahoga County board at this point. I also began to realize that walking through the detailed steps with this county board helped me as much as it seemed to help them. I started understanding firsthand what the board—all the boards—needed from my staff and me as Secretary of State for Ohio's 88 counties to plan for and be prepared for the upcoming election.

There were still a majority of the counties in Ohio that were not using paper ballots, except for absentee voting. For these counties, they were essentially running two elections—one with touch screen voting machines with voter verified paper audit trails (VVPAT) for in-person voting, and the other with centrally counted optical scan paper ballots for absentee voting. Each type of ballot had to be processed differently and the results combined using a single server that performed tabulation. If a scanner was of the type that allowed for scanning with a second, separate control for tabulation, scanning of absentee ballots could occur in the day or two before Election Day, so that as soon as the polls closed, instantaneous absentee results could be tabulated and released from ballots already scanned.

Interestingly, many boards of elections believed it acceptable to not count absentee ballots received on Election Day until they counted provisional ballots, more than ten days after the election. When Cuyahoga could perform that function accurately in its election night count, it was no longer credible for any other county to state that it could not accomplish this. The old practice was banned.

Speaking at a pre-primary press conference on preparedness for the 2008 Presidential primary election

Understanding the properties of paper ballots to expand or contract with unexpected numbers of voters, my staff and I decided that backup paper ballots were needed for Ohio's counties using touch screen voting. We would implement this for the 2008 Presidential primary election. The howls from county boards of elections (especially Franklin County) and some newspaper editorial boards, especially the Columbus

Dispatch, were at times deafening. A convenient criticism was about cost and having thousands of unvoted ballots left after the election, for which my office was reimbursing anyway using federal HAVA funds that had already been appropriated to Ohio by Congress.

Our directive to the boards required counties with touch screen voting systems to have backup paper ballots available if they were needed or desired by a voter. A voter could simply vote the backup paper ballot as a preference, even if lines were not long. My office created posters and other written information and required boards to use them and to include their use in training. Some boards embraced them; many others did not. Poor or inadequate poll worker training because of resistance to these backup paper ballots resulted in many voters who requested paper ballots being handed provisional ballots that were not counted until at least eleven days after the election. In even my own voting precinct, when I asked for a paper ballot at the Presidential primary election, I was handed a provisional ballot and had to gently call out the poll worker on the issue.

The Union County Board of Commissioners (Union County is adjacent to the northwest of what was then recalcitrant Franklin County), filed suit against me to stop me from requiring boards of elections to print backup paper ballots. The commissioners there did not want to fund this required board of elections expense. I won the lawsuit, and backup paper ballots were required for the March 2008 primary in every precinct where touch screen voting machines were in use.

The ACLU had filed its lawsuit in federal court in Cleveland against the Cuyahoga County Board of Elections for not having scanners in the voting precincts at the primary election, but we prevailed in this matter as well. There were times in the 2008 primary election, and even more so in the general election, when forces on both the right and the left disagreed with our actions, all at the same time. At one point later in the year as lawsuits piled up in the general election, I shrugged my shoulders and said, "No way will I ever get reelected with this much controversy, so I'm just not going to sweat it. I'll just do what I think is right." During times like these when it was hard to know where the next blow would come from, I would sometimes catch a glimpse of myself in a mirror with my shoulders looking hunched. I seemed figuratively to be waiting to duck my head for the next object hurled my way.

My staff and I were clearly unprepared from a communications standpoint in the primary election season for the vitriol and ferocious attacks we experienced. We were making decisions and moving to bring about quick and timely change in Ohio's election processes. These attacks were in the form of editorials, sharp criticism in quotes in news articles from elected officials, party leaders and election officials, lawsuits, blog posts, academic studies, and they were from all sides—the right, the left and the middle. I used to have a saying that I could fill a wall four stories high with portraits of all the people in and out of Ohio government who thought that *they* had been elected Ohio's Secretary of State and could best tell us how to administer Ohio's elections. If the size of their portraits were relative to the extent of their protests and admonishments, some of those individuals' portraits would have been giant sized, like those seen in the full-scene Renaissance-era paintings in the Louvre in Paris.

The attacks were the worst from my hometown newspaper, the Columbus Dispatch. I couldn't figure out what I had done, but I remembered a conversation I had had in September 2007 with one of its executives about the deputy director of the Franklin County Board of Elections, Matt Damschroder. This executive told me that "they" had told Matt Damschroder that they wanted him to stay at the board for five years after he was hired. I had thought at the time that was a strange thing to be coming from a newspaper, but I dismissed it then. Matt had supported me in my election, even attending a fundraising event in Upper Arlington held for me by the late Democratic activist Barbara Sokol.

When Ken Blackwell was still Ohio Secretary of State, Matt had openly criticized him, even though the two of them are Republican. Matt had taken a $10,000 check for the local Republican Party that represented the interest of the Diebold company during the HAVA-required voting machine procurement process several years earlier. He had been disciplined for it by the Franklin County Board of Elections, but he was neither prosecuted nor fired for facilitating the transaction. This same executive had informed me that the Dispatch believed that Matt had redeemed himself by speaking out against Ken Blackwell, who had engaged in at least one self-imposed news blackout with the Dispatch.

Progress Ohio, Ohio's premier Democratic progressive nonprofit organization, headed by Brian Rothenberg, had made a public records request of Matt's emails from his board of elections email account. The records were voluminous. When I had the opportunity to review them, it was my birthday in February 2008, exactly one month before the primary election.

My "birthday present" in these emails was to feel like a patient who had been limping around for weeks who finally saw an x-ray of her broken leg and finally knew why she had been limping. Matt Damschroder's emails were replete with conversations with staff at the Dispatch ranging from the reporter assigned to cover me to the editor to the associate publisher. In it were a myriad of emails from various other Republican local election officials from other counties in the state, often copied to personnel at the state Republican party. Then the two most astounding things jumped out at me in my perusal of Matt's emails: his invitation to the reporter assigned to cover me to come to his house for dinner—and the reporter's acceptance of the invitation.

Other email exchanges were with Candice Hoke, the professor at Cleveland State University's Marshall College of Law who headed the law school's HAVA-funded Center for Election Integrity and who sat on our Voting Rights Institute Advisory Council. In those emails she encouraged Matt to testify against the central scanning of ballots in the ACLU litigation being waged in Cleveland. She was recruiting one election official to testify against another to foil an election process in her county that was permitted by Congress. I was discovering this within a month of the election.

When I was in Washington, DC attending the National Association of Secretaries of State's conference, I called the editor of the Dispatch, Ben Marrison, at a session break. I told him I didn't want the Dispatch reporter assigned to me covering me any more. I told Ben that I did not think the reporter could be fair and objective if he was having dinner at the home of Matt Damschroder (one of the reporter's best sources who was at the same time one of our office's biggest critics). Ben seemed shocked—I'm not sure at whether I actually called him and made the request, or at the allegation I lodged, or both.

I supplied to him the emails I had reviewed. I also supplied them to the newspaper's associate publisher. Ben asked for a meeting. I agreed. At the appointed date and time Ben, the reporter in question, and another reporter appeared at my office for the meeting. With Patrick Gallaway and Jeff Ortega on one side of the long conference room table, with me at the end of the table and with the three representatives from the Dispatch on the other side, I listened as Ben Marrison flatly told me that at his paper there was a bright line between news and editorial content and that they were and could be fair with me. I argued, citing examples to back up my contentions. Nothing much was accomplished. I couldn't tell them what to do, only how I viewed what they did. After that time it seemed to be just brief periods when this newspaper would let up from its sharp criticisms and sometimes editorialize in my favor.

After the primary election, any short riptide of respite created a mini-tsunami of backlash about how wasteful backup paper ballots had been—how few were used and how many were left. In the Dispatch's view, it was wasteful and unnecessary. Since that time I have seen a change in the newspaper's outlook on this and other reforms made during my administration. At the time, however, the criticism was strong and intense. Regardless of what it cost, (which was not significant,) my view was that ensuring every voter is enfranchised was not something that could be priced. I still believe it today.

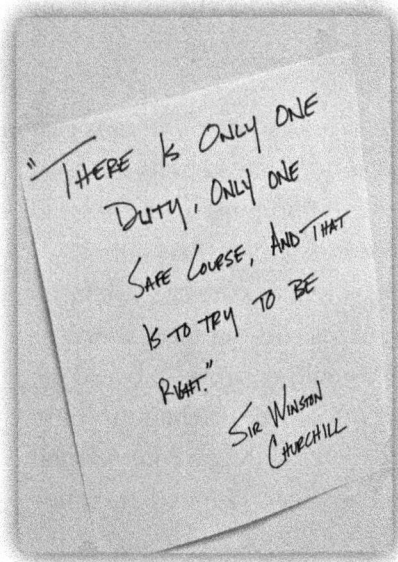

Sign posted in the CRC room where voter calls were handled during the 2008 elections, with quotation from Sir Winston Churchill

Primary election day, March 5, 2008, was a true Ohio day, weather-wise. There were ice storms, flooding in the Ohio River valley, power outages, and yes, even a bomb threat or two at the state's polling locations. Added to that was an ever-vigilant Obama campaign for President. Governor

Strickland had voted early and touted the fact he had voted on a touchscreen machine that primary election day (he did not ask for a backup paper ballot as we were promoting for voter peace of mind and enfranchisement).

The Voting Rights Institute (VRI) had established a pilot voter hotline, called the Citizen Response Center ("CRC"), to take calls from voters statewide about their voting experience and to trouble shoot and get messages to local Secretary of State representatives who were working directly with boards where voters needed help. The VRI had created "Share your voting experience" cards that had already been circulated in the state and that were required to be included in poll worker packets. Voters could take them from the polling place and call our office with issues, comments or problems. This program was designed to ease the burden of calls for boards of elections already busy communicating with poll workers on Election Day. It also helped provide another source of information for voters receiving busy signals when trying to contact their boards about voting problems.

With Ohio's polls open for thirteen hours, once voting is closed, it's closed, unless there is a court order to keep polls open longer. In the morning we learned of flooding in Southeast Ohio counties that prevented voters from reaching their polling places. State law would not allow voters to vote at the board of elections in lieu of their polling places without a court order. We had learned in 2007 that if we could convince a board of elections to go along with letting my office sue them in court, we could accomplish what we needed by filing a complaint and an agreed entry by all parties and get nearly immediate relief from a judge.

In this case, because I was venued in Franklin County in Columbus, the state's capital, we filed a lawsuit in Franklin

County to give voters in flood-affected counties some needed relief. We were blessed to draw Judge John Bender, former Governor and Secretary of State Bob Taft's chief elections counsel and my first-ever election opponent. We received immediate cooperation from Judge Bender, who readily understood the issues with little explanation. As the day went on and more flooding occurred, we were able to amend our original complaint to add more counties as needed.

If an Election Day is going smoothly, the day seems almost interminable, because as the state's chief election officer, you're waiting for the proverbial other shoe to drop. When the clock finally reaches 7:30 p.m. there is a huge sense of relief, knowing the polls are closed. I did not know that feeling in the 2008 primary election. There were bomb threats reported in Trumbull County. In Franklin County, precincts were running out of provisional ballots, presumably because of the county's resistance to the backup paper ballots and provisional ballots being used instead. I was talking with former state Democratic chair and now board of elections director Denny White, by cell phone and seeking the help of our then field representative, Katherine Thompson. I asked for her help in getting extra ballots from the warehouse to the precincts in need. The fact that Franklin County was running short on provisional ballots may have accounted for the huge numbers of backup paper ballots that remained after the election. I had been told that poll workers in training sessions were told not to worry about the backup paper ballots. There was vehement and continuing disagreement with my directive on these backup ballots, especially in Franklin County.

I talked with the director of the Darke County Board of Elections on the far western side of the state who was operating the server tabulating the votes using a generator. The frozen conditions there had downed power lines, creating power outages there that meant no power at the board offices. Poll workers were having difficulty traversing icy roads to bring the ballots and election materials to the board for tabulation. I stayed in periodic contact with her by cell phone, amazed at her calmness under these trying conditions.

Every county sheriff is required to assist his or her county board of elections if called upon on Election Day. The Secretary of State routinely notifies sheriffs of this responsibility by memorandum before each statewide election. Like other secretaries of state before me, I had transmitted this memorandum to the county sheriff in each county. The Darke County sheriff would not assist unless the board paid for it. The sheriff stated he did not have the staff to do it and maintain his regular responsibilities. I called the director of the Ohio Department of Public Safety and asked him if the Ohio State Highway Patrol could "spot" for the sheriff's deputies so that they could assist poll workers in bringing in the ballots. I received the help I needed.

In Sandusky County, a county using optical scan paper ballots, some precincts were running out of ballots. The county used a "ballot on demand" system to print ballots on blank, numbered ballot stock to replenish ballot shortages, but the county's machine had broken down. In this Presidential primary election Senator Hillary Clinton, supported enthusiastically by Governor Strickland, (who even traveled to Iowa to campaign for her,) remained a viable candidate even into the Ohio March primary. Radio personality Rush Limbaugh had urged many conservative Republican voters to switch parties in the primary to vote for Hillary, because it was believed that John McCain could defeat Hillary Clinton more easily than he could defeat Senator Barack Obama, who was in the lead for primary wins throughout the country. Many boards of elections had not planned for enough Democratic primary ballots for a phenomenon of what later came to be called "Rush Limbaugh" voters. Some of these boards were concerned about cost and potential budget battles with their boards of county commissioners.

I called Barb Tuckerman, the Sandusky County board's director. "Have voters been turned away for a lack of ballots?" I asked. She answered directly that they had. "How many voters do you think have been turned away?" I asked again. She had trouble coming up with a number. "Just ball park it, Barb," I said. She paused and responded, clearly flustered and concerned, "Three hundred or so," she said. That was it. I couldn't allow the polls in Sandusky County to close on time. It was time to get a court order to keep the polls open. We were able to do that quickly with the help of the Attorney General.

Once a local court order was in place, we followed it up quickly with a directive to the other 87 county boards of elections that they were to close on time but not release any election results until 9:00 p.m. when the polls in Sandusky County closed. We did not want voters in Sandusky County receiving news reports of voting results and influencing their votes or confusing them that the polls were closed, when they were still open in their county. Our communications section's job in situations such as this was to work with local news media to disseminate the information that polls would remain open in the county for extended hours. Meanwhile, I was holding regular media briefings with state and national reporters on what was occurring throughout the state, while my field staff was holding scheduled briefing calls with our elections administration staff in Columbus and conferring with our VRI staff on the Citizen Response Center phone lines.

We had tested our new election night reporting system, which was now completely contained in Ohio and redesigned so that users could customize the reporting of just the results they wanted to see. We had inherited a system devised by contractors for former Secretary Blackwell that could not be modified without the contractor being reengaged. The backup server for the system had been operated by Smartech in Tennessee, the same company that managed the Bush White House political email system and that was the subject of much speculation about its potential use in 2004 to allegedly "rig" or steal Ohio's election. All I knew was that any backup to our system should be in Ohio, so we maintained the backup server in our Cleveland office. We knew that in the 2004 controversial Ohio Presidential general election, Ohio's election night website had received 42 million hits in a period of just several hours. We had stress tested our new reporting system for an even higher number of hits in such a short period and were satisfied that it would hold up. It's ironic, though, when things go smoothly, that kind of capacity is not needed. The reporting system was a success, receiving many compliments, especially from some veteran Republicans in and out of state.

Then there was Cuyahoga County. Within a half hour of the closing of polls there, the Obama campaign went to federal court to seek extended polling hours where there were alleged ballot shortages. It wasn't a countywide order that was sought, but rather, what I considered, "cherry-picked" precincts. I was furious, remembering how Al Gore had "cherry-picked" counties for recounts in Florida in 2000 and how well that had served him and the rest of the country. Ohio Democratic Party Chair Chris Redfern called me to talk to me about what was happening with the Obama campaign (I was making public statements about cherry-picking"). I hurled my "cherry-picking" allegations right back at him to the point that even over the phone I could imagine him backing up and looking for the nearest exit. "Okay, okay," he said.

Jane Platten was furious, too. She had carefully planned each step of this pivotal election, and it had been executed well. The federal judge ordered several precincts be kept open until 9:00. Five additional voters voted. Some precincts that he ordered reopened had already been closed, and precinct judges could not be reached to reopen them, because the lawsuit had been filed so close to 7:30 p.m. when the polls were required to close.

Voter turnout in the 2008 Presidential primary was the largest in Ohio history—46%. Because of the hotly contested Democratic Presidential primary, turnout was highest for Democrats (regular and Limbaugh Democrats). One of the latent effects of this turnout was that many so-called "Democrats" were targeted for persuasion and turnout efforts in 2010. When contacted by Democratic candidates and parties, they seemed frustrated, claimed they weren't Democrats and slammed the door in the faces of many of my canvassers in my 2010 U.S. Senate primary. Rush Limbaugh's influence in Ohio has been lasting in more ways than he would anticipate.

The near aftermath of the Ohio primary election saw a cautious consensus that the primary election had gone fairly well—for Ohio. National media had been fully expecting disaster. Ohio experienced plenty of disaster that day, but it was externally caused disaster, and for the greater part of that day's experiences, Ohio was prepared. We later learned that one of the most vocal critics of the backup paper ballots, Lake County, actually had to use them but didn't tell us. The criticisms of the cost of backup paper ballots dogged us. But like seatbelts, which in the 1960's were optional at best, election officials and voters came to appreciate the change. At the time we simply endured the stinging criticisms lobbed our way. ≈

Chapter 17

Bloody Sunday

After the primary election, there was a sense of relief. We experienced a brief respite before we had to dive in again and be fully immersed planning for the general Presidential election. Rick and I actually had some down time. It was May 4, 2008, and an early Sunday evening.

Our son, Johnathon invited us to dinner at his girlfriend, Erika's, family home just northeast of Columbus, in Westerville. The three of us traveled there together in our pickup truck with our then three dogs riding in the capped truck bed behind the cab. The dogs, especially Jake, the oldest, had traveled the state, and a pickup truck like ours with screened side windows allowed these lovable critters to walk around in the truck bed while taking in the sights, smells and sounds of all of Ohio when they traveled with us. So it wasn't unusual that they would go with us that night. They slept, looked out the screened windows and waited patiently in the back of the truck while we visited with John and Erika and Erika's family.

Erika's dad, Mo (short for Mohammed), came to the U.S. in the 1970's from Iran before the Shah's regime fell. He is a successful engineer in the U.S., who had to scramble when the home regime fell and he lost his funding for school midway through college. He had heard that college was affordable in West Virginia and struck out for the hills to test his fortune. He met a beautiful, blonde, blue-eyed West Virginian named Pam who had Nordic roots and was a math major. After graduating and marrying they ended up in Columbus. They have four beautiful children, two of whom have the striking dark Persian beauty and the other two with the fairer characteristics of their mother.

Erika can best be described as what any young girl would imagine a Persian princess looks like with her dark hair and almond skin and piercing blue eyes. My young man and only son, John, was stricken at first sight. She has proved to be a steadying and edifying influence and is soon to be his partner in life. She is someone of whom Rick and I have grown very fond.

L. to R. Erika, age 21, me and son John, age 21, after Profile in Courage Award ceremony, May 2008, at JFK Library and Museum in Boston

Enjoying a family meal with an immigrant family is a rare treat. The closeness, importance and easy enjoyment of being together is as delightful as the food Mo cooked every Sunday evening for their weekly communions. One particular Iranian family tradition is smoking rose tobacco in a "hookah" at the end of a good meal. As Rick and John and I sat on the back patio with the family and enjoyed this new experience, Pam asked where our dogs were. She invited them into the backyard to join us. We hesitantly acquiesced, since McGuffey the hound dog and Lane the ornery mutt (whose "underdog" emails during my Senate campaign a year later would raise me several thousand dollars) were at constant competition with each other. They were still working out their puppy energy.

At one point the two dogs began chasing each other through the backyard, the neighbor's backyards and onto the patio. Lane darted under one of the hoses of the hookah, pulling the whole hookah onto the ground and causing a commotion of the first order. The dogs were retrieved and the evening cut short with profuse apologies and no hard feelings from Mo and Pam and company.

I had inadvertently left my cell phone in the truck only to return and find I had ten missed calls and five voicemail messages in the period of less than two hours on that Sunday night. I sat back and wondered to myself what was up. If only I had known that while I was chasing a white-lightning, hookah-breaking little dog through the backyards of people I didn't know in a northeast suburb of Columbus, the fate of Ohio's chief law enforcement officer, Attorney General Marc Dann, was being discussed by the state's top Democratic leaders, and they were looking for me to join them.

Things had reached a critical mass with a brewing scandal involving questionable hiring practices, fraternity-type antics and an extramarital relationship between General Dann and a top female staffer. Earlier, realizing that Marc was having difficulties but not fully informed of them, I had suggested to the First Lady, Frances Strickland, that perhaps some family mentoring was in order for all statewide office holders and their families to help them with the personal adjustments to the changed circumstances of their positions. When I served as a judge, Chief Justice Moyer's wife, Mary, had initiated a Judicial Family Network for the judges of the state at all levels. The organization helped families adjust to life with a family member in the judiciary. Rick had chaired it for a year, and many participants around the state found it beneficial. When I brought up the idea of mentoring, she shook her head and looked away as if I had just said I was thinking of bringing Al Capone to dinner at the Governor's residence.

The Sunday evening of the dog and hookah escapade, Governor Strickland had been trying mightily to reach me to the point that his people had called my daughter, Kate, and my chief of staff, Tom, (who had walked to my house from his house just several blocks away to try to locate me. None of them was able to reach me during this time of political "crisis." In the cab of the truck with all three dogs in tow, I listened to all five voicemail messages and attempted to call everyone back until I reached someone who could brief me on what was going on.

I was directed to call in to "Free Conference Call.com" when I arrived home to join the other Democratic state officials and the party chair to discuss Marc Dann's political future. I thought it weird that something of such a serious, dramatic and newsworthy nature would occur on "Free Conference Call.com." I shook my head as I dialed in and listened.

I was shocked at what and whom I heard: Governor Ted Strickland, his chief of staff, John Haseley, Lieutenant Governor Lee Fisher, state Democratic Party chair Chris Redfern, legislative leaders Ray Miller in the Ohio Senate and Joyce Beatty in the Ohio House, Senator Sherrod Brown and Treasurer Richard Cordray had agreed that Attorney General Marc Dann needed to resign in light of recent revelations that showed mismanagement in his office, extracurricular staff activities that were the subject of investigation and that he had been conducting an extramarital affair with a female staffer.

When Ted Strickland took office, his first Executive Order had been about ethics in government. As part of this initiative, he required all state government staff under his authority (all the people on the call, except Lee Fisher, were separately elected and not subject to his direct authority) to abide by gift restrictions of $20. State law set $75 as the reporting threshold for gifts. But this $20 restriction was not a reporting requirement; it was an outright ban. I learned that this resulted in at least one of his cabinet members having to refuse a gift from her staff in recognition of her service because it exceeded $20.

What I heard on the call that Sunday night was a plan to seek General Dann's resignation. Apparently, he had already been asked to resign by the Governor, and he had refused. The letter that was intended to be from all of us had already been crafted. The call I joined was for the purpose of getting every statewide officeholder's assent and sign-on to the letter. John Haseley read it to the group assembled on the call. One line raised red flags for me that read along the lines that General Dann had not upheld the standards of "honesty and integrity" that should be expected of Democratic officeholders in Ohio.

I had seen a lot of Democratic (and Republican) officeholders in my years. What Marc did was not vastly different than what I had seen in the past—not pretty, but I wasn't sure any of it was an impeachable offense warranting resignation. Then, I countered to myself, 'Maybe I don't know everything,' remembering Frances Strickland's shuddering reaction to my mentoring suggestion for office holders and their families.

Listening to John Haseley read the carefully crafted letter, I kept thinking, "Just what *are* Democrats' 'standards of honesty and integrity?'" The only picture in my mind I could see in trying to define it for any political party was a video of someone trying to nail Jello to the wall. "Oh, boy," I thought. "This is a mess." I balked at signing the letter, especially signing on to that particular statement. It was so vague it could be used against the Pope, I thought.

The definition of integrity to which I commonly ascribe is, very simply a consistency of actions with values. When judging the integrity of any office holder, a judgment of what is consistent between actions and values belongs solely to the voters. For anyone to presume that voters elected anyone to public office because of perceived adherence to any party's standards of "honesty and integrity" was folly, I thought, and I still do. No one but the voters, and especially not the governor of a state or its other office holders, can take away the power of another duly elected officer holder that is given to him or her by the people. I said I wasn't comfortable signing the letter. I was the only holdout.

Finally, John Haseley offered to take out the "honesty and integrity" sentence. I reluctantly agreed to sign on, later regretting that I had.

The letter agreed to was as follows:

> Dear Attorney General Dann,
>
> We write to you tonight to ask that you resign your position as Attorney General of the State of Ohio.
>
> We believe that your actions have irreparably harmed your ability to effectively serve the people of our great state.

The work of the Office of the Attorney General matters more, and is far more important, than any one person. In many, many cases it is all that stands between the people and the powerful.

Sadly, we no longer have even the most remote hope that you can continue to effectively serve as Attorney General and that is why we are asking for your resignation.

We also want to make you aware that if you do not choose to resign, Democratic members of the Ohio House of Representatives will immediately introduce a resolution seeking your impeachment. We sincerely hope that this action will not be necessary and that you will act in the best interest of the people of Ohio by tendering your resignation Monday morning.

Sincerely,

Ted Strickland Governor
Sherrod Brown U.S. Senator
Lee Fisher Lt. Governor
Jennifer Brunner Secretary of State
Richard Cordray Treasurer
Ray Miller Senate Minority Leader
Joyce Beatty Chris Redfern

The call was ended with an announcement that the Governor would call General Dann with the letter and ask him again to resign. We would reconvene the conference call the next morning to discuss what to do in the event General Dann refused to resign. I joined that call the next morning while in my car, announced my presence, put my phone on mute and just listened. General Dann had refused to resign, which was not surprising to me. (The Governor's staffers on the call had seemed shocked that General Dann would not resign on the

Governor's request.) The Governor was planning to call a press conference. Several on the call said they wanted to be there. I said nothing and continued to listen.

The matter went forward, national news was made and Marc responded with his own press conference after he had fired his closest top staffers, including his communications director. Just before he held his press conference, Marc called me. Talking to me as if I were his sister, he wanted me to know that he had had an affair with a female staffer (which was pretty much publicly known by this time), that he had admitted it to Alyssa, his wife, and that she was supporting him. Now he was going to bare his soul to the world. I said, "Marc, are you sure you want to do this?" He assured me it was the best thing to do. I kept questioning him, trying to get him to think it through, until he said he had to go.

We hung up, and I walked into one of my assistant's offices. Emily said, "Marc Dann is giving a press conference now." I said, "I know. I just talked to him." Emily and one of the other staffers in the office looked at me in disbelief that I already knew what was unfolding in front of them. What my staff often didn't seem to grasp was that, the office holder often knows things that happen even when away from the office, because people race to be the first to tell them, or they have been informed as a courtesy before news is made. Often, even when traveling hours away, I knew more about what was happening in the capital than my own staff who were closer to that scene.

Emily had live video pulled up on her computer for the press conference. I watched briefly until Marc said, "I wasn't prepared for this office. I didn't think I would win." I slapped the flat of my palm on my forehead. "You never say that," I moaned. I couldn't stand to watch the rest of the 40-minute meltdown where he let media representatives have a field day with him with no press secretary to step in front of him at the podium and say the press conference was over.

After the press conference, General Dann hunkered down. Speculation swirled about his resignation. There would have to be a special election if he resigned before September 25th of that year, less than two years into his term. I was interviewed by one of the media outlets and when asked about my reaction to his situation said simply, "It is what it is." This didn't exactly please the Governor's staff, but I did not want to fuel the swirl. Reflecting back, I would have preferred watching all hell break loose while a white, rambunctious dog broke a hookah at an Iranian-American family dinner than being a witness to what amounted to a Kabuki drama.

General Dann hired expensive, high-powered counsel from Texas to examine a constitutional challenge of what was happening to him in Ohio. Opinion overall was divided. A Columbus city councilwoman expressed to me her disgust and opined that he needed to resign for his transgressions against his family and women. I remained silent and listened with genuine interest in learning how people processed this information in light of their own life experiences.

Obviously, the woman who expressed this opinion is one of high integrity whom I respect. She was also fairly new to politics and hadn't seen the world of "good old boys" where I had cut my teeth in the 1970's as an Ohio statehouse staffer. The good old boys taught me that politics was about one thing, loyalty. They partied hard on lobbyists' expense accounts, took what they could within reason, hired their friends and relatives, yet kept their word when they made a promise and took care of their constituents, sometimes cutting deals to scratch each other's backs to keep their words. In a state as diverse as Ohio, each legislator, (which is where Marc came from as a state senator before he was attorney general,) represented the uniqueness of his or her constituency, and somehow, things got done. I'm not saying it's ideal, only that it did result in getting things done.

General Dann had previously represented a constituency in the Ohio Senate that was essentially my old Senate boss' district. The area is one of an extremely depressed economy, with its once thriving steel industry largely gone. But it's the people of the area, and all of Ohio for that matter, who are extraordinary in the face of the toughest challenges. In Youngstown, I have talked with early retirees in a home and on the street who were protesting because Delphi was allowed to bail on their retirement and health insurance long before they were eligible for Medicare. I have been bowled over by the quiet intention of the volunteer Mahoning Organizing Collaborative, which has indexed and cataloged all blighted property in Youngstown in the wake of record foreclosures.

So it wasn't a surprise to me that an adopted "Valley" boy, Marc Dann, was going to hold out and not capitulate. During the campaign and even into office, Marc had been like a brother to me—the kind you want to hug and punch all at the same time. Rick had worked as his counsel during the 2006 campaign, even as he counseled my campaign staff and me along the way. When Marc won, Marc asked Rick to leave his private practice and run his office. Rick politely declined his generous offer, knowing that he couldn't afford to give up his practice, potentially be done in a four-year term and have to start building his practice all over again, this time four years older. In Marc's case, that would have happened in less than two years.

General Dann's and his top staff's political analysis of the 2007 Cuyahoga County Board of Elections overhaul had proved to be short-sighted, but he came through in the end, personally representing me in both the common pleas trial court and the

Ohio Supreme Court hearings (which by this time were heavily covered in the news). Marc did a very good job, too.

Appearing with Ohio Attorney General Marc Dann at a 2008 pre-primary election press conference on election preparedness

General Dann was willing to investigate irregularities of the Franklin County Board of Elections, a board closely and zealously protected by the Columbus Dispatch newspaper to the point that one of its executives asked for a one-on-one meeting with me in early 2008 which I naively granted. In the meeting, the executive spoke of "working to take people out" (referring to local elected officials) when they did not act in agreement with the editorial board. The indirect message was that I was to leave alone the Franklin County board's Republican deputy director, Matt Damschroder. I did not heed it.

Marc Dann had called me after hearing about anomalies in ballot layout in Franklin County in 2007. Investigation later showed the server's audit function had been disengaged. Marc had said, "Send me a letter, referring it to me." He was known for taking the Eliot Spitzer attorney general approach of crusading for "the people" for what he believed was right in spite of opposition. He was loved already for some of his fearless and groundbreaking work.

The longer Marc held out after that disastrous press conference, the worse the situation became, and the worse I felt for him. By this time, the Cleveland Plain Dealer had run a huge picture of him with a scathing article that chided him for acting like he did—how dare he act like what the Plain Dealer implied was a stereotypical Youngstown crony when he was really from Cuyahoga County's Shaker Heights?

Shaker Heights is a well heeled, gentrified, but aging Cleveland suburb that I had once sued for race discrimination while in private practice. The city had used its various building permit processes to stop an African American woman from opening what my opposing counsel called a "players" nightclub there. My underpaid crusade in that case caused consternation among countless upstanding citizens who had been previously vocal in opposition to her plan. I sued many of them personally for race discrimination after a racial epithet was hurled at her restaurant kitchen designer at a neighborhood meeting.

Several of the large white-shoe downtown Cleveland law firms become involved, placing an African American former bankruptcy judge as lead opposing counsel. They went after me personally in addition to working against my client. They filed a motion for sanctions in our case and we eventually lost the overall case in federal court. When I ran for Secretary of State almost fifteen years after that lawsuit, a lot of those involved must not have associated me with the lawyer who worked out of the basement of her house and scrapped with them for all she was worth. I received hearty support then and even in the 2010 U.S. Senate race from many people in Shaker Heights, Ohio.

During Marc's holdout period, I had talked with lobbyist, former state Democratic party chair, mentor and friend Paul Tipps, who was in frequent communication with Marc and who encouraged me to call him. When I did, Marc was nearly dumbfounded but happy to hear from a political friend on the inside during his self-imposed exile. I was the only one of the statewide office holders who had called him since the letter was made public asking him to resign.

When I talked with Marc that afternoon I was more interested to know how he and his family were faring. He was grateful I called. We talked about whether he would resign. I told him I regretted signing the letter and wished that I had not succumbed to that pressure. He held no grudge and then shocked me when he said he fully planned to resign but wanted to wait until after September 25th, to avoid a special election mid-term. He did not believe that Democrats could hold the seat in a 2008 special election. He was hiring lawyers to help him stay in office to help the party in spite of the party. I shook my head when I hung up.

All kinds of legislation in the General Assembly were moving quickly. The Speaker of the House was Jon Husted, who became my successor in the Secretary of State's office. Early on in Governor Strickland's administration he had forged a working alliance with Speaker Husted, feeling even grandfatherly toward him for at least a short time. At this juncture, Speaker Husted suggested that the Governor-appointed Inspector General, Tom Charles, be given investigative authority over the Attorney General, a separately elected office holder. Governor Strickland agreed to the suggested arrangement. It may have sounded like an expedient solution to a sticky political problem, but there was a hitch. Marc Dann, like Rich Cordray, Mary Taylor and me, was a constitutional officer. How could one constitutional officer exercise dominion and control over another without specific constitutional authority to do so?

Governor Strickland's chief of staff, John Haseley, called me to inform me of quickly moving legislation extending gubernatorial power over the Attorney General. Coincidentally, I had that day received a call from Delaware County First Assistant Prosecutor Bill Owen, the hearing officer in the Cuyahoga County board removal process the previous year. Bill said that if Marc Dann did resign, it would be important to "lock down" computers and other equipment that may hold evidence in the investigations that would ensue. One of General Dann's top people who had been fired by him had "spoiled" such evidence on his departure. As a former judge, this suggestion made eminent sense, so I mentioned it to John Haseley at the end of our call, in the event General Dann resigned.

John Haseley's call about legislation to create new power for the Inspector General had gone over with me like a lead balloon. In the same conversation I pushed back, saying that the governor-appointed Inspector General should not have that power over another constitutional officer. I also was concerned that the next step would be to extend it to the other separately elected statewide office holders such as Rich Cordray, Mary Taylor and me. I told John that I would have appreciated being consulted before a position was taken favoring this legislation, that he was putting Rich Cordray and me at political peril to be "next" and that a "witch hunt" sometimes produced things that weren't real but took on lives of their own. John was abruptly defensive at my challenge.

The bill was approved by the all-Republican controlled legislature that day. That evening, despite my objections voiced to John Haseley, the Governor quickly signed the bill giving the Inspector General his new power in time for an all-out raid on the Attorney General's office the next morning. This new law facilitated the Governor's actions in using the state Highway Patrol to effectively "raid" General Dann's office the next morning. Officers demanded that Marc hand over his Blackberry cell phone and his computer. I am told that

Inspector General staff stood back and watched somewhat in shock at the swiftness and intensity of this action taken against a sitting office holder. In a matter of hours, Marc threw in the towel and walked out of his office, leaving his diplomas on the wall. He made an impromptu media announcement that he was resigning. His once foster daughter, Mia, who worked for me as a publication designer, stood with him on a sparse stage as he made his announcement. He had demanded that Governor Strickland appear on the stage with him. It looked uncomfortable from what could be seen in news reports. When the deed was done, Marc walked ignominiously off the stage with Mia in tow.

I was in a state of utter shock, feeling sick and wondering if I had somehow unwittingly, in passing along a prosecutor's suggestion, given a shot of adrenalin to move forward a situation that was the ugliest, bloodiest coup I had witnessed in my political experience. Dumbfounded, I shuddered at what had just happened. As in the Roman Senate death of Caesar, the worst political deaths are imparted by those closest to the often unprepared and bumbling victims.

This kind of political family bloodletting extends its effects well beyond the political family. Real families and reputations suffer as political bludgeoning occurs. The aggressors who impatiently crusade for bloody redress and fail to leave resolution to the existing legal framework often sidestep the law themselves. In Marc's case it was a perfect scenario for two political parties to collude and ignore the state Constitution with a law that was contrived for political expediency on both sides.
For the families of the bludgeoned real costs include jobs and houses lost, kids ridiculed and whispered about at school, perished marriages, and the psyche of a community damaged for years. To front row onlookers to such debacles, it is a sobering lesson that, in politics, nothing is sacred.

When any entity, be it a political party, a government, a corporation or even a "family," believes that the end justifies the means, the means will become more brutal with each incident of power unchecked. In Marc's case, this exercise of power bore a mighty fury.

When the Inspector General undertook an extensive investigation even after General Dann's resignation, I was called on to be part of the investigative team because my office had jurisdiction over campaign finance. When I attended the first meeting of the team, suffice it to say I stuck out like a sore thumb in my tan pantsuit with turquoise shell and pearls in a room of blue and black suits and uniforms. My reaction was visceral, and sharp pangs hit me hard in my stomach as I listened to the plans ahead for investigation and prosecution.

The extensive and costly investigation resulted in two misdemeanor ethics violations. Ohio's former Republican governor, Bob Taft, pled guilty to four ethics misdemeanor violations while in office and never left office. The former governor's resignation wasn't pushed because it was to Democrats' advantage to leave him in office as an object of enmity during the 2006 campaign.

The personal aftermath for Marc and his family was not good. Their house went on the market in an area already depressed for lost jobs in a dormant manufacturing "valley" that is called Youngstown. It is an area that once more took it on the chin for corruption in politics. The children survived the chaos and have moved on. Marc still practices law in northeast Ohio.

A year after this troubling political debacle for which some Democrats congratulated themselves for having rooted out corruption, I was receiving the first Stephanie Tubbs Jones Award at the Cleveland City Club from the American

Constitution Society of Northeast Ohio for work in the 2008 Presidential election in Ohio. Marc was in attendance. I walked over to his table and tapped him on the shoulder. He stood up, apparently shocked that I would voluntarily greet him. I hugged him and asked how he and his family were. He was upbeat and grinned like the "brother" I knew.

A few minutes after I had returned to my table before the award ceremony, he lumbered over to me grinning even wider and said, "Just let me know when you're ready for me to endorse Lee Fisher against you in the Senate race." I had seen how politics can distort the human condition like the mirrors of a fun house, but amazingly, Marc Dann could still laugh. ≈

Chapter 18

A Voting Rights Institute for Ohio

Throughout my campaign for Secretary of State I had premiered the idea of creating a "Voting Rights Institute" in the office. The institute's purpose was to bring together the various interested parties who wanted to see Ohio's elections improve, to be a think tank for needed legislation, and to provide direct service to voters. I knew that establishing a function like this in the office would leave the understaffed elections section in a better position to provide prompt and responsive service to the state's 88 county boards of elections. The local boards were funded by local boards of county commissioners, some more generous than others, but many boards of elections were so destitute that one board of elections operated out of what was once the "ladies lounge" (restroom) at the county courthouse and stored voting machines in a dilapidated building across a large parking lot from the board "mini-office."

Moreover, many newly minted and long-established voting rights organizations had longed for a formal way to participate with the secretary of state's office, having been all but shut out by the previous administration. They were looking for an opportunity to be heard, conferred with and involved. After hearing from many of them on the campaign trail, I knew they had opinions, and I knew those opinions would be voiced regardless of whether or not their speakers were embraced. From my experience in forming a drug court in Franklin County, I knew it would be valuable and even essential to bring them "to the table" as we were developing needed changes, even if we did not agree on all points.

I did not know of any such organization, a "Voting Rights Institute," in any other secretary of state's office in the nation, but it seemed right for Ohio. It turned out to be the first of its kind in the nation as a division actually operating out of a secretary of state's office. The VRI proved to be invaluable and gained national recognition, with its members and advisory council members being recruited to serve on national voting rights committees and working groups.

Kellye Pinkleton, organized, cheerful, resourceful and a tireless advocate for voting rights, became Director of the Voting Rights Institute

Kellye Pinkleton was the perfect person to launch the Voting Rights Institute in my administration, with her always-cheerful demeanor, can-do attitude, sardonic wit and incomparable organizational skills and "follow-up" methodology. She had been the field director of my 2006 Secretary of State campaign, and when Richard Cordray and I combined our field operations, she oversaw both.

As we began to form the organization of our administration during the transition period, I never doubted Kellye for a moment that Kellye was the perfect person to direct the activities of the new Voting Rights Institute in the office. I trusted her to create and shape a groundbreaking division of the office that would work with everyone from representatives of the Ohio Republican Party to Black Box Voting. Black Box was a radical (some called it "rogue") organization that had obtained the source code for the Diebold voting system and began testing of its efficacy, with disturbing results (that weren't significantly counteracted in our own voting machine study.)

VRI's Dean Hindenlang sits at front of room with staff members from various divisions of the Secretary of State's office who operated the Citizen Response Center, known as the CRC

Kellye and her team made visits to various county boards of elections to familiarize them with the CRI as a new service arm of the Secretary of State's office and show them how the VRI could help them and the public. She learned from them their concerns and helped pass on ideas from one to another about innovative ways they were undertaking voter registration, such as printing a voter registration form to be included in the City of Chillicothe's water bills. She and her small but edgy staff had printed the business-sized cards, "Share your voting experience."

Even though some boards had been a bit intrepid about the use of these cards, as time wore on, they started to see less stress on their offices in Election Day calls. Voters were able to call the Secretary of State's Citizen Response Center (the telephone number listed on the cards). The CRC was staffed by at least ten people for nearly two weeks during the 2008 general election and for three weeks during the 2010 election. At the time of the 2008 general election Ohio had more than 14,000 voting precincts and nearly 8 million registered voters. If a call came in, especially on Election Day, with a particularized problem, we were able to gauge if help was needed and dispatch our area field representatives to the board of elections to make them aware of where help was needed or to provide us with more information.

We wanted the Voting Rights Institute to "take the heat off of" boards of elections so the boards could do what they do best— administer elections at the county level and deal directly with voters. During the four years it was in operation, that's what it did. I've found few people like Kellye in my years of experience, and we continue to work together today on advocacy efforts such as Fair Elections Ohio, a nonprofit organization formed to protect voting rights in Ohio, and Courage PAC, to encourage citizen advocacy.

The VRI provided what could otherwise have been called "boring" statewide duties with ways citizens could have direct and meaningful access to their government and its most fundamental democratic processes. Its initiatives included:

> **Grads Vote** – a collaborative program with the Governor and the State Department of Education to provide every graduating senior (even in charter schools) with a voter registration form and information about voting absentee and becoming a poll worker

Ohio College Vote – an interactive, web-based program so that Ohio college students in and out of state could learn the nuances of the laws on where and how to vote, and how to organize voter registration and absentee voting activities on their college campuses, including how college administration officials could assist

Vote in Honor of a Veteran – a program to honor the service of veterans and promote participation in democracy, which received bipartisan support from now Speaker of the House Bill Batchelder, allowing particular veterans to be honored with on the website and pins to be worn to remind people to vote in honor of a veteran

Vote@17 – a program (conceived of at the dinner table at Rick's home farm with his 18-year-old nephew, Jacob, a senior at West Branch High School,) to inform 17-year-olds that they can vote in a primary election if they will be 18 years old by the general election, using school visits and assemblies, bookmarks and a special web page dedicated to these special new voters

NVRA Leadership Team - conducted voter education to implement critical provisions of the National Voter Registration Act (federal law) requiring designated agencies such as state and local Job and Family Services agencies and the state Bureau of Motor Vehicles to conduct voter registration as part of their regular course of business, allowing for settlement of one of the major lawsuits inherited from the previous administration

Youth Poster Contest – themed, "Vote Today . . . Shape Tomorrow," with more than 900 submissions from children in grades three through twelve

KidsVoting – collaboration with and funding of this nonprofit organization's recruitment of high school poll workers and its work with elementary schools in conducting mock elections to expose children to voting at an early age

Client Empowerment/501(c)(3) – a program near the end of our term to educate community leaders about how to involve their groups in voting through understanding the nuances and applications of laws and practicalities of voter registration and absentee voting, offering underserved voting populations the opportunity to work together in developing ways to better involve their constituencies

"Find a New Direction" – development in cooperation with the state Department of Rehabilitation and Corrections of educational materials and conferences on voting rights of those leaving incarceration that included widespread education and training of corrections staff, probation officers, inmates, and social services agencies serving parolees and probationers (as many leaving incarceration believe they are no longer able to vote in Ohio—ever— because they are a "felon")

New Citizens Initiatives – launched to register and educate newly naturalized citizens, including direct work with federal courts where naturalization ceremonies took place

Address Confidentiality Legislation – in collaboration with domestic violence and women's groups throughout the state, developed legislation to protect victims of domestic violence and stalking by providing them with a safe and secure address through the Secretary of State's office by which to vote absentee and receive their mail

Overseas Vote Foundation Partnership – work with this nonprofit web-based resource to provide military and overseas voters with web site tools to provide online registration and absentee ballot request to simplify voting

Poll Worker Recruitment "Tool Kits" – analysis of statewide statistical results on demographics and community-based groups of poll workers to offer advice on how to better utilize veterans, students and other identified groups who have been engaged and are likely to remain deeply engaged in election work

Secretary of State Debate – conducted and promoted by the VRI's Advisory Council, the first state-sponsored, televised statewide debate for the party nominees for Secretary of State, including third-party nominees

L. to R. Democratic candidate Maryellen O'Shaughnessy, Republican Secretary of State Jon Husted, and Libertarian candidate Charles R. Earl; at podium, Donita Judge, Advancement Project's lead attorney for the State of Ohio and VRI member: VRI-sponsored Secretary of State debate, 2010

"Operation Forward Democracy" – development of a pilot project to encourage veterans to serve on the "front lines" of democracy as poll workers

U.S. Post Office Change of Address Voter Registration Study – spearheaded a Pew Charitable Trusts-funded half-million-dollar academic study with national visibility that included two Ohio postal districts, along with areas of Kentucky and Indiana, requiring cooperation with two Republican secretaries of state (Trey Grayson of Kentucky and Todd Rokita of Indiana) to ease burdens for boards of elections in last-minute registration by making it easier to change voter registration at the time other address changes were made when voters moved

The Pew Charitable Trusts in March of 2007 undertook a 25-person focus group in a several-day session at the conference center at Pocantico outside of Tarreytown, New York. Pocantico is the site where the famous John D. Rockefeller home called "Kuykuit" is located. The old Rockefeller home sits atop a windy hill overlooking the scenic Hudson River. Pew's Center for the States wanted to explore whether to fund a national election integrity initiative, which it ultimately did, called, "Make Elections Work." Just two months into office, I was among a select, bipartisan group of elected and non-elected election officials from around the country from whom Pew was seeking counsel about whether to fund a $2 million dollar program. Attendees included secretaries of state from Kansas, Indiana, Minnesota, Pennsylvania, California, Ohio and state and local election administrators from Michigan, New York, Wisconsin, Missouri, Texas and Ohio (Matt Damschroder from the Franklin County Board of Elections), along with a representative of the Elections Center, an educational organization for elections officials, funded in part by voting system manufacturers.

The topics discussed were fascinating, and not only did I lend my thoughts and experiences, but I gained insights into what lay ahead for my staff and me in election administration as we prepared for the 2008 Presidential election. I had met my Secretary of State colleagues from around the nation just weeks earlier at my first National Association of Secretaries of State (NASS) conference in Washington, DC. There I had found much in common in philosophy and approach with Robin Carnahan, Missouri's Secretary of State. It was at Pocantico that our group studied her office's website. I came back to Ohio enthused about what she had done in just over two years in office (elected in 2004) and asked my staff to move in the direction of a website with the same clean appearance and ease of navigation as her state's website.

During one of the evening receptions before dinner, Robin asked me where I was staying at the conference center. "I'm in the big house in a beautiful room on the third floor with windows on three sides," I said.

"You must rate," she said. "I'm in the horse stables."

"I think it's because I'm from Ohio," I said, keeping my amazement to myself. (Matt Damschroder was in the big house as well.)

When I had walked into my room at Kuykuit earlier that day (an elevator in the house took me to the third floor), I was frankly astounded. It was as if I had stepped back in time to the 1940's— even down to the white ceramic, gear-like fixtures in the bathroom. The furniture had once been new, purchased in New York City. It was as if what was once new was preserved as it looked when bought to furnish the room, like in Miss Havisham's house in Charles Dickens' *Great Expectations* (sans cobwebs).

There was a fireplace in the room, with woodwork painted a creamy white and the carpet a low pile light steel blue. A wooden and upholstered bench was placed under the window. Perched on my knees on the bench, I surveyed the beautiful view in wonderment inside and out, and imagined the lives that had filled this room. The Hudson River looked peaceful as the sun was getting ready to set. No wonder John Rockefeller and his family had chosen this site, I thought.

When I lay in bed that first night, the windows rattled fiercely and repeatedly as the winds whipped the stately structure. With windows on three sides, it was to be expected. From those same windows in the daylight I could see many of Nelson Rockefeller's carefully placed sculptures throughout the spacious gardens and grounds. Little did I know until I took a formal tour of the house while there that I was sleeping three stories above a private art gallery in the lower level that contained original paintings and drawings of Andy Warhol and Pablo Picasso and colossal collections of historic dinner china. With my penchant to visit the art museum in nearly every major city I visit, I was astounded.

After traveling the highways and byways of Ohio, meeting humble people, hearing their stories, eating lots of chicken and way too much fast food, I was now in the home of a famous Ohioan, John Rockefeller, one of history's richest men, and among significant relics of his, his family's and our country's history. As I took in my surroundings for the first time, I said quietly under my breath, "Thank you, Ken Blackwell." Ohio's "problem child" status at least rendered me a decent room at Kuykuit.

Often at the National Association of Secretaries of State's (NASS) twice-yearly conferences, secretaries of state or their staffs offer presentations on programs that work in their state.

They share ideas and approaches on improvements to voting and election administration. When my office and I presented what we were doing with the Voting Rights Institute, other secretaries and their staffs were incredulous that we could bring such diverse groups together for a common purpose. I believe the combination of an open approach taken by our administration, the dire circumstances and reputation Ohio faced since the 2004 Presidential election, and Kellye and her staff's forward-looking and positive outlook combined with an inclusive and proactive approach made it work. Several states duplicated to some degree the VRI and its aims. Unfortunately, my successor disbanded the institute and its advisory council.

Serving on the NASS Elections Committee for four years, I recall a particular conference call among the secretaries of state from around the country who served on this committee. I was very surprised to hear nearly all of the approximately fifteen or more secretaries of state on that call say that they did not consider it their office's job to conduct or promote voter registration. They saw themselves as administrators of elections. All I know is that a component of the Secretary of State's job in Ohio is voter education. We took that seriously, and the VRI was there to help make that serious intention a reality.

The VRI Advisory Council was pivotal to the VRI's success. By 2010, the representative from the Ohio Republican Party had quit the council, but we still maintained Republican membership on the Council. The Council had divided into six standing committees and even more ad hoc committees during our administration. VRI Advisory Council members, citizens and organizational representatives served as unpaid advisors on policy issues, legislation and outreach efforts to bring people more in touch with their government. I personally met and spoke on telephone conferences with the council members on a periodic basis. They often testified in the Ohio legislature for us on bills that could help or hurt Ohioans' voting rights and elections.

In its advisory role, VRI often undertook various research projects in addition to the Pew project on voter registration, adding to our body of knowledge for effective voter engagement. VRI Advisory Council members were offered access to many Secretary of State's office activities, serving in official roles as representatives for voting rights at statewide election summits, and attending and participating in semi-yearly election officials conferences, never before having been recognized or included. They labored with our staff and Ohio's elections officials on required planning for continued federal funding under the Help America Vote Act.

After four years of work, the VRI's advisory council at the end of our administration still consisted of:

Sibley Arnebeck, Citizen Activist Representative
John Burik, C.A.S.E. Ohio
Rick DeChant, Veteran Services & Programs, Cuyahoga
    Community College
Adele Eisner, Citizen Activist Representative
Phil Fry, C.A.S.E. Ohio
Dwight Groce, Social Studies Consultant, Ohio Department
    of Education
Lois B. Harris, Director, The Ohio State University Office for
    Disability Services
Suzanne Helmick, Senior Consultant, Kids Voting Central
    Ohio
Candice Hoke, Esq., Center Director, Center for Election
    Integrity at the Marshall College of Law at the Cleveland
    State University
Leslye Huff, Esq., Voting, Civil and Human Rights
    Activist/Huff Law, LLC

Pete Johnson, R.Ph., C.A.S.E. Ohio

Donita Judge, Esq., Project Director of Redistricting and Staff Attorney, Advancement Project

Renee Klco, CERA, Manager, Precinct Election Officials, Franklin County Board of Elections

Kevin J. Knedler, Chairman, Libertarian Party of Ohio

Greg Moore, Executive Director, NAACP National Voter Fund/Ohio Voter Fund

Jeanette Mullane, President, Ohio Association of Election Officials

Ron Olson, Steering Committee Member, C.A.S.E. Ohio

Douglas J. Preisse, Chair, Franklin County Board of Elections & Chair, Franklin County Republican Party

Norman Robbins, Ph.D., Research Director, Northeast Ohio Voter Advocates

Dora Rose, Esq., General Counsel and Director of Voting Protection, Ohio Democratic Party

Peg Rosenfield, Elections Specialist, Ohio League of Women Voters

Matthew Segal, Executive Director, Student Association for Voter Empowerment (SAVE)

Representative Vernon Sykes, Ph.D., Director, Kent State University Columbus

Petee Talley, Secretary-Treasurer, Ohio AFL-CIO

Jocelyn Travis, Co-Convener, Greater Cleveland Voter Coalition

Stuart Wright, League of Women Voters of Metropolitan Columbus

Considering the diversity of this small group of people led by Kellye Pinkleton, it was no wonder that Kellye's email signature has included the following:

"Never doubt that a small group of thoughtful, committed citizens can change the world; indeed, it's the only thing that ever does."

- Margaret Mead

Even in the tumult and complexity of new technology, social change, population and demographic movement and corporate/citizen battles for which "class warfare" is claimed to be a taboo moniker, the power of such a small group of people known as the Voting Rights Institute's Advisory Council is immeasurable and always will be. ≈

Chapter 19

So Goes Ohio, the Nation

During my tenure as Ohio's Secretary of State, I co-chaired for a year the NASS Elections Committee with none other than the Secretary of State of Florida, Kurt Browning. Kurt was the sixth Florida Secretary of State to follow the famed Katherine Harris, who ended her term in 2002. His term started just five years after her term ended. The less than one-year average term of each Secretary of State who followed Katherine Harris illustrates the tumultuous state of elections administration after the 2000 Presidential election.

As Ohio's Secretary of State, I followed Ken Blackwell, who had served for two four-year terms, and whose actions in 2004 were deemed by many to be the cause of sufficient rancor in Ohio and elsewhere about the fairness of Ohio's and U.S. election practices. The irony was not lost on many that the co-chairs of this core committee of the nation's secretaries of state were from the two least likely states anyone anywhere would entrust with helping to influence election administration policy for the fifty states and other territories of the country. But maybe Kurt, from a Republican administration, and I, an elected Democrat, were just the people to chair the committee, because of our states' battleground statuses.

Ohio and Florida are rich in electoral votes and often "swing" from election to election, reflecting the changing moods of a national electorate. From an election standpoint, their shared fate is high scrutiny. Their fate is also highly publicized for election irregularities and controversy about matters that are otherwise seen as common (and even expected). I suggest that their over-studied and too-often-tinkered-with processes are indicative of the present nature of the tactical, procedural focus of present-day campaigns in tandem with local traditions that have shaped local elections practices over the years. For anyone who has looked at a flawed process and wondered if it was due to nefarious intentions or just plain tragic stupidity, there's usually a combination of both. Suffice it to say that when partisan political operatives try to take over the rules for governing elections processes, a jumbled-up mess is usually the result. Conversely, the ideal election scenario involves inclusiveness in planning, a commitment to fairness above partisan interests and transparency. When that is permitted to occur, the process strengthens voter trust.

I keep a red, white and blue tagboard sign from one of the Democratic National Conventions I have attended that says, "So Goes Ohio, the Nation." Many believe this to be true of their home state or town and have some formulaic explanation for its importance. This I can say, however, about Ohio. No Democratic Presidential candidate has won the presidency without Ohio since Senator John F. Kennedy won the presidency in 1960, and no Republican candidate for President has ever won the presidency without Ohio. Because of Ohio's diversity, it is a battleground state, a swing state and often referred to by veteran campaign politicos as "ground zero."

So it was with the 2008 election. In the 2008 primary election season, as March 5, 2008, the date of Ohio's primary, neared, the number of media interviews per day increased. Nearly one-third of my time was spent prior to the primary giving newspaper, radio, television and Internet interviews. Moving into the 2008 general election season brought requests for interviews at the same rate, and they grew in number, complexity, uniqueness of location and stature of interviewers with each day. Dan Rather, John King, Mary Snow, Carol Costello and John Roberts of CNN, Rachel Maddow of MSNBC and Greta Van Susteren of Fox News

interviewed me. Brazil and Russian television outlets wanted
interviews. I met with the editorial board of the Washington
Post (all women, as opposed to the Columbus newspaper's
generally all male interviews I had experienced). Interviews on
National NPR news and syndicated shows occurred, with
personal visits to my office from the Wall Street Journal and the
New York Times. It was because of Ohio and its role in the 2004
Presidential election, and I suppose because there was a
secretary of state in Ohio who was trying to change Ohio's
reputation and taking some hits in the process.

The Republican-controlled Ohio legislature had discovered that
I knew how to use the directive power of the Secretary of State's
office to implement changes I saw necessary for election
integrity, and they didn't appear to like it. They wanted to add
limitations on that power. What they were suggesting in May of
2008 was agreeable to me—creating temporary and permanent
directives and requiring a period of public comment before
issuing permanent directives. Under the new law I would have
the power to amplify this new law with rules. So I agreed to it.
They could have forced something much worse upon me, but I
believe they knew that to do that could have created more havoc
than accomplishing what they wished—to exert legislative and
political control over my executive decisions.

The new law intended to limit my directive power took effect
September 12, 2008. This deadline was in fact a blessing. It
caused my staff and me to issue all of the directives we really
wanted for the 2008 general election before the new bill took
effect. (Several of them were issued at 11:58 p.m. on September
11, 2008, thanks to the hard work of David Farrell, my very
organized and dedicated Director of Elections and Patricia
Wolfe, the office's long term elections administrator. Pat is a
Republican who was initially hired by Bob Taft in the 1990's.

Both Ken Blackwell and I retained her. She stayed on in Jon Husted's administration as well.

While we were working to beat the political clock that was meant to slow down or stop the rate of change coming from Columbus, the state's 88 county boards of elections were receiving clear guidance from the early issuance of these directives so they could better prepare for and anticipate changes or enhancements they would need to their policies and procedures for administering elections in their counties.

It was routine for me to personally review directives. Most often I reviewed them electronically, redlining the changes I wanted to see and inserting comments and questions. David Farrell, working with legal staff, had developed a drafting and review protocol so that I was the last person to make comments on the directive or advisory to the boards of elections, and I could see who had drafted it and reviewed it before me.

My executive staff kept a running list of work for me and provided it to me by email daily. As I traveled the state, I used mobile wi-fi to keep up with these tasks. Senior staff learned early on that, even though they had ready access to my schedule, time in the car was not time for one of them to call me; I was working. If they did call, I knew it was important. Once I reviewed a directive, it was returned to the office's general counsel, to David Farrell and to the original drafter for any further comments about the changes I had asked for. Often, there were comments back, and the more skilled the elections attorneys became, the more I acquiesced to their comments to my comments. Our goal was to issue the directive once and not have to clarify, modify or change a directive. When a modification was needed, which was rare, it resulted in grumbling from the state's 88 boards of elections and contributed to uncertainty about what we were asking.

Restoring trust to Ohio elections began with earning the trust of the state's 88 county boards of elections members and staff.

Once the vast majority of directives were issued before September 12, 2008, I began traveling to boards of elections around the state to discuss with them how they would implement the directives for the 2008 Presidential general election. In a few instances, I learned of some problems the directives caused. As a result, we made modifications or permitted waivers to be issued. It was satisfying for both board staff and secretary of state staff, including me, to see this give and take to better prepare for November 2008.

Directives for the 2008 Presidential election ranged from continuing the earlier directives for backup paper ballots for counties using electronic touchscreen voting systems, to rules for observers at polling places and counting stations, to the submission of plans for polling place arrangement for two lines in touchscreen counties, one for paper ballots and one for machines, to strict rules on challenging voters before election day and on the basis of foreclosure records, to forbidding the taking home of voting machines by poll workers, to requiring bipartisan teams to transport ballots to boards of elections from the polling places, to rules on the counting of "double bubble" votes on optical scan ballots and conducting post-election audits. The number of directives issued grew past 100 in 2008. This became a cause for the Ohio GOP to issue a press release criticizing the Ohio Secretary of State for issuing too many directives.

As I saw it, the directive power of the Secretary of State was like the mortar on a walkway of uneven stones. We wanted a smooth pathway for voters. The directives at least smoothed the spaces between the uneven rocks legislated in place by a one-sided legislature that lacked "big picture" understanding of the nuances of election administration causes and effects and that appeared intent on tilting the playing field in its party's favor. In my book, it doesn't matter which side you're on, a win isn't real if you have to tilt the playing field to get it. The only tilt I ever wanted was toward making sure it was easy enough for voters to step onto the field and play. That's what democracy thrives on— participation.

One election official challenged me by an email that was simultaneously copied to all 88 county boards of elections to clarify how we would deal with the fact that absentee voting began before the close of voter registration. This meant (and still does) that Ohio has a five to seven-day period where the equivalent of "election day registration" for early voting takes place. It's been in the law since at least 1981. However, when the Republican-controlled legislature expanded absentee voting in 2005 to anyone who wanted it and without reason (apparently to incentivize votes against a statewide ballot issue in 2005 that would have done the same thing), it created a Frankenstein whose life force it had not anticipated, especially in the wake of an Obama campaign that was perfecting grassroots organizing. Once again, the Republican dominated legislature created that which it did not intend—a perfect mechanism for registering more voters and providing them with absentee voting tools and opportunities.

In my first campaign in 2000, the conventional wisdom was that absentee voters were predominantly Republican and therefore were not a good indicator of overall outcome, especially in a city. Today, the grassroots organizing efforts that became the norm for Democrats beginning in 2008 have resulted in heavy early voting by Democrats. That makes it no surprise that in 2011, the Republican-controlled Ohio legislature passed a law that forbade boards of elections from mailing out absentee ballot applications unsolicited en masse. This has been a practice of larger counties like Cuyahoga County since 2006, It has resulted in significant relief of congestion at polling places there, endemic in the 2004 Presidential election.

This election official who challenged me on the early voting and registration overlap was the same one who made sure I could see in his board office when I visited that he had placed rubber, fake poop on a memorandum on his desk from one of the elections attorneys in my office. I acted like I hadn't noticed this juvenile demonstration of apparent dissatisfaction with what was in the letter.

Once this elections official challenged me "publicly" among the state's election officials, I did not back away. Rather, I issued a strong directive that required boards of elections to comply with this law. The directive specified that they had to do so in such a way that any attempts at voter fraud would be detected and stopped. No voters who registered and voted on the same day during this early voting window were permitted to vote on electronic voting machines. They had to vote paper, optical scan ballots so that the boards of elections could verify their eligibility to vote before their ballots were opened, processed or counted. All other previously registered voters were permitted to vote electronically during the early voting period.

This challenge and my response were the beginning of the "voter fraud" allegations in Ohio during the 2008 Presidential general election. This was the precursor to marathon and cumulative litigation in state and federal court that confirmed Ohio's battleground status in Presidential elections. The most serious challenge emanated from the eventual state elections director Matt Damschroder, who is said to have brought to the attention of Republican operatives that the HAVA-mandated statewide voter registration database contained "mismatches" with the state Bureau of Motor Vehicles database. Federal law does not require disqualification of voters whose records show a "mismatch" as compared with other government database information Rather, local boards of elections are simply required to make efforts to resolve discrepancies and clarify information to ensure maximum accuracy of voting rolls.

A list of voters is about as static as people's lives. A voter list on any given day is simply a snapshot. Added to that dimension is the fact that Ohio's voter database was compiled from the "ground up," giving the benefit of the doubt to local elections officials, since they are "in the trenches" with voters. At the time this provision of HAVA for an up-to-date statewide voter database was developed, local elections officials were in the best position to easily access new information about a voter (name and address changes, for example) and to resolve any discrepancies. The database had been consultant-created and was inherited from Ken Blackwell (who had contracts in place where literally one consultant's job was to manage other consultants' work). It was designed so that "mismatches" were flagged for voter registrations for more reasons than were required by federal law. Moreover, the system did not provide for a safety valve for data entry errors at the local level that did not exactly match what was in driver and Social Security records.

The Ohio GOP made a public records request for a list of all "mismatched" Ohio voters. The Columbus Dispatch newspaper followed with a similar public records request. The system was not configured to produce lists of mismatches. It had been designed only to show discrepancies upon the entry of a voter's name when a match could not be produced with the other state and federal databases. I asked my staff to try to produce a list of all "mismatches" in response to the public records request. My IT staff was frank with me and told me that to modify programming at what was then less than a month before the election would damage the system and affect the ability of boards of elections to produce accurate voter lists.

The Ohio GOP filed suit against me in federal court. It happened that the assigned judge, Columbus federal Judge George C. Smith, reached his decision against me the day I had reluctantly agreed to be interviewed remotely via satellite by Greta Van Susteran of Fox News. My media staff had advised me not to take the interview. "Palestra," a "youth" television crew powered by Fox News had shown up at my office on a day when I was traveling in the state and demanded an interview. Their report was that I had refused to meet with them when I was not even in the office in Columbus. My staff did not think we would be treated fairly in any interview with national Fox news. I believed in Greta van Susteran, that her instincts as an attorney and for fairness would prevail. I was wrong.

Van Susteran's interview was hostile, and I couldn't have looked worse in that interview, with makeup overdone by a makeup artist at the recording studio. Filming occurred before a one-foot square black-screened camera with ultra bright lights and a satellite feed through a plug in my ear. The bright lights have a tendency to make the interviewee look either drunk or sleep-deprived with slightly closed eyes because of their brightness. Seasoned interviewees learn to ignore the lights and keep their eyes open wide enough. By the evening broadcast, choice portions of Judge Smith's federal decision were woven into the interview, making my answers to questions look like poor excuses for losing the lawsuit. Words above my image said essentially, "Federal court finds Ohio Secretary of State violated Ohio election law." Rick has never heard me groan so loudly watching a television interview of myself as I did that night.

Despite the van Susteran portrayal, we went on to win the appeal of Judge Smith's decision. But the Ohio GOP asked for a decision from the entire court, *en banc,* and we lost again. I was to speak on a panel at the National Press Club in Washington, DC the next day, on October 15, 2008. The evening before, when the Sixth Circuit Court of Appeals, *en banc,* rendered the decision, I talked with Rich Coglianese, the capable assistant attorney general assigned to provide counsel to the Ohio Secretary of State. Rick and I were at dinner at the Rusty Bucket at the bottom of the "hill" in the suburb where we lived, Worthington Hills. The decision just didn't ring right, and it was really bugging me. Rick and I talked about theories for appeal and agreed there were avenues. With Rick's encouragement, I called Rich Coglianese right from the dinner table to explore an appeal.

Rich was skeptical and informed me that we had at best a 40% chance of prevailing in the U.S. Supreme Court. I sighed and gave up. That night, sitting in my den, Kent Marcus, Governor Strickland's chief legal counsel called me asking why we didn't appeal the decision of the circuit court.

"Rich said we had a 40% chance at best," I said into my cell phone. Kent and I talked further about it, and he, like me, agreed it was worth a try to appeal the *en banc* decision. "Here," I said, "Do you want his number? Maybe you can convince him. Go ahead and call him, yourself. I have to be on a plane at 6:30 in the morning to go to DC. I need to get to bed."

That was the last I heard from Kent, and I didn't think much more of it. My new scheduler flew me to Dulles instead of Reagan, leaving us with a 40-minute town car ride to my hotel, the Phoenix Park Hotel. When we arrived at the hotel, it was still morning, and luckily, the hotel had a room available for me. I crashed for a nap with little sleep from the night before.

Of course, there's a reason there's a term called "bed head." That's what I had before I had to go to the National Press Club and be filmed on a panel on C-Span. I'd learned the tricks of turning your hair upside down, brushing it, spraying it and letting it dry before you stand upright, so that when you do, you could be a very scary witch in a Walt Disney princess cartoon movie. Then you gently brush it down, style it, spray it, don't move and look like, well, maybe a fashionable member of the 1980's band, Devo, but at least you're presentable. That's what I did to get ready for the National Press Club.

NYT photo from the National Press Club, October 2008

A reporter from the New York Times, Ian Urbina, covered the Midwest for the Times and was a frequent caller about Ohio election issues. I was on my cell phone with him as I was walking into the press club and finally had to exit the conversation to be ready to discuss election issues with Gracia Hillman, one of the commissioners of the U.S. Election Assistance Commission, South Dakota's Republican then Secretary of State, Chris Nelson, and a statistician for AP who was an expert at determining voting trends to be able to "call" a state for a Presidential candidate even upon early and minimal voting returns. I held my own in the discussion.

A photographer from the Times attended the Press Club event and shot a pose of me that caught the distinctive "Devo" hairdo as particularly curled and set. While some said it was a great picture, I knew I was wearing an adaptation of "bedhead" gone Devo. Such was my life at the time.

Later that evening, I was at the National Democratic Club for dinner and was sitting with some folks from DC when my cell phone rang. It was again Ian Urbina from the New York Times.

"Brunner," he said, "are you holding out on me?"

"What?" I said, "What are you talking about?"

"I heard you were going to SCOTUS," he said. Being a lawyer, I immediately knew he meant, the Supreme Court of the United States.

"Not that I know of," I said in all earnestness. "I didn't think we could win. But wait, maybe we did and they didn't tell me. I wanted to. Lemme call you back," I said and hung up quickly.

I called Rich Coglianese. "Rich," I said when he answered immediately, "did we go to the Supreme Court?"

"Didn't anyone tell you?" he said. "Oh, boy, I'm sorry. I thought Eleanor told you."

"No, no one told me," I said, feeling a tinge of anger. I kept a cool head, because logic told me the result was what mattered. I copped a cheerful attitude and said, "Well, that's what I wanted to do, so that's great." Obviously, the Governor's office had convinced the Attorney General to file the suit, but they forgot to tell me.

I called Eleanor, my general counsel, who apologized profusely, and who confirmed that we had, in fact, gone to SCOTUS. Rich had told me that they had to get the petition filed before 8:30 p.m., because the justice assigned to the matters retired early each night. We needed to get it to him before him before he went to bed. I had to laugh at that one thinking of Eleanor and I doing our "handoff" of the executive summary of the EVEREST Report. I called Ian back and told him what I knew.

At that moment, Jayme Staley, who was with me said, "We need to get you out of here."

"Why?" I said. "No one knows me in here."

She motioned with her head toward the large television screen in the Democratic National Club. I looked in time to see footage of me on CNN's Lou Dobbs show. According to Jayme, people were starting to stare. Just then my brother called. He was living in South Carolina but in Boston for business.

"Jen," he said. "Are you doing alright? I'm watching you on Lou Dobbs." It really was thoughtful of him to call, but it was the final indication I needed to get out of the Democratic National Club. Jayme and I exited and returned to the Phoenix Park Hotel for the night.

Two days later the U.S. Supreme Court in a unanimous decision handed down a victory to the Ohio Secretary of State and her crew that the Ohio GOP didn't have standing to bring their lawsuit. Eleanor brought the news to me and threw her arms around me, practically jumping up and down at the same time. It was one of the most exciting moments for the lawyers in our office and the 2008 Ohio Attorney General's office under the graceful direction of General Nancy Rogers, who had been appointed by Governor Strickland to replace General Dann until the election of a new attorney general in the fall election.

General Rogers and I had held a meeting August 15, 2008 for all the political party and Presidential candidate attorneys from local, to state to national, to introduce them to the attorneys involved in election law issues from my office and the attorney general's office. As described in the Ohio Secretary of State General Election 2008 Report, it was:

> "... the first ever legal forum in Ohio aimed at avoiding unnecessary and disruptive litigation prior to the Presidential election. Representatives of Presidential candidates, political parties and the Ohio General Assembly as well as election law practitioners attended the forum. The forum provided attendees with information regarding the Secretary's preparations for the election, including a master list of directives and advisories in effect, and information to enable and encourage efficient and preventive communication prior to the filing of any litigation."

We gave the attorneys attending direct line telephone numbers and email addresses for those attorneys who would be handling matters for the upcoming general election. We exhorted the attorneys to call them with questions, issues and things that would ordinarily land in court but could be discussed, mediated and resolved without litigation. It was not that we didn't want the extra work, it was that we wanted the election to proceed as smoothly as possible, especially without interference with boards' activities. Senator John McCain's lead counsel was Trevor Potter of Caplin and Drysdale and Senator Barack Obama's lead counsel was Bob Bauer of Perkins Coie. They participated by telephone.

We had hoped this unusual and unprecedented "peacepipe" meeting would lessen the legal battles that inevitably lay ahead in Ohio, a key battleground state. Eleanor and I tried to venture guesses on how many lawsuits would be filed during the general election season in 2008. I projected 8 lawsuits. As it turned out there were fifteen, with several of them being new actions that revived dormant, leftover Blackwell actions that were not yet resolved. Appending a claim to an existing lawsuit usually guarantees that the lawyers filing it know which judge will get it, and in my case, Judge Algenon Marbley had pending an opportune lawsuit involving the Ohio Secretary of State that provided a sturdy platform for civil rights litigants seeking redress of their claims.

It was clear the Obama campaign was watching and analyzing the directives issued. Sometimes within an hour of them being uploaded to the website, we would receive a call from Kent Markus on behalf of the Obama campaign, questioning the finer points of a directive, asking what we meant, did we think of this, why did we say or do that. It was clear to me that the stakes were so high for both sides that my job as Secretary of State was like getting precious cargo through a wicked sword fight. Even though I may have been on the political team of one side, it was clear that, had my own side believed my actions were wrong on the law, they would not have hesitated to whack away at me as the Republicans felt free to. The lawsuits, like those in the primary election, came from both sides, despite our best efforts to promote dialog and cooperation.

On June 10, 2008, the Ohio legislature had adopted a capital appropriations bill and of its own volition appropriated to the Secretary of State $3 million dollars for mailing absentee ballot applications to all Ohio voters. The funding was also supposed to cover return postage on the applications. The only problem was that the $3 million dollar sum was not enough money to get the job done in a state of 8 million registered voters. The Republican-controlled General Assembly never conferred with my office on how much would be needed.

During one of our office's weekly legal and legislative meetings after the appropriation had been made, elections attorney Brian Green addressed the matter on the week's agenda. "Secretary, we've looked at this, and our best recommendation to you is that you simply divide up the money appropriated and give it to the boards of elections and tell them there's not enough to pay for everything they're required to do here," he said.

We all agreed that the language of the amendment was not mandatory for the boards of elections—it was mandatory for me to tell them how to spend it. The attorneys who worked on the issue knew that anything other than what it appeared the legislature had intended would likely result in significant controversy. I understood that, but I saw that simply splitting up the money and sending it to the boards could create uncertainty and even greater controversy. Any semblance of uniformity in application would likely dissipate, still leaving open the question of whether or not undertaking the mailing and paying for the postage was mandatory.

In the past, especially during the six months before his 2006 gubernatorial election, Ken Blackwell likely would have ducked the issue of whether it was mandatory and, if so, what to do about the underfunded mandate. The closer it was to the general election in 2006, the more he told boards to ask their local prosecutors about legal interpretation of the election laws. It resulted in varying degrees of opinion throughout the state and created disparate implementations of the law. I saw this particular situation to be a legislatively created morass at best. It could have been avoided with some good, old-fashioned bipartisan discussion. Our office could have informed the legislative leaders that $3 million dollars was not enough, and either more money could have been appropriated, or the intended activities could have been modified to fit the budget.

Faced with these after-the-fact revelations, it made sense to me to level with the boards from the outset, interpret the language as permissive and set out a fair method of reimbursement. I made sure boards understood that their chances of full reimbursement diminished as more counties opted to participate. For those boards whose funding from the county commissioners for any such cost overage was doubtful, opting out was permitted. Other boards that were willing to take their chances could opt in. In light of insufficient funding, this was the honest and responsible approach to take with the boards, and it was important to let them know as soon as we could what the situation was. They were making plans for the largest turnout election in a four-year cycle. (Any new board director or deputy director felt they had been "initiated" when they had completed the administration of a Presidential election.)

On July 18, 2008, we issued a directive explaining to boards of elections the import of the new state appropriation:

"... the capital bill appropriated $3 million in state funding to pay for some aspects of the absentee voting process in Ohio.

* * *

The capital bill required the Secretary of State to establish, in advance of September 5, 2008, the method by which the $3 million appropriation will be made available to the boards. This directive establishes that method.

All counties are eligible to receive a portion of the appropriated $3 million. It should be noted, however, that the $3 million appropriation is insufficient to compensate county boards of elections for the mailing of a notice to every registered elector of the state (currently 7.953 million registered electors), and it is insufficient to compensate county boards of elections for this expense and the additional expense of paying electors' return postage on absentee ballot applications. Therefore, this directive attempts to equitably apportion reimbursement as is contemplated by this law.

* * *

Each county board of elections is therefore eligible for a minimum amount of money in proportion to the number of registered voters in the county on August 6, 2008, compared to the total number of registered voters statewide on that date. For example, a county whose registered electors comprise 10% of the total registered electors in Ohio on August 6, 2008, is eligible to receive 10% of the $3 million appropriation, or $300,000.

* * *

Priority of Use of Funds

The Secretary of State's office was not contacted about this appropriation or its enabling language by whoever initiated it and we remain uncertain of the amendment's origins. It is unfortunate for boards of elections that our office was not provided the opportunity to offer suggestions or comments that may have improved the implementation of this law and resulted in a realistic appropriation to support the intended use of the funds.

Regardless of these circumstances, our office believes it incumbent on the state's elections officials to place the interests of the voters above administrative concerns of election officials, and therefore, because of the shortfall in state moneys to fully fund this new mandate, our office has prioritized the uses of the funds.

* * *

Participation is not Mandatory

The capital bill does not mandate that all boards of elections send an absent voter's ballot application to each voter. Rather, the capital bill simply instructs that if boards of elections do so, in conjunction with the notices of election sent pursuant to R.C. 3501.19, some or all of the postage to do so may be paid for using money appropriated in the capital bill."

It was this last section of the directive, that the mailing of the absentee ballot applications was permissive and not mandatory, that caused a strong reaction from the leaders of the Ohio General Assembly. They did not discover that, however, until a point close in time to the September 5, 2008, mailing date for the applications.

In early September 2008, I had received a telephone call from then Speaker Jon Husted about his concerns. He was clearly agitated. Finally, he asked me to level with him. In the world of partisan wrangling, a question like that from someone of the other party means that the guards must come down and the two office holders speak as statespersons and public servants. They share a common bond of public service; although, they each face different political pressures. In the world of decent bipartisan relations, the two sides realize the particular political pressures each faces and consider it in reaching a mutually acceptable solution. In difficult situations, such a question can bring a sense of relief, because potentially more can be accomplished working together. It is unspoken that what is said in such discussions is not the subject of public accusations or press releases. I had learned this from many years of working in state and county government, especially in legislative dealings.

The Speaker wanted to know if I thought there could be equal protection problems if some people received absentee ballot applications in the mail in some parts of the state and not others. A court had not yet addressed the question. I was concerned, though. I hesitated, and trusting that this was one of those "candid" conversations, I said with honesty, "yes." In that conversation I also pitched for more money for the boards if he and Senate President Bill Harris wanted the bill's provisions to be able to be carried out.

It became clear that the Speaker of the House and the President of the Senate had intended for the amendment in the state's capital budget to be mandatory for boards of elections. But, as drafted, it was not. After I gave the Speaker my assessment, the conversation ended quickly. Later that day, he drafted a letter to me and released it to the media, quoting me on the admission that there could be equal protection problems with some boards sending out applications for absentee voting and other boards not. But he had provided no solution, except that I do the impossible task that the legislature had attempted to mandate. I lost trust from that point forward, and communication

Rick and me in front of Mile High Stadium in Denver in 2008 prior to Barack Obama's acceptance speech

was not the same again until I worked with him on his transition to the office at the end of my term.

The controversy didn't end there. As I was flying to Denver, Colorado for the Democratic National Convention where I was serving as a delegate by virtue of holding statewide office, Speaker Husted and Senate President Bill Harris sent a letter to the state's 88 county boards of elections. In the letter they essentially told the boards not to follow the directive, that they were required to do the mailings. In my years of working in and around the state legislature and the Secretary of State's office, I had never seen this type of activity take place. One branch of the government was attempting to act in the stead of another. Not surprisingly, the boards of elections started calling the Secretary of State's office to ask what they were supposed to do. Time was critical for election planning.

I learned of this action after I arrived in Denver, close to the end of the day in the Eastern Time Zone, but still during the afternoon in Denver. Rick and I went to the convention for the proceedings that evening. A cell phone lay on the seat beside me in the arena. I checked the contacts in the phone and determined it was Ohio election attorney Don McTigue's cell phone. I called his home to let his wife know that I had his phone. When he found me to retrieve it, I told him about the troubling letter to the boards of elections from the two highest legislative leaders in the state and the confusion it had already caused. He said quickly, "You know, there's a statute, a criminal statute, that forbids anyone from interfering with the conduct of an election."

It's been said that one person's "junk" is another person's "treasure." In this case, his misfortune gave me the good fortune to hear his thoughts on the problems before me. He gave me some insightful advice, and I agreed it was a good approach.

After the evening's proceedings, I sat up late at night in my hotel room, researching and crafting a letter to the two state legislative leaders, citing the section of the law Don had mentioned. I did not mention in my letter that interfering with the conduct of an election could subject persons to criminal penalties. I figured their attorneys could figure that out for them. My staff reviewed the letter and seemed somewhat apprehensive about sending it. They often were about some of the things I wanted to do. But I persisted.

The letter worked, and the legislative leaders backed off. Several weeks later, I saw Matt Shuler, then chief of staff for the Senate. He had always been one I could trust for a straight answer, and we worked well together, even though we are of different parties. He shook my hand firmly and said with a laugh, "Boy, you really know how to use brass knuckles." I knew what he meant, smiled and said, "I've learned from playing tennis that if someone hits the ball hard at you, just position your racket and hold on firmly. It will go back at them just as fast as they hit it to you." We both laughed. I figured they had seen the criminal penalties. Nothing more needed to be done.

As circumstances would have it, the larger, urban counties that usually experienced long lines took their chances and mailed absentee ballot applications to their voters. The smaller, rural counties decided not to. One of the explanations given by Patty Johns, director of the mostly rural Wayne County Board of Elections, was that so many political organizations and parties mailed absentee ballot applications in her county (a largely Republican County) that a similar mailing from the board could be a source of confusion for voters and simply duplicative.

In the end, the counties that mailed the applications were reimbursed at 100% of their expenditures. Not all of the money was used. The remaining nearly half million dollars was used in

2009 to settle one of the largest lawsuits left to me by Ken Blackwell. The suit had been brought by the League of Women Voters and others to correct thirty years worth of election problems in Ohio. We used the fact that we had the funds as a "carrot" to bring ongoing settlement discussions to closure, pointing out that we would lose these funds for settlement if they lapsed at the end of June 2009.

A key element that helped bring settlement discussions to a close was our agreement to a six-year consent decree that would bind the Secretary of State to implementing certain election procedures for the next six years. Examples included requiring election preparedness plans from each county board of elections, continued use of backup paper ballots and uniform poll worker training. This also involved continued use of the "flip chart" instruction booklets (which the judge was impressed with) that we had developed for poll worker use on Election Day. These flip charts were often used before Election Day for poll worker training by many of the less populous counties. Because it was a consent decree, if the Secretary failed to follow the terms of settlement, the court retained jurisdiction to order compliance.

Richard Cordray's policy staff had at first refused to let my attorneys and me agree to a six-year consent decree. His staff said that no consent decree should extend beyond my term of office, a year and a half. I knew that other state agencies had signed lengthy consent decrees, such as the Department of Youth Services regarding living conditions for juvenile prisoners. At the time I was running for the U.S. Senate and would not be holding a second term. I remembered the advice of David Royer of the Franklin County ADAMH board, that the best test of success is what happens to your program when you're gone, I also believed that unelected staff in the Ohio Attorney General's office did not have the right to decide questions of discretion that lay with the Secretary of State by virtue of having been elected.

I had been the person to suggest six years. I remembered my staff attorneys' reactions when I suggested it. They were shocked. Previously, I had been vehemently opposed to a consent decree for any appreciable length of time. I did not want to be bound by a consent decree, and most office holders would not. I realized, however, that it would help the state's election officials have consistency of instruction and procedures for the next two statewide and the next presidential elections. I also understood that six years was enough time for these newly developed "best" practices to become standard procedure.

Since I had taken office in 2007 I had observed a high turnover of local election officials as new technology was required by HAVA. A significant number of the "old guard" of election officials were leaving or retiring. (Many members of this "old guard" were also quite vocal in opposition to the new election technology and the changes it necessitated.) As new election officials were trained, they would not question these changes. Instead they would learn how to do the work needed, thinking this is how it had been done for years. They had no other point of reference. I had learned this lesson observing the judges on my court as the TIES Program was implemented. New judges accepted the drug court with little question, as if it had always been there. So, I fought for the six-year decree.

I called Rich personally and exhorted, cajoled and even used guilt to convince him that we needed six years. I reminded him of our earlier days of campaigning together. I should not have had to do this and told him so. Within a day or two, he called me and said he had instructed his staff to let us agree to six years.

As we neared final agreement on the six-year settlement decree, the state budget was tanking. Governor Strickland was looking for every source of funding that was not tied down to balance the budget at the end of the year. His staff spied our leftover funds from the 2008 absentee ballot appropriation and tried to take it. Antoinette Wilson fought hard to keep it and succeeded. I was prepared to take this one to the mat. I was separately elected; the funds had not been appropriated to the Governor but to the Secretary of State. Fortunately, I did not have to personally "get into it" with the Governor or his chief of staff.

We reached the settlement with the League before the end of the fiscal year. The leftover absentee ballot funds from 2008 that I had never asked for were used to cement practices that improved Ohio elections. Ironically, the six-year consent decree now binds Secretary of State Husted and his state election director, Matt Damschroder, to continue administering these reforms, including using backup paper ballots.

In 2008, as we moved closer to Election Day, the issue of "voter fraud" was a steady drumbeat of the Ohio GOP. Press release after press release was issued by the state Republican party to the national media. This fueled something akin to a media-fed hysteria that not only broke loose in Ohio, but it reverberated around the country. "Voter fraud" was the perfect foil for lawsuits and other protests, especially in battleground states like Ohio and Wisconsin. Around the country, the GOP challenged everything from early voting laws and practices to "mismatches" in the federally required statewide voter databases of states.

My staff at every level had begun to endure hate telephone calls and hate letters and emails. Concerned for their safety Ohio State Highway Patrol guards were posted in the lobby of our high rise building. Even our computer servers had to be shut down for at least a day when it was discovered they had been hacked. Because of our strong working relationship with MicroSolved, security experts used in the EVEREST voting systems study, we were able to deal with the problem quickly and effectively, though at a cost of nearly $50,000.

Finally, the national media frenzy, fueled by voter fraud claims and twenty-four hour news, and especially ramped up by Fox News, reached a point that death threats against my family and me were called into my state office. Finally, I received a letter at my home from Jackson, Mississippi, from a man who railed against my work as Secretary of State. My home address and telephone number were unlisted.

It was at this point that the Governor assigned members of the Ohio State Highway Patrol to guard Rick's and my home twenty-four hours a day and to escort me in an unmarked car with plain-clothes security detail officers wherever I went. One would travel with me, while the other traveled in a separate car ahead of the other office and me. It was quite a production to get me anywhere now. It also was the last time for seven weeks that I would go anywhere alone or travel in any other vehicle other than a patrol vehicle, except when I broke protocol to take my son, John, to the hospital for pleurisy in the middle of the night. I told the trooper in the marked car at my home that I was leaving to take care of my son. He was not happy. I called one of my plain clothes officers who said to keep him informed. I was shocked when I sent a text message to him at 4:00 a.m. that all was okay and received an immediate response. He must have kept his Blackberry phone by his pillow.

As timing would have it, our home in Worthington Hills was for sale, since Rick and I were building a condominium unit downtown. The housing marking was failing, and we kept chasing lowered property values with our own cuts in the sale price of our home. On the final day of our six-month contract with our realtor we went into contract for the sale of the house. The next day a patrol car was in my driveway for our protection. That protection and surveillance continued even through the move to our downtown condo. I can't imagine how difficult it would have been to sell the home with a patrol car sitting in the driveway. We missed that by just one day.

Barely visible, but always there, one of the members of my security detail stands behind Patrick Gallaway behind the podium on election night 2008

Suffice it to say, it's quite an experience to hand out Halloween candy and have parents of little ones comment on how nice it is to have "the police" in the driveway, or to grocery shop with two men in trench coats walking behind, or to have them in accompaniment to the doctor, a dinner with children at a restaurant or furniture and appliance shopping for a new home. The members of the Ohio State Highway Patrol could not have been more professional, kinder, more conscientious or dedicated. Rick and I will always have respect for this institution and its officers. The plain clothes officer who kept his Blackberry by his pillow had informed me one Saturday morning before the Ohio State-Michigan game (to which he was escorting Rick and me) that he had popped the question to his girlfriend. He asked me to officiate his wedding ceremony, which I was honored to do six months later. I have often seen him accompanying Governor Kasich since he took office.

The officers of the Ohio State Highway Patrol protected my family and me from October 22, 2008 until the day I certified the results of the election on December 15, 2008. They worked with the Columbus Police for frequent patrols past my children's homes in Columbus. They had accompanied Rick and me to multiple Columbus Crew soccer games, including the Major League Soccer semi-finals at Crew Stadium, experienced Whole Foods concept grocery store with us, traveled the state from north to south, participated in pre-purchase walk-throughs at our new condominium, accompanied Rick and me to two closings within two days, attended parties and receptions with us and met all of our children. I began to learn about their families and even met some of their children. I consider myself blessed despite the unfortunate circumstances that brought us together. Most people do not consider how personal lives must be compromised to ensure the safety of those who lead in service. I had not until then. I have new found respect for the sacrifices of these leaders and for those who protect them. Governor Strickland and I discussed this after the election. We agreed that it certainly takes some adjustment to live that way.

One of my four detail officers who worked various shifts to be with me for sometimes sixteen-hour days actually apprehended one of the people who had made threats against my family and me. This caller had used his cell phone. Allison Marshall in my office had quickly copied down the number from the office phone's caller ID function. The caller was incarcerated on a $1 million dollar bond by a municipal judge. However, his situation involved decompensation from his treatment for mental illness after his mother had died recently. At the Columbus Dispatch Christmas party I talked with Franklin County Prosecuting Attorney Ron O'Brien who informed me as a "crime victim" that the defendant was dealing with mental illness, which had been clear to me from the description of him at the time of his apprehension. Ron asked if I would be satisfied if the felony were reduced to misdemeanor telephone harassment. I assented on the condition that the young man complete Judge van der Karr's mental health court docket that I had been involved in helping him start as I started operating the felony drug court docket. Ron agreed.

By Election Day 2008, I believed the State of Ohio was ready to run a smooth election. Most of that day I felt like a caged lion. I was expecting a crisis, but none occurred. During the morning, still nervous for what the day could hold, I received a call from James Hardy, my field representative from Akron. James is an amazing young man. In his early twenties, he was elected to the Akron School Board and later became its president. While serving on the board, he had the chance to intern for former President Bill Clinton at his foundation in New York. James took the opportunity and during his internship commuted from New York City to Akron to be available for school board meetings each week. His political acumen was extremely on target, and he was a good face to the public in that part of the state for me. So, when he called me Election Day morning to say that representatives of the Ohio Democratic Party were trying to distribute literature to people waiting in line to vote, I knew this needed immediate attention.

Ohio law requires people campaigning outside a polling place to remain at least ten feet from people waiting in line to vote. Ohio Democratic Party representatives were approaching voters waiting in line as the polling place opened and handing out copies of the ballot language for statewide ballot issues (there were four of them). Apparently these reps thought that people would take less time to vote if they were familiar with the lengthy ballot issues ahead of time, and long lines would be alleviated. The campaign workers undertaking this questionable leafleting were wearing large ID information packets around their necks. When James advised that they were in violation of the law, one of them told James he had no business telling them that they could not do this. She then said to him that she knew me and that she would call me and have him fired. I have no idea who it was, but firing James was the last thing I would have done.

I called ODP's voter protection coordinator, Dora Rose, whom I had first met with Candice Hoke, who operated the Center for Election Integrity at Cleveland State University Marshall College of Law. I told Dora that these folks in Akron needed to cease and desist. She began arguing with me, saying that what they were doing was legal. Eleanor sat across from me as I made the call from my desk. I was incredulous that after all the preparation, blood, sweat and tears my staff and the boards and I had put into making this a successfully administered election, my own party, after all of the battles fought, would work in such a counterproductive way. Such internal rage as I had no idea could exist, welled up in me like a volcano exploding into the sky. I felt like the little girl in the Exorcist movie whose head spun around. Out of my mouth, spewed, "Dora, don't f*%# with my election." I looked at Eleanor sitting across from me whose face showed a combination of being stunned, amused, and not knowing quite what to say. Poor Dora was unnerved. It was not one of my banner moments.

Next I called Chris Redfern and told him that I could not believe that my own party was working against me to screw up this election. I was less than eloquent or tactful, and a few more expletives came from my mouth. He called me out on that; I apologized, regrouped and said that I needed him to call off these workers. He did. I had expected shenanigans from the Ohio GOP, but not this kind of difficulty from some in my own party looking for what I characterized as a reason to be relevant.

Later in the day, I talked with Jane Platten about how things were going in Cuyahoga County. She told me that she had heard that attorney John Climaco was considering filing an Election Day lawsuit. She did not know why.

I called John Climaco. Apparently, he was representing the Obama campaign in the area, and there was concern about ballot availability in several precincts in Cuyahoga County. He said he needed to talk with Jane Platten but had not been able to reach her. I gave him her cell number and later, after 6:30 p.m. received a voicemail from him that there was no need to go to court. That was as close and harrowing as it became on that Election Day when, ultimately, more people would vote in that election than had voted in any other election in Ohio history. Amazingly, at this election more people voted for President Obama than had voted for any other Presidential candidate in the history of Ohio.

I sat in my office as the hands on my desk clock snuck silently past 7:30. It was 7:32. Shocked, I clenched my fists, went into Antoinette's adjoining office and said, "We did it! We did it!" We had made it through an Election Day in Ohio where there were no long lines, no extended hours at polling locations, not even significant calls with questions or problems that day. Blissfully, Ohio's election was boring.

Patrick Gallaway, with the help of Jeff Ortega, Kevin Kidder, and Luisa Barone, had briefings planned for 8:30 and 10:30 p.m. so that I could address the media with updates on the election returns. There was so much media interest in Ohio's Presidential election (even Al Jazeera was there), we had to rent space in the large Statehouse atrium and set up two levels of tables for reporters. There was a podium at the front of the room on a dais and a large seal of the Secretary of State of Ohio behind the podium.

Media setup election night November 2008 in the Ohio Statehouse Atrium.

My "heat" as State Senator Eric Kearney had once called my security detail, was with me.

At the 8:30 briefing, all reporters were there. We could report no problems, and it was a matter of waiting for the results to come in. Mary Snow of CNN sought out Patrick and apologized, saying that she and her team were heading to Chicago, because there was nothing going on in Ohio. She had spent at least the two previous weeks in Ohio, reporting from various areas throughout the state.

Problems had been anticipated in Ohio. They never materialized. Soon after the 8:30 briefing, one after another of the networks began calling Senator Barack Obama the winner of the Ohio Presidential election. Later, I heard from someone who had been standing in Grant Park in Chicago near Oprah Winfrey that, when she heard the Ohio results, she began to cry.

Antoinette Wilson (right) and me November 4, 2008, at the Ohio Statehouse after Ohio's Presidential results were called by the national television networks before 9:00 p.m.; Jayme Staley took the photo and gave a copy to each of us

We had done it. We had ensured an election where we had prepared and done everything humanly possible so that each who was eligible and who wanted to vote was able to vote—and it was fair, without long lines or lawsuits to disrupt the process. This was how it was supposed to work. Antoinette and I sat on a sofa in one of the Statehouse anterooms outside the press area with Rick, our children, his parents, and some of our close friends. When Rick and I and his parents walked through the parking garage underneath the Statehouse with my security detail to return to the car, two African American women whom I did not know walked up to me in the garage and simply said, "Thank you." ≈

PART IV

✦

THE NATIONAL LANDSCAPE

Chapter 20

Profiles in Courage

"For no thought is contented. The better sort,
As thoughts of things divine, are intermix'd
With scruples and do set the word itself
Against the word:
As thus, 'Come, little ones,' and then again,
'It is as hard to come as for a camel
To thread the postern of a small needle's eye.'
Thoughts tending to ambition, they do plot
Unlikely wonders; how these vain weak nails
May tear a passage through the flinty ribs
Of this hard world, my ragged prison walls,
And, for they cannot, die in their own pride.
Thoughts tending to content flatter themselves
That they are not the first of fortune's slaves,
Nor shall not be the last; like silly beggars
Who sitting in the stocks refuge their shame,
That many have and others must sit there;
And in this thought they find a kind of ease,
Bearing their own misfortunes on the back
Of such as have before endured the like.
Thus play I in one person many people,
And none contented: sometimes am I king;
Then treasons make me wish myself a beggar,
And so I am: . . . but whate'er I be,
Nor I nor any man that but man is
With nothing shall be pleased, till he be eased
With being nothing."

From the "Life and Death of Richard the Second," Act 5, Scene 5
- William Shakespeare

"Don't a lot of Profile in Courage award winners go on to lose elections?" asked veteran Dayton Daily News Reporter Bill Hershey in one of our numerous interviews during my tenure as Ohio Secretary of State. Presumably he meant that Profile in Courage Award winners generally go against the popular grain to follow their consciences, even when the cost involves them no longer holding the office. To those from the school of pure politics, I imagine behavior awarded as politically courageous is to them seen as a bit (or a lot) quixotic. I have seen and heard the juicy rationalizations used by some veteran and even some novice politicians that, "It's more important to elect me than to elect me on the principles on which I stand, because even though you can't count on me to stand on principle, I will look out for you somewhat better than that other schmuck." I don't believe that will work much longer, and I believe the American people are tired of suffering it.

By September 2009, in a face-to-face meeting, Senator Bob Menendez, chair of the Democratic Senatorial Campaign Committee, in so many words told me that "out of duty to my country" I should drop out of the U.S. Senate race because I wasn't raising enough money. His inference was that an uncontested primary could help Democrats attain another Senate seat (outgoing Republican Ohio Senator Voinovich's seat). It was apparent that the sentiment was that any Democrat who could win was better for the country than any Republican—to allow Democrats to retain their majority control of the U.S. Senate.

As for Bill Hershey's question, I couldn't deny that Profile in Courage winners, and many Senators who had been profiled in President Kennedy's book, often suffered less than desirable political fates under contemporary, popular political opinion. But then, that's why they give the award.

If an award winner is lucky, the award is given to them in time to help complete the job, bolstering their resolve to do what they know they must do. No matter how pure of heart the public servant is, tests inevitably come and the question internally asked is, "So this is public service? I didn't bargain for this." Those thoughts came to me when the death threats to my family and me became multiple, the media criticisms blistering and the national controversy about Ohio swirling to the point that, walking into a MLS Crew Soccer game with my plain-clothes guards, someone in a group in the parking lot shouted out, "Jennifer Brunner, how about that ACORN?" (ACORN is a now defunct group that registered working class and low-income voters, with some highly publicized problems that were exploited by right-leaning groups, Fox Television Network and CNN, this engendered a "voter fraud" frenzy in 2008. Since that time, many media outlets and reporters have recognized that actual voter fraud is a miniscule fraction of less than a percent).

When the JFK Profile in Courage Award is given in the early stages of reform, it helps at later points of doubt to encourage that public official to fight on, to continue to listen to the voice of conscience that became reason and purpose in the first place and to say with courage, "How can I not?" It seemed as if the bipartisan JFK Library and Museum Board, guided by Caroline and Ted Kennedy in 2008, must have been able to hear that voice, knowing its exhortation was sorely needed—especially in Ohio.

I am certain I am not the first or last elected public servant who has seen the circumstances under which I labored to be as the winds, rain and lightning of an angry and stormy night sky. It was as if my job as Ohio's chief election officer was to guide the fragile structure known as "public trust" through the turbulent and unsettling winds set into play by the might and frailties of human triumphs and failures that characterize America's historic, political democracy. It was incumbent upon me to do all I could to make a reality of my unshakeable belief that the empowerment of one is the strength of many, honoring the proposition that one vote becomes power beyond measure.

I had been derided before the 2008 Presidential primary election by many election officials, some partisans and even some voting rights advocates for the EVEREST voting machine study that exposed for Ohio and the nation disconcerting risks and flaws in the nationally sanctioned means by which the most basic expression of democracy is exercised—voting. The last thing I would have imagined in those early stages leading up to the 2008 Presidential election was that anyone was watching or would offer encouragement to bolster the internal rudder needed to see the journey to a safe landing. But that's what the Profile in Courage Award did for me in 2008.

After the silver platinum award lantern, a replica from the U.S.S. Constitution, was safely ensconced in my state office, I would look at it and say to myself throughout 2008, "Well, *they* think I have courage, so I must." I would muse this to myself more than once, often daunted by the particular task in preparing for an election at "ground zero," as Ohio was frequently called. From my desk I could look up to see the engraved lantern sitting serenely on its mirrored base in a glass-topped box atop a brushed aluminum pedestal. It was designed by Ed Schlossberg, Caroline Kennedy's husband, and produced by Tiffany's. It came in the largest turquoise Tiffany's box I have ever received.

Later I became immensely grateful for this external recognition of my service, especially when others failed to respect or recognize it when I chose to run for the U.S. Senate. In running, I hoped to do even a fraction of the good that Senator Kennedy had done to empower individuals in our nation. As the only woman Democratic officeholder statewide, I ran for the Senate to try to achieve for women greater political parity for a state that has yet to see a woman Senator or Governor elected in her own right. Standing firm had taught me that, often, the public demonstration of commitment matters as much as the outcome. For these reasons and more, the good the award has done since its inception in the late 1980's is immeasurable. I would venture that President Obama's Nobel Peace Prize so early in his Presidential administration was in part recognition of the enormity of the task before him both to restore and transform the social and economic fabric of United States of America as a peace-loving nation of the world.

I learned I was being considered for the award in March 2008, just weeks after Ohio's 2008 Presidential primary election. I still do not know the names of those who nominated me, but I remain grateful. Cuyahoga County Commissioner Tim Hagan, a close friend of Senator Ted Kennedy, had called me one morning as I was scuffing around at home in my slippers and white fuzzy bathrobe. I had chosen to take a radio call-in interview with a Newark, Ohio radio station at home rather than at the office. On my way into the study to be behind closed doors away from my curious cats and barking dogs, my Blackberry in my robe pocket started ringing. I saw Tim Hagan's name light up on the digital screen. I vacillated on whether or not I had the time to answer it, but I did so because it was Tim.

"Hey, Jennifer," he said. "Senator Kennedy just called me, and he wanted to know if I thought you would be a good candidate to receive the Profile in Courage Award this year." My mind was racing as I slowly sunk into the beat up leather desk chair in our study. I thought to myself, "I think there's only one Senator Kennedy, and that's Ted Kennedy." I had earlier that year seen him in a local DC restaurant for lunch at the next table when I had lunched there with a high school friend, Craig Huffman and friend Eric Lee, when attending a National Association of

Secretaries of State conference. Despite being encouraged to walk over and introduce myself to him, I hadn't wanted to bother him, so I just observed him quietly as I sipped my soup, imagining he would prefer privacy to glad-handing over his lunch.

As Tim continued, I thought, "Profile in Courage Award. I've heard of that. I think that's pretty big." Tim told me he had told his friend, Senator Kennedy, that he thought I would be a good candidate for the award. Tim said, "Listen, if this happens, it's going to happen fast, so you'd better be ready. You should be ready to make the most of it." It was still sinking in, and I had to close my jaw. I thanked Tim, and we said our good-byes. Slipping into judge mode once more, I became stoic, put this revelation in a proverbial box and dialed the call-in number for the Newark radio call. I concentrated on the interview, listened carefully to the questions asked and answered them in a straightforward manner for Newark's radio listeners. I quietly mentioned the subject of the Kennedy award with Rick, my mother and a few of my top staff. Then, I put it out of my mind. Several days later, Erin Duffy, my scheduler, came to me with a smirk, telling me that I had a call scheduled the next day with Caroline Kennedy.

Caroline had called the Secretary of State's office's general number for Business Services that day. It was a general call-in number for the public. She had reached Liza Farnlacher, one of my business services customer service assistants, who fielded calls from the public day in and day out. Liza forwarded the call to Erin and then said to her supervisor, "Caroline Kennedy just called here," to which her supervisor matter-of-factly said, "She did not." Liza is well read and happens to belong to the Mensa Society, so she had no doubts about who was actually calling. To say the least she was thrilled.

The next day I was at Rick's law firm office for the call. As scheduled, my Blackberry began to go off with a call from an unidentified number. It was Caroline Kennedy. "Hi, this is Caroline Kennedy. Is this Jennifer?" I had stumbled through the dumbest salutation I have ever made. "Uh, why yes. It's—it's good to hear your voice," I said.

Caroline began by mentioning that the bipartisan board of the JFK Library and Museum had met and wanted to award to me a Profile in Courage Award. She then asked, "Would you be willing to accept the award?" I couldn't imagine anyone ever saying no, and I said yes immediately. She mentioned a timeframe in May, that I would be delivering a speech at the award ceremony and that I could invite my family and friends to attend. By the time I hung up the call, I was ecstatic. It's great to be recognized, and it's even better if it helps your state and you accomplish a tough task—like cleaning up Ohio elections in twenty-two months. This was big for Ohio, especially after 2004. The fact that *Ohio* was being recognized for something *good* about elections was phenomenal at a time when many members of the media were fully expecting an electoral meltdown in the fall.

By this time, the partisan attacks, along with what I called do-gooder, "we can do it better," attacks were steadily escalating in response to the reforms my staff and I were crafting to make ready the Ohio battleground for a contentious Presidential contest in November. I worried about my staff at all levels. It wasn't easy. At this point, my directors were under stress. The Sunday before Caroline's call, for some reason, William Seward came to mind. All I really remembered about him was the reference to "Seward's Folly" and the state of Alaska.

I researched and read more about him. He was a lawyer and generally regarded as ethical and having integrity. William

Seward had been Governor of New York and Secretary of State
under Presidents Abraham Lincoln and Andrew Jackson. He was
a progressive reformer and responsible for the purchase of
Alaska, called "Seward's Folly" by some. I could relate precisely
to the situation in which he found himself.

Seward oversaw the U.S. purchase of 6,000,000 square miles—
Alaska and the Aleutian Islands—for $7,200,000 US Dollars,
what amounted to a few cents per acre. Horace Greely, of *The
New York Tribune*, said that Alaska "contained nothing of value
but furbearing animals, and these had been hunted until they
were nearly extinct. Except for the Aleutian Islands and a
narrow strip of land extending along the southern coast, the
country would be not worth taking as a gift." After Seward died
in 1872, gold was found in Alaska in the 1890's and later, oil. The
last Monday in March each year, Alaska celebrates "Seward's
Day."

I remember smiling to myself, thinking that he, too, (a different
kind of Secretary of State,) took his licks for doing what he
thought was right. As a member of Lincoln's cabinet, Seward
was also the target of a failed assassination attempt at the same
time that Lincoln's was successful. Lewis Powell stabbed
William Seward in the face and neck as he lay recuperating in
his bed from a fall from a carriage. The metal brace on his jaw
prevented the knife from reaching his jugular vein.

After reading about Seward, on a whim, I dug out the 1991 book,
Longing for Darkness, edited by Peter Beard. My sister, Andrea,
had given it to me in 1997. She knew one of my all time favorite
movies was "Out of Africa," based on the book by Isak Dinesen,
a Danish author who managed a farm in Africa. Dinesen realized
great levels of self-actualization as a result of her struggles and
triumphs in that tough environment so foreign to her. The
Beard book was primarily about Kamante, Dinesen's beloved

African servant who was of immense help and a trusted friend to her. The last two pages of the book contained photocopies of two letters handwritten by Jacqueline Kennedy to Kamante. When Caroline and I talked, I told her I had just read her mother's statements on courage the weekend before. I spoke of them in my remarks upon accepting the award:

> . . . she [Jacqueline Kennedy] spoke to Kamante of the young people of the 1960's who were fighting for civil rights. She said, "They had allies in an earlier time, who knew that courage was endurance as well as abandon."

> I then understood that endurance is the mortar that holds together the bricks of courage. It also illustrated that those who hold elected office must endeavor with endurance to better the lives of the people they serve, even if it can only be for the time they are in office. I have come to learn that this is enough to make a difference.

The simple words of Jacqueline Kennedy made tremendous sense to me during that time and seemed to be the words of encouragement I needed to give to my staff. I emailed those words to them on that Sunday. Ironically, the next day, Tim Hagan's call came.

In May of 2008, when Caroline Kennedy introduced me to supporters of the JFK Library and Museum at the gala the night before the award ceremony in Boston, she laughed that I had quoted her mother's definition of courage when learning of receiving the award about her father. In 2009, when I attended a fundraising event she held for my U.S. Senate race in her New York apartment, she had asked me to arrive early. She pulled out her copy of the book, signed and filled with doodled cartoons drawn for her by Peter Beard, himself.

She remarked offhandedly that she had been cleaning and found the book. Clearly, this was not a "cleaning" coincidence. More than once she has demonstrated her exceptional kindness and thoughtfulness. I smiled to myself, touched by this gesture. Amazingly as she opened the book a handwritten note from Kamante to her, decorated with an African bird feather, fluttered to the ground. We as a nation are blessed that she has honored and cared for the symbols and heritage of her parents' time in the presidency. She has shown exceptional stewardship of the public and private remembrances kept and available for Americans and citizens of the world to see and experience at the Kennedy library. Referred to time and again as "Camelot," I see the time she, her brother and parents occupied the White House as like no other, where modernity was celebrated with dignity and grace as we barely could see the cusp of change about to sweep the social fabric of our nation.

Writing my acceptance speech for the award was a task that only I could tackle, because it had to be from my heart. It forced me to put into words my beliefs about public service. But it had to have meaning for more than just me. Trying to write what is supposed to be an epoch speech when nearly every moment of the day is scheduled, and you're seldom alone is a challenge. Even when the time to write is "scheduled," there always seem to be issues that crowd into that time, diminishing it to a frenetic few minutes and sometimes to just a quick jotting down and review of bullet points before a public address. But this time, this speech was too important—and the JFK Library wanted it in advance and planned to post it on its website.

There was only one place I could think of where I could isolate myself from the issues of the day long enough to write a decent speech that meant something to me and hopefully to other Ohioans and Americans. It was a place that has given me solace for years. I sat in my car under a tree alongside the greenway at

Schiller Park in the German Village section of Columbus just south of downtown. There's something about sitting in the comfort and cocoon of your car, in warm weather maybe opening the windows and a sun roof, if you have one, under the canopy of a mature tree, being able to look up from your reading or your lunch and see joggers, walkers and their dogs and children enjoying an oasis of nature in the middle of a richly historic, residential area. At this park in early 2005 I had read Congressman John Conyer's report on the 2004 election during one of my lunch hours while still a judge on the Franklin County Common Pleas bench. I remember feeling my stomach turn as I read the details of how people lost their opportunities to vote in 2004 in Ohio and about the irregularities of that election for which there was no decent excuse.

That morning in 2008, I sent emails to my staff that I was working on the speech and would be in soon. I kept writing, sitting in what had been Ken Blackwell's Chrysler 300C, hemi-engine, white-leather-seated, sleek-mobile (he paid cash for it, so I was stuck with it). As I wrote, I cried, thinking of how this award was about so much more than me. It was about Ohio. It was about a rap Ohio never deserved, yet bore with the same kind of grim hardiness that the people of Ohio have shown time in and time out under tough economic and social circumstances. Ohio deserved a break, and this seemed to me to be one to seize for them. I wanted to highlight that in my speech, so I said:

> I come from the State of Ohio, whose history is mired in political traditions and machinations with a claim of 8 of the nation's 43 presidents. Since Ohio's statehood in 1803, many of the state's citizens have served as Presidential cabinet members whose activities have helped shape this country throughout its history. Ohio has been a state that is critical to

the direction of the leadership of our country.
In the last Presidential election, Ohio supplied the
needed electoral votes for our current president's
victory. Many have questioned the efficacy of our
last Presidential election in Ohio. I simply
questioned its fairness of process.

It pained me to see the representation of my state in
2004 with long lines at polling places, accusations of
unequal distribution of voting machines in some
counties, and certainty by many that Ohio's election
was stolen or tainted. I love my state, and I love my
country. Whether or not this characterization of
Ohio's 2004 Presidential election is accurate, I see it
as my challenge to change Ohio's elections to instill
voter confidence. Voter confidence in Ohio's
elections does not stop with its electorate—I knew
from the national interest in my own election in
2006 that what happened in Ohio mattered to the
country.

I finished the speech that day and gave it to Jeff Ortega and
Patrick Gallaway. They reviewed it, along with Brian Clark, (a
newer member of our media staff.) After commenting on it, and
within a week or so Antoinette, Jayme Staley, my political
director, Patrick, Jeff, Brian and I met in the library of Rick's law
office for me to practice it in a quiet setting, focusing on the
speech's delivery. As I would get to the passage about Ohio, my
voice would break, the tears would well in my eyes, and I would
have to start over again. When I delivered the speech at the
award ceremony, to my relief, my voice stayed strong about
Ohio, but I felt my throat catch as I spoke of the sacrifices made
by my family. I had no idea at that time, how many more
sacrifices my family would make leading into the November
election.

The Kennedys could not have been kinder. The lead up to the Profile in Courage Award Ceremony at the JFK Library was the annual gala and dinner the night before the award ceremony. It had been billed as "black tie." I had carefully shopped for the perfect formal dress for this event, buying it in New York City at Bergdorf Goodman—a navy, tailored

The dress with train for the Profile in Courage gala; my sister, Kathy to the left, and daughter Kate to the right, helping me get ready in the hotel room

taffeta full-length, deep v-neck, sleeveless dress with a double train from the back waist band. I had shopped online for the perfect shoes (at just the right height and size of platform to avoid having to hem the dress), faux sapphire earrings and necklace and even a satin purse. To me, the ensemble was nothing short of fabulous. I didn't tell Rick for a couple of weeks just how much the dress cost (and he didn't think to ask about the accessories). When we sat over our every-Friday Mexican lunch after the Bergdorf-Goodman shopping trip, he dared to ask. I had him play a guessing game based just on price range. That was about as much as I let him know, but it was enough that he stunningly pointed out that the dress cost as much as his first new car.

Jayme Staley saw to the finer details of planning, such as making sure the other award winners, including an Ohio student winner from Indian Hill near Cincinnati, received hand-delivered to their hotel rooms formal, signed commendations from me and a small congratulatory gift that included Ohio's famous peanut butter and chocolate "Buckeye" candies. All of my family (and I mean all of them) came to the event in Boston—including my mother and stepfather, John, my three children and their significant others, my sisters and my brother, my nephews, my sister-in-law and her husband and their boys, and my parents-in-law. The Kennedys had said it was okay to invite my whole family, and I thought they'd understand if it really was my whole family, or pretty close to it. My sister, Kathy, painted my nails for me. My son's girlfriend, Erika, styled my hair. Rick wore his tux with a satin navy cummerbund to match my dress.

When it was time to attend the pre-award ceremony gala, a sleek black town car awaited us outside the Boston Harbor Hotel. Rick and I slipped onto the back seat, both in wonder about what was to happen. As we exited the car after it drove up the curved driveway and parked in front of the JFK Library, photographers began snapping photos as we exited the car and walked up the windswept sidewalk into the library. I appeared in the Boston Globe the next day, looking elegant but somewhat windblown. Rick bragged that he had the best looking elbow— all that showed of him in the picture. We walked into the museum and were introduced to Anne Aaron, our cheerful main contact for the award ceremony. Soon after, Ted and Victoria Kennedy entered the building. Senator Kennedy was dressed in his tux pants and a leather bomber jacket, carrying his tuxedo jacket, which he promptly donned. Both were all smiles, relaxed and friendly.

I had had an earlier opportunity to spend some one-on-one time with Senator Kennedy when I had been in Washington, DC several weeks before. He had just ten minutes to see me. I had arrived late, delayed after talking with Ohio's senior Congressman, Republican Ralph Regula from Canton, who was serving out the last year of a long and illustrious tenure before his retirement. Congressman Regula had wistfully shown me his framed picture and handwritten letter from President Ronald Reagan and seemed still as taken as I was with the lovely view from his large office window of the Capitol building, acquired as a result of his senior status.

When I arrived nearly breathless to Senator Kennedy's office, it was precisely at the end of the ten minutes I was to meet with him. A young gentleman in his office whom I only remember as "Henry from Nantucket" and who was a full six feet seven inches tall said we had just missed him. He said then, "Wait a minute, I think we might be able to catch him before he goes on the Senate floor, if you'll follow me." Even though I'm five feet seven inches tall, trying to keep up with Henry from Nantucket was like being a puppy dog trying to follow a full-grown greyhound.

As we approached the Senate tram in the underground passageway between the buildings, Henry paused momentarily but then brushed his hand into the air saying, "Naaah, we can walk faster." Antoinette Wilson, who had been with Jayme Staley and me and is barely five feet tall, just could not keep up. As I looked back at her, I was torn between keeping up with Henry and not leaving her behind. I could see her struggling to keep up through her usual dignified demeanor. She took one swipe at the air in front of her, and breathlessly waved us on. So, to stay apace with Henry's gliding lope, I walked long strides interspersed by periodic two-step clips to propel me forward as fast as he seemed to glide. Jayme managed to stay with us.

Henry led us to the President's Room off of the Senate Chamber. I figured out what room we were in when I noticed gilded letters on the underside of a registration book propped open on a stand atop a tall, impressive wooden table. I was directed to sit on a tufted reddish leather sofa in the opulent room to await Senator Kennedy. It had been his duty that day to escort the Prime Minister of Ireland onto the Senate floor. That accounted for his need to keep a precise schedule.

I sat there quietly, wondering if this room was the anteroom for presidents past who waited to be escorted to the Senate, when Senator Kennedy walked into the room with a smile from ear to ear and heartily introduced himself. He sat on the tufted sofa next to me and talked with me in preparation for the Profile in Courage Award ceremony in the next two weeks. I passed on a joking message to him from Tim Hagan, to which Senator Kennedy threw back his head in that laugh that only he could do. He asked me about my mother, if she would be attending the ceremony and was delighted she was living in Louisiana, where Vicki's family was from. He then posed for a picture with me.

My next stop was to see Senator Sherrod Brown. I told him where I had met Senator Kennedy, in the President's Room. Senator Brown corrected me on the room, saying it must have been the Senate Reception Room, but I held fast. I knew what I had read on that book. Later, in checking with my high school friend, Craig Huffman who works for the Senate, I learned I had in fact been in the President's room. The President's Room had been completed in 1859, a renovation which added new Senate and House wings and a cast-iron dome. Presidents had used the room to sign legislation at the close of each session of Congress until about the time my father was born in 1933, when Congressional and Presidential terms of office were changed and differed. While the room is occasionally used by presidents, it's used primarily by senators for interviews and press conferences and is only accessible on a guided tour with a Congressional staffer—like Henry from Nantucket.

My feet ached after keeping up with Henry. I could barely walk through Union Station at the end of the day to take the Metro to the airport. I wouldn't have traded that experience for anything, no matter how much my feet hurt. The photo of Senator Kennedy and me was sent to me shortly before he died in late August 2009. The virtual video tour on the U.S. Senate's website shows the red, tufted sofa to the left of the fireplace.

As for the Profile in Courage Award gala the night before the ceremony, I had been given an itinerary and order of events to prepare for the festivities. The part about "heralding trumpets" piqued my curiosity. As Rick, the other awardees and I entered with the Kennedys, there were, in fact, heralding trumpets. But truth be told, I didn't really notice them. The trains of my gown were just a few inches longer than my full-length dress, dragging the ground behind me. Rick would accidentally step on them, jerking me back and giving great entertainment to Caroline, Ted and Vicki Kennedy. Rick would say, "I'm sorry, honey." I would gather myself and say, "Oh, it's okay," and a few steps later it would happen again. I felt terribly overdressed, even for a gala of 600 people at the Kennedy library. But I reared myself up and carried on with grace as if I were its epitome.

I moved into the room, directed to my assigned table. The room was filled with round tables that seated eight people each. I missed the obvious—place cards with our names on them. I was directed to sit between Caroline Kennedy (on my right) and Ed Schlossberg (on my left). "Surely, I shouldn't separate husband and wife," I thought in my colloquial and polite Midwestern way. So I moved around the table. Caroline's college roommate's husband, George, said, "Excuse me, I think you're standing in front of my seat." I was directed to my own seat, marked by name card, which indeed was intended to be between Caroline and Ed.

Often, we look up to people, whether we see them on television, in newspapers or in magazines. They are part of the fabric of our lives, woven into the history of how things have unfolded. Even though we age, we can't believe that they do, too. They become larger than life. Some of them wonder from day to day how they got there, in awe of their circumstances as much as we are of them. Others have lived that way for as long as they can remember. When I was younger I learned to overcome shyness by adopting the attitude that in any conversation I should work to make the other person feel comfortable. Adopting this attitude has made it easy for me to talk with anyone, whether a Kennedy or a probation officer who has come to discuss a probationer's progress. We are all people. We all have children, parents, dogs and cats, and we all laugh, grieve, joke, play and cry. We're born alone, and we die alone. Some of us are called on to reach great heights, bear heavy responsibility or simply to be kind. These callings of character and service know no stations in life.

It came time for each winner (Debra Bowen, Secretary of State of California was being co-honored with me, and William Winter, former Governor of Mississippi was receiving a lifetime achievement award) to make brief remarks during the dinner. I decided it would be good to tell the anecdote about Liza in my office not being believed by her supervisor that Caroline Kennedy had really called the Business Services section of my office. People laughed. Ted Kennedy laughed, and the remarks were well-received, so well-received that Senator and former Presidential candidate John Kerry, sought me out after the dinner and said incredulously, "Where were you in 2004?"

The next morning pre-ceremony was a breakfast buffet on the seventh floor of the library for award winners and their families, JFK Library staff and the Kennedy families. There is a portion of the seventh floor that looks much like a welcoming living room with a beautiful view of the Boston Harbor. Near the window is also a guest register. I looked at the guest register and noticed that recently the Prime Minister of Ireland had been there and signed the register. I smiled, thinking of my waiting in the President's room of the Senate as Senator Kennedy escorted him onto the Senate floor.

On the seventh floor of the JFK Library there are numerous personal effects of Jack and Jacqueline Kennedy. Two small paintings of Caroline and John from Jackie's bedroom are in the mantel area above the fireplace. There are sculptures, relics and implements that would look normal for nearly any home or office, except they are wrapped in the history of our country.

That morning Caroline and Ed sat on the sofa across from Rick and me and informed us that their teenagers were at home in New York and that they had entrusted them with the responsibility to get themselves up and to school on their own. Rick and I laughed when we heard Caroline and Ed calling them, saw them roll their eyes and laugh, because sleepy voices had answered the telephone after they should have been out of bed. Some things are universal.

As ceremony time drew near, we traveled down the elevator to the first floor and were treated to a personal tour of the Kennedy library by Ted Kennedy, himself. It was clear how much he loved the library. As we made our way to the room in which President Kennedy's desk was on display, we saw in front of it an elevated dais with five chairs on it for a live a media interview by CNN. There was a chair for each of us.

Senator Kennedy, Secretary Bowen, Caroline Kennedy, Governor
Winter and I sat in the chairs before the camera to talk about
the award ceremony to be held later that morning. John Roberts
of CNN took the opportunity to try to question the authenticity
of authorship of Caroline's dad's *Profiles in Courage* book, based
on the then recent autobiography by Ted Sorenson. He
intimated that Ted Sorenson had ghost written the book.

Caroline demonstrated her nerves of steel. She didn't miss a
beat. She shot back, live on camera, "John, the book was written
before I was born. I wouldn't know the details." He persisted
with more speculation. She drew blood, outright challenging
John Roberts on this live interview, saying, "I don't know why
you're so fixated on this issue." He stammered in response,
saying defensively that he wasn't fixated. Touché. He dropped it.
Silently, I was cheering her on.

As we moved into the ceremony, Secretary Bowen changed to a
white suit. I had my one suit I had carefully selected and hadn't
thought of wearing different outfits for the press conference and
the ceremony. My attire for the day was an eggplant-colored Via
Spiga suit (that I bought at Overstock.com) with a turquoise
green shell and white pearls Rick had given me. My brown Cole
Haan shoes I was lucky enough to find at Marshall's (broken in
well by keeping up with Henry from Nantucket), and my Bulova
leather-banded watch I found through another good buy at
Overstock. Who would have known? I think I understand the
satisfaction many men find hunting. I get the same adrenaline
rush with a quality bargain-hunting find, and there's a lot less
mess.

It was ceremony time. In true warm and kind Kennedy fashion,
not only was the ceremony designed to honor the award
winners but also to recognize their families and *their*
contributions to public service. Ted Kennedy opened the

ceremony. During his remarks, he introduced my mother and asked her to stand and be applauded. She beamed, all five feet two inches of her. I was proud of her. There were seats for each of our spouses behind us on the stage. Ted Kennedy introduced Rick each of the others.

In his introductory remarks Senator Kennedy explained why the board of the library had chosen each of that year's recipients. I was surprised at how detailed his remarks were about my work:

> "Our next honoree, Ohio's first woman Secretary of State, Jennifer Brunner, showed similar courage on that issue. She was well aware that the confidence of voters in Ohio had been deeply shaken by scandals and voting irregularities in several recent elections. After taking office last year, she immediately set out to correct the problems.
>
> She began by proposing that all poll workers be recruited impartially and trained properly, so that future elections would be managed by trained professionals, not partisans.
>
> She called for the resignation of all four members of the Cuyahoga County Board of Elections, which includes Cleveland, after two election workers in the county were imprisoned for election offenses.
>
> She then decided full review of state ballot procedures was essential, and it found "critical security failures" that made easy tampering possible in the voting machines.
>
> She immediately ordered the state's touch-screen voting systems to be replaced with a reliable system of paper ballots that could be optically scanned.

Her decision was met with immediate resistance from all corners of Ohio's political world. Local politicians and even newspaper editorial boards insisted that her decision was "injecting a culture of fear and intimidation" into the electorate and that there wasn't enough time to change the current system before the state's Presidential primary in March.

Despite the strong political winds against her, she kept moving forward and insisted that every vote had to be counted correctly on election day.

The results speak for themselves. Voter turnout was heavy, but the paper ballots saved the day, and restored the basic right to vote in a state that had lost confidence in its election system and its elected officials as well.

Ohio Senator Sherrod Brown says of Brunner, 'I've rarely seen anyone in public life so focused and persistent in fighting for the right causes.' As we honor her here, I know President Kennedy would agree."

I had invited Senator Brown and his wife, Connie, to the ceremony, but they were unable to be there. I was grateful for his kind words and surprised that Senator Kennedy had gone to the effort to get my long-time friend's comment. As for Senator Kennedy's final words of introduction, nothing could have made me happier than to think that President Kennedy would have had good things to say about my work. I was shocked and humbled when I heard these words.

At award time, California Secretary of State Debra Bowen was introduced first, delivered her speech and received her award presented by Caroline Kennedy. Then it was my turn. For my

Receiving the JFK Profile in Courage Award from Caroline
Kennedy May 13, 2008 at the JFK Library and Museum

part of the award ceremony, Caroline opened with brief
remarks, saying:

> "Ohio Secretary of State Jennifer Brunner took office after a
> series of Ohio election problems had badly shaken voter
> confidence in her state. In the face of blistering political
> opposition, she has made difficult and sometimes
> controversial decisions in order to restore the integrity and
> the accuracy of Ohio elections. She has stood her ground
> with voting machine vendors and political partisans, and has
> been unwavering in her determination to see that every vote
> is accurately recorded and counted. For her dauntless
> commitment to the enfranchisement of every Ohio voter, we
> are happy to present Jennifer Brunner with the 2008 Profile
> in Courage Award."

Delivering remarks upon receiving a JFK Profile in Courage
Award, John F. Kennedy Library and Museum, May 13, 2008;
Ted Kennedy and award lanterns to right

It was certainly surreal. I was nervous. My delivery of speeches is much better when I can look straight into the faces of my audience. Yet, I had prepared remarks that I was supposed to deliver, and I had poured so much of my heart into the words that I didn't think I could afford to stray from them. It was clearly not my best delivery, but I got through it, and afterward, the comments from my family, and especially my friends, were overall positive.

Governor Winter was more relaxed and impromptu. The applause for him was thunderous, and deserved. Governor Winter had been a brave pioneer for desegregation and education reform in Mississippi. I thought of our foster son, David, now benefiting from Governor Winter's reforms, and I was glad to be sharing the stage with this octogenarian who was as vibrant as ever and who had done so much in public life. In a quiet moment, he and I talked about his time in the Governor's office in Mississippi. We talked about the joys of campaigning and meeting people in their own environments, hearing their stories and taking what we learned from them into office. He confided that he liked the campaign better than governing. Considering his achievements in governing he must have been one heck of a campaigner.

A contingent from Ohio, including nearly all my top staff, had paid their own way to come to Boston to see the award ceremony. Such loyal, hard working and generous staff is a hallmark of a successful administration. Pictures were scheduled immediately after the ceremony followed by a luncheon with the Kennedy family and the award winners and their families. My only regret was that I was unable to personally see the Ohio contingent and thank them for making the trek to Boston. Many of them toured the library, and quite of few souvenirs were bought at the museum store that day. I thanked them in writing when we returned to Columbus.

After photos, the award winners were whisked back to the seventh floor for the luncheon. At lunch I was seated between Ted and Vicki Kennedy, with no problems finding my correct seat this time. Rick and I have been keeping a "memory board," a cloth board covered with crisscross ribbons for holding ticket stubs and other mementos, going for about seven years now. The first one has expanded to five more. Quietly, at the end of my meal the night before and after the luncheon, I collected the place cards for myself and the people seated on either side of me—just in case my grandchildren didn't believe me some day.

Senator Kennedy and Vicki could not have been kinder or better conversationalists. Vicki and Rick had already found a kindred sense of humor, especially after dress-stepping incident the night before. Then Senator Kennedy wanted people in the awardees' families to tell something humorous about each of the award winners—potentially embarrassing things. As family members relayed amusing anecdotes, Senator Kennedy threw back his head and laughed. It is how I like to remember him.

As we were nearing the end of our time with the Kennedys, Caroline had been talking with my brother, Dan, his wife Chris and their two boys, Nathan and Garrett. She asked them not to leave just yet, as she had something for them. She left for another floor in the library and returned, giving them a signed copy of the children's book she had authored. We were touched by her personal gesture. That is why I am convinced she didn't just happen to find her own copy of Peter Beard's edited book, *Longing for Darkness*.

When the ceremony was over, Rick and I, our children, our family members and our friends returned home, each of us still glowing from the honored and special time. Once home, I remember standing in front of my kitchen sink at dusk and looking down at my menagerie of cats and dogs, thinking to myself, "Did that really happen?" Later, when the actual award lantern arrived, shipped to my home, I received a call from then Speaker of the House, Jon Husted, who started the conversation with the statement that he had never talked with a Profile in Courage Award winner before. I told him I was just opening the award as he had called. Ironically, he became my successor in office. Despite my having to break an unpleasant tie vote in 2010 on his residency for the Montgomery County Board of Elections in Dayton and his responsive lawsuit filed in the Ohio Supreme Court, we had a smooth transition from my administration to his and remain collegial to this day.

About four days after the Profile in Courage Award ceremony in 2008, Senator Kennedy suffered a seizure that was the first evidence of the ganglion tumor that had been discovered near his brain. I sent a card wishing him well after his diagnosis and surgery. In true Kennedy class, Vicki and the family acknowledged my card.

I recall watching his funeral on my bedroom television as I was getting ready for an event I was to attend in 2009. Standing there in my robe with a towel turban over my wet hair and tears in my eyes, I was stunned to see the reaction of so many people in Washington who turned out to meet the funeral cortege. I was touched by the large contingent of staffers who turned out to honor him and his family. I forgot to look for Henry from Nantucket.

When I was campaigning for the Senate, the Westside Democratic Club west of Cleveland held a forum and asked me to keynote. During the question and answer session, I was asked which Senator I would most like to emulate if I were to be elected to the Senate. Hands down, I told them it was Ted Kennedy for his principled stands on things that matter to everyday Americans, and especially to those in need.

Thanks to Ted Kennedy, we have curb cuts for wheelchairs that are not easily found off the cobblestone streets of Europe. Our medical privacy is protected; more children have health care; environmental protections have been institutionalized and troops have been honored and protected. Today, work is underway for an institute in his honor, the "Edward Kennedy Institute for the United States Senate." It will be dedicated to educating the public about government, "invigorating public discourse, encouraging participatory democracy, and inspiring the next generation of citizens and leaders to engage in the public square." It is to be located adjacent to the JFK Library on the University of Massachusetts Boston campus.

I am grateful for even the brief time that my life crossed paths with Senator Ted Kennedy and his wife, Vicki—and with Caroline and Ed. I share Senator Kennedy's passion that young people see public service as a calling. I believe young people who value public service for its own sake are our country's greatest hope for democracy to endure and flourish in the days and years ahead. Edward M. Kennedy's life is a testament to that. I only hope that my work served in some small way to assist in helping to foster its achievement. ≈

Chapter 21

State Politics under a New President

If war has been said to be the ultimate failure of human relations, political battles that take no prisoners are the war games in preparation. It doesn't matter whether the battle is between political parties or within a political party. It doesn't matter whether the political party in question is in power or has fallen from public grace. When people fail to realize or lack the courage to recognize that "politics" is really about relationships between people, it is the beginning of the entity's demise.

I wanted Ted Strickland to run for governor. When I was a judge, Scott North, an attorney and eventual Strickland staffer came to talk with me. It had already been announced that I would be leaving the bench to run for Secretary of State. Both Scott and I wanted Ted to run, and Scott, who knew Ted better than I did, was among a small group of people working to convince him to run. The Governor's race was still undetermined with then Republican Governor Bob Taft term-limited. I knew Ted had cosponsored federal legislation as a Congressman, working with then U.S. Senator Mike Dewine, (defeated in 2006 by Sherrod Brown and four years later beating Richard Cordray to become Ohio's Attorney General) to provide for greater access to mental health treatment in the criminal justice system. While the measure was not funded at the time, I was thrilled that Ted was part of a bipartisan effort focused on something I cherished mightily. (As the drug court judge, my court also provided for mental health treatment.) I saw it as refreshing when traditional partisan "enemies" put down their weapons to work for the common good.

When Ted began his race for Governor, one of my favorite experiences was having appeared with him in Summit County in Akron, Ohio, at a Democratic party event where he was essentially introducing himself, a Southeastern Ohio Appalachian, to a populous and largely Democratic bedroom community of metropolitan Cleveland, Ohio. He and his wife, Frances, came to the event together. At the time he was still opposed pre-primary by Columbus Mayor Mike Coleman, who traveled in a swanky converted bus that was said by some to have been the Clinton traveling bus used after the 1992 New York City Democratic National Convention. While Mayor Coleman attended the event with an entourage, Ted and Frances walked in somewhat tentatively without fanfare and asked where the party room was for the event. It made me smile.

At this diehard Democratic event I was nervous for Ted and wanted him to gain the acceptance of this group, at least to be given a chance. Mayor Coleman and Akron Mayor Don Plusquellic were known to be great friends and political allies. Ted gave a refreshing and heartfelt speech, and the open-minded people of Akron gave him a chance. At the end of the dinner, with just Ted left standing up from the head table on the dais, a rank-and-file party member, an older woman, approached Ted and asked him if she could give something to one of his staffer people, not wanting to burden him.

"Do you have someone here who I could give this to?" she asked, clutching a small white piece of paper. He wasn't sure what she was asking. I said, "She's looking for a staff person here for you." Humbly he said, "Frances . . ." trailing off, "well, she could take it." I had to close my jaw. Here was a guy running for Governor, and he seemed as down to earth as anyone. The woman ended up giving her note to Ted directly. I told him there that I was so glad he was running for Governor and that he was just the kind of candidate I wanted to see in office.

Later in 2005, Ted and I were both in Geauga County, a conservative, northeastern county with rolling hills and bucolic communities to the east of Cleveland. It was Ted's birthday that day. He was well accepted by this special breed of Democrats who held their event at a lovely country club on a small lake. He had turned 64 that day, looking vibrant with blonde-haired charisma and a winning smile and blue eyes with a twinkle. His candidacy and the promising ticket that year stoked new life into hopeful Democrats around the state. The reaction of the crowd that night was a testament to that promise and hope for a state that had no idea of the trials that lay ahead.

Ted introducing me at fundraising event in Ashtabula County in June 2006 during our respective campaigns for Governor and Secretary of State of Ohio

In August of 2005, in Highland County, a county Ted had previously represented in Congress, I watched joyful, hope-filled Democratic rank-and-file, people of no great means, queue in a long line after the outdoor picnic speech he gave. They waited to greet him, shake his hand and get his autograph, even once with a black marker on the back of a tee shirt being worn by a man. I had not seen this in my political life, even though I had been involved for nearly thirty years.

I had the opportunity to talk with Ted at length after that dinner. We stood by a graying, split rail fence on the strip of grass outside the cement platform of the wood-framed picnic pavilion on that sunny Sunday. I was surprised he would talk so long after this upbeat event, thinking he must have more places to go. He seemed to be enjoying himself and felt strongly about our shared interest in seeing real justice for incarcerated mentally ill inmates. This had been the subject of his work as a psychologist at the Lucasville state prison, the scene of prisoner riots in 1993 that garnered national attention.

Ted spoke to me of a particularly memorable and extremely intelligent mentally ill inmate at Lucasville whom he had helped gain a commutation from outgoing Governor Richard Celeste in 1990. Ted and I both understood from first hand experiences, he as a prison psychologist, and me as judge that, while the prison system is not an ideal setting for anyone incarcerated there, it's especially harmful to mentally ill inmates. These inmates usually experience longer incarceration for the same crime committed by a person who is not mentally ill, especially when prison behavior affects length of sentence. Ted spoke honestly and with disgust about Lee Fisher who, as a newly elected Ohio attorney general (elected in 1990), worked politically to reverse certain commutations granted by Governor Celeste at the end of his term, including this particular one. I was astonished and impressed that Ted could recall with such specificity the details of this particular inmate's case. It had been fifteen years.

Ironically, Ted would in less than a year believe he needed Lee Fisher to sign on as his gubernatorial running mate, bringing with him his own years of political juggernauts and unmatched fundraising prowess, especially in the Jewish political donor community. Lee would be Ted's lieutenant governor in a joint candidacy and for the apparent purpose of pushing Eric Fingerhut, another Jewish candidate, out of the gubernatorial primary. When this happened, it left only Brian Flannery as Ted's primary election opponent.

Flannery, who believed strongly in reforming the state's education system, was poorly funded and used questionable tactics to attack Ted on an extraneous, truth-stretched and sensationalized allegation concerning one of Ted's votes in Congress of "present" when the Republican-controlled Congress voted on a resolution condemning a psychological study on damage caused to victims of child sex abuse. The meta-analysis examined fifty-nine different studies, based on college samples, and reached the conclusion that:

> Many laypersons and professionals believe that child sexual abuse (CSA) causes intense harm, regardless of gender, pervasively in the general population. The authors examined this belief by reviewing 59 studies based on college samples. Meta-analyses revealed that students with CSA were, on average, slightly less well adjusted than controls. However, this poorer adjustment could not be attributed to CSA because family environment (FE) was consistently confounded with CSA . . . Self-reported reactions to and effects from CSA indicated that negative effects were neither pervasive nor typically intense, and that men reacted much less negatively than women. The college data were

completely consistent with data from national samples. Basic beliefs about CSA in the general population were not supported.

Ted, a psychologist, was not willing to turn an academic psychological study (that was later duplicated in separate research with the same results) into writer Nathaniel Hawthorne's Hester Prynne, branding it with a scarlet letter. The subject was considered taboo, and its results were being "abused" by organizations that promoted sexual deviance. He has been hounded ever since because of it. It was a low blow for Bryan to use it, and Ken Blackwell, in the waning days before his 2006 gubernatorial campaign as Ted's opponent crashed and burned, tried to revive it to no avail.

Later during the 2006 campaign, watching Ted Strickland move through the crowd at the renowned Circleville Pumpkin Show (just south of Columbus), Rick and I were astounded watching people crowd around him, wanting to touch him, talk to him, shake his hand and get his autograph, almost as if he were a Presidential candidate. Up to this point, the last statewide politicians from Southeast (Appalachian) Ohio to my memory were former Governor Jim Rhodes, from Jackson County in his early years, and Vern Riffe, Speaker of the Ohio House of Representatives, from Scioto County in the southern most part of Ohio. Regardless of where they came from, I had never seen this reaction to a politician, especially a state candidate.

When I met Ted's closest advisor and confidante, John Haseley, who hailed from Athens, Ohio, (and who has often been described as "Smilin' John"), I found him to have deep eyes that peered into you when he smiled, with a somewhat shy demeanor and humility in his gait. John was the quiet person about whom I had heard from many was someone of substance and who got things done for Ted. John had originally worked for

former astronaut and Senator John Glenn and had worked his
way up to chief of staff in Ted's Congressional office.

From the Congressional office, John moved into the statewide
campaign manager role for Ted's gubernatorial campaign, and
upon a decisive statewide victory, to Chief of Staff for the new
Governor Strickland. John did little public speaking, but two
days after the election, he spoke of how the campaign had
paired counties with similar interests in different parts of the
state so that the counties (especially in Southeast Ohio) that
knew Ted well could "adopt" other counties with similar
interests that didn't, such as in the far northwest corner of the
state. It worked beautifully with Ted capturing gubernatorial
victory in 72 of 88 counties, unheard of in recent memory.

As Ted and John settled into the Governor's office, they carried
the simple, country humility of the campaign into how the
administration's inner circle was organized, establishing their
offices in the actual Statehouse, with wooden cubicles just
outside the Governor's office for key folks like John Haseley, the
new chief of staff, and Kent Markus, Counsel to the Governor.
They eschewed the posh, secure offices on the thirtieth floor of
the Riffe state office tower. The Governor's office began to hold
monthly meetings of the Democratic elected statewide office
holders in this Statehouse office. But as the rigors and demands
of the office, including minding the shop at the state
Democratic Party, grew heavier, the meetings would be canceled
and eventually seldom called, except in crisis.

In each meeting I was the only woman and was often the first
one there, with Ted seated at the relatively small, round wood
table in the corner of his expansive office, appearing on time as
scheduled. It was exciting for all of us in the beginning, having
swept the state and captured all executive offices except State
Auditor. There was the camaraderie—and the unspoken

competitiveness, coyly kept in the background, like brothers and sisters dressed for a fine family dinner, full of anticipation and trying not to pinch one another.

Even after the well-intentioned plan to hold the periodic meetings got lost in the rigors of tending the state, routinely, when a newsworthy event was about to happen, each elected statewide office holder would receive a peremptory call from John Haseley to give us advance notice of what was about to occur. One such incident was an intern taking home a backup computer disk with information about all state employees. The intern had left it in his car and it was stolen. It necessitated that the state pay for all state employees to take advantage of a credit protection program. The safeguards of that program, however, prevented any ability to obtain instant credit for discounts at retail stores. It was a hazard of what happens when a new administration takes over. Unless it can be discovered soon enough what the previous administration set into play, practices are unwittingly tolerated before they can be discovered and corrected. The sheer size of Ohio's state government made discovering a practice by an intern like finding a needle in a haystack, until someone sits on it.

When in 2009 state budget revenue forecasts started teetering, the Democratic statewide officeholders were called in to the governor's office for a briefing. The forecasts, demonstrated on charts, were like ominous storm clouds before a tornado. Not even all of the office holders were there to see them, some having sent surrogates.

Over the four years of my term in office, I watched as one person, John Haseley, worked tirelessly to successfully manage the Governor's office, be a friend and confidante to Ted Strickland, work with Cabinet Secretary Jan Allen, to oversee scores of cabinet agency heads and their activities and more.

The task of moving forward a 60,000-plus-person operation known as Ohio with a legislature firmly in the control of the other party, along with overseeing the operations of the Ohio Democratic Party in the nation's seventh most populous state was a tall order. It was unfathomable to me how one person could do it all. It was a lot of plates to keep spinning at once.

As for Ted, I observed up close something that I suspect voters have learned about their elected officials over time—a humble, sweet man with a preacher, prison psychologist background who was at great risk of not emerging from the meat grinder of elected office as the same cut of meat as when he entered it. In nearly every state, the governor is the head of his or her party in that state. In Ohio, Ted's successor, John Kasich, had to work to change the makeup of his GOP state party's governing body to ensure that he had a party that was in synch with his vision. He did so with aplomb. But for any governor, this de facto party leadership position is an added and often complex burden.

It's all too easy for old-time machine political party politics to fill the gap left when such a party leader becomes enmeshed in the affairs of state. It's worse when that mentality seeps into and becomes part of the social mores used in governing. When nubile politicos, who much like children in a dysfunctional family, believe that they, too, must exercise counter-intuitive behavior to get ahead or even be noticed, "the emperor has no clothes" situations could fill a wardrobe. Moreover, when this same mentality so often found in the bowels and gutters of party politics is accepted by members of the media with a sniff and a shrug as if watching gladiators from afar, it's hard for things to get better.

Suffice it to say, as I watched high school students sing during the prelude to one of President Obama's 2011 visits to Ohio, rosy with anticipation for just a glimpse of the President, I silently hoped that their enthusiasm would never tarnish. I hoped that the frayed, gilded curtain of politics, public office and political leadership would never be fully parted for them to see what often lies behind it. We can't afford for them to lose hope.

The fewer and fewer of experienced, would-be candidates who make the foray into running for or returning to public office remind me of the tired and sweaty fighters in the ring who get up with great effort just once more from the seeming knockout punch—delivered by the media, their political parties or even the deluded public. They shake the sweat and blood from their eyes, giving it one last swing to say, "No, I will not be broken by this." Sometimes they succeed, and sometimes they don't. But when they keep trying, we ponder what it is that keeps drawing them in.

The American public is a quiet and watchful group. Those who have fought in the ring out of a sense of public duty, regardless of outcome, regardless of party, remain admired by many while still scorned by others. There are no clear winners in politics.

Admirers often see the winners as principled fighters, as catalytic sparks for change. The hope and the goal is that, after the fight, win or lose, those who began as principled fighters can still identify who they are and why they're there. The hope and goal are that such fighters can express and articulate into words and actions what they've learned.

The essential hope and goal are that these fighters can inspire the high school students, college students, people of color and differing sexual orientation and gender identity, nationality, religion, people with unpronounceable names, the downtrodden and poor, that each of them matters. With the changes that are ahead—telecommunications, travel, a global economy, and more—the politics of the future must reflect this diversity of personhood, human needs and interests.

In 2010 when politics' traditional, conventional wisdom failed Ted Strickland and so many others, the costs were irretrievably devastating. The conventional political tools (used by both parties) of money, power, bullying and retribution could not save them from a complete loss of Democratic control of Ohio government (loss of every statewide office and the majority control of the Ohio House and further losses in the Ohio Senate.) Similar Democratic devastation was the norm around the country. To many this was unthinkable. To me it was a symptom of a need for real political change, a necessary prerequisite to moving to a higher ground of political and democratic involvement, so that "politics" can be seen more in the context of the "body politic" and less in the resigned sigh of, "that's just politics."

On the night of the general election of my last year in office, November 2, 2010, I was no longer a candidate for any office. My job was simply to make sure the election ran smoothly for the statewide races. As vote counts came in, all of the down ticket statewide races were clearly going to Republican candidates, except for Ohio Attorney General Richard Cordray. His numbers were precariously close to those of former U.S. Senator Mike Dewine, who was seeking a return to office, having lost in 2006 to now Senator Sherrod Brown. Ted's numbers were not as close as Rich's, and challenger and former Congressman John Kasich was winning. The night was wearing on, and no improvement was being seen for either Democratic candidate. I left the Secretary of State's office just before 9:00 p.m. and traveled to the Hyatt Regency for media interviews held where the Democrats were gathering for what was supposed to be an election night victory celebration.

Lee Fisher's inevitable and interminable concession speech was underway. I focused on my interview that was occurring at the back of the large room. I was barely acknowledged by anyone in the room, trying to slip in and out quietly. Once the interviews were completed, out of respect, I headed over to Franklin County Clerk of Courts Maryellen O'Shaughnessy's private gathering room. She was running on the Democratic ticket to succeed me.

When I entered the room, she said apologetically, "I'm afraid I'm not going to be able to hold the seat for you. I'm sorry." I gave her a hug and asked if she had conceded yet. She told me she had not. Her campaign manager, supplied by the Ohio Democratic Party, had never joined her that evening. Instead, he had remained in the "war room" of the Ohio Democratic Party to gather and compile statewide election results. He had given her Jon Husted's cell number and told her she could not concede until Ted or his people told her she could. I challenged her that it was her own race, and she should do whatever she wanted to do. She refused to cross the line and did not call Jon Husted until she was permitted to do so by party leaders. She did what the party expected of her, waiting until Ted conceded much too late, himself, into the evening. She stood with the other losing Democratic candidates on stage. I watched it on television.

As for Ted's loss, the results continued to come in late into the evening. I had learned from Brian Shinn before I left for the Hyatt that evening that the Strickland campaign, along with veteran attorney Don McTigue and some Democratic operatives at the Franklin County Board of Elections, believed there were an inordinate number of provisional ballots voted in The Ohio State University campus area. They also believed they could find a way under Ohio law to open these ballots and count them election night. They decided that these ballots had been voted provisionally in error. Their theory was that, instead of being given paper ballots when voters expressed that preference over voting on electronic machines, they had erroneously been given provisional ballots. Knowing how the deputy director of the Franklin County Board of Elections, Matt Damschroder, was adamantly opposed to using these backup paper ballots (the board had nearly run out of provisional ballots at the 2008 primary election when they were first mandated), it may have been plausible. However, it was not provable. Brian and I both knew that what we were being asked to do was not authorized or permitted by law, regardless of whether or not any mistakes had been made.

As I walked in to the Hyatt ballroom, Kent Markus, Governor Strickland's chief counsel, began calling my cell phone. I saw his name show up on my caller ID and ignored it. He called again.

I answered it without saying hello. I simply said, "Kent, I'm getting ready to do an interview. I need to call you back, and I'm not talking to you about provisional ballots." Before he could say anything more, I ended the call.

When I returned to my state office, I learned that Kent Markus had not let up. Brian Shinn, Mike Rankin and another one of the office's election attorneys came to my office. We needed to deal with Kent on the provisional ballot issue in Franklin County. With the three of them seated around my desk, I dialed Kent on my speaker phone in my state office. The conversation that ensued was astounding.

Kent informed us that the Franklin County Board of Elections was poised to take a vote on the opening of provisional ballots from the campus precincts where they believed voters had been given provisional instead of regular paper ballots. Kent wanted to know if I would break a tie vote in favor of Democrats who would vote to open them. I told him flatly "no," then thought better of previewing such a vote. I qualified that I would obviously have to see the question, but if it involved opening provisional ballots election night, I could not support that. The law did not permit it.

He continued to argue, "But they're not provisional ballots. They're regular paper ballots voted in error as provisional ballots." It was one of the lamest legal arguments I had heard.

I knew why he wanted them opened. If Governor Strickland's vote count could be moved up, he would not have to concede, and there could be a legal fight over provisional ballots, giving the Governor a fighting chance to still win the election. This is why one Republican tactic in Presidential elections has been to push as many voters as possible into provisional ballots. They are not counted until almost two weeks after the election. They are contained in secrecy envelopes within identification envelopes. Legal nitpicking often results in their invalidation, affecting the final vote count. These ballots are thought to be more likely to be Democratic votes. Once a paper provisional ballot is separated from its stub (which contains an identifying number), it is forever secret and unable to be identified with any particular voter. A *provisional* ballot means the validity of the vote is in question. That is why the ballot cannot be counted election night—the eligibility of the voter must be ascertained before a ballot may be counted.

The Governor's chief legal counsel was asking me to—how else do I say it—break the law. I had liked and trusted Kent, and this seemed out of character for him. I wondered about the pressures he was acting under and whether they existed by circumstance or by command. There was never a doubt in my mind about what I would do. I said, "Kent, I took an oath to follow the laws and the constitutions of the State of Ohio and the United States. I will follow them. That is my duty."

He verbally backed away, realizing how this discussion sounded. "I'm not asking you not to follow the law. I would never do that," he said. He further tried to explain his position.

I countered, exasperated, "Kent, I was elected Secretary of State by the people of Ohio, not you. This is one situation the Governor and you cannot control."

Clearly frustrated, he sputtered, "You don't understand. There are serious political consequences."

I had had it. I said in the most steely way I knew how, "Kent, when I look at the Ohio Revised Code for reasons to open provisional ballots on election night, I don't find 'serious political consequences' as one of them." Brian Shinn looked as if he had just seen a slapstick comedy riff in the middle of a church service, except what he and the two other attorneys in the room had heard with their own ears was about as light-hearted as a machine gun.

Governor Strickland continued to hold out. He would not concede the election. We learned that his campaign was starting to make statements to members of the media impugning the integrity of the election. When we heard this, I directed media staff to begin a proactive release about the statistical impossibility of a Strickland win. We needed to protect public trust in the election results. Patrick Gallaway had just left the office. We called him to come back to the office as quickly as possible. We began to struggle with the wording of a release. I was incredulous that we were having to defend the integrity of the election against claims of the Governor of our own party. Then, as quickly as a sleight of hand, Governor Strickland conceded. I called Patrick and told him not to come back. It was done.

Ted Strickland had only spoken to me once since the primary election, and since that time he never spoke to me again. I have been systematically excluded from Ohio Democratic Party activities, including the epic $42 million dollar labor and Democratic effort to fight back a 2011 ban on collective bargaining. This even led to false claims that I did not support labor in its effort. At the times I made attempts to participate, appearing at state party functions, my presence was not acknowledged. I have believed and always will believe that it is the office that deserves the respect, regardless of the like or dislike of its holder. There is a reason that once elected, the title of "Honorable" continues with the holder until death.

Since leaving office, Governor Strickland formed a consulting firm that on its website described itself as "connected." His firm moved into the same building as my law firm which had already occupied an entire floor there. His firm is situated on the floor directly above, locating itself on the same side of the building as the attorneys' offices on our floor, including mine. In an effort to extend an olive branch, in 2011 I offered to work with him on reforming redistricting for legislative districts in Ohio; I had a statewide initiative petition already drafted to amend the state constitution. My offer was declined.

A year later in 2012 I handed over that petition as a contribution to good government groups. Those still aligned with the former governor offered groups the equivalent of the "next shiny object"—funding and the promise to gain enough signatures to qualify for the ballot. They took it and generally lost control of the effort. As the ballot issue campaign struggled for traction, emails exhorting women to support the effort were sent from Frances Strickland and former State Representative Joan

Lawrence. The issue failed miserably at the 2012 general election.

Even had I known the "serious political consequences" I would face, nothing would have changed my decision on November 2, 2010. If I had to do it all over again, I would still opt to take the political beating I have, rather than capitulate.

That Ted Strickland's successor, John Kasich, unveiled massive changes borne of doctrinal differences of nearly galactic proportions should have been no surprise to anyone. John Kasich told people what he was going to do; they voted him into office, and he and his troops began the march up the hill. As the banner of the first battle unfurled, Ohio public workers found themselves stripped of collective bargaining rights. While Governor Kasich fired the first shot at what many on both sides of the aisle had perceived as a malaise of government inaction, those who had not taken him seriously realized that their current remorse was much worse than their previous indifference. The shock morphed into rage and then activity that produced a backlash that knocked the wind out of the confidence of most of Ohio's new Republican leaders. Senate Bill 5, the public employee collective bargaining ban, was defeated by more votes than put John Kasich into office.

Ted left office at age 69 and soon after was bested in his bid to chair the DNC by Florida Congresswoman Debbie Wasserman Schultz. Standing at the Statehouse with a bullhorn, calling out Governor Kasich amidst throngs of union members and their supporters, he placed himself squarely in the middle of the battle for public employee collective bargaining rights in Ohio. Had he been reelected, he would have instead been negotiating with them as their employer in the middle of a second term. Ohio was a battleground once again. ≈

Chapter 22

Deciding to Run for the U.S. Senate

In January 2009 before the Presidential inauguration of Barack Obama, I sought Ted Strickland's counsel about whether or not I should run for the open U.S. Senate seat being vacated by former governor and Senator George Voinovich. By then Treasurer (later Attorney General) Rich Cordray and I had discussed and agreed that we did not ever want to run against each other at any time in the future. He had made it very clear that he intended to run for governor one day. I had served as his treasurer when he ran for the U.S. Senate in 2000 and lost in the Democratic primary to Ted Celeste, brother of former Ohio Governor Richard Celeste. I believed Rich's opinions about the office he stated he had desired to hold to be well formed. I had had a professor of Gerontology at Miami University who had told me at one juncture, "You'd be good in politics," to which I replied spontaneously, "Yes, I'd like to be a U.S. Senator." The professor's immediate remarks were, "Well, I didn't mean that."

By this time, many Democratic women from throughout the state had already quietly made it clear to me that they were counting on me to run for higher office. Never has a woman been elected to the U.S. Senate or even Governor in her own right in Ohio. As it became apparent that Senator Voinovich would not run for reelection, some women would walk by and whisper in my ear, "Do it!"

Never before had a woman currently holding statewide office been a candidate for U.S. Senate (there have only been five women elected to statewide executive office in Ohio their own right). Democrat Mary Boyle, a Cuyahoga County commissioner, had run for the U.S. Senate in 1994 and in 1998, narrowly losing a bruising primary battle in 1994 after the party favored the son-in-law of retiring Senator Howard Metzenbaum, Joel Hyatt. He lost to Mike DeWine that fall. Republican Bernadine Healy, a physician, cardiologist, and a former head of the National Institutes of Health, professor of medicine at Johns Hopkins University, professor and dean of the College of Medicine and Public Health at The Ohio State University and eventually president of the American Red Cross had also run that year in the Republican primary and lost to Mike Dewine.

By early January 2009, new state representative John Carney had asked me to swear him into office. He represented the part of Columbus where I had largely grown up, known as "Clintonville." The swearing in ceremony was in the shelter house at the Columbus Park of Roses—a place where I had attended Girl Scout functions, and as a mother, marching band functions for my daughters. There was a casting pond at the park on which I skated so much as a youngster that I had even once been taken from it in an ambulance after suffering a concussion playing crack the whip on the ice with my friends. Swearing in this new state rep at the Park of Roses meant a lot to me.

When I arrived at the shelter house, I learned that I was only to swear in the new state rep and that Rich Cordray was the speaker for the event. I was disappointed to say the least, and it was made clear to me that I was to make no remarks. Rick had accompanied me, and it was in moments like this that I not only felt disappointed for myself but for him as well. Why would he waste his time to come and be with me for some perfunctory act that nearly anyone could have performed? Despite that, we always tried to enjoy the circumstances we were in; rank and file Democrats make that easy. Some of them expressed disappointment that I did not speak other than to swear in the new state rep.

Our next event that night was to attend a pre-Presidential inaugural private dinner for the top officers of the Ohio Association of Public School Employees Association, known as "OAPSE." Rick and I were attending at the invitation of Joe Rugola, who, in addition to being OAPSE's president, served as president of the Ohio AFL-CIO, succeeding Bill Burga. Joe had said that he wasn't inviting just anyone to this event and really wanted me there, so Rick and I traipsed on a Saturday night from the shelter house of my youth to a swanky hotel dining room in northeast Columbus.

It was at this event that I first met John Haseley's wife, who stated matter-of-factly that she and John started dating "at the same time he and Ted did." We all had laughed at this one. She is obviously a very understanding and tolerant wife for the high toll politics takes on families. To my surprise, Rich Cordray appeared there as well. No other statewide officials had been invited.

During the dinner, Joe Rugola brought both Rich and me to the front of the room. Starting first with me, Joe said, "Now, Jennifer here ran a great election in 2008, and she should be so proud of that, but I think even Jennifer will agree that we have to think of the future of our party beyond Ted Strickland, and that's Rich Cordray." I watched some of the few women in the audience become wide-eyed with dropped jaws. Luckily, my training as a judge caused me to quickly set a stone-face. I gave it my best vacant-eyed smile, not letting any discomfort show about what amounted to a public ranking ceremony by the highest union official in the State of Ohio.

We left to go to our next event, which was a reopening of the Columbus Symphony Orchestra. We were guests of former U.S. Senator John Glenn, who was narrating the program. We enjoyed the symphony performance and relished the time spent with John and Annie Glenn that evening. Senator Glenn and I talked of the experience of holding public office. Rick talked more with Annie, who is so easy to talk with about nearly any subject. She has a way of making a person feel comfortable with her sparking eyes and sweet smile. Seeing the Glenns was the highlight of our entire evening.

The next morning, a Sunday morning, I woke up at 6:00 a.m. This was highly unusual, since weekends were when I caught up on my sleep from less than six-hour nights of sleep during the week. I lay on my stomach, head on the mattress without a pillow, looking at the wall, and the words came into my head slowly and with decisiveness, "I will not be Betty Montgomery."

I like Betty Montgomery, the first woman to be elected Attorney General and Auditor in Ohio. She is Republican. Betty Montgomery's first foray into statewide office happened when she ran for Ohio Attorney General in 1994 against then one-term incumbent Lee Fisher. She ran a great race and defeated him. She was just the third woman to be elected to executive statewide office in her own right in the history of Ohio. (Former State Auditor, now Lieutenant Governor Mary Taylor and I were the fourth and fifth, elected in 2006—Ohio became a state in 1803.) Betty was the best thing the Ohio GOP had going for it in 2006, enjoying wide popularity among rank and file members, with even Democrats on her staff singing her praises. She had served two terms as Ohio's attorney general (defeating Rich Cordray who ran against her in 1998), was term limited and then served a term as State Auditor. She decided to run for governor in 2006, but so did Jim Petro, who had been elected and served two terms as state auditor in 1994 and one term as Attorney General, and also Secretary of State Ken Blackwell. Ken Blackwell had been appointed state treasurer in the early 1990's when then President Bill Clinton tapped State Treasurer Mary Ellen Withrow to serve as U.S. Treasurer.

In 2006 Bob Taft was Ohio's term-limited governor. Governor Taft first expressed the desire to run for Governor in 1990. He was told by the GOP elite that it was not his turn and to stand down and run for Ohio Secretary of State so that George Voinovich, mayor of Cleveland and a former Lieutenant Governor for Governor James Rhodes, could be the GOP gubernatorial nominee. In 1990 Bob Taft beat Secretary of State incumbent Sherrod Brown for that office, while George Voinovich defeated former attorney general and secretary of state Tony Celebrezze for governor. As a result, the Democrats lost control of the apportionment board that drew state legislative district lines.

Bob Taft's "turn" came up in 1998. He was opposed by Lee Fisher (four years after Fisher was defeated as an incumbent by Betty Montgomery for Attorney General). In 1998, Ken Blackwell, like Bob Taft eight years earlier, said that *he* wanted to run for governor, after serving a partial appointment and being elected to his first full term as Treasurer of Ohio. Blackwell, like Taft, was told to wait *his* turn and moved into the "holding pen" of the secretary of state's office. By 2006, Ken Blackwell was term limited and it was finally his turn (according to the logic of politics). Except, the real choice of the Ohio Republican Party seemed to be Jim Petro. Betty was convinced to get out of the race, in part because "they stepped on my air hose," she once said in a joint television interview with me. (She was losing in the money race but not in popularity.) Petro swung to the far right as he ran television commercials where a man and woman's hands were one over the other with a "voice-over" that Jim Petro believed marriage should be between a man and a woman, even though he had previously opposed the 2004 Ohio constitutional amendment to ban same sex marriage.

It was like too many bees swarming on one lone flower in the sun—Betty was convinced to run for attorney general again, an office she clearly loved. Blackwell was in it to win it; many Statehouse regulars, including some high-powered lobbyists, backed Petro. Already to the far right, Blackwell won, since primaries usually reflect the more extreme swing of the party. No one knows whether Betty Montgomery would have been able to beat Ted Strickland, but most believe she would have done eons better than Ken Blackwell did, and polls were showing that she could. Ted Strickland's win 60.54% to 36.65% over Ken Blackwell was like a victory lap around the ice for a hockey player who knocked the puck into the goal with one swing of the stick—no real sweat. So, after what Joe Rugola did and said the night before, no way was I going to get slated for a seat on the bench like Betty Montgomery. I learned from her and owed that much to the women of my state.

I talked about it with Rick that day, and we were still thinking about how kind the Glenns had been to us the night before and how weird the prelude to it had been. Already, I had been the only statewide Democratic office holder to not be on the stage at Richard Cordray's and Kevin Boyce's joint swearing-in ceremonies for Attorney General and State Treasurer, respectively, after the 2008 general election. At my own swearing in, our daughter Kate had made sure that not only each office holder, but his spouse had a place on the stage.

For the Ohio delegation breakfasts at the Democratic National Convention in Denver, each of the other statewide office holders had been tapped to host the delegation breakfasts. With four men and one woman and three breakfasts to host, it seemed that the party could only compartmentalize by gender. I was placed on par with the first and second ladies, Frances Strickland and Peggy Fisher as cohosts. It was clear that the party barely knew what to do with female office holders then. While male Democratic office holders had convention floor seats reserved for their wives, Congresswoman Betty Sutton and I had to fight for seats for our husbands.

They say, in politics, timing is everything. That same Sunday, my friend and colleague at the time, Robin Carnahan, Secretary of State of Missouri, called me on my cell phone. She had already declared her candidacy for the U.S. Senate for the seat of retiring Missouri Senator Kit Bond.

"Well, are you in?" she said when I answered the phone. "What do you mean?" I said. "You know what I mean," she laughed. "Are you running for the Senate?"

"I don't know," I said. I went on to recount to her the happenings of the last twenty-four hours, and she cut me short saying, "Well, you'd better make up your mind, because your senator is going to announce tomorrow that he's not running for reelection."

"How do you know that?" I said. "Oh, I have my ways," she laughed. We talked a bit longer and said our good-byes.

Then, Dale Butland, a long-time aide for Senator John Glenn called me to alert me that Senator George Voinovich would not be running for reelection. I was sitting at the dining room table working on bills when he called. Soon after, Rick called downstairs to me from his study. "Hey, there's a blog post that Voinovich is going to announce tomorrow that he's not running for reelection." He started down the stairs and came up to the table. I looked up and smiled, "I know."

Monday, the next day, the weather was icy, and I was traveling up interstate 71 from downtown with an aide when my cell phone rang. It was Lee Fisher. He wanted to know about whether I had plans to run for the Senate. I said I was considering. I asked him the same question in return. He said he was considering it, too. We both agreed that we should talk and decided we would try to get together at the Presidential inauguration in DC.

Newspapers started speculating. Multiple Democrats' and Republicans' pictures appeared on the front pages of newspapers all over the state. Of course, I was the only one wearing a pink jacket, a perquisite of being a woman office holder and candidate. Some women are adamantly against a woman leader wearing pink, but why not? If it looks good on you, go with it. Women have more freedom that way. Dan Rather during one interview in my office had remarked how nice my light green jacket had looked for our television interview. I told him with a smile that women are more fortunate because we have a wider variety of colors to choose from. He could not disagree with me that no man could ever wear a pale green jacket trimmed in black and pull it off with credibility.

Antoinette had counseled me that I needed to meet with Governor Strickland to discuss whether it was feasible for me to run for the Senate rather than for reelection. He met me the night of his chief security detail officer's birthday. I arrived at the residence in Bexley on the east side of Columbus as Ted and he were returning from a dinner in Columbus. After Frances presented the security detail officer with a small cake, and he blew out the candle, Ted and I began our discussion, alone at the kitchen table at the residence.

"Governor," I said. "I want to run for the Senate, but I need to know how you feel about it. I have multiple levels of consideration—personal, family, professional and political. For the political I have to determine if I can raise the money, if I am a viable candidate and if I have party support, and you're the key to party support, Governor. If you have a problem with me running, I need to know." Ted looked uncomfortable.

We retired to the study where we sat in front of a crackling fire, each of us in leather tufted wing back chairs angled toward the fire but leaving us with the ability to face each other as we sat there. He put together the tips of his fingertips from each hand. "Ah, the Senate," he said. "That is a very deliberative body." He looked slightly up and didn't say much. I began to wonder if he wanted to run for it. He had considered it in 2005 when he looked at polling numbers for then Senator Mike Dewine and publicly suggested Sherrod Brown should run for governor. Still, silence.

I finally said, "Governor, do *you* want to run for the Senate?" He paused, seeming to be caught off guard. Stone faced, he said, "That would not be prudent at this time." He went on to ask who else was considering. I tossed out the names: Congresswoman Betty Sutton, Lieutenant Governor Lee Fisher, Congressman Tim Ryan. We rolled through each name, considering each one. Tim was not likely to run. He had no opinion on Betty; he had to be reminded of who she was. As for Lee Fisher, he said strangely, "Ultimately, I don't think Lee will run." He said it twice. In hindsight, I believe he thought it to be his "out" from having to make a decision. As I mulled over this conversation in my head multiple times after that night, it was as if he didn't want to tell me not to run and be responsible for that, but neither did he want to give me his support. He simply eventually said, "Follow your heart." I told him I wanted to run. He said nothing.

If I had been more cerebral in my approach, I would have asked whether he would commit or had committed to support or endorse Lee if Lee ran. But, when I heard the words, "follow your heart," I did not want to stop and draw out any potential negatives, because what I was told to follow already knew what it wanted to do. After two hours, beginning first at the kitchen table, then at the fire and then back to the kitchen table and with a lot of Diet Coke, I had not been told to stand down, even though many would argue I was needed for my office after 2010—to serve as a member of the state apportionment board in 2011. This was clearly a big political drawback to my running for any other office rather than running for reelection. Democrats had lost the privilege of drawing legislative district lines in 1990 when Sherrod Brown and Tony Celebrezze were defeated for Secretary of State and Governor, respectively, and thereafter when Bob Taft beat Lee Fisher for Governor in 1998.

At the 2009 Presidential Inauguration for President Obama, I stayed at the Phoenix Park Hotel, one of the union hotels in DC with a great location close to the Capitol. Lee stayed at the Mayflower Hotel, site of Ohio Democratic Party inaugural activities, bringing with him his full state security detail. Ted and I had discussed in our fireside chat about Ted attending the inauguration; he had not decided if he was going to go. I had been shocked and said, "Governor, you have to go to the inauguration. You need to be there." He said he probably would go but stay only one night. I asked where he would stay, and he said he was thinking of just sleeping on the couch or floor of his DC office. Again, I discouraged that, but he said he didn't want to spend the money. Sure enough, the morning of the inauguration, I was walking to the long lines to attend the inauguration and saw Ted, John Haseley and several others about to be interviewed by a television crew in front of the Ohio office in DC. They had indeed slept at the State of Ohio Washington office, Ted looking as clean and pressed with every soft blonde hair in place as he always did, and John looking disheveled like someone who had just spent a fitful night in an office.

As for my Washington meeting with Lee, he surprisingly had agreed to meet with me at my hotel to discuss the Senate race. At the last minute he sent me a message backing out. He wanted me to meet him at his hotel, at the Mayflower. That didn't work for me, so I demurred, and we agreed we would meet in Columbus after the inauguration.

The inauguration was a joyful and stressful time. To be among such a diverse group of people, many of whom were not "the usual political suspects," and whom a decade or two ago would likely not have had access to such an historic event, was amazing. The lines were long to get onto the grassy area in front of the Capitol and the Washington Mall behind it. Once we were in, what was even more amazing was the rapt attention paid to our new President's words—the silence of the audience as he spoke must have been sobering for him. He was elected on a message of change, and people were thirsting for a new way, a new time and another chance at greatness for the country they loved. I have experienced no other time like that, and it was a sheer privilege just to be there. I was grateful that Rick, our daughter, Kate, and I were there to witness it together.

Later that evening, I wore the Bergdorf-Goodman dress from the Kennedy award ceremony to the inaugural ball, figuratively cutting the cost of the dress in half by wearing it a second time. I recall talking with many Democrats at the various events at the inauguration, some of whom were supportive of the prospect of my Senate run and others who were concerned with only the prospects of Democrats being able to draw the legislative district lines. Many of them seemed to forget that at least two Democrats, Ted and me, had to win reelection before any Democrats could control drawing the lines. It was clear to me from the comments of the naysayers that the proverbial battlefield lines were being drawn. It even seemed as if land mines had been planted well before my arrival.

During that visit to DC, I was scheduled to meet with New Jersey Senator Bob Menendez, who was then chair of the Democratic Senatorial Campaign Committee, known as the DSCC. I had snagged the meeting with the help of Senator Glenn, who first had called Nevada Senator and Majority Leader Harry Reid, who referred him to DSCC Chair Menendez. Senator Glenn had dutifully and kindly called Senator Menendez' office to open up for me the opportunity to meet with him while I was in DC for the inauguration.

The meeting with Senator Menendez was established before I left Columbus for DC. Jayme Staley, my campaign political director, who accompanied me and had set the itinerary for the DC trip, was so nervous for the meeting, she left the informational packets for the meeting in the car with our driver. Senator Menendez met with me for less than fifteen minutes and challenged me on each point I made. Finally, I said, "Look, what do you want to talk about? Is it money? I raised almost $2 million for the Ohio Secretary of State's race, and that was a down ticket race where Sherrod Brown and Ted Strickland were also running. I raised money from all 50 states and from Americans in Canada, Japan, France and Mexico. I won the state with 55 percent of the vote, defeating my opponent in his home county. I can do this, and I'm going to run," I said looking him straight in the eye. He was clearly unnerved.

"Ted Strickland still carries a lot of weight in this town, and people listen to what he has to say," said Senator Menendez. I brushed it off mentally. I thanked him and left with Jayme, who was shocked at what I had done in that meeting. The driver returned to pick us up and Jayme doubled back with the folders she had left in the car, taking them up the stairs and back to his office.

At the inaugural ball, Doug Kelly, Executive Director of the Ohio Democratic Party, began berating me in front of others attending the ball, saying that I should not run for the Senate but only for reelection, because of the apportionment board. Jayme called him away from me and chided him out of earshot that he had no business talking to an elected, statewide office holder that way, especially in public. He called (twice) the next day, apologizing profusely. Charlie Brown, brother of Sherrod Brown and one-time attorney general of West Virginia, was at the Ohio ball. I'll never forget campaigning for his race for attorney general in Weirton, West Virginia, where the houses are far apart and set up high, with steps up that seemed to go on forever, when it was less than 3 months after I gave birth to Laura, an exceptionally big baby. Charlie questioned me on the wisdom of running. Yet, he stated that this was a once-in-a-generation time that could be like being in the Senate during the Johnson Administration of the 1960's or the FDR Administration of the 1940's where major legislation to bring greater social equality and economic opportunity to millions could occur. It was an exciting thought, even if Charlie was less than enthusiastic about my run.

I introduced myself to Senator Tom Harkin from Iowa, and talked with Governor Tom and his wife Christie Vilsack of Iowa. The men seemed nonplussed about my run for the Senate. They seemed to know the issues of the state ahead of time and did not warm to the idea. It seemed that any real DC establishment excitement about my candidacy had been nipped in the bud, and I did not understand why.

During that trip I had a meeting with EMILY's List's political director, Jonathan Parker. EMILY's List was formed in 1983 by Ellen Malcolm, who perfected the art of bundling checks for women candidates with an organization named for the principle that "Early Money Is Like Yeast," hence, EMILY's List.

One of the first things Jonathan Parker said to me was that he had received a call from John Haseley, Governor Strickland's chief of staff, earlier in the week. I stiffened. I thought that was extremely odd. Parker went on to say, "You shouldn't run if Ted Strickland endorses Lee Fisher." My eventual Senate campaign manager, David Dettman, used to shake his head and say, "Here was a guy telling you not to run against a guy if another guy endorses him, and that's coming from EMILY's List?"

When Jonathan Parker had mentioned the call from Ohio, instead of questioning why John Haseley had called him, I immediately became suspicious of Jonathan Parker and decided to pull back from providing him with any significant information. A smarter me would have called John Haseley right after this meeting and asked him why he was conferring with EMILY's List (which supports women candidates). But smarter "me's" usually don't show up for most people until it's well over.

After I returned to Columbus, Parker would call me at least weekly to ask me what was going on. Eventually I wouldn't answer his calls until after I had declared my candidacy. EMILY's List was involved with the campaign, but it refused to endorse my candidacy and even discouraged at least one of my regular donors from contributing to my campaign. EMILY's List was in constant contact with staff at the DSCC and seemed to be more focused on being in step with the Washington establishment, setting a high fundraising bar in a short time to test my "viability" as a candidate, based solely on how much "dough" I could raise on my own before they would supply any proverbial "yeast."

Later, one of the staffers the organization sent to Columbus to assess our campaign and give us guidance was heard at a party attended by my DC media consultant trashing my campaign. He almost took it to blows with her. The DC rap was set up and heard time and again, "Great candidate, but she can't raise money." This is what happens in party primaries, especially to women. As Betty Montgomery put it so visually, the party establishment "steps on the air hose" for funding and then turns around and says that she can't raise money, often damaging the candidate for years to come.

When Lee and I finally met to talk about the Senate race, it was mid- to late-January. We met at Rick's law office, a converted, stately, Victorian house. We met in the main conference room. Lee's two state security detail members sat in the library with Jayme Staley across the hall. In the conference room, I sat at the end of the table facing Lee, who was seated at an angle to my right. I told him very directly that I was running. He said he hadn't made up his mind. Finally, I faced him, looked him squarely in the eye and said, "Look, if you and I run for the Senate, one of us will no longer be an office holder. I can come back. I don't know about you." With two statewide losses already under his belt, that statement seemed to particularly unnerve him. We agreed that when/if either of us announced, we would inform the other before doing so. Soon after my direct challenge, he got up and left, practically bolting out the front door and without letting his security detail know he was leaving. I walked into the library to see the two plain clothed officers sitting in informal, lounged positions at the large table.

"Uh, he just left," I said pointing with my thumb over my shoulder. They immediately jumped up and briskly walked out the front door. ≈

Chapter 23

Kickoff

"Jennifer, think about it," said Paul Tipps. "How many campaign managers survive from the beginning to the end of the campaign? Usually, there aren't many. Who may be the right manager for the beginning of a campaign may not work later in the campaign." Paul made great sense as usual. He was talking about how rare it was that a campaign manager like John Haseley lasted the entire Strickland campaign for governor in 2005 and 2006.

It was early 2009. I was preparing for my run for the U.S. Senate. Now it was my turn to pick a manager. Antoinette, my consummate political advisor for more than seven years by that time, was tied up in my state office as Assistant Secretary of State. I needed her where she was. She and Jayme Staley, my campaign political director, conferred and agreed that I should talk with Susan Markham from EMILY's List, who was looking to leave and wanted to manage a U.S. Senate campaign. Susan fervently believed in electing more women to office.

During the inauguration of President Obama in Washington, DC, Rick and I scheduled coffee with her at the Corner Bakery across from the historic Willard Hotel. I had just attended a DSCC breakfast there with Cincinnati attorney Stan Chesley, who glided me through the room, introducing me to Senators from around the country whom I had only seen on television before this. Meeting Susan afterward was an easy walk across the street.

We talked, and I observed Susan's passion for the work of electing women. Even though she had two small children, a

¤388

husband and a solid career in DC, Susan believed in me and believed she could handle the job in Ohio, her home state. When I asked her on the spot in the restaurant if she would be my manager, I remember the shocked look on her face, her hands held apart in a taut gesture, her pausing and saying, "Okay!" It was much more than Antoinette and Jayme had prepared her for or than she expected. The catch was that she was still at EMILY's List. I had not yet met with Jonathan Parker, so when I did, I asked that Susan be permitted to be my "tracker" at EMILY's List, assigned to monitor my U.S. Senate campaign. He agreed.

Several weeks later, when I saw Minnesota Secretary of State Mark Ritchie as we were both in DC, he had told me about a great "new media" consultant who had not only created and managed his website but produced his television ad, John Rohrbach. I met with John at Reagan National Airport at a table in a café right on the lower level promenade and signed him on. Using his laptop placed on the café table as we sat over our coffee he set up a Facebook page and YouTube site for my campaign. Things seemed to be whirling to where I wanted them to go.

On this trip to DC, I again met with Jonathan Parker at EMILY's List, along with Susan, and we decided after watching events in Ohio since the inauguration, it would be best for me to announce before Lee Fisher. By this time Lee had formed an exploratory committee and had begun raising money for a potential Senate run without actually declaring his candidacy. I was hearing through my own political intelligence that he was asking quite a few people at the time their opinions on his running, vacillating in what he would do and not seeming to be sure at all that he would make the run. He collected checks for his exploratory committee.

Shot from announcement video for the U. S. Senate; made in my home; kitchen in the background

Susan orchestrated the announcement event in part from DC and completed it on an extended visit to Columbus in February 2009. Our announcement date was set for February 17, 2009, the day after President's Day. We had decided to announce via an Internet video, as my friend, Robin Carnahan, had done for her Missouri Senate race. John Rohrbach produced the video, coming to Columbus with a cameraperson and scouting locations with tips from Susan. We shot video from morning until night. Susan did an impeccable job getting us from site to site with all the people we had recruited to appear in the video. We even recruited Susan's parents, who lived in town, and David Farrell's parents, who drove from Springfield, Ohio, to Columbus to be in it.

The weekend before, Rick and I had attended Sherrod Brown's mother's funeral in Mansfield, Ohio. Emily Brown died at 88 years old, having been one of Sherrod's best campaigners. She registered voters in Mansfield, Ohio, even into her 80's. She was a community organizer, and her works in her own right extended statewide, as a past President of the Ohio Council of YWCAs. The outpouring of love and grief on her death was palpable.

Emily Brown's funeral was held in the Mansfield church where she was a member. Near the front of the church I was seated to the right of first lady Frances Strickland, with Ted on her left. Rick was next to me, with Jayme Staley next to him and Lee

Fisher next to Jayme. It was a bit awkward with political folks still speculating about what would happen in the open Senate seat race. I had already talked with Sherrod by telephone, who at first argued with me about why I would want to run for the Senate, even though he had encouraged me to do so in early 2007 after he, himself, had taken office.

Speaking by phone on a Saturday morning in early February, he had said, somewhat exasperated, "Did you read Connie's [his wife's] book?" (about his 2006 race). I told him I that I had and that I believed I had a duty to run, to move women forward, since no woman had been elected to the U.S. Senate from Ohio—and besides I wanted to be involved in policy making. When I talked to him of my duty to run, I recalled that Sherrod had told me that his two brothers, Charlie and Bob, had pushed and even chided him with that same sense of duty in late 2005, that he had a duty to run for the Senate. Sherrod became very quiet, and then, in the gravelly voice that has developed over years of giving speeches, he barked out, "Go for it!" This was the old Sherrod that I knew from my years of working with him. These were the words that I needed to hear, said in this way and from my greatest political mentor and teacher.

At his mother's funeral, as I listened to him give his mother's eulogy and talk of her passion for electing women candidates, I couldn't imagine not having his support. "How could he not?" I mused as I sat in that church pew, sharing in his grief for the loss of such a special woman.

On the day we kicked off the campaign, EMILY's List had already sent to Columbus a fundraising consultant to work with me on raising money through "call time," that is, telephoning donors. Kari, the consultant from EMILY's List and Susan Markham were an imposing duo. It was as if they literally stormed in and took over. According to Jayme, they dictated what supplies should be purchased and with which funds, pushed to move my campaign office to rented space and set goals for raising funds, which if met, could provide me with the coveted EMILY's List endorsement. The EMILY's List fundraising consultant sat with me as I made calls, and used a green, electronic egg timer strategically placed in front of me to time each call and remind me to keep my calls short so that I could dial more and raise more. She left it for me as a "gift."

When what is known as "call time" is undertaken, the time spent on the phone is supported by at least that much, if not more time, in preparatory work of selecting the calls to make, researching the donors, pre-calling the telephone numbers to make sure they're accurate, and entering data into a specialized computer database to record when calls are made and the results of the calls. There are actually companies that most candidates use that specialize in this recordkeeping. Candidates who use this system (which includes most federal candidates) also enter their political contribution information into the system, making campaign finance reporting to the Federal Election Commission much easier, especially when having to aggregate contributions toward a limit over several reporting periods.

When contact is actually made via a fundraising call, or there have been a significant number of calls made to a particular potential donor, follow up letters are key—ideally by email or fax, but if necessary, by regular mail. Often, a contribution will follow. In recent years, fundraising consultants urge that candidates push for on-the-spot donations by credit card, having the candidate hand the phone to the consultant to take down the financial information, while the candidate moves on to the next call in the pile of call sheets set before her.

It is not unusual for there to be a bulletin board in the call room with daily and hourly fundraising goals posted in plain sight. Call time is sacred, uninterrupted time, requiring permission to get up and leave the room. When I had to travel for my duties as Secretary of State, a call-time staffer was posted in the car in the back seat, necessitating I use my own car, so that I could make calls enroute from one end of the state to another. We had two cell phones, my own Blackberry that appeared to the caller as a blocked call, and a flip-phone that was the "call back phone." When a message was left, it was the call back phone number. If the call back phone rang while enroute, I had to silently mouth to the person in the back seat who the caller was as the staffer furiously fished out the right call sheet from his or her alphabetized accordion file. Call time managers see the candidate at some of his or her most undignified moments, especially if the call back comes in at the time when she's juggling French fries and a burger while eating on the road.

When pressing state business interfered with car-time call time, I could feel the piercing glare of the call-time staffer into the back of my head as I carried out my state-required duties. This is the way it has been done since television advertising has become the standard means to disseminate a candidate's message. It's starting to change with the advent of Internet and social media. But, until that form of media is available and widely used by people of all ages and geography to *receive* a candidate's message, television and its attendant expense, along with the variety of consultants needed to make it work, continues to require this insane method of raising excessive and ever-increasing amounts of money.

On February 17, 2009, I called Lee Fisher mid-morning and informed him that I was announcing that day. He sounded alarmed and said he would be announcing in a few weeks. He was actually in Youngstown, Ohio that day, apparently with the

Governor. What he did was rush to Columbus, along with the Governor, quickly assemble a team of elected officials with as many women as he could and announce at approximately 6:00 p.m. that he was running, so as to keep me from having a news cycle to myself. As ridiculous as many on my team thought the move was, he succeeded in placing his name in contention along with mine on that kickoff day, and from that point on, especially when he gained the Governor's public endorsement, I was characterized as having run against Lee rather than vice versa.

Within days after Lee and I announced we were running for the Democratic nomination for the U.S. Senate, Antoinette had advised me to call John Haseley, the Governor's chief of staff, to ask that the Governor not endorse in the race or to at least wait. Major occurrences in history often hinge on inconsequential events. I called John, who committed that he would speak to the Governor about not publicly endorsing. It was reported to me that the Governor announced his endorsement of Lee Fisher that evening. I called John, completely baffled how this could have happened. John told me he had not been able to reach the Governor, that the Governor had lost his cell phone. Much later, in recalling these events, I remembered that the Governor traveled with at least two plain-clothes troopers, each of whom could be reached by phone.

By late February, Susan Markham was still on board, planning to leave EMILY's List and move to Columbus by May 2009. She planned to maintain her residence in DC, leaving her family for intermittent trips to Ohio. She would live with her parents in central Ohio when she was in Columbus. At the end of February, I traveled to see my mother in Louisiana, a trip I had planned since before I ran for the Senate. My plans were to travel directly to a federal election board meeting in Orlando in my role as Secretary of State upon leaving Louisiana. I asked Susan to please allow me to have a two-day visit with my mother, and then we could pick up in between meetings in Orlando. Being a relentless manager, she said okay and then scheduled a live blogging session for me while I was at my mother's home. She and John Rohrbach gave me "issues" sheets, with Rohrbach actually writing sample answers for me to potential questions that would be asked of me and answered by me online.

I was hesitant about this, as I wasn't sure these answers were what I really believed, especially without seeing the research to back them up. But this is also a standard practice. I was used to being an expert at what I did as Ohio Secretary of State, having previously served in the office and after that, practiced election law for 13 years. I had developed independence, having served nearly 5 years as a judge. Is this how it really worked in Congress? Candidates and Congresspeople just stuck to canned issues papers?

While Rick and I were staying at my mother's home, I received an email message from a woman in Cuyahoga County telling me I should not be in the Senate race. She was married to a former state senator and had been a supporter in my Secretary of State's race. She basically said it was not my turn—it was Lee's turn to run for the Senate. She talked of Lee's in-laws who had both served on Cleveland City Council, that his mother-in-law had set the tone for women in politics, with women gathering in people's homes to support candidates, making large pots of pasta for campaign workers, and so forth. I was shocked. Rick and I on separate occasions had written to Connie Schultz, Sherrod Brown's wife. She is an unapologetic and outspoken feminist who was a popular columnist for the Cleveland Plain Dealer. Strangely, Connie said to be careful not to play the 'gender card.'

I mulled this over for several months as my Senate campaign progressed. "What exactly *is* playing the "gender card?" I thought. Here is what I concluded: playing the "gender card" is perceived as a negative when it's used to accuse someone of wrongdoing and to assign blame based on this kind of discrimination. It's legal to fight this kind of discrimination, and that's how many lawyers rightfully make their living.

But, conversely, does a female candidate really help herself if she fails to ever acknowledge she's female or call out societal wrongdoing when she sees it? I don't think so. I've watched many women, and even some men of color, fail to acknowledge their differences from the majority of office holders. It's disappointing to the underrepresented group; otherwise, it wouldn't be a big deal that a candidate like that is running.

In my view, it's especially incumbent on candidates who are from proportionately underrepresented groups in elective office to understand what it is that makes their group different or special in comparison to the majority. It could be certain health care issues. It could be issues of assimilation, language, family dynamics or housing issues. When a candidate or office holder takes a stand for how these may be lacking or inadequate or need improvement as they affect a certain demographic group, is that wrong? I don't think so. In fact, improving services or the workings of businesses, services and access in these areas may improve service, responsiveness and access for all of us. That's the beauty of democracy—addressing the needs of one often addresses the needs of many.

It was also during this stay at my mother's home that I received an email from Caroline Kennedy, excited about my run for the Senate and offering to do an event for me in her home. I set up a call with her and EMILY's List for the first morning when I would be in Florida.

My first morning there, before the conference call with Caroline, I had woken up to an email from Susan Markham, written at 6:35 a.m. that she had decided she could not manage my campaign, that it was logistically impossible with a husband and two young children in DC. I was very surprised, not having known the internal struggle she had been having. I tried all morning to reach her, but she did not answer my calls. Finally, I sighed and wished she would have reached this conclusion sooner so that I could have at least enjoyed my visit with my mom. I realized she would not be on the call with Caroline Kennedy later that morning. I learned later that she felt terrible for many reasons—for where it left me and for losing the opportunity to do something she was so passionate about.

I was left to conduct a planning call with Caroline Kennedy with people I had not even met yet. As the call began, with Caroline in New York, me in Florida, Jayme Staley in Columbus and EMILY's list in DC, the representative from EMILY's List said while Caroline was on the call that the organization ordinarily did not become involved with events such as this. "Why, in heaven's name," I thought to myself, "then, did you want to be on this call?!?" I grimaced, glad for no video telephone at the time, and quickly took control of the call. I advised that my staff would handle the event. I never understood why EMILY's List would harpoon an event that any other sane person would have danced a jig in their underwear to get. So much for the sanity of campaigns.

After returning to Columbus, I had to start from scratch to find a new manager. There was already friction from EMILY's List in my having taken on a senior advisor, Jerry Austin, a long-time political veteran who gained significant stature in managing former Ohio Governor Dick Celeste's 1982 gubernatorial campaign, and who did not want to manage the campaign, but rather, be senior advisor. Jerry had pitched to me on his strong desire to be there for an Ohio "first," as he put it, to help the first woman be elected to the Senate from Ohio. Jerry had suggested a manager for me with whom the chemistry just wasn't there. EMILY's List had suggested managers, one of whom demanded on our telephone interview that I give her an answer the next day, because she was also interviewing with my opponent, Lee Fisher. Before I could call her before her noon deadline the next day to politely decline, she called me at 8:30 a.m. to turn me down first. She was the first of three managers Lee had in his campaign.

I finally settled on David Dettman, a former campaign consultant with more than twenty years of political consulting experience in federal and state races. David most recently had managed Progressive Majority's Ohio office, providing key help in recapturing the majority in the Ohio House of Representatives in 2008. He came highly recommended by the first labor union local, Laborers Local 310 in Cleveland, that had endorsed me in my race for Secretary of State in 2005 and whose chief political officer, Jim Goggin, actually had called and asked me to run for the U.S. Senate. In his endearing Irish brogue, Jim struggled to get out the question in early 2009. I was expecting as the call began that he was going to ask me not to run. I stammered incredulously, "You mean you *want me to run?*" What a breath of fresh air. He highly recommended David, whose father had also been a Laborer, a fact of which David is very proud.

Before the Progressive Majority engagement, David had worked for the National Democratic Institute in Ukraine and in places in the Middle East, doing democracy-strengthening work. In Ukraine, he unofficially helped Viktor Yuschenko achieve victory after Yuschenko had been poisoned and the election re-voted in what became known as the Orange Revolution. David told me that there were times when Viktor had been flying from one point in Ukraine to another when his plane had not been permitted to land by government officials. At times during the Senate primary, David said his experience during Yuschenko's election in Ukraine had prepared him well for this primary election campaign.

It wasn't until David was well-ensconced in the campaign as my manager that he admitted that he had promised his wife before this campaign he would never manage another campaign again. After that tumultuous primary campaign, I think his resolve will not dissipate, and he will from now on be able to keep his promise to her. ≈

Chapter 24

Dirty Tricks

Lee Fisher has more than once said with pride that he has never lost a primary election. He also said, after beating me in the 2010 Democratic primary election for U.S. Senate, that I made him a better candidate. Unfortunately, that didn't seem to come to fruition when he lost by 18 points to Rob Portman. Lieutenant Governor Fisher spent more than $3 million dollars on our primary election, running nearly $1.3 million in television advertisements against me. I ran no television advertising. I raised just under a million dollars. I lost that primary with a margin of just over ten percent. It startled many Washington campaign observers when the results were announced.

As can be expected, a U.S. Senate campaign is very much a Washington affair, but the votes are still counted in Ohio. There is a political establishment in Washington, among not just members of the Senate and their staffs and campaign staffs, but also among political consultants and journalists, all of whom pass judgment on candidates for the exclusive club known as the U.S. Senate. Senator Sherrod Brown once told me that, upon being elected and beginning his tenure in the U.S. Senate, Senator Patrick Leahy from Vermont literally said, "Welcome to the club." I did not fully understand this when I began the race. I just knew how to campaign statewide in Ohio and how to win. With deep family roots throughout Ohio, nearly five years as a trial judge spent working closely with jurors (all of whom are registered voters) and now my time working with the state's 88 counties and their political and elected officials, I understood what it took to win with Ohioans. But it still takes money.

As the campaign got underway, we watched Lee spend money on expensive law firms, multiple consultants and staff. We heard of focus groups in which questions were being asked about not just me but about my husband and son. We were told that these focus groups preferred Lee in still shots and not video. Lee seemed petrified about the fact I am a woman. Soon after he announced for the Senate, "Women for Lee" was formed. Lee was so nervous about the "woman thing" that "miraculously" two African American women jumped into the primary at the last minute before the filing deadline, one from Cleveland and the other a former staffer for him in the Attorney General's office. Neither qualified for the ballot with insufficient signatures on their petitions. Paul Tipps said this was the oldest trick in the book—trying to water down support with more than one candidate in a "constituency" group, if that's what you can call women.

Today, especially among Democratic candidates, there seems to be some kind of wisdom that people need to be grouped and categorized. They are Women, Farmers, Veterans, Jewish-Americans, LGBTs, African Americans, Latinos, Hunters, Students, Pet Lovers—and more. I haven't figured out if this is supposed to make a candidate look stronger; perhaps it does. But, in a time when being united is a rare treasure, I've never understood why some seek to divide us into splinter groups and compartments that most of us don't neatly fit into. From a campaign consultant's view, it may be easier not to have to think hard enough about a message that will have broad appeal. Polled and micro-targeted messages may seem a safer bet, but there is always the danger that some of their meanings will collide. Moreover, when political party officials brag that they know "everything about" a particular group of voters, it may actually turn them off, especially if they feel their privacy is invaded.

Categorizing people into splinter groups and then targeting messages to them can be a prescription for trouble in the wrong hands. Uncoordinated messages can turn into accusations of lies or being less than fully truthful. I've told my children for years, "If you lie, you have to remember what you said." (I also added for my children's benefit that, "If you lie, your mother will always find out," which usually left them wide-eyed after hearing that ominous last maxim.)

Common sense tells us that most voters want a candidate to stand for something. They're disillusioned by wishy-washy answers from candidates that don't really tell them anything, except that the candidate prefers to play it safe. Most voters understand that they will not agree with a candidate on every point. Most voters would rather know *where* the candidate stands on a variety of issues and that the candidate is willing to 1) listen, 2) be honest with them, and 3) work hard for them. No one needs to be "grouped" into an interest group to figure out if they like the candidate, especially if the candidate is telling them the truth. That is the human message, and it works with nearly every group.

My first public "debate" with Lee was in Cincinnati. Its characterization was changed to a "forum" at his campaign's request. There was much dithering from Lee's campaign in agreeing to a final format for what could be called a "forumbate." During the planning stages of the forumbate, Lee at first refused to appear on stage with me, asking for separate appearances at the same event. Finally, after much dogging of him by various Democratic bloggers, which I'm sure David had nothing to do with, Lee agreed to a format where each of us sat at café tables on stage and took turns speaking at separate podiums. I went in with a giant briefing notebook with the iconic World War II Rosie the Riveter on the cover. By this time Rosie had become my campaign mascot.

Rosie the Riveter from WWII became our campaign mascot; this version was a downloadable campaign window sign

In preparing me for the event, David simply said to me, "Just be yourself. You know these issues. They just need to get to know you—to like you." So I listened to him. It was great advice (I later won Hamilton County in the primary).

The riff coming out of Washington after the debate was that I was trying to win the race on personality. Within days after the debate, I wrote a blog piece and highlighted in an email to supporters that people on unemployment should be permitted to work part-time, subtracting their part-time earnings from their unemployment benefits. That way they could be working to help them get a "foot in the door" for the chance at a full-time job. I had my folks tracking Lee Fisher's website after an appeal he made asking for ideas to help create more jobs in Ohio. The idea had come from someone writing to Lee, and I decided run with it. Lee had done nothing with it. My email premiered the idea and was entitled, "The Lack of Jobs is Taking its Toll . . ." It began with a message I had received from an out-of-work electrical worker from Cincinnati, a member of the IBEW. It read:

"Last night I was on my Facebook accounts and read a message from a friend from the Cincinnati local of the International Brotherhood of Electrical Workers. He said to me:

'. . . the lack of jobs is taking its toll. In Cincinnati we (the IBEW) have approximately 600 electricians unemployed and 3000 unemployed across Ohio with nothing in sight or out of town.'"

* * *

I went on to describe the policy that would help people like this electrical worker:

"In Ohio and many other places in the U.S. we need some common sense solutions-like letting people work part time when they can find it but not cutting off their unemployment benefits. Few states allow this, so why not pick up this regulation from the states for now and get people working again, even if only part time?

Most people on unemployment are receiving just a portion of what they were earning. They still have their mortgages to pay, prescriptions to pay for, cars to fuel and repair, and kids' lunches to buy--so why not let them do it with reduced benefits? They would have longer to find a sustainable job for the same overall benefit cap while small businesses could safely begin to grow right now.

The wages they receive would most likely be substantially less anyway than their weekly benefit, but if they could take the job, it could lead to a full-time position and they could still receive partial benefits while working without giving up their unemployment benefits completely.

You can read more here. It's time to get people working again. I hope you'll join us. Have a great day."

The next day I received an email from my mentor and friend, Senator Sherrod Brown, entitled, "Your last email," advising, "You can't win this race on personality; it has to be about issues and how badly the state will be served if we go back to the Portman policies that got us into this mess." He said that a message like he suggested would play much better to Democrats. It was clear he had angst about a contentious primary between Lee and me. But trying to stop that was like trying to stop two kids in the backseat from fighting over which video they will watch on one DVD player. It wasn't going to happen.

After Lee had left his position as the state's development director and Ohio lost two major employers, DHL in Wilmington and NCR in Dayton, the GOP referred to him as Ohio's "failed jobs czar." Lee Fisher referred to Rob Portman as a former "trade czar." Ohio was bleeding jobs, and Lee had quit the agency that was in the best position to help the state grow jobs. All of it was fair game. But to Ohioans, jobs, not Portman policies, mattered. I responded.

> **From:** jennifer brunner
> **Date:** Tue, 26 Jan 2010 19:07:11 -0500
> **To:** Sherrod Brown
> **Conversation:** Your last email
> **Subject:** Re: Your last email
>
> Sherrod --
>
> Thanks for your advice. The email wasn't an attack on Lee. When Lee and I appeared together in the Cincinnati Forum last Wednesday, he went after Portman in his home territory. People were pretty offended, because even Democrats in Cincinnati like Portman.

I have been talking about issues from the get go. They're all on my website http://jenniferbrunner.com/index.php/issues/ and in my blog http://jenniferbrunner.com/index.php/blog/index_new/ and all over Daily Kos http://www.dailykos.com/user/Jennifer%20Brunner and other blogs like Huffington Post. When we filed our petitions last Wednesday, we handed the reporters a briefing notebook with clips, blogs and posts all filed by issues.

. . . if I talk about "jobs" I'm somehow impugning him. I think his folks have been churning this in DC. The email was to show empathy and caring for the plight of so many people in Ohio. Everywhere I go, even to the eye doctor, I talk to people who have someone in their family affected by this recession, and they are working hard to get by. Ohioans are good people, and they deserve credit for that by being treated with respect.

I don't think I have the money to educate the public about anything more than what I will try to do for them. Rather than tear Portman down . . ., I would rather show voters I have ideas that will help them and that I care. I don't believe that's trying to win on personality, but rather, trust. If I can't win the right way, then I don't deserve to win.

There will be a time to focus on Portman as more people focus on the race. Right now I'm collecting the votes to win the primary, taking this one step at a time. Thanks for reaching out. Hope you are well.

Jennifer

Sherrod repeatedly declined to endorse me. I continually asked. He didn't endorse in the 2008 Presidential primary in Ohio, either, and I'm told that he received phone call after phone call from the two candidates, asking like I had, for reconsideration of his position. He never relented—in either case.

Interestingly, even though I could not hear from Sherrod the words of endorsement I sought, my daughter, Laura, who lived in New York City, heard from one of Sherrod's Columbus staffers. After obtaining her telephone number from her former coworker, he left her an odd message that he was going to be in the city and "would love to hear what you think about your mom running for office." Laura only knew him through serving him at the downtown Columbus Starbucks coffee store.

At about that time, David informed me that inquiries were coming from some of Sherrod's Ohio staffers about the level of racial diversity in staff of both the Secretary of State's office and in the campaign. There was clearly no problem in that area, and I wondered why the question was even being raised. I challenged David on the claim that the inquiry had come from anyone associated with Sherrod. David held steadfastly to his assertion. Later in the campaign when he talked with one of Sherrod's Cleveland staffers, he was cautioned that we needed to be careful about our attacks on the banks (Sherrod sat on the banking committee in the Senate at the time). We were obviously being watched, and it was surprising how much, especially when there was a refusal to endorse my candidacy after I had been told to "go for it."

A short time after I had announced my candidacy, this same staffer called me to ask me what Sherrod and I had discussed before I had announced. The staffer claimed that Sherrod could not remember our conversation when we had discussed my running for the U.S. Senate. I relayed the conversation and

Sherrod's encouragement to "go for it." The staffer said that that sounded like Sherrod, but I was asked to please not say that he had encouraged me to "go for it." I countered that I was not going to lie. I was asked to simply say I had discussed it with him and that we were friends. That was difficult to do, and I honestly cannot say I complied with that request.

Sadly, the Sherrod I had known in the 1980's who, when Secretary of State, had to be talked out of risking arrest for violating a bogus ban on registering voters outside of welfare offices in Cincinnati (I and others convinced him to do a press conference on the courthouse steps instead), was now asking me—not even directly—to stuff any evidence of his support. I was disappointed, but I didn't want to stop believing in the reasons I had worked for and supported him in the first instance. That is one of the difficulties when being personally acquainted with the candidate or office holder. It's difficult for the *individual* who is the candidate or office holder to live up to the ideals that form the basis for political support; this is often difficult to accept. I am certain I have disappointed some in my own elected and political circumstances, as much as I tried not to and did not want to disappoint them.

David figured out early that I could write. He respected me, which went eons further than the plentiful not-too-experienced campaign operatives who are trained by various state and national political organizations. Some staffers of this ilk seem to wish that candidates were nothing more than cardboard cutouts to be easily manipulated and moved from situation to situation. These same staffers are easily flustered by the candidate's family members and their wants and demands and seem especially good at rolling their eyes when they think no one is looking. They spend inordinate amounts of time calling each other from around the country to share the latest political gossip or blog post, and often they let go the menial tasks with a "silo" mentality that precludes them from helping on a variety of tasks where the need is critical but not exciting.

I have found that the best campaign staffers are those who can do the actual tasks called for, are willing to work hard until the job is finished and are teachable on political strategy. Every statewide campaign I have run has started with the typical political operatives and ended with hard working Ohio regulars who know how to do the tasks and who learn the politics as they go. It is the manager who most needs the political experience, along with the patience and judgment to keep staff working together and to communicate to them their value to the effort. They can be taught political ropes that primarily involve trusting their common sense. If they learn to trust their common sense, they are even better at anticipating the dirty tricks that come along the way.

Dirty tricks in campaigns are nothing new, and it's especially disheartening when they occur in primary elections. A primary election is like a family fight. Rick and I often told our children that family disagreements were to be kept within the family; in public we all stood together, no matter what. A political party is, in a sense, a family of core values, beliefs and activity. So when one member assails another publicly, it can get ugly.

I surmised that much of Lee's consternation at having me for an opponent was because of my gender. He had experienced his first electoral loss at the hands of a woman—Betty Montgomery. Also, it's difficult to openly attack a woman effectively when you're a male candidate, and it often backfires. So dirty tricks, which routinely happen in primary elections, were a greater challenge with a woman opponent. He or his folks had to get the job done quietly and not leave a trail. One of my political mentors, Don Kindt, once chided another staffer that, "In politics, you're not supposed to leave tracks. Pointing out her deficiencies in that department, he exclaimed, "You've got your goddamned footprints all over the walls and the ceiling!" (When I heard him actually say this, I thought I would fall off my chair, trying not to laugh, just imagining the visual.)

Suffice it to say, Lee Fisher's supporters and staff had learned well to cover their tracks. That's why I was so relieved for the primary election to be over. It took awhile to get used to not feeling like I needed to look over my shoulder before nearly every move I made. Whether it was having a "tracker" with a video camera in my face as I traveled to even the remotest part of the state or opened my campaign headquarters in Columbus, or having the finance director's laptop computer stolen from campaign headquarters, while others in the open were left undisturbed. This campaign was anything but fun as it got underway, despite the fact that I was a candidate who loved to campaign.

The Ohio Department of Taxation sent an electronic notice to the Business Services section of the Secretary of State's office that Rick's law firm corporation had not filed all necessary paperwork with the department and needed to be canceled. My state office thereafter canceled his corporate charter. I never knew it happened until afterward. It was an electronic transaction. The information was publicized. My daughter, Kate, who managed the practice, sought information from the Department of Taxation about why a notice had gone from Taxation to the Secretary of State's office and what needed to be done to reinstate the corporation. The reasons given for the cancellation by the Department's staff kept shifting. Finally, someone in the department admitted that it had gone back through 11 years of its records and that a particular document was missing in its files; the Department's claim was that none had been filed. The law firm's accountant still had a copy, stored in dead files in his garage, showing it had been filed. Kate supplied it to the Department, paid a reinstatement fee, and the corporation was reinstated. The director of the department had given Fisher a large contribution, and one of Department's top administrative staff was a Fisher supporter.

Meanwhile, documents had been delivered to a Cleveland Plain Dealer reporter by "a Fisher supporter," as he described it. Other outlets pounced on it after the first publication. Here was AP's report:

Tax woes muddy U.S. Senate contest in Ohio

July 16, 2009

COLUMBUS (AP) — A series of sloppy tax filings by the husband of U.S. Senate candidate Jennifer Brunner has become a source of growing tension between the two Democrats seeking to replace retiring Republican George Voinovich.

As the campaigns of Secretary of State Brunner and her rival, Lt. Gov. Lee Fisher, have been embroiled in the issue, Republican Rob Portman has run away with a fundraising lead in the race for the coveted seat. Portman is a former congressman and Bush cabinet official.

Brunner has been peppered with questions about tax irregularities over the past week following a series of political blog entries by The (Cleveland) Plain Dealer. Fisher, in turn, has been confronted with accusations by her campaign that his camp fueled the mess.

As this was being debated in the news media, the director of taxation, himself, was interviewed and discussed the situation. It was prohibited for him to discuss publicly the affairs of a particular taxpayer. David attempted to negotiate the situation with John Haseley, the governor's chief of staff. They met at the downtown Starbucks. David called out the Strickland/Fisher team as "bullies," to which David reported Haseley pounded the table and got up to leave. David didn't flinch and basically shrugged his shoulders as if to say, "Okay, go ahead." Haseley apparently thought better of his exit, returned to the table, and they discussed what was wrong with Fisher's approach. Regardless, we needed to seek redress for what had occurred. A complaint was filed with the State Inspector General about the tax commissioner's actions. Our complaint went nowhere, especially after we had listed John Haseley as one who knew about the transactions in question.

It was clear that my and my family's entire background had been well researched. (One former Ohio Democratic Party staffer told us that the party kept files on members of my family—my file was described as thinner than my family members' files.) "Hits" were timed to drip out, one-by-one, and kept us scrambling. The difficulty of running against a Lieutenant Governor endorsed by the Governor, with all of us in the same party, was that to hit back at the Lieutenant Governor regarding his behavior in office was tantamount to an assault on the Governor.

We heard reports that Lee had been telling donors I was dropping out of the race (so donors would have a disincentive and not contribute). The Governor was reported to have said that I couldn't raise money. It affected my bottom line on fundraising, but I was still contending.

The first part of July 2009 was pivotal, and it was just before the July 15 campaign finance reporting deadline. Among the documents delivered to the Cleveland Plain Dealer reporter were property tax records on my then 22-year-old son's condominium that Rick and I had helped him purchase. Rick's name was also on the deed to help John qualify for financing. John, in youthful oblivion, thought his mortgage payment included his property taxes and insurance (PMI). Even though property tax bills came to him, he ignored them. Rick and I didn't know taxes had gone unpaid. Rick and I had both been consumed with the Senate race and holding down the day-to-day work of our respective jobs.

When we learned about the property tax problems, I went online and paid the tax with a credit card. Sandy Theis, a former Plain Dealer reporter and consultant to my campaign, counseled our son, John, about how to talk to Plain Dealer reporter Mark Naymik. John wanted to talk with him to set the record straight. I was not in favor of it, but John was insistent. He had traveled with me as my driver in my first statewide campaign, and I knew he could handle himself. Rick was upset. John youthfully thought he could make it right. I steeled myself. I knew I had to get through it. Attacking my child, however, was unforgivable, and I would never forget it. That's what mothers do.

David was furious that Lee Fisher had had any part of going after my son, saying that the test was that if the story reported depended solely on the child's last name, that is, in other circumstances it would not be newsworthy (late payment of property taxes), it was off limits. When I chose to run, I knew Lee Fisher was my likely opponent. I knew of his reputation to be hard-nosed, bragging that he had never lost a primary election (even though he had lost two general statewide elections by that time). But, I never thought he would stoop this low. I had worked so closely with him and his family as his campaign's legal counsel when he ran for Governor in 1998. I had introduced my children to him over the years, even taking John as a boy to his campaign office in Cleveland to meet him in

1998. I thought there would be a line that would not be crossed, but I was wrong.

All my forbearance in not attacking Lee seemed like a worthless sacrifice, and it no longer seemed the politically prudent thing to do. I would never attack his family, but I was ready to hit back at him for what he had done to my son and husband. Naymik's coverage of the situation illustrated the classic textbook campaign tactic of what my pollster, Celinda Lake, called, "knock her off her pedestal." It's a ploy to diminish a woman candidate's standing when nothing significant can be found in opposition research about her. By attacking her family, she is knocked off her pedestal. Naymik's article made it look like Mom and Dad were bad parents. The article was critical and stinging. John's quotes were at the end of the interview:

> . . . Brunner said in an interview that his parents bought him the condominium but he was responsible for the taxes as part of the deal. He said they bought it for him so he could work and attend school at Otterbein College.
> "It's my fault," he said. "My parents were nice enough to buy me the condo and I rewarded them by getting behind on the taxes. I love my parents and they are the most honorable people I know."
>
> * * *
>
> Brunner's campaign said it was unaware of the bill until the Plain Dealer called.

In even a moderately funded campaign "self-research" is conducted to learn of such problems. They are taken care of before they become issues, and the team is prepared with an answer if the subject arises. We would have had a stock answer ready when the issue was raised by the other side. But in this campaign, we were fighting for survival.

At the point when a "Fisher supporter" went after my son, I had had it. My consultants had never stopped asking me to hit Fisher hard. I had continually refused, knowing that it could hurt the Governor. Also, many of my supporters would be disappointed if I were to go negative. But at this point, I was a mother first and a candidate second. A mother lion will protect her cub at nearly any cost.

My shot at protecting my "cub" was to call out Lee to honor pay equity for women, especially in the Department of Development he had just resigned from as Director. His second successor, a female, was being paid more than $50,000 per year less than he had earned, while Lee as the former director still attended department events, cut ribbons and performed ceremonial duties on behalf of the Department as if he were still its director.

When Lee left the Development Department, which was necessary ethically, since he planned to and did solicit contributions from the principals of the businesses to which the state had awarded development grants, he dropped the extra state salary he earned for his Department. His first successor, a man, was paid more than his second successor, a woman. Her predecessor stayed on at a salary that was $40,000 higher than hers.

The release was direct, and it also got the Governor's attention.

FOR IMMEDIATE RELEASE

July 9, 2009
* * *
US Senate Candidate Jennifer Brunner Calls on Lee Fisher to Abide by Pay Equity Laws and Raise the Salary of his Woman Successor

COLUMBUS-U.S. Senate candidate Jennifer Brunner today called on her opponent, Lee Fisher, to do more than talk about getting support from women voters. "Fisher should fight for equal pay for women, starting with the woman who has taken his place as director of the Ohio Department of Development," Brunner said.

* * *

Brunner challenged Fisher to give more than lip service to pay equity for women and to use his continuing influence with the department to honor President Obama's first act signed into law, the Lily Ledbetter Fair Pay Restoration Act. Since leaving the department, Lee Fisher continues to assume visible responsibility for the agency's public activities, allows his picture to be featured prominently on the department's website, and carries out the public duties of an agency director, despite having ceded the position . . .

* * *

"While Lee Fisher continues to take for credit for the activities of the state department responsible for adding jobs to our economy, he silently acquiesces to the obvious pay inequity for the woman who handles the day-to-day responsibilities that he . . . once performed," said Brunner.

"Women across the country still earn just 78 cents for every dollar men earn, and for women of color, it is even less. Instead of zigzagging across the state to capture the limelight for Development Department achievements, Lee Fisher should be pushing for the woman who holds his old job to get a pay raise—she's doing the work he used to do, and he's showing up to take the credit," stated Brunner. "I challenge Lee Fisher to fight for the basic principle that we are all created equal," said Brunner.

The Lilly Ledbetter Fair Pay Restoration Act is named for an Alabama woman who, at the end of a 19-year career as a supervisor in a tire factory, learned she had been paid less than men who did comparable jobs. . . . The Lily Ledbetter Act was President Obama's first bill signed as our nation's new President.

Brunner is currently serving as Ohio's Secretary of State. She is seeking the U.S. Senate seat now held by George Voinovich, who is retiring. Brunner would be the first woman from Ohio to serve in the Senate.

- 30 –

When this release went out, I was in Dayton speaking with the editorial board of the Dayton Daily News. Listening to the multiple voicemails on my Blackberry after that extended meeting, I first heard John Haseley's voicemail message where he clearly wasn't "smilin.'" His voice was raised, and it sounded like he was speaking through clenched teeth, "Jennifer Brunner!" he exclaimed and addressed me in his voicemail. His message mentioned the media release from that day, and he hissed, "This goes beyond the pale!" The chief of staff for the governor demanded that the Secretary of State call him back.

The next message was from Governor Ted Strickland, himself. He addressed me by title, with "Madam Secretary . . ." Governor Strickland asked that I return his call. I ignored Haseley's call and returned Ted's call. When his staff put him on the telephone in answer to my call, he began the conversation as a psychologist would likely have, along the line of, "Just what were you thinking when you sent out that press release?"

I mentally noted the open-ended question. But before I could get the answer out, Ted raised his voice. It was shaking, and he was clearly angered. When I was given a chance to respond, I said directly, "Lee went after my son." That didn't seem to phase the Governor. "Of course," I thought, "he doesn't have any children, so he doesn't know what it's like." I went on.

"Governor, I never want to hurt you, but if Lee hits my family, I will hit back, and if you're near Lee, you'll be hit, too. I don't want to, and it's not my intention to hurt you, but I think you need to communicate to Lee just what your endorsement means." Emily Puffenberger, my driver and my campaign fundraising assistant, Alisha, sat in shocked silence at hearing firsthand a heated argument between two of the state's top office holders.

Apparently, someone on Ted's team had been following my tweets on the social networking site, Twitter. There were two that had particularly bothered Ted and staff. At that time a new biennial state budget had expired, and the state was operating on an interim budget. Someone on the Governor's staff must have grossly miscalculated the political effects of cutting the state's library system budget, because library supporters all over the state were flooding legislative and the Governor's offices with emails. Ohio has been known nationally for its excellent library system, and many counties had no local library-funding levy, depending largely or entirely on the state for funding.

With more than 200 individual libraries throughout the state, each library, with one or more computer terminals, became more than 200 mini-campaign offices to fight for restored library funding throughout the State of Ohio. I, for one, agreed with library supporters, thinking this was an illogical item to cut, with joblessness on the rise, and many Ohioans cutting their Internet service in favor of using it at the library. Libraries throughout the State of Ohio had to cut their hours, and there were dozens of library levies on the ballot the next year in 2010.

Eighty percent of them passed.[4] In 2012, one hundred percent of them passed.

During the heated telephone discussion about my press release, the Governor pivoted topics and asked, exasperated, why I would mention the libraries. I had just over a week earlier "Tweeted" the following two messages on July 1:

> Ever think that someone (in this case, OLC) would have to tell librarians to quiet down? Post your best library memory.

> Best library memory: riding bike in summer to Clintonville library, carrying back 7 books in my bike basket & then not being seen for days.

When asked the pointed question about why I had talked about libraries, I said matter-of-factly to the Governor just one word: "Conscience." There was silence on the other end of the phone. He countered, asking me how I would find the extra revenue to balance the budget. I answered quickly: "I would delay the

---

[4] The Ohio Library Council reported on November 3, 2010, the day after the election:

"Yesterday, 30 of the 38 library issues that were on the ballot passed. Statewide, 80% of the library issues were successful. Overall, 23 of the 29 new library levies were successful . . .

. . . Ohioans are using their libraries more than ever. Statewide circulation of library materials has increased, but the biggest growth has been in the number of people who come into the library and use the services available to them for free. Public libraries continue their commitment to providing outstanding service to people of all ages in Ohio: the internet to help people find jobs, homework help centers and early literacy programs to improve children's education, and a variety of services for all of Ohio seniors."

income tax rollback for those making $200,000 or more. You could save more than $900 million dollars right there."

He then asked bluntly if I wanted a tax increase. I said, "Governor, it's not a tax increase, but even if it's called that, I'll be right by your side defending you." He was quiet again and then said resolutely that there would be no new revenue, that it would be the slots at racetracks as the solution to the state revenue shortfall. Moving to "the slots" for state revenue was an about-face move on the governor's part, after just three months before having been reported in the Youngstown Vindicator to have said that a legislative move to place slot machines at racetracks was "a very, very, very wrong action" that he would likely veto if adopted by the legislature.

Soon after our heated exchange, the proposal for slots at racetracks went into the state budget, but it was quickly challenged by a referendum effort brought by a group thought to be backed by one or more principals for newly voter-authorized casinos, but which never reported the real sources of its funding. The referendum resulted in delaying the law that authorized the video slots. The Governor's intended revenue to fix the budget gaps was stalled.

In the end, Ted Strickland did just what I had suggested, but not until September 30, 2009. When I received word of the policy change, my campaign immediately issued an email in his support, telling supporters, "Time to Stand With Governor Strickland." The email pointed out:

> Some say calling for the repeal of tax cuts for the wealthy is risky politics. The Republican smear machine is already gearing up to attack Governor Strickland. As the Governor has demonstrated, it takes courage to lead -- even when it means that you open yourself up to partisan attacks. The

Governor knows that you have to put the good of your constituents and your desire to be a public servant above hardheaded partisan politics. I commend him for his courage, support his call for the freeze of the irresponsible tax cuts, and call on the legislature to do its duty with the same courage and compassion that Governor Strickland has demonstrated.

It still took almost another three months to get the measure passed, stalling resolution of state revenue shortages until more than five months after our heated discussion, until late December 2009. His inability to resolve the state budget until within less than a month before his re-election year began contributed to a tough campaign ahead. While he fought hard under trying conditions that had pervaded many state and local governments all over the country, he lost his reelection bid in November 2010.

As we neared the end of that dramatic July 2009 call, I asked the Governor how we would resolve our disagreement. I could almost hear his jaw constrict, as he said tautly, "I don't know." And it was never the same after that.

At the Ohio Democratic Party annual statewide dinner just a month before the heated telephone exchange between the Governor and me, the party had given its Democrat of the Year award to a group of attorneys for their election protection work in the 2008 Presidential election, the same election I was responsible for supervising and for which I had been recognized with the JFK Profile in Courage award. While these attorneys had been great partners, their work was less relevant in 2008 than it had been in 2006 when Ken Blackwell was running elections.

Before this time Governor Strickland had declared to me in a one-on-one encounter in his gubernatorial office before other office holders had arrived that, other than endorsing Lee in the primary, he was remaining neutral in our U.S. Senate primary contest. It clearly did not play out that way.

The day after I lost the Democratic primary election for the U.S. Senate, the Ohio Democratic Party held a "unity luncheon." A small but elite group of the state's top Democrats, office holders and statewide candidates met in the back room at a local Italian restaurant called, "Tony's." The long tables were situated end-to-end to form a rectangle with an open center. Governor Strickland and Chair Redfern sat at the tables perpendicular to me on my right. Lieutenant Governor Lee Fisher and his campaign manager sat directly in front of Rick to my immediate left, me and State Treasurer Kevin Boyce to my immediate right. At first I had been informed that Rick was not permitted to attend, to which I replied that if he did not go, neither would I. The party relented. Ohio Attorney General Richard Cordray did not attend. David Dettman sat at the tables perpendicular to my left. He was clearly angry to be attending this luncheon, but it was his duty, and he fulfilled.

The luncheon was carefully scripted. We had each been given the "script" ahead of time. It indicated that Chair Redfern would open the luncheon meeting and introduce the Governor for remarks. After the Governor's remarks, the U.S. Senate primary loser would speak, followed by the primary winner.

When Governor Strickland spoke, he did not look at me. He did not mention my name. He did not even mention the primary election. He talked about jobs in an empty, hollow, distant fashion, like a rote campaign speech. They followed the script.

It was my turn to speak. I said directly, "I thought this was a unity luncheon, but the Governor never mentioned the primary election."

At that point, Kevin Boyce (as he later told me) thought to himself, "Well, that took courage."

I continued, "So let me tell you why I ran for the Senate." I discussed that I ran because I owed it to women in Ohio to run. No woman had ever been nominated in a contested primary for the U.S. Senate in Ohio, let alone been elected to the Senate. I continued. The election reforms I had made were like new wounds healed. I said that by not running for reelection, these reforms would not be subject to the stresses of vitriolic GOP campaign criticism that was surely to come in a Secretary of State reelection campaign in a year that would determine the makeup of the state's apportionment board.

When it was Lee's turn to speak, he told the group that I made him a better candidate. I knew he was right. The luncheon was intended to be prophylactic, but it was full of holes.

When Lee and I had talked privately outside on the restaurant patio before the luncheon began, I told him he needed to give money back that he had accepted from a Goldman Sachs executive. I advised him to study the banking industry's practices in light of the TARP bailout and the banks' effect on the economic well-being of most Americans.

I told him how inappropriate it was for his campaign to have come after my son. He started to hold up a finger and protest as if he did not have control over that activity. He took one look at my sideways glare, and he stopped mid-sentence.

While David had suggested that obtaining various political leaders' endorsement was less than optimal in the primary election campaign, Lee had worked the many endorsements he gained to his advantage. He obtained local political leader endorsements early. It had dampened local institutional Democratic support for me in critical places like Toledo, Dayton, Akron and Canton. He was able to do this because local Democratic officials were reminded of tax supported grants they had received "from him" as the state's development director. Private practice attorneys were reminded of the contracts they had been awarded to perform outsourced legal services when he had served as Attorney General.

Despite this, when Lee and I were on a level playing field, competing head-to-head for the party endorsement in "independent" Democratic Party counties like Wood County (home of Bowling Green State University just south of Toledo), I won the endorsement, even though he paid for automated, pre-recorded robo-calls to the voting members ahead of time and even with a public roll call vote. Lee won endorsements in places like Stark and Columbiana Counties, where there was no notice of endorsement and no opportunity to compete. The county chairs there simply moved the machine forward for him.

When I attended the Stark County Democratic dinner (to which I had received no invitation), I was told I could sit in the back of the room with board of elections officials who were attending. One member of the northeast Ohio black caucus, Demeatrious St. John, standing about six feet five inches, walked up to me asking what I was doing sitting "back here." I answered that I was told this was where I was to sit. He said, "You're not sitting there. You come with me." He led me to a table at the front of the room to sit with some women who were happy to have me with them.

My presence made many people uncomfortable at party events like this. Lee could rarely deliver a riveting speech and usually didn't stick around for the whole event. When I was afforded a chance to speak at these events, I could see distress in the many faces of the audience. There was a lot of dissonance going on at these events—people wanting to follow their hearts, as the Governor had told me to do, but being told they had to get in line with what a few leaders wanted. In these political party situations, because discipline was enforced in a variety of ways, folks tend to stay in line.

At this event, then-Congressman John Boccieri approached me, calling me "Jen" and telling me that I should run for reelection for Secretary of State and not for the Senate. By this time I had been running for the Senate for seven months. In the Secretary of State's race in 2005 and 2006, he had been a state senator then and the last "hold-out" candidate for the office before petition filing deadline in early 2006. In December 2005, he received a call from then Ohio AFL-CIO president, Bill Burga, who told him that the federation would be endorsing me for Secretary of State. Later, in the summer of 2006, Boccieri traveled to Cleveland where I was making fundraising calls. He ceremoniously walked into the office there, wrote me a check for $500 from his campaign fund, and he made some vague comment about the state apportionment board and to remember him at that time.

At the Stark County Democratic event, Congressman Boccieri asserted that he had "stepped aside" for me to run for Secretary of State. He seemed to be saying that this gave him a right to direct my path now. This kind of bravado was close to a phenomenon. I looked him straight in the eye and said, "John, you stepped aside because Bill Burga told you the AFL-CIO was going to endorse me, and even if you had stayed in the race I would have beaten you." This time he was quiet. He shrugged his shoulders, turned and started to walk away, throwing out, "Well, good luck making your decision." I spoke to his back. "I've already made it. I'm running for the Senate."

Toward the end of the campaign, Lee Fisher adeptly used the limitations of my office as Secretary of State against me. With Ken Blackwell having pledged his support to George W. Bush's reelection and even serving as a co-chair of that effort in Ohio in 2004, I pledged not to support any candidate or ballot issue so long as I served as Secretary of State. I had said that an "umpire can't wear the jersey of one of the teams." That meant that if I lost, I could not endorse Lee in the general election. This was a question Lee and his supporters kept asking me repeatedly, and I couldn't understand why. His sister-in-law asked me at the Cleveland Human Rights Campaign dinner in Cleveland. Even his wife Peggy, just before the historic Cleveland City Club debate, stopped me in the dining room where the debate was about to get started and asked me whether I'd support him if I lost. Over and over again I explained that I would like to but can't because of my job.

Paul Tipps kept sending warning emails to Rick to not let me get too tired. On a bus trip to Athens, a reporter from the Dayton Daily News rode along. She baited me saying, "I think Lee's going to win. How much support will you give him if he does." Tired, her statement had irritated me, especially in light of all the dirty tricks that had been played. I simply held up my hand with fingers curved to my thumb, signifying a zero. I added that I couldn't do so because of my job. The answer should have been given in a different way. She reported it as it happened; we tried to soften it with the reality of the job restrictions. But the article and the way it was stoked by the Fisher media staff angered some Democrats.

In addition, Lee's folks apparently looked at some Republican polling and hit me on my having to administer a law on political party affiliation in primaries, dubbing statements required by law upon changing party affiliation to be "loyalty oaths." A high school student from Shaker Heights obviously was put up to asking a question on this complicated legal issue in the public questions portion of the Cleveland City Club debate.

Many Republicans had jumped parties in 2008 to become "Rush Limbaugh" Democrats so that they could vote for Hillary Clinton, apparently with the thinking that Barack Obama would be more difficult for John McCain to beat. When this new breed of "Democrats" (or anyone changing parties for that matter) asked for a different party ballot than previously voted, they were required by law to sign a statement that they supported the principles of the party's ballot they now were voting. We already knew there were many of these Rush Limbaugh Democrats, because our supporters had been ordered off porches by angry people whose names appeared on Democratic walking lists of registered voters but who declared angrily that they were not Democrats.

During that time I had a sixth sense that something was terribly wrong. This had happened in earlier election campaigns and even during the 2008 election season when death threats emerged. Later, soon after the election, Dave Heller, one of my media consultants, told me he had been on a panel in DC with a Republican media consultant who informed him that at about the time I'd had that sense, the GOP had seriously considered running ads against me in the primary. Republicans preferred to run against Lee Fisher than me.

Congresswoman Marcia Fudge had told me at an Akron event during the primary, "People are saying they don't know how you're going to beat Lee Fisher, but they don't know how Lee

Fisher will ever beat Rob Portman." Rob Portman was raising eye-popping sums of money.

Lee Fisher spent more than $3 million dollars against me in a primary race, leaving himself with less than $1 million dollars to enter the general election race. By this time, Rob Portman had $7.6 million in the bank with no primary. I had been, as the Washington, DC publication, *The Hill,* put it, "meagerly funded from the start of the race" and spent "considerably less—about $800,000." The publication reported that I had stayed within single digits of Fisher in the polls.

It can never be said that I ran Lee Fisher out of money—he ran himself out of money. I had no television advertising—I couldn't afford it. I had claimed in the primary that his dollars raised for an early fundraising lead were "low hanging fruit." He didn't figure out how to climb that tree, and he eventually ran out of money, donating $100,000 to the Ohio Democratic Party to help the rest of the ticket.

Sherrod Brown announced the move and is reported by the Huffington Post to have said:

> "Few times in the course of a rigorous, frenetic and difficult campaign do candidates step up and do something spectacular -- and unselfish," Brown said in an e-mail to supporters. "Lee Fisher just did."

> . . . Lee donated his last $100,000 to the Ohio Democratic Party for its get-out-the-vote effort. That will matter not just to Lee, but to the governor, to members of Congress who are under siege, to our ability to hold onto the majority in the Ohio House of Representatives, and most importantly, to the people of Ohio for years to come."

In his campaign email, Senator Brown cited, ". . . Lee's generosity and act of courage and statesmanship" and exhorted his own followers that, if inspired by Fisher's acts, to donate to the Ohio Democratic Party's federal account for which he said money was needed most, or to "head over to Lee's Facebook page and simply thank him for stepping up like few politicians have."

Despite his protests that he was not giving up, Lee Fisher stepped aside so that other candidates could have what little money he had left. Rob Portman beat Fisher by 18 points, winning in 82 out of 88 counties. ≈

Chapter 25

Going Grassroots

By the end of September 2009, New Jersey Senator Bob Menendez, chair of the Democratic Senatorial Campaign Committee, had summoned me to DC for a meeting. I had had numerous face-to-face sessions with J.B. Poersch and Martha McKenna, both political directors for the DSCC. Martha had traveled to Columbus and interviewed me one morning at my home. (David had "pre-interviewed" her to make sure she wasn't coming to Columbus to ask me to drop out of the race—Lee's pernicious mantra.) The DSCC was clearly trying to determine whether it should become involved in the Democratic primary and to what degree.

I had also had meetings with Campbell Spencer from the Obama White House. She was assigned to cover the political affairs of the Midwest. She traveled to Columbus and met in my home with David Dettman, Antoinette, Rick and me one weekday evening. The President stayed out of the race. One of his top White House advisors, David Axelrod, had been a political consultant to Lee in the 1998 Governor's race, and Lee had hired Axelrod's firm with whom David Plouffe, the President's 2008 campaign manager, was now associated. Campbell kept in close contact with our campaign, and by late September, when Lee's efforts to dry up my funds appeared to be having some success, she met with me in a coffee shop in DC, appearing anxious and concerned. At the same time, we were cutting ties with EMILY's List.

Campbell said she just didn't see how I could prevail without being able to raise more money. I was adamant that I would not drop out, and I stressed with principle and zeal that I could do this—and that I had to. I could practically see her shaking her head when we each went our separate ways from that coffee shop. I last saw her on International Women's Day, March 8, 2010. She accompanied Valerie Jarrett, an advisor to the President, to Ohio, who was a speaker at a small reception for the event. I told Campbell quietly that I thought I could win the race. The grassroots efforts had taken hold by that time. Apparently, Washington was noticing. As we stood there, she said quietly, "I hope so."

The International Women's Day event was held less than two months before the primary election. It was one that Frances Strickland and Peggy Fisher assiduously worked for months to keep me out of, despite my being the only Democratic female state office holder. At first they cited the reason that they did not want to include Republican State Auditor Mary Taylor, so they could not include me. It was a nonpartisan event. Supporters of my Senate campaign such as Barbara Gould and Lana Moresky were offended that I was not included in the planning. Each of them participated in multiple and lengthy planning meetings.

Eventually, the event's organizers indirectly asked for my help, as organizational strength seemed to be lacking. One of my staff persons, Robin Dever, was a gifted planner. Antoinette had returned to her consulting firm by this time and had agreed to raise funds for the event through a nonprofit structure. Antoinette asked me if Robin could assist. I reluctantly agreed, only because it was a good cause and promoted women in leadership. The morning of the event I learned that the program agenda had been completely changed. Peggy Fisher would be introducing Valerie Jarrett, the luncheon speaker. I would be introducing former House Minority Leader Joyce Beatty at a panel of women for a mid-morning workshop. Joyce was late. There was not any particular role for me at the luncheon, and I do not recall being invited to attend it. I was invited to attend a Latino luncheon at which a recently appointed court of appeals judge from Toledo was the keynote. She later lost her election. I attended the private gathering with Valerie Jarrett later in the day by crashing it.

In the Senate campaign, EMILY's List refused to endorse me in the primary, even after a personal meeting with Ellen Malcolm, the founder of EMILY's List (EL). At that meeting EMILY's List repeated its two criteria for endorsement in my race: 1) that the Governor didn't endorse the Lieutenant Governor, and 2) that I selected a media consulting firm that EL approved of. As Jonathan Parker put it, there were two check boxes that would keep EL out of my race, and because the Governor endorsed Lee Fisher and I did not choose a media consultant of which they approved, I was ineligible for endorsement. I believe other reasons would have appeared had I even selected whom they wanted, as Lee had the Washington establishment well in his pocket by this time. EMILY's List, to my disappointment, had become establishment.

My DC-based consultants, including my pollster, had said from the beginning that it likely would be too difficult to win the primary without help from EMILY's List. A few had done it, like my friend Elaine Marshall, Secretary of State of North Carolina, in her Senate race in 2010. After Elaine won not only a primary but a runoff election to be the Democratic nominee, EL endorsed her in the general election. Elaine was just not able to get over the finish line first in the general, but she did not give up and continues to run.

The media-consulting firm EL was pushing me toward wanted $50,000 up front just for retaining them, and that year, in 2009, the firm was handling Michael Bloomberg's mayoral reelection in New York City. EL was aware of the two consultants I chose to use, as they had been in the "mix" of those they knew I was interviewing. There had been no prior admonishment not to hire them. It was only after I did so that the second "check box" materialized. I believed these two consultants were the best. I had carefully scrutinized TV ads by many and been wooed by four different media firms that traveled to Ohio to make their pitch. I selected the people I believed made the best commercials. The EL endorsement was never a sure thing, and it was never promised that hiring one of EL's endorsed consultants and paying the $50,000 upfront fee would secure me the coveted endorsement. I used my best judgment and did not look back.

If this campaign taught me anything about proverbial glass ceilings it was that women do best when they embrace who they are. Using the same methods to achieve power that are used by those who keep it from you doesn't really get you where you need to go. David didn't beat Goliath by fighting Goliath's way. He did it by using what he knew and doing it well. When he created confusion and caught Goliath off guard was when he let the stone fly from his sling. It's about timing more than anything else. I firmly believe the moneyed ways of Washington are numbered in their days. Things will change when more women are elected and form a critical mass in the decision making process. I do not believe that toeing a line drawn with more testosterone than women will ever have or want will make it happen any faster.

As for raising money as EL wanted, my fundraising staff and I had kept pushing the way we knew how, which had been honed to nearly a science. With the help of my call-time manager, Alisha Woodward, now National Director at Emerge America in San Francisco, I became proficient at "double dialing," We had two phones on the desk, and Alisha dialed as I dialed. If she actually achieved a connection with the potential donor, she had to ask them to hold for me, and we had to hope I hadn't reached someone on my end, too. Surprisingly, it was a very efficient system. We developed almost a rhythm, allowing my call-time manager and me both to leave messages from me and to move closer toward sending a solicitation letter to potential donors after so many calls to them had been made. Ironically, it was Lee Fisher who had taught me that once a potential donor has been called several times, it's okay to send them a letter (or today, an email) expressing understanding of their busy schedule, telling them why you called and making the solicitation for a specified amount.

In 2006 when I ran for Secretary of State, these follow up letters sometimes resulted in receiving $1000 contributions in the mail—from people to whom I had never even spoken. In 2006 we also had thoroughly researched our donors and knew their interests. My daughter, Kate, being an outstanding writer and a proficient student of people, could write letters that sold her mother and netted significant contributions. Ironically, after Lee was elected Lieutenant Governor on the ticket with Governor Strickland, and I was elected Secretary of State, Lee interviewed her to be a speechwriter for him. She made it to the final interview with him. When he informed her in no uncertain terms that he was difficult to work for, describing himself with an epithet that begins with "a" and ends in "e," she asked me, "Mom, do I have to take the job?" Of course, my answer was no, and she withdrew her candidacy before any offer was made to anyone. Looking back, had she gone to work for him, well, that would have been interesting.

There was and still is a class of large donors who contribute only after a candidate has been persistent with them, calling sometimes up to seven or eight times. It's almost like a game that is played to see how badly the candidate wants the contribution from them. I found it demeaning and resented it. Seasoned call time managers don't seem to differentiate between these "plum givers" and more nubile givers who feel like they're being hounded, especially since the practice of "call time" is widespread in the number of candidates who do it and the geographic range of the calls they make. When you're in the Midwest you can continue with call time until 8:30 or 9:00 p.m if you're calling California. You call New York, Boston and Florida during the morning or earlier afternoon hours. You can call Texas and Chicago during your lunch hour, because it's not yet lunchtime there.

Call-time databases usually contain a field associating them with how they were obtained or according to interest. Candidates sometimes share databases with one another. There are names from databases based on interest, such as clean energy advocates, doctors, airline pilots—you name it. A list of big donors in a charitable event program is often researched and compared against existing political contribution databases, and new prospects are identified. As a candidate, I had definite impressions of what other candidates' donors were like, based on my conversations with them. Some groups of donors were definitely not fun to talk to, while another group of donors would have invited me into their living room if I'd been at their door instead of on the telephone. By looking at the "source" of the donors' names, I often knew before the call whether it would be pleasant.

In my campaign, the combination of the state of financial affairs for many traditionally large donors, the rumor-mill churned by my opponent and his supporters about whether I would stay in the race and the chatter in Washington made it increasingly difficult to make call time productive. As that began to show in quarterly campaign finance filings, "She can't raise money," became the next assessment of my efforts, further drying up funds from traditional donors. A candidate who can't raise money usually doesn't win elections, so who wants to give money to someone who can't win? That slogan was pitched to the media, political columnists, reporters and party insiders, "How will you win when you're not raising as much money as Lee Fisher?" became the persistent question. Having to answer that question from the media eats up time in an interview that could be spent talking about issues. When that manufactured reputation sticks, it's a tough one to shake. When all was said and done, even a year after the election, a former Secretary of State colleague from the northeastern states who was running for the Senate, was said to have state at a meeting of national women donors, "Jennifer is a great candidate, but let's face it, she can't raise money."

There was one more layer in this challenge. Many of those who had contributed to my Secretary of State race in 2006, some individuals as much as $10,000, had been strategic and, as a block, supported me through the Secretary of State (SOS) Project, a national organization formed in recognition that fair elections ensure fair outcomes. This fact has been recognized in the wake of the disastrous 2000 Presidential election in Florida and the 2004 Ohio Presidential election. Many of these donors were glad to take my calls, but they would not contribute to me until they were assured that my successor Democratic candidate for Secretary of State would be a consummate defender of voting rights. This meant that I had to actually recruit a candidate to run in my place, which I did in Marilyn Brown, a progressive Democratic county commissioner from my own county, in Columbus, Ohio.

Unfortunately, Marilyn exited the race after an attorney who was a state representative from Southeast Ohio, Jennifer Garrison, moved forward aggressively with substantial union support. Coming from more conservative Southeast Ohio, Jennifer Garrison, a Democrat, proved to be a traditional, anti-choice candidate who was also said by many to have shown antigay proclivities in one of her previous campaigns. When I campaigned for the Senate, especially in Southeast Ohio, I was questioned about whether another Democrat could win my seat. In Ohio, "Brown" is an excellent ballot name. I assured them that they couldn't lose with either a Brown (Marilyn) or a Jennifer (Garrison). People seemed satisfied by that.

I had had a private moment with the Governor in late June of 2009, after both Marilyn and Jennifer had addressed a meeting of the state's county chairs the night before in Columbus. He volunteered to me in that meeting that he had not recruited Jennifer Garrison and that he was not endorsing her. Other information I had was not consistent with that, before or after, even though I wanted to believe him. It was at that June 2009 meeting with the Governor that I was able to say to him that I understood why he had endorsed Lee Fisher, even though I was not happy about it. He pointed out to me that, even though he had spoken at that same meeting which I also had attended, he had not publicly spoken in favor of either Secretary of State candidate or even of Lee. It was at this meeting he declared to me that he planned to remain neutral going forward.

Several months later in 2009, I had the opportunity to attend an event at the Governor's residence and to talk briefly with Frances Strickland, Ted's wife. She bluntly said that "they" were most likely going to have to write off the Secretary of State's race without me and focus on the Auditor's race, all to keep the apportionment board majority that Democrats then had with Ted and me. The fallacy of the argument about the apportionment board was that everyone assumed Ted and I could not lose. When I would remind naysayers in my Senate race that Ted or I could lose reelection bids, no one really believed me.

Perhaps the most confounding argument made against my running for the U.S. Senate was from Democrats who said that Ohio could not afford to lose me in the Secretary of State's office. When publicly challenged in this way by a male attorney at a Cleveland law firm meet and greet, I countered, "So, if you do a great job and seek more responsibility, and someone says, 'We can't afford to lose you where you are,' would you stick around?" There was no argument with that, especially from aspiring young law firm associates. Besides, organizations like Laborers Local 310 *wanted* someone like me in the Senate; I had proved a strong supporter of the issues they cared about.

To those who wanted the status quo, I often had to explain that my staff and I had "shored up" the institution of elections in Ohio. I recited to them the "David Royer maxim" that I knew to be true, that the greatest measure of a successful program or organization is what happens when a leader leaves it. Any good leader must strengthen it so that it is largely self-sufficient and with a strong culture and protocols that foster its success, with or without any particular leader.

I also pointed out to many Democrats that a great deal of the vitriol in the 2008 Presidential election (to the point of death threats) was due to GOP gamesmanship that appeared designed to build a negative record with which to defeat any reelection bid I would make. By not running for reelection, I told many, as I later told the attendees at the post-primary unity lunch, the reforms we made to protect Ohio's voting process would not have to be rehashed on the airwaves in the 2010 election. The newly healed wounds would not suffer unnecessary stress. No one ever argued with that.

I also know who I am. While I can be a decent caretaker, I'm motivated best when there is an opportunity to help make things better—to reform them. I ran for the Senate because I wanted to be a part of crafting public policy, especially at a time when I believed our country could use all hands on deck. I had learned a lot and given a lot as Ohio's chief elections officer, and even as a state trial court judge. The national experience and exposure among my contemporaries afforded me good working relationships already throughout the country. My work with national and international media outlets in reforming Ohio elections positioned me well for a Senate post, and being a woman U.S. Senator from Ohio could give my state greater visibility and leverage as it did for Maine, Washington and California, where both U.S. Senators from those states are women.

When asked on what committees I wanted to serve, I said without hesitation, the Senate Judiciary committee, to work on prison and criminal justice reform and fairness in civil trials.

Speaking as a U.S. Senate candidate at a 2009 health care rally in support of passage of President Obama's health care plan later dubbed by the GOP as "Obamacare"

I wanted to work on federal election issues, help shape foreign policy, assist farmers, laborers and veterans, fight to see more women in office, work for better health care coverage, work for more policies that assist families, such as workplace flexibility for working parents and better child care and elder care policies, to name a few. What better place to be a part of helping people's lives improve than in the U.S. Senate?

And for me, running for the Senate was freedom. I was not bound by the neutrality of being a judge or as the arbiter of fair elections. I could freely speak my mind and in the process work to solve difficult problems—to help people. When David discovered that I could write he encouraged me to do so. I frequently posted on Internet websites, in diary threads on Daily Kos and Huffington Post. My campaign developed a strong web presence, revising and adding functionality to our initial website with the help of Blue State Digital, which even today on its campaign website proudly posts:

> For Barack Obama's historic Presidential run, Blue State Digital developed and managed an online campaign operation that was unprecedented in size, scope, and influence.

We worked hard to attract new subscribers to our integrated email list and website and began using email strategically to push out clear policy statements on a wide variety of issues. This approach was critical to a twenty-first century grassroots campaign that could now be super charged by the medium of the Internet.

As a practice that sometimes confounded our Washington-based consultants, David would map out a series of upcoming communications with our supporters. We brought on a former blogger who had written under the name, "Yellow Dog Sammy," Jeff Coryell, an accomplished lawyer and artist, who further honed his online skills and became our New Media Director. Eventually, David, Jeff and I learned to perform "Wizard of Oz"-type feats, looking and sounding eons bigger than we three individuals were behind the "curtain" of the Internet and social media.

We used our "netroots" presence to build a healthy grassroots presence. With the help of Tiff Wolf, formerly of Progressive Majority, we developed "tables" or dialogs between the campaign and groups of supporters from

Jeff Coryell

throughout the state. She set up regular conference calls with them. I remember a particular call with a strong and early group of women supporters from throughout the state. One female supporter quietly challenged me, "Promise us you won't drop out." The way she said it hit me hard. She voiced what I suspect many wanted to know. If they were going to work this hard for me, how committed was I? I promised I would stay in the race, and once I make a promise, I do everything within my power to keep it, and I did keep it.

Not long after that, I sat at the dais of a 600+ person veterans' luncheon in Columbus next to State Auditor Mary Taylor, a Republican. That day the newspapers throughout the state had announced her decision not to run in the GOP Senate primary. Her state party immediately endorsed Rob Portman, said to be George Voinovich's handpicked successor. At an earlier juncture, I had talked with Auditor Taylor at a local restaurant while she was having breakfast with a McCain campaign leader. I did not know who he was when I approached her.

"Hi Mary!" I said cheerfully as I walked up to her table. Newspapers at that time were speculating about who would be in the race for Senator Voinovich's seat. I continued, "You know, if you and I run against each other and each of us wins our primary, Ohio will elect a woman to the Senate. So, do you just want to have a joint press conference now?" I thought the man sitting with her was going to spit out his eggs. Mary laughed.

A few months later when we sat next to each other at the veteran's luncheon, she said quietly to me from my right, "Don't drop out." I looked sideways at her and said quietly, "What?"

"Don't drop out," she repeated. I whispered, "I'm not." She continued, "I mean it; don't drop out." I stepped it up. "I swear I won't," I said. "Even if I go down in flames, I won't drop out."

Mary was quiet for a moment. Then she said with emphasis, "If you even think for one minute about dropping out, you call me, and I will talk you out of it," with almost staccato emphasis. "I've got it," I said. I was frankly amazed. I began to see that the reason that had convinced Sherrod Brown to tell me to "go for it" was the reason I had to see this race through, no matter what. If I dropped out, I would disappoint women, even though many were disappointed when I eventually lost the race.

Talking with Mary after the 2010 election was over, she reiterated that it was important I did not drop out of the race; otherwise, women would be farther behind in Ohio than they are now. Mary went on to join the Republican gubernatorial ticket as former Congressman John Kasich's Lieutenant Governor running mate. As Ohio's current Lieutenant Governor, she stands in good stead to run statewide for whatever office she wishes in the future.

Before the time she decided to run for Lieutenant Governor instead of for reelection as State Auditor, there were stories I believe to be true that Mary was being told by her party to step aside in running for reelection in favor of former state

Representative Josh Mandel, who was making his first statewide run. It was said he could raise more money than she. But, she was the only executive statewide office holder the Republicans had managed to elect in 2006—and she was qualified for the job. She was the first Certified Public Accountant in state history to hold the office of state auditor (and only the second Republican woman to be elected to statewide executive office in her own right).

Apparently the GOP didn't think she could win reelection, because she was not raising eye-popping sums of money. But . . . she was doing a good job, and she was the incumbent. It was apparently more politically important that someone, anyone GOP, occupy that office to stake claim to the state apportionment board, no matter who they were. Money, and lots of it, is, more often than not, the admittance to political power.

I have said that politics is about people, but ironically, it's also about power. In a democracy, when people hold the power, there is some semblance of balance. In an oligarchy, where power rests with a few, (whether it be according to royalty, wealth, family ties, education, corporate, or military control,) balance can be feigned, but it is not certain. Aristotle coined the phrase, plutocracy, when the few in power are rich. In this scenario, a grab for more than one's share of power is not limited to the rich when undue control is exercised by, for example, labor, business or other political leaders. This is the case, whether exercised in government or in the operation of a political party or a labor organization. Such imbalance of power will eventually destroy the organization and inflict needless suffering until its demise.

Public service should be examined in light of how to use power that is gained through the competition of ideas in the political process. Wayne West, Sherrod Brown's last assistant secretary of state, used to say that "good government is good politics." I believe he was and is right. I discovered first, as a judge, and became further convinced, as Secretary of State, that when those holding elected public office bring people together and empower them, it is government at its best. This is also the embodiment of democracy.

A grassroots campaign empowers many to effect change by electing someone they believe will achieve it in public office. People who work in grassroots campaigns work hard. But they are willing to do it, because they know better in this type of campaign who the candidate really is. A grassroots campaign tests the authenticity of a candidate for public office. It also helps the candidate to learn, really learn, about his or her constituents. Voters have the opportunity to see and hear the candidate firsthand, unvarnished. Not every candidate looks good that way, and many political consultants will be the first to tell them. But candidates can learn and grow—just as people do. The best of politics, and ultimately public service, is about people—nothing more and nothing less.

Had I the opportunity for a "do over" in my Senate race, I would have parted ways with EMILY's List after the second quarter of 2009, June 30th (instead of September 30th). I believe the organization may have felt the same way. We just didn't have the same philosophy when it came to how to campaign. Moving earlier to our eventual strong grassroots campaign would have saved me monthly finance consulting fees that weren't even keeping up with funds raised. (For example, $10,000 per month was considered "reasonable" or even low for a national fundraising consultant, even when the fee wasn't being covered by funds raised).

Going grassroots actually was what allowed me to keep my promise and stay in the race. While establishment forces can control to a great degree the traditional, large donations and ensure that they are verboten to a challenger or renegade, these same forces get very nervous when they realize they cannot control small contributions, especially when they start to appear en masse. My theory for why the organization, "Citizens United" chose such a name was to appear as other "citizens united," organized or not, who participated in ways they never did before in electing Barack Obama President of the United Sates of America. An oligarchy generally abhors the masses.

By October 2009, we were so desperate to raise funds, that grassroots fundraising was the only way to escape being squashed like a bug by the giant thumbs of those who could control the flow of traditional campaign money. I suggested to David that canvassing could be used to raise small dollars in large amounts. David counseled that we would first need to use our volunteers to gather signatures on my candidate petitions to get them trained. In the meantime, I continued making calls to a somewhat lesser degree. With all three of my finance call-time managers from EMILY's List gone, I at least did not have that overhead to bear.

During this seemingly nomadic period of the campaign, "miracles in the desert" started to occur. Campaign workers seemed to have come out of nowhere to replace the ELers who had left. We also decided to move our basement offices to some less accessible on the 5th floor of a building less than two blocks from my home, since the first offices were easily infiltrated.

Two "miracles" in particular occurred during this period that left me dumbfounded. They seemed to happen at moments when my resolve to stay in the race was at some of its lowest ebbs. Discouraged one afternoon, I headed upstairs from our basement offices to wait on the street for Rick to pick me up for our weekly lunch. He wasn't there yet, but a large van pulled up in front of the building and parked in front of me. Our climbed five nuns, each dressed in simple white gowns and habits with rich, purple aprons and rope belts.

"Hello!" said one of them exuberantly. "We've been working at a soup kitchen in Newark! We're here to have a picnic lunch! Do you know where we can go?" Newark was 45 minutes away. "Okay," I thought. "This is really weird." I helpfully directed them to a nearby park area and gave them my card, since after all, I was still their Secretary of State. They were delighted. I told Rick of this at lunch, still blown away by the weirdness of this encounter. It was if I had seen an apparition of the Virgin Mary when I was just about to jump off of a cliff.

"I'm very discouraged. I'm wondering if I should drop out," I said, feeling very beaten down. "But, it's so weird these nuns just pulled up when I was standing there waiting for you," I said.

Rick leaned over the table toward me and looked at me pointedly, " What do *you* want to do? Do you *want* to drop out?" he queried. Conflicting thoughts raced through my head. Of course it would be good to be done with all this, but I knew I had promised, and I could not quit now. It would further entrench the tactics being used against me. "No," I said. "Then don't," he said simply.

The second miracle occurred again when I was leaving those basement offices, trying to keep my chin up in the face of low dollars. A tall young man walked in and said, "Hi, I'm Adam Niswonger, and I'm here to volunteer for your campaign. Can you tell me who I should talk to?" Adam Niswonger, with no previous campaign experience, but who liked my stands on the issues, eventually helped organize the field operations of the

Adam Niswonger, driver of the Courage Express, when we delivered the bus after its last official run from Valley View Farm to WBNS-10TV studios

campaign. He found a bus on eBay for sale for $2050, supervised its conversion and actually had a commercial driver's license and drove our bus when we put it on the road. It was Adam who traveled with me to the farm outside of Alliance where we had retired the bus. He drove it on its last journey to Columbus to give it a new home, at WBNS-TV, sharing with me our "last supper" at the McDonald's outside of Canton on the way.

Adam was special and another reason why I went the distance. He was unemployed when he appeared at our campaign office. He and his wife had moved to Columbus for her to take a job. She had encouraged him to get involved. So he did, and our campaign was the better for it.

After the ELers left, new staffers like Adam, Matt McSorley, Deb Steele, Mallory Mitchell, Matt Johnson, Derek Clinger, Vince Bruni and Christa Johnson, Dustin White, and stalwart Mary Woods, who worked for pittances—or for nothing, sought the chance to make a difference. They were dedicated beyond belief and inspired each other and other workers and volunteers to get involved. The growth of our campaign started becoming organic. Luckily, David, who had academically studied how campaigns could grow organically was delighted to see this and fostered it. David also kept cutting his salary to keep us going. His wife and son who had moved from Cleveland to Columbus to be with him moved back to Cleveland. It was hard on them, and I could only imagine from the hell my family and I were living through what was also being experienced by those around me.

In March of 2010, I had been invited to Germany to speak at an overseas voting forum, along with several other secretaries of state. Rick was excited for the trip and had paid for a ticket to accompany me. In the crisis-to-crisis times of campaigns, a trip like this is usually not appropriate, but David did not want to tell me no, and it was a short trip. As often happens, the universe did it for him. It turned out to be a sort of "Irish Blessing." On St. Patrick's Day, Lee Fisher asked the Ohio Democratic Party to endorse him, just eleven days before the start of early voting. Serious efforts were needed to combat his last ditch effort to squash me like a bug.

Just days before we were to leave, we discovered our passports were expired. We could have walked them through renewal by going to Michigan, but we started thinking better of it. It was just a day or two before the Cleveland St. Patrick's Day parade— an event we were sternly told by many in Cuyahoga County we should not and could not miss. (I keep an obnoxiously grass-green leather jacket that I rarely don other than in March just for this purpose.) We called off the trip. Rick was terribly disappointed, and I was glum, too.

But, it couldn't have been a wiser decision. The campaign challenge that followed was one of the most gripping times of the campaign.

Within a week of St. Patrick's Day, on March 24, 2010, the Ohio Democratic Party would be holding an executive committee meeting. The state central committee of the party is sixty-six members, half men and half women, each whom are elected at the primary election by the voters in the party every two years. The state central committee serves as the party's central governing body.

When the central committee reorganizes every two years after an election, it elects a chair and thereafter expands its membership with appointees selected by the chair and becomes the party's executive committee. Knowing the makeup of the executive committee, I didn't stand a chance if the question of endorsement went to a vote. The members of the executive committee were handpicked and controlled by the chair who answered to the Governor. An endorsement of Lee over me would have cut off my ability to use the party's voter database, the lifeblood of a grassroots campaign.

Two days after Lee's request for a party endorsement, late on a Friday afternoon and just five days before the meeting of the party's executive committee, Adam informed me we were losing full access to "Vote Builder," the party's voter database. Alarmed, I asked him to describe what was happening. He ended his explanation with, "Don't worry, I already have a download in progress, so if we have to create our own database, we can build one with what we have." We called an IT expert to come to our office to talk with us about how to build our own database if we had to.

The benefit to the party in allowing any campaign to use the voter database is that whomever uses it has the opportunity to enhance it with information gained from the person-to-person contact that happens in a grassroots campaign. We were doing massive amounts of phone banking. One of my volunteers, Eugenio Kinbur, came in nearly every day and conversed in Spanish with Latino voters. Gene spends his winters in

Guatemala, taking a bus there, working on green initiatives and coming back to Columbus every spring. For the data we gathered the party had every reason to want a campaign like ours to be using the database, but that wouldn't matter if there were a party endorsement. We would be cut off and left for dead.

I immediately contacted Chris Redfern, the state party chair, describing for him the nature of the problem. My first email alerted him to the problem. My second email informed him that we were having difficulty accessing the data our volunteers had gathered. Adam had detailed the specific problems in a memo I provided to Chris:

"Our experience using VoteBuilder was stellar until yesterday, March 18, 2010, when we lost the ability to export files directly from the voter file, based on targeted lists we created. . . .

. . . this prevents us from producing targeted lists for direct mail – therefore making the database nonfunctional. I placed a call to Carter on Thursday, March 18, 2010 without getting a call back.

Three of our users (Mary Woods, Derek Clinger and I) have been stripped of certain options that we need to interact with the data and with our volunteers. . . . We no longer [can] . . . setup our volunteers with the virtual phone bank. We now must go through the process of requesting a user account which has to be "OK'd" by Carter each time we want to set up a volunteer. . . . We have also been stripped of the ability to create and edit reports and labels – and the ability to download lists into label and letter formats.

We have also lost the ability to locate polling locations, create survey questions and scripts, monitor the system, edit a list in script view and view canvass results. . . .

Chris Redfern called me almost immediately after receiving this email. Within an hour full access was restored. During our conversation, he indicated that he was required to call the meeting of the state executive committee but that he could control whether or not there was a vote on endorsement. He said to me more than once in that conversation, "When you win . . ." I was shocked that he would say that, as he, more than anyone else, had assiduously worked to create the impression of extreme neutrality in our race.

But I was convinced, despite any intentions he expressed to the contrary, that he could not control a sequence of events that could happen at an executive committee meeting—only the Governor could. If the shutdown to our data could occur on his watch, so could a party endorsement. I could not afford for there to be any endorsement request even entertained by the Ohio Democratic Party.

One or more of my women supporters had called Chris to test his intentions. He assured them that the question of the vote on endorsement would not be called. We all wanted to believe him. But the bylaws were subject to interpretation, and we believed the question would have to be called. While we worked over the weekend to put contingency plans in place so we would have access to our data, David and I convened a telephone conference call with Antoinette, Rick and four of my key women supporters from throughout the state. Jeff Coryell joined the call from Cleveland, already working furiously to set up an email template and functionalities so that supporters could email executive committee members and sign a petition, all to stop a party endorsement. Our call was scheduled for late morning on

Saturday. It took us an hour to hash through our options. We finally decided the only option was to appeal to our supporters to bombard the party executive committee with emails and call for no party endorsement, especially this late in the campaign. I was a members of the executive committee by virtue of my office. I would be getting these emails as well.

I could practically sense Jeff's sweating out the details as he continued to work in Cleveland to launch this counterattack. David and I worked through what the email would say, with Jeff's careful review and comment. It would be emailed to several hundred thousand people that Saturday, and it explained:

"I'm Ohio Secretary of State Jennifer Brunner. On May 4th, I am competing against the state's Lieutenant Governor for the Democratic nomination for the U.S. Senate seat now held by retiring Sen. Voinovich. Polls show each of us has strong support for the nomination.

The Ohio Democratic Party has so far remained neutral in this primary. Just last week my opponent delivered a letter to the state party asking for its endorsement. The Ohio

Democratic Party Executive Committee meets Wednesday, March 24, 2010, and its bylaws require endorsement consideration to move forward. Early voting begins in just 10 days on March 30th. Until now, the party has remained neutral. We need your help to keep it that way--not just for me, but for Ohio.

A state party endorsement at this late date provides no conceivable benefit for anyone but my opponent. As Democrats, we're all in this together. A party endorsement would alienate supporters of the candidate not endorsed and hurt party unity after the primary election.

Let's face it, the real fight here is against electing Rob Portman, whose record of free trading and hard core conservative voting as a Washington insider in Congress has lost jobs for Ohio and will take us backward not forward. Help us keep the Democratic Party unified and stop an endorsement in the U.S. Senate race in Ohio. Please sign our online petition for NO ENDORSEMENT in the U.S. Senate primary on May 4th!

Tell the Ohio Democratic Party to let the voters decide. Please forward this to your friends and family and have them sign, too! Sign the petition now."

Once supporters went to the petition to sign it online, they were given the option to email all of the state executive committee members to tell them not to endorse. Jeff sent test emails to David and me. We approved them, and finally, Jeff pushed the fateful "send" button.

Rick and I left the house, going to his cousin's housewarming party in Delaware County just north of Columbus. I tried hard to focus on the conversations I was having at this beautiful home with people who really could have cared less about politics or about the fact that my Blackberry was running out of power from vibrating, after receiving so many emails as a member of the state party executive committee. I was aghast at the power of electronic communication.

Soon I was getting complaints from the Hamilton County Democratic Party Chair, and Rick was receiving complaints from a Mansfield state representative, that too many emails were coming in. Finally, Chris Redfern sent me a cryptic message that these emails could hurt me with the party. By 11:00 p.m., Chris Redfern emailed me, saying, "I have received many many complaints about the numbers of emails being sent to Executive Committee members. I believe these emails may be counterproductive to your efforts. As I have told you many times this week, the Party will not be considering endorsements [sic] in your race next week"

I could not rely on this. I countered:

> Just found your email, as I, too, have been inundated with emails. . . .

> I understand that the emails may be annoying. . . . If Lee Fisher would withdraw his letter, I could cut off the emails. As I see it, members of the executive committee are performing their own form of public service, since the bylaws of the party call for an open process and that the party is open to all Democrats. If they were to endorse Lee because they are upset about this, it would make the party look even worse.

> . . . Not ready to turn off the emails yet. It's the only avenue I have to let the committee know what else is out there

besides pressure from Lee and purported (I hope) pressure from the Governor as pushed by Lee.

* * *

The emails continued through Sunday. More than 74,000 in total were sent among about 100 executive committee members.

By Sunday evening, I knew we could not have what some considered an intrusion continuing into the Monday morning work day, especially since many executive committee members' email addresses were through their businesses.

"If Lee were smart," said David, "he would put his head down, get through this, and get the endorsement. The executive committee is stacked with folks who would vote as they were told by the establishment." I agreed. I was still concerned, though, that this could turn sour on us.

"But I can't have people getting their workdays interrupted by political party emails," I said. In a telephone conference on what to do next between David, Jeff and me, Jeff pointed out that our website software had capabilities to ask people to write letters to the editors of newspapers. I agreed that would be better, and David pointed out that it would give us the opportunity to tell people how they did and inform Fisher (whose wife was on the state central committee as well) how many people opposed an endorsement. We agreed it was the way to go.

Monday morning before 7:00 a.m., Jeff turned off the emails to executive committee members. We issued a new appeal by email, informing our supporters that more than 74,000 emails had gone to state executive committee members in less than 48 hours, and now they needed to write letters to the editors of their local papers to push for Lee Fisher to withdraw his endorsement. David wrote:

On Saturday, Jennifer Brunner asked you to go to www.handsoffourprimary.com to tell the Ohio Democratic Party (ODP) not to endorse in the U.S. Senate primary. You have spoken collectively with strength and vigor. In the first 48 hours you sent over 74,000 e-mails to members of the ODP's Executive Committee and added your names to our online petition. Some of those on the committee have talked to us since your emails and said they don't want to see an endorsement process go forward on Wednesday, and we're glad.

Your voices are being heard. Shouldn't Democrats be focusing even now on what it will take to beat a Cincinnati Republican who is the epitome of Washington elite and has the banking and special interest money to prove it? Now, Jennifer's opponent needs to withdraw his request for endorsement.

Please send a message to Jennifer's opponent to withdraw his request for endorsement, if you have not already done so, to demand a clean primary election where the voters decide. If you have already signed the petition, send letters to the editors of Ohio newspapers. To sign the petition please click here

* * *

The last thing Ohio Democrats should do is "stack the deck" against a competitive primary.

Democrats need to be smart and let this process move forward without an endorsement. We'll have enough challenges in the fall. Jennifer's opponent must not tear our party apart with a painful endorsement fight. Please stand with Jennifer for a fair primary.

Keep spreading the message that our opponent must

withdraw his request for ODP endorsement. And please forward this to your friends and family and have them sign the petition, too!

Sign the petition and send letters to the editors today.

Thank you.
David Dettman
Campaign Manager

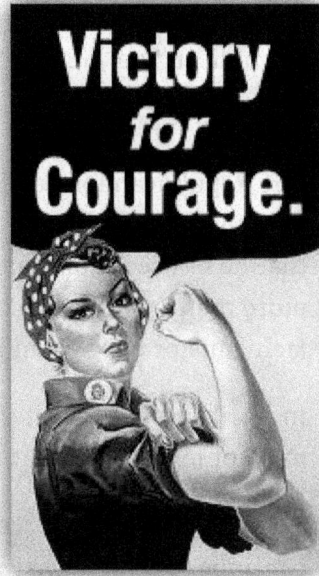

Victory for Courage.

By the time Lee Fisher withdrew his endorsement that morning around 10:00 a.m., more than 500 letters had been sent in less than four hours through our website to editors of newspapers throughout the state. It was a huge victory for our campaign, and we used it to celebrate our victory and continue to raise money online. The ever faithful Rosie the Riveter had a new slogan, "Victory for Courage."

By April 30, 2010, less than a week before the primary, Mark Naymik of the Cleveland Plain Dealer, the same reporter who interviewed and reported about my son in July 2009, wrote a comparison piece on Lee Fisher's and my fundraising styles. He harkened back to an earlier piece he had written a year earlier on our race, where I had referred to the character in actor and director Mel Gibson's "Braveheart." At that time Lee was making an early push to show financial strength to push me out of the race. Naymik reported Rob Portman's totals, with no primary, to already be far surpassing even what Lee and I combined were doing. He reported:

"While Fisher and Brunner will be forced to spend millions battling each other for the chance to succeed retiring Republican Sen. George Voinovich, candidate Rob Portman is banking millions.

The Republican former congressman and Bush administration official from Cincinnati will announce today that he's raised more than $1.7 million this quarter and has more than $3 million in his campaign account. He is not facing major opposition in the primary yet."

In April 2010, a year later, I was still in the race, and Naymik had not forgotten about the "Braveheart" analogy, stating:

"Asked last year if she would consider dropping out if she continues to trail Fisher in the money race, Brunner referred to Mel Gibson's bloody portrayal of Scottish rebel William Wallace in the movie "Braveheart."

Laughing, she said, 'I'll be shouting, 'Freedom!' as they cut out my gizzards.'"

It was the battle over primary endorsement and our grassroots victory over Lee Fisher that brought our race to the proverbial moment, as in the movie "Braveheart," where I was perceived as such a threat, that I would in fact be shouting "Freedom!" as they were doing me in. By this time, I was raising more money through grassroots fundraising than I had through my last quarter using traditional call time. We weren't rolling in the dough, but it paid for field staff, literature and "Courage cards." Our printing vendor was mailing our literature to Democratic voters on the same day people were mailed their absentee ballots by boards of elections. Incredibly, we could find no evidence that Lee was making these same absentee ballot-related mailings. He appeared to be relying solely on television and some earlier mailed pieces with gloomy storm clouds on it, railing against Congress.

Here, a photo extracted from a campaign YouTube video http://tinyurl.com/8r93mfh with Tuscarawas County Perry Township Trustee Matthew Micozzi, after helping him fill potholes in the cash-strapped township where he often did this work on his own time

Once we succeeded in shutting down the party endorsement, we observed that the Governor went visibly on the stump for Lee. The Mahoning County Democratic Party held an event the Sunday before the election, but we could find no invitation from the chairman inviting me to attend. The turning of the screws was no longer quiet, but by this time, neither were we.

We had already experienced conventional fundraising events being shut down, even with printed invitations. We found another way, holding "cupcake parties" all over the state, traveling in our bus to get there, creating canvassing packets on the way for our volunteers and creating YouTube videos of our experiences. We were pushing out our videos and messages through social networking and email, raising dollars online and in person. The establishment knew we were surviving without it, or at least in spite of it.

My motivating songs at that time were from the band, Need to Breathe, "The Outsiders," and Bonnie Raitt's, "I Will Not Be Broken." In President Obama's first campaign for President, it was at about this time that large contributors started moving his way. In my case, with the Governor openly backing Lee Fisher in a primary and members of the Governor's team covertly "disincentivizing" potential backers, that didn't happen. At least one lobbyist told me after the primary that the pressure was so intense against him and his clients being involved in my campaign that they were told that "not even the wives" of his clients could contribute.

A strong and thriving grassroots campaign freed us of the establishment pressures. Ours was an iconic campaign. We could see it in the eyes of the people we met, and so could the establishment. Once the video tracker who followed me told Christa, who was filming for our campaign, that I had something in my hair, and she should take it out. It was dandelion fuzz. Christa stopped her own filming of the event, walked up to me and pulled the fuzz out of my hair. We both laughed.

Early in the campaign the Dayton Daily News had written an article with profiles of each of the Senate candidates then in the race. On the Republican side, Tom Ganley from Cleveland was called, "The Businessman," Rob Portman, "The Congressman," Lee Fisher, "The Contender," and I was called even then "The Renegade," with an independent and politically rebellious streak. I couldn't have moved to a grassroots campaign without that. Along with David's proclivity to take on the establishment and his willingness to be paid less to stand for a principle, it's doubtful we would have otherwise survived to that point.

We were surviving, leaving the establishment to guess how well, while Lee was fretting as he always did. Lee pushed his advisors to buy more television time. They threw in nearly $1 million on top of the $300,000 they had already spent for television, mostly in the Democrat-rich Cleveland area. We had spent too much money initially on staffing and office overhead when we began as a traditional campaign and had not turned to grassroots early enough. Without at least $150,000 of television to counter Lee's television time, we could not survive it. We were outspent on television about $1.3 million to zero, and overall in campaign spending, we were outspent 4 to 1. Lee told me afterward that he told his advisors not to underestimate me. But it wasn't me; it was the people—on the campaign, in the trenches, on the Internet, who made the difference. ≈

Chapter 26

Women

Some of my most ardent supporters were a group of women from various parts of the state. They each stepped up, one-by-one, summoning great courage.

Nearly as soon as I announced my candidacy, Lee Fisher began a "Women for Lee" organization, showing fear of gender's potential effect in the race. I frankly thought it was meaningless. Women don't ordinarily vote as a block. They are as diverse as any population that shares only a single attribute, and that is not limited enough to be uniting. While some said we should start a "Men for Jen" group, I didn't see that as smart or viable, either.

When a woman runs for office, she is subject to scrutiny of her appearance, modulation of her voice, her demeanor and her reactions, much more than men. She has to avoid appearing sexual, or she is not credible. However, she must be well put-together, or anything in her attire or styling that is out of place will distract from her message. She cannot screech, but she must keep her voice well modulated, and she cannot make excuses or assign blame where it is not warranted, or she is accused of being weak. Hence, she must coyly put on lipstick before she speaks but not incessantly push her bangs away from her face. She must be serious but remember to smile without being glib. But most of all she must be smart and work hard, and it never hurts to have a sense of humor.

When reasons why women do not run for office are studied, they generally boil down to three: they believe they are not qualified, they cite concerns with family and child-rearing obligations, and they have never been specifically asked. Some women stay out of the fray, because they see politics as just plain dirty, which it can be. Most women run for office because of something they want to get done, not for the typically male reasons of wanting power or prestige. As late as 2012, I asked a male former candidate why he was considering running for Congress. This man had not run for office for about 25 years. The question stumped him, leaving him temporarily speechless. I heard the wind up, "I don't know . . ." He thought some more, "...you know, the prestige associated with the office. And I could raise a lot of money and be influential in the process and really have some power in the caucus." It was almost textbook.

When I ran for the Senate, we covered the silver-painted reflectors of our bus, situated at the front of the roof, with decals for the number "18." People wondered what that meant. Some saw it as the Jewish number signifying life. That sounded good to me. But what it really signified was that, if elected, I would be the 18th woman in the U.S. Senate (out of 100). I had watched a 2006 video made by the women of the Senate about their experiences, showing what it meant and even showing what life was like with the responsibilities of being a wife and mother and serving their constituents. For this video party affiliation did not matter.

Even after leaving office I still speak to students, and I am not afraid to talk about the dearth of women in elective office. No woman—or man—should be. Whether we are male, female, straight, gay, lesbian, transgendered, bisexual, African American, Latino or Latina, Asian, American Indian, young or old, foreign born and naturalized or with ancestors on the Mayflower, our experiences shape our judgment. Our government must represent our diversity, which is our strength as a country, and in Ohio's case, as a state. That's why it matters that we elect candidates from diverse backgrounds. They will think of things others without their life experiences can't even envision. When our diversity is reflected in our government policy, we collectively improve our lives.

Some of us never stop fighting for that. Lana Moresky had been Senator Hillary Clinton's Ohio state finance director for Senator Clinton's Presidential run in 2008. I was first introduced to Lana in 2005 by Antoinette Wilson. The two of us traveled to Cleveland to meet to Lana, along with a group of amazing women activists that included Nancy Cronin, Ellie Sullivan, Elaine Fortney and Renee Lipson.

Lana Moresky, an original ERA warrior, who is now a member of the Ohio Women's Hall of Fame

Lana was an original fighter for the Equal Rights Amendment, having worked in Iowa and elsewhere for passage of the ERA in the 1970's. One impactful story she tells is of working with another activist to set up "shop" in a Missouri hotel, methodically going through the local telephone book to look for women to call and taking advantage of the extra phone in the adjacent hotel room as the maid was cleaning it. Lana continues to be active with the National Organization of Women, the Feminist Majority Foundation and countless other organizations that work to protect and strengthen the rights of women, including their right to make decisions about their bodies and their health. Early on she exhorted people to support me, held fundraising events and traveled to New York City to the fundraising event Caroline Kennedy held for me in March of 2009.

For Lana, it was a tough choice. Lee Fisher was her neighbor in Shaker Heights, and both of them are Jewish—with both of them involved in various, related causes in their community. Lana was a strong supporter of Governor Ted Strickland, and he had appointed her to the Ohio Board of Regents, a plum appointment charged with overseeing the operation of the state's robust university system. Lana believed she owed it to the political establishment in Cleveland to be clear about her support for me. When she one-by-one spoke with its members and declared her support for me, she was repeatedly challenged. With each defense, she became stronger and even angrier and showed strength in the face of threatened retribution. She was at nearly every event I appeared at in Cleveland. She drove to nearby counties where I was appearing, usually bringing another supporter or two with her. She made calls and talked about my candidacy to countless women and men in and out of Ohio.

The long anticipated Cleveland City Club debate for the U.S. Senate race was held on April 13, 2010, just weeks before the primary election. Lana attended, once again bringing others with her. She even traveled with me that day in the Cleveland area on the Courage Express, our converted school bus, as I made the rounds of seven speeches that long day.

She drove me in her car as we ended the day so that we could, together, visit Elaine Fortney, one last time. Elaine had chosen to be removed from life support the next day in the nursing home in Cleveland where she was being cared for with Lou Gehrig's disease. Elaine, still a relatively young woman, had been one of my two Cuyahoga County coordinators for our successful 2006 Secretary of State campaign. She was in a wheelchair by that time, and with the help of energetic Ed Monroe, they were an indefatigable team. Elaine was a quiet and amazing organizer of exponential description who never gave up and was able to mobilize more volunteers than anyone I have ever known—in the state's largest county, heavily Democratic. To have Elaine working on your campaign was the luckiest break a candidate could ever have.

On our way to see Elaine in the nursing home, I finally confided in Lana, who was driving the car, that I had had a routine medical procedure the previous day for which 1% needed a catheter. I confessed that I was a "one percenter." I watched her foot hit the brake in the car, "What? Are you wearing one now?!? You did that during the debate today?" she asked incredulously. "Yes," I said quietly, embarrassed but grinning. I thought Lana was going to wreck the car. She regained composure. Her reaction was amusing. A woman has to do what she has to do. She resumed driving for us to see our dying friend.

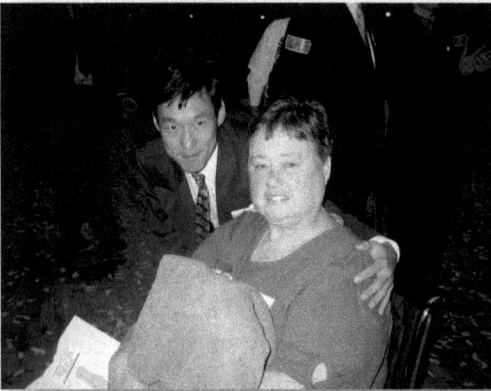

Ed Monroe and Elaine Fortney on election night in 2006

When we arrived at Elaine's room, Elaine pointed out the literature from my Senate campaign tacked onto the bulletin board beside her bed. Elaine smiled effusively when Lana and I came into her room. She couldn't speak, but she motioned in approval at the pictures on my computer when I showed her the Courage Express. She made me promise to win the race as I left, and by choice, she died the next day. It was tough for all of us.

After the well-attended Cleveland City Club Senate debate, Lana was elated at what had transpired at the end of the debate. She said, "What you did today was exactly what a feminist does. You don't just talk it. You actually do it." What she was talking about was the fact that throughout the debate, Lee Fisher had assiduously referred to me as, "Jennifer," while I largely and respectfully called him, "Lieutenant Governor Fisher."

Before the luncheon and debate began, both sides had been required by the Cleveland City Club to convene in a small room outside the dining room. We were to effectively "draw straws" to determine who would go first and also who would get to choose in which order we would ask a final question of each other. Lee refused to come in the room. I remember seeing him pacing outside the room like my dogs do when they need to go outside.

Lee left the task to his second campaign manager, Jay Howser, to cover the pre-debate formalities, even though the City Club administration clearly expected both candidates to be together for this pre-debate ritual. Sitting at the table in the small room with Lee's campaign manager, I drew the favored "straw" for determining the order of the final question. Impulsively, I said, "I'll ask the last question." David, who was quietly leaning against the wall in the room, asked the debate conveners if he could confer with me for a minute and asked that they hold my choice for the moment.

We moved away from those seated at the table. "Wait a minute," he whispered to me. "If you ask the last question, he gets the last word when he gives his answer. Don't you want to ask the first question and let him ask the last question? Then you answer last." He was right, and I couldn't believe I hadn't thought of that. But a good campaign manager is strategic, and David was all that. I returned to my seat and asked if I could change my preference. The City Club management obliged. I would ask the first question and get the last answer.

Cleveland Plain Dealer photo adaptation: Lieutenant Governor Lee Fisher (left) and me during the Cleveland City Club Debate in U.S. Senate Democratic Primary, April 13, 2010

Lee Fisher's press secretary was sure David and I had planned the entire turn of events (ah, the wonders of Oz). When Lee asked me the last question, he used my first name at least five times. I felt indignation rise within me. Throughout the debate I could not recall him once referring to me as "Secretary Brunner," while I made it a point to be respectful, calling him "Lieutenant Governor Fisher." This was not easy, because I had been his lawyer before; we had considered each other friends; he had contributed to my first judicial race (even with the reputation of being notoriously close-fisted with campaign contributions). All I could think of at the moment before I provided the last answer was Hillary Clinton's Presidential debate with President Obama (in Cleveland) where commentator/questioner Tim Russert bullied her so roughly that I lost respect for him, despite his stellar reputation. (I resolved it for myself based on the fact that some people after heart surgery have angry bouts, and Tim Russert soon after that debate died unexpectedly of a heart attack.) I remember being disappointed that Hillary didn't haul off and at least verbally punch him. But she didn't. I decided then and there that I would not let anyone do to me what had been done to Hillary in her debate.

The voice was coming from afar in my head, moving closer, "No . . . you cannot . . . let - this - one - go. You ran for women and girls. You owe it to them . . . speak up . . . Do - it!" There were high school students in the luncheon audience. I knew I had to do it. The debate was being video recorded by the City Club and recorded for replay on Cleveland public radio. This was not going to be pretty.

Before giving my answer to the last question, I called out Lieutenant Governor Fisher on why he couldn't address me by my elected title. I pointed out that he had called me "Jennifer" throughout the debate. From the recording:

"Well first of all it'd be wonderful...I have not once referred to you as Lee. And it would be wonderful if you referred to me by my title, which is Secretary of State Brunner, but (applause from the audience) I'm just as glad people know me by my first name because it will be on the ballot. . . .

I went on to answer his question, a politically meaty one, which was whether I would endorse him if I lost. I continued,

"Unfortunately, Lt. Governor Fisher, I serve as Secretary of State while I run for this office, and I cannot publicly make any endorsements of a candidate or an issue. I am a very dyed-in-the-wool Democrat, unlike my mother, and I will do everything that I am permitted to do as Secretary of State to make sure that I continue to be a very good Democrat."

Upon making the public observation about his use of "Jennifer," I had watched the audience. I saw mouths drop open, especially from women in the audience. It was a gutsy move, but I had to make it. It clearly unnerved the Lieutenant Governor's press secretary, and soon after the debate he put out a statement about how many times I had called Lieutenant Governor Fisher, "Lee." He claimed about five or six times.

It was this occurrence that had struck Lana. But this is why I ran. David used say from his work in Ukraine that the first people to step out in a revolution get shot or their heads cut off. But their sacrifice means something when others keep coming, and change finally happens. Lana is busy helping other women candidates and she always will be until she can't go anymore.

Janet Carson, Chair of the Geauga County Democratic Party in northeast Ohio

Janet Carson and her husband Terry are the heart of the Democratic Party in Republican-dominated Geauga County, just to the east of Cuyahoga County. It's easy to imagine that she and Terry were once quasi-hippies from the 1960's and 1970's when you see them together. They clearly delight in each other's company. His eyes light up, and she throws back her curly brown head in laughter. They have a booming insurance agency where they work together with their son, Andy. Janet has taken the reins of the Geauga County Democratic Party with aplomb and serves on the Geauga County Board of Elections. She can shake things up, but with precision. Janet is a key actor in the Ohio Democratic Party Women's Caucus. Their daughter, April, is a successful lawyer and an Afghanistan veteran who, with the help of her mother, raised money and supplies for an Afghan orphanage when she and her husband, James, also an attorney, were stationed there.

Both Janet and April traveled to Indianapolis in 2009 to attend and hear me speak at the national conference of the National Organization of Women. April and James held a successful fundraising event for my Senate race in their home in DC. April kept giving to my campaign until it hurt. She inspired reticent givers to step up by her example and her frequent exhortations. Janet traveled with Lana to Caroline Kennedy's event in support of my Senate candidacy in NYC in March 2009. Like Lana, Janet held fundraising events and meet-and-greet events for me. She rode the bus with me, traveled to be there to support our race and generally remained watchful for us on matters, state and local. At the time when Lee Fisher sought the late March state Democratic Party endorsement in the Senate primary, and our campaign experienced the temporary disruption of access to "Vote Builder" that late Friday afternoon, what I didn't know until well after the election was that county parties like Janet's were also affected.

After the women's Democratic caucus in her county endorsed me, she received at least one telephone call from Democratic state party headquarters threatening loss of county party privileges from the state party—no visits from statewide office holders, loss of access to the statewide voter database and more if support of my campaign continued. Janet and Terry lost access to the database as primary election day neared, cutting off their ability to do the grassroots work in their county that was so important to success. At the time our campaign experienced problems with access, reasons had been cited that some county parties were downloading too much information. I never put it together until after the election, and neither did she. She remains a friend and committed supporter of electing more women to office to this day.

Kathy DiCristofaro (left) beats the drum during an educators rally in support of a statewide referendum vote on S.B. 5, a bill that would have banned public employee collective bargaining

Kathy DiCristofaro is a college professor at Youngstown State University with skill and expertise in communications. My only regret about Kathy is that I was never one of her students. There are few like her who have the ability to read a situation, see the chicanery in it, call it out, smack it down and smile afterward, even if she gets whacked back and the short end of the stick. She doesn't stop and hasn't stopped fighting.

Kathy has more common sense in the tip of her little finger than most people would if they had the chance to use three brains. During the primary, Kathy facilitated her county's women's Democratic caucus endorsement of my Senate candidacy. (Her county party, too, eventually lost access to the state party's voter database.)

Later in the campaign Kathy stepped in to ensure the success of a critical fundraising event in Trumbull County (next to Mahoning County where the City of Youngstown is located) that had been organized by several supporters in the area. She took an event for which planning was not meeting its marks and turned it into one of the most successful events of the campaign. It provided healthy funding and key political and public support.

Kathy is a skilled warrior who can throw great cherry bombs with strong aim. Having Kathy on a campaign team creates positive gains for any campaign. Yet, she remains patient and committed in mentoring new women candidates. Kathy continues to help other women running for office in her area. Anyone who has Kathy in their corner is fortunate indeed. We still exchange advice and stories, and she continues to work for women candidates.

Cindy Demsey is a lawyer in Cleveland who practices law with her husband, Richard. She is a key leader in the Cuyahoga County Democratic Women's Caucus, a pivotal women's

Democratic organization in the Cleveland area. Cindy finds ways to maneuver through the gauntlet presented by male-dominated organizations that seek a women's branch, even when the organizations lack a commitment that demonstrates the intrinsic rather than utilitarian value of highlighting women.

The Democratic political climate in Cleveland is steeped in tradition, division and pressure, and more recently, in prosecuted corruption. Cindy experienced plenty of pressure against supporting me, especially in her visible role with the women's caucus. She pushed ahead nevertheless.

At one organizing event at Lana's home, Cindy encountered a young man in a suit as she walked toward Lana's door. He was taking down license plate numbers from cars parked in front of Lana's home. Cindy called him out for the intrusion, but she was not in a position at the time to file an official request to learn if public records had been used to further political purposes. The political climate there still infers retribution. She later became angry enough at what she saw in this climate that she was willing, but there was not enough time and the information was no longer fresh enough to allow us to pursue it.

Both Cindy and Richard Demsey, her husband, became avid financial supporters of my campaign. By the end of the campaign, Cindy was also volunteering tirelessly, making sure Brunner signs were posted near polling places all over Cuyahoga County on Election Day. While there were many others who stepped up, it is this small group, along with Barbara Gould, in Cincinnati, who made all the difference.

Barbara Gould is a brilliant woman, an accomplished philanthropist and a savvy political strategist. She is married to the Pittsburgh-born, successful founder and executive board chairman of a multi-national, nationally traded medical test manufacturing company. Barbara's husband, Bill Motto, started his business from his garage with $500 and the goal to find a more effective way to transport human samples from medical offices to a laboratory. He had gained discipline and experience in the U.S. Navy before he worked in medical sales. Barbara, herself, has been a successful businesswoman, with her own jazz record company and a design business, to name a few. She was Bill's interior designer when he was a single father, raising several young boys. Eventually, Barbara moved in with Bill, and it went from there.

Barbara Gould, a very special friend and supporter; any friend, cause, organization, group or candidate she supports is blessed

The tireless and effervescent Barbara Sokol from Upper Arlington, a suburb of Columbus, first introduced me to Barbara Gould. These two Barbaras had served together on the Cincinnati Opera Board. I must say, my life has been full of wonderful Barbaras (including my mother). Because I've been fortunate in this way, I subscribe to the principle that everyone needs at least one Barbara in her or his life.

In 2005 and 2006 and thereafter, Barbara Gould expanded her renowned philanthropic generosity to strategic and political generosity. At the time I met Barbara, she was heavily involved in local, state and national Democratic politics. Her husband Bill is and has been a strong Republican, but he respected her for her views. The 2006 statewide elections were her first foray into statewide politics. She expanded her work into Presidential politics in 2007, as an early supporter of President Barack Obama. He won Hamilton County. I am certain I would not have won Hamilton County in the 2010 Senate Democratic primary election without her.

Barbara Gould has a keen mind. She learns from every situation. The more she does, the more she gains in political acumen. She is routinely sought out for not just financial but strategic, political help. Barbara has ideas, admonishments, cautions, exhortations and insights that continue to make her the target of pleas of assistance, even when she makes it clear that she is not pleased with the course of events.

She is a Jewish woman who has escorted a gaggle of Buddhist monks to Cincinnati arts events. She set up a Career Closet for Success for students at Cincinnati State University. She works directly with causes and organizations seeking to improve conditions of incarceration and reentry and the increasing problems of homelessness for previously incarcerated individuals, some in the most desperate straits. Barbara orchestrates Christmas celebrations for Bill's many grandchildren, never failing to delight them with thoughtful and numerous gifts. She is literate, a poet and has not stopped thirsting for knowledge and self-improvement. In one of my first extended telephone conversations with her, our discussion was interrupted when I heard her tell one of the workers at her home where construction was going on to "catch that snake" that just crawled up the stairs but not to kill it. I knew this woman was special.

Barbara Gould began her support of me cautiously. She expects respect, because she is a lady in the truest sense, whose many facets are like a beautiful, glistening mosaic in a community mural. She can cut through layers of crud, whether placed sloppily or meticulously by ineptness or nefariousness, (and she can usually call out which it is). She had been a supporter in my Secretary of State's race, and we continued our friendship and relationship throughout my tenure in that office.

Barbara was a key supporter of Governor Ted Strickland. She felt great pressure to hold back in my Senate race. With much encouragement from Jayme Staley, Barbara decided in the summer of 2009 it was time to publicly declare her support for me. I was on my way back Indianapolis after speaking at the national conference of the National Organization of Women. Barbara had not been treated well when she decided early on to support Senator Barack Obama for president. She had been "demoted" and even forced to resign from the governor's committee for maintaining the residence. At first she held back on my race. I suspect she did not want to go through similar treatment in this primary election.

When she called me in the car (where I spent most of my time) to tell me she was ready to express public support, we discussed sending an email announcing her support. After the announcement some in the Strickland/Fisher camp were incredulous she had stepped out of line in this way. But Barbara is strong and independent. She has compassion and passion. She supports firsts—first women, first African Americans, history making firsts that uplift people. She was taunted about her support of my candidacy even as she attended an event at the Governor's mansion. Still the Strickland crew kept her close. They needed her fundraising abilities, and, as his poll numbers dipped in the general election, her creative solutions and common sense advice. In the usual bravado of many sitting elected officials and their staff, they expected her to jump when they said jump.

Barbara should have been respected for her exceptional support, intuitiveness and political and tactical brilliance, which often eclipsed the value of her phenomenal financial support. After she endorsed my candidacy she received threatening telephone calls from highly situated Democrats for endorsing me.

Undaunted, Barbara was "all in" to help me win my primary in spite of these sometimes ugly challenges. Together we devised the campaign's "Innovation Tour for Ohio Jobs," where online supporters could suggest businesses in Ohio that were creating innovation and jobs for our campaign to visit and highlight. Not surprisingly, Barbara's husband, Bill Motto's company, Meridian Bioscience, located in northern Hamilton County, was a great entrepreneurial example.

It was an initiative admired by many, and Republican Rob Portman used something similar in his winning campaign in the fall. Our invitation to submit nominations for stops on the tour, sent in October 2009, recognized Ohioans' tough times but offered some solutions:

Our email read:

> "Although times are hard, the future of Ohio is bright --
> thanks to the spirit of innovation, creativity, and hard work
> that has been a beacon for Ohio and its people since the
> days of Thomas Edison and the light bulb, Granville Woods
> and the mobile railway telegraph, Josephine Cochran and
> the dishwasher, and of course The Wright Brothers and the
> airplane.
>
> My campaign for the U.S. Senate is launching our
> "Innovation Tour for Ohio Jobs." The history of Ohio maps a
> trail of innovation over time and geography that sets Ohio
> apart from so many other states. In times like these, when
> we focus on what has made our state realize progress, I am
> struck by the wealth that is our very people. I have often said

At Meridian Bioscience, Inc., L to R: Bill Motto, founder and
Executive Chairman of the Board, Jennifer Brunner and Jack
Kraeutler, Chief Executive Officer

479

that our diversity is our greatest strength. When it comes to ways to promote economic progress for Ohio, we need only start with our people to see our potential. My Senate candidacy is about the kind of leadership that will empower that potential to grow jobs and progress for a state that deserves so much.

Our Innovation Tour for Ohio Jobs encourages Ohio's entrepreneurs and assists small businesses with big ideas by highlighting their outstanding vision and creativity. I'll be traveling across the state, promoting the work and efforts of innovators and visionaries in technology, business, health care, agriculture and education to help bring together the people and resources that make jobs and progress happen for the people of Ohio.

I urge you to nominate Ohio businesses, organizations, individuals, or institutions . . . nominate local projects that reflect and promote our state's history of innovation, creativity, and hard work. That's how we've always brought more jobs to Ohio.

* * *

My Innovation Tour for Ohio Jobs means utilizing the talent, hard work, and creativity of everyday Ohioans to come together for solutions. . . . Ohioans have what it takes, and with leadership that's focused on public service -- doing what's right for our families, our communities, and our state and country -- we can do what we've been struggling to do for so long, to create more jobs for more Ohioans.

* * *

The online nomination form is simple and quick, and there are so many cutting edge businesses, programs and projects that are just waiting for you to nominate them. They will benefit from the publicity and promotion of being included in the Innovation Tour for Ohio Jobs and will be on my mind as I show Ohioans some of the things I want to do for my state as its next U.S. Senator. Please take a few minutes to visit the site and submit your nominations. And thanks for your help in making Ohio, the state that you and I already love and treasure, even better."

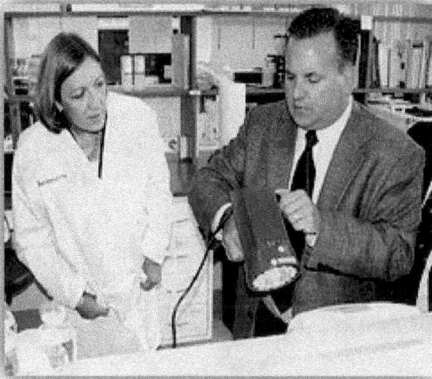

At BioEnterprise, a biomedical innovation business incubator in Cleveland

We received so many nominations of businesses working to innovate that we could not visit enough of them. For those we did visit, I was astounded to see what was happening in Ohio, especially in the biomedical and clean energy fields. I never understood why Ted Strickland did not emphasize this work more in his campaign for reelection in the fall of 2010. I truly believed he would have convinced the voters with his sincerity that an effort was being made to "Turn Around Ohio" (the Democratic campaign slogan for 2006). He could have showed Ohio what I saw in that Senate primary and plaintively and credibly asked for just a little more time to finish the job. Instead, it seemed as though the message, coming from Washington, not to return to the "failed Bush policies of the past," was a dismal failure that didn't move voters who soon too easily forget.

Barbara helped "cook up" the network of intimate fundraising events in people's homes throughout the state called, "Cupcakes, Coffee and Conversation." These were small fundraising events in people's homes where vast varieties of cupcakes and coffee were served. It was a chance to bring women and men together to talk about the issues facing the state and the country. These parties were a smashing success, and they, too, have been imitated since.

First "Cupcakes, Coffee and Conversation" or "cupcake party" held in Cincinnati; it was a smashing success with more than one hundred women and a few men attending; it was repeated throughout the state during the campaign and has been copied by others since

Barbara and I both saw the report issued in late 2009 by the Center for American Progress and by Kennedy cousin, Maria

Shriver, "A Woman's Nation." That report was the genesis of the series of Women's Forums, which the campaign did in two waves in twelve locations around the state.

The first wave of forums highlighted the findings in the report and also issues involving women's health care. Chandra Yungbluth, my executive assistant from my state office, who must have never slept during that time, worked in her off hours setting up this logistically difficult feat, while attending each forum. She continues to work for women, labor and minorities today as a political director for the United Food and Commercial Workers in southwest Ohio.

L. to R. Jaladah Aslam, Jennifer Brunner and Kellie Copeland together at first regional women's forum in Akron for U.S. Senate Democratic primary, Spring 2010

The second series of forums focused on solutions for legislation. Both women and men attended them.

Suffice it to say, Barbara was a critical partner in the venture that was my Senate campaign. When I lost, she, like no other, was able to help me claim victory from its difficulty, to grow from my experience and to better hear my own voice.

To this day, I often wear a special necklace that this small, committed group of women gave me for my birthday after I left office. It is a silver and gold cupcake on the most tenuously delicate chain that accentuates its fragile yet unique beauty. The "icing" on the cupcake is of small diamond chips.

Each one of these staunch and sometimes scared supporters rode the Courage Express campaign bus with me, attended or held a cupcake party and continues to work to this day toward the goal of helping more women be elected to public office. Together we learned that the courage to demand respect and accountability is transformative.

One person's transformation can be powerful and contagious. Simultaneous transformations can bring about systemic change. My Senate race, as difficult as it was, helped many women face their fears, find their voices and resolve to do something and to keep doing it, no matter how difficult the obstacles. Soon it will not be unthinkable for a woman to be elected to the Senate from Ohio, or to be elected governor for that matter, and when this happens, it will engender power that is shared and that transforms many. ≈

Chapter 27

An Iconic Campaign

"Face it, Jennifer, yours was an iconic campaign," said Barbara Gould, after the campaign was long over and we continued to marvel at one "copycat" move after another. My campaign involved emails from dogs, cupcakes, a converted silver bus bought online through eBay and named by supporters, silk sunflowers in clay pots and "Courage cards" that I hear many student volunteers on my campaign have used for bookmarks. I had wanted to prove that a campaign like President Obama's could work at a more local level than for the presidency of the United States. Like an experiment in a lab for the cure of a pernicious malady, trial and error is necessary to perfect the cure. Not every experiment works the first time, but much can be gained from each trial that allows the next one to succeed.

My dog, Lane, at my laptop; campaigns now routinely send emails from the candidate's dog, but when Sandy Theis suggested I use "Laney the Underdog," the ploy made USA Today with the question of whether the Senate campaign was "going to the dogs." That little dog raised me several thousand dollars online.

I had declared at the Cleveland City Club debate in April 2010 that I was running for the Senate to change the Democratic paradigm. Despite all the years I had spent developing an

485

expertise in political finance, even being hired as a political finance expert for USAID consulting work in Serbia after I left office, it took campaigning for the U.S. Senate for me to directly see how *too much* money has damaged our political system.

Today, the major test of the success of a campaign is how much money has it raised. Control over the outcome of a race is largely based on money. He or she who has the most money is statistically much more likely to be the winner. Even with the growth of online tools to reduce campaign costs, the amount of money raised remains the greatest predictor of success in an election campaign.

There are many silent and powerful individuals who understand that those who can control political money can best control who is elected—except when the money is obtained largely in small donations from many individuals. In my view, that is the best explanation for the January 21, 2010, U.S. Supreme Court's "Citizens United" decision. Grassroots campaigns not only reach people in smaller and more personal ways, using the volunteer efforts of many, they also raise dollars that way, too. When dollars are raised this way, it's harder to control the candidate or the elected official.

When a corporate-sponsored group gets the "green light" to masquerade as a group of "citizens united" to place massive amounts of corporate dollars onto the political battlefield to tilt it, most Americans see we have serious problems. I believe this fake "citizens united" effort is a "last ditch" before there is a dramatic shift in how we communicate with one another, especially when it comes to political speech. I believe future campaigns are moving and need to move toward Internet-assisted grassroots campaigns. This shift should make massive amounts of funds less necessary to be able to be a "decider" in government. To me, the "Citizens United" decision is a clear indication of a fear of power shifting to the masses, in a democracy that is already more than 200 years old.

Significant power in this country has been held for centuries by a relatively few persons, some of great wealth, who would like to keep it that way. They benefitted most when the middle class was strong. But as they poured more money into the political coffers of members of Congress, they became proverbial kids given the keys to a candy shop, stuffing their faces without any oversight from their parents. Now they complain of stomachaches but continue to eat the candy, thinking that it can make them feel better.

Because I was permitted and left alone to research and write policy statements in my Senate campaign, I saw this most clearly in the practices of the financial industry, which have in recent years given more than 40% of political contributions nationally. Campaign finance as we know it today came about after a combination of the 1970's Watergate scandal, where emergent campaign laws primarily codified the way dollars were raised, making what some would call "corruption" legal, and making television advertising the rule rather than the exception, even for campaigns within a small geographic area. Television advertising is still used as being more efficient in reaching large numbers of people. But it is now overused, in part, because media consultants who produce the commercials charge based the amount of time purchased. Today the cost of running for office is astronomical, especially in a state like Ohio with at least eleven potential media markets for television.

The profession of "political consultant" is now practically an industry. Most "media consultants" are those who work with the campaign on messaging, working closely with a polling firm. Polling is valuable to help shape a message. I learned in my Secretary of State's race from watching audiences' faces that a largely Democratic audience related better to the description of good elections as "free, fair, open and honest," while a largely Republican audience related better to elections that are "safe, reliable and trustworthy." I asked my pollster, Celinda Lake, to test it. I was right. Polling can help a candidate wisely apportion limited resources. Knowing how hard it was for some people to give, but who gave anyway, we were constantly conscious of not wasting their hard-earned money. Polling helped us do that.

Media consultants are generally paid some small consulting fee, and they sometimes earn a percentage of advertisement production costs for a television or radio ad, which are billed through to the campaign. Largely, however, media consultants get their fees based on a percentage of the amount of television time bought. If a consultant's fee is 7%, a $2 million dollar television and radio buy for ad time earns the consultant $140,000 for a campaign. Often, they work on several campaigns at once at a variety of levels and locations. Today, with the amount of money spent in campaigns, political consultants can live pretty well.

A cash-starved campaign is an easy target for scorn and jeers by establishment insiders, including political consultants, the media, and even local political afficionados who believe in their "unerring" ability to read the tea leaves without even knowing what tree or flower they came from. Most "politically sane" people whose candidacies are deprived of the "mother's milk of politics"—money—get out when they can, run for cover, cut a deal or retreat in relief or shame. But most "politically sane" people in politics fear those who aren't, especially if they're already officeholders and not wingnuts. Mark Naymik, the Cleveland Plain Dealer reporter, said, "Jennifer Brunner can sneak up on voters." It is just such conditions that can germinate an iconic campaign.

As difficult as it was to deal with the "under-the-table-in-the-dark-with-a-knife" tactics of an Ohio primary election, the combination of being starved of cash and having promised women I wouldn't drop out forced me to find a different way to campaign. I am grateful to those in the Democratic Party in Ohio who unwittingly helped me do this and create an "iconic campaign" that has inspired many new candidates see what can be done, believe in themselves and run for office.

The most demonstrable icon of our iconic campaign was The Courage Express. For Christmas 2009, one of my Secretary of State staff people, Katherine Thomsen and her fiancé, then state Rep. Dan Stewart, gave me a copy of Paul Wellstone's watershed book, *Conscience of a Liberal.* Both Katherine and Dan had read this book, each having been a candidate and both being passionately committed to Democratic and progressive causes. When I read it, it was as if the scales fell from my eyes. Paul Wellstone described politics as a means and not an end. He put what many love about fighting for political causes and parity in such clear and simple terms.

As I read Paul Wellstone's book, I found myself almost gasping at the clarity with which he spoke and wrote. He illustrated how he figured all of this out, writing of traveling the state of Minnesota in his green and white bus and how he took on the most difficult of circumstances, inspired and empowered others, and in never giving up, transformed their lives. Even after his death the mental health parity act was signed into law years later and his efforts remembered. His family's Wellstone institute has trained countless people to run for office, staying true to the reasons why he stepped up in the first place, to help people.

I started bugging David that we needed a bus to travel the state. He probably had a better understanding of its difficulty rather than its charisma than I could or ever did until I rode in it, with its very worn shock absorbers. All I knew was that we would have little or no television advertising, so we had to garner as much "earned" (free) media as we could. An iconic bus was the ticket.

It was a weekday in the spring of 2010. In Youngstown, while having lunch with local supporters and labor leaders in a private, second floor room of a Youngstown area restaurant, my phone rang. David's name came up on my screen. I excused myself from the table and answered the call out of earshot. David was short on words and long on excitement.

"I need to know if you'll okay us buying a bus," he said quickly. "There's one for sale on eBay for $2050, and it's nearby in Licking County." I was delighted. "Sure!" I said, excited.

"Okay, you're okay with that? You sure?" he continued. "Yes, yes, go ahead. I think it's great. It's what I've wanted to do," I continued.

So it would be done. We were going to have a bus. I went back to the table feeling excited and smug at the same time. "I just bought a bus," I thought to myself. "Wow," was all I could think.

By the time we bought the bus that, of two for sale, was in the best condition from Southwest Licking Schools, we were learning what it meant to own a school bus when you're not a school district. You can't keep it the orange/yellow color that schools use. It has to be inspected by the highway patrol. The tailpipe needs to be changed. The bus needs insurance. For six months, alone, the license tags cost $1000. And there was work to be done inside the bus. We found discarded, laminated table tops, and Adam, with the help of Vince, Matt, Deb Steele, Christa and others took out some seats and turned others around to set up a train-style interior with seats on each side of a table facing each other throughout the bus. The bus had mobile wi-fi, so it could be a traveling office, and an electrical outlet was rigged on the bus to use for charging laptop batteries and for a printer. When all was installed, our campaign staff could literally "cut the turf" creating walking lists from the Internet, using Vote Builder, (the party's enhanced voter database), so that at each stop we could hand out canvassing packets to waiting volunteers.

David asked me to choose a color to paint the bus. Some thought it should be two-toned with one color at the bottom and another at the top, like Paul Wellstone's bus in green and white, or in navy and white. I knew that some prison buses are navy and white. Two-toned was not going to do it.

The Courage Express became our campaign's homespun substitute for television, traveling nearly 6000 miles in three weeks throughout Ohio; the bus was a symbol that captured hearts and minds during the campaign—and attracted lots of free television coverage throughout the state

Tiff had already started using the term, "Brunner Brigade," coopting the World War II icon of "Rosie the Riveter" as our mascot. In keeping with that theme, I closed my eyes and imagined a good color for the bus. Somehow, silver came to me, like an airstream trailer. David liked it. Others thought it sounded weird, but I knew it would be just perfect, and it was.

Campaign manager David Dettman, gesturing toward the bus to demonstrate its potential. With campaign staffers Matt Johnson, Vince Bruni, and Derek Clinger looking on

We needed to paint it. That was a problem. David, with help from some folks in Cleveland, lined up some off-duty painters from one of the unions. The painters were apparently scared to death of anyone finding out they had helped me. By this time, pressure was intense from the Ohio AFL-CIO, my former client, for me to stay out of the Senate race. Bill Burga had retired, and Joe Rugola, an early supporter of Ted Strickland, was at the helm. He had tried to talk me out of running, along with Ron Malone, now a labor leader, once Sherrod Brown's campaign manager and Assistant Secretary of State, but my impassioned statements of how I could champion workers' rights that I made at that breakfast at Plank's Restaurant in Columbus left him saying to me, "I was supposed to ask you not to run, but I'm not going to."

The Plumbers and Pipefitters, all but three locals of the International Brotherhood of Electrical Workers and several locals like Laborers Local 310 didn't heed the admonishment from the Ohio AFL-CIO or members of the Governor's team to not support me and stay out of the race. All of the United Food and Commercial Workers locals decided to support me and were bold enough to tell the Governor ahead of time, who asked them not to. They declined to follow his request and reiterated they would be supporting me. So, when David asked how we should get the bus to the union painters who would do the job, he was instructed to secure a warehouse for painting the bus, deliver the paint and then pick up the bus at the end of the weekend.

We secured a warehouse in Marion, Ohio, with the help of Vaughn Sizemore, a business friend and colleague. David wanted to know the name of the person to notify that the bus had been delivered. He was told simply to ask for "José Pinto," which means "Joe Paint" in Spanish. David told me that the pressure was so severe against helping me that we could not say how we managed to get the bus painted or it could be very bad for those who had helped. He mentioned something about the trunk of a car.

The bus received one coat of paint sprayed on professionally with some areas where, if you looked really hard, you could see a little yellow peeking through. Adam conferred with me and

Cindy Demsey on outside design and content. Staff made their own stencils, and they worked weekends to complete painting the navy letters for the words on the bus. Christa Johnston made amazing YouTube videos about the creation of the Courage Express, many of which I didn't have time to watch until the campaign was over. When I saw the full chronicle of the campaign through her series of videos, it was the only time I cried after losing. It was, after all, an iconic campaign.

Our bus needed a name. I suggested to David that we email our supporters and hold a contest for naming the bus. On April 5, 2010, our email challenged our supporters:

> "Two weeks ago, we bought a school bus (on eBay!) that once carried students in Licking County. Because this bus will help us directly reach Ohioans, we want you to be a part of helping us name it. You can . . . use our online form and give us your ideas for a great name for it. We've painted it silver to help Rosie look great and to give you lots of options.
>
> You can also use our online form to tell us where you think we should take our bus in Ohio. You can tell us what's going on in your community and when, so we can reach more voters and get them engaged for the Democratic primary and beyond. And we're still looking for help to keep our bus rolling and our volunteers and staff working along the way to get out our people-powered message and get people to the polls. Your donation of $5, $10, $25 or more right now means we can pay for gas, more literature, more phone banking, and staff and volunteer expenses."

By April 7, 2010, two days later, we had more than two hundred names to choose from, including some snarky names from apparent Fisher supporters and from GOP and Tea Party detractors, like "Hopelessness Express" or the "Tea Party

Express." While reviewing suggestions, I was a passenger in Rick's and my truck traveling south on Interstate 71 after having left an event. Cruising down that highway, discussing it with those in the car with me, we collectively reached a decision. I sent this email to David and Jeff:

On Wed, Apr 7, 2010 at 9:34 PM, Jennifer Brunner wrote:

Top contenders:

Buckeye Battle Bus
The Courage Express
The Courage Coach
The Bus for Us
No. 18 Express
Silver Rosie

And the winner is . . .

The Courage Express
Sent from my Verizon Wireless BlackBerry

Campaign staff and volunteers apply the name to
the bus with handmade stencils and paint

495

Jeff immediately reserved Internet domain name, and The Courage Express was born. "Express" sounded fast moving and forward moving. "Courage" was a given. It was already on our literature and on small, business card-sized "Courage cards" that we were able to distribute widely and inexpensively in our grassroots campaign. We eventually added three more words to the bus, spread along the top on each side: Courage, Commitment, Compassion.

One of the most touching emails of the campaign came from Rick (who seemed to get a higher open rate on emails than anyone else, including me). He encapsulated in his email the emotion about buses that I saw on the faces of many who climbed aboard the Courage Express:

> "I'm Rick Brunner. My wife Jennifer Brunner is Ohio Secretary of State and she's running for the open U.S. Senate seat in Ohio.
>
> In rural Eastern Ohio, my Dad's 30 year off-farm job was being a school bus driver. The school bus parked by the barn marked our farm on the hill and was part of the directions to my boyhood home.
>
> The bus route calibrated the rhythms of our farm chores and family meals. The ritual cleaning of the bus punctuated both the beginning of the new school year and summer vacation. The empty bus was a place where my dad imparted life lessons and sad news like my grandfather's passing. The bus was the vehicle that took me to my high school activities. The bus opened the world to me and led me to where and who I am now.
>
> Rolling into the final weeks of this campaign on The Courage Express, a Licking County public school bus that we've painted and refurbished, seems more than right to me.

This rejuvenated bus is a bold, firm statement about the values of everyday Ohioans and their part in and value to this campaign. It brings back the excitement of the first and last day of school, high school football games, victory parades, marching band and making friends. The bus was the vehicle from which Ohio's rural kids launched their lives and now it will launch a remarkable courageous leader and my best friend to the United States Senate.

We're celebrating the kick off of our statewide bus tour today at TheCourageExpress.com. I hope that you will visit the site and join in the fun

* * *

The school bus that we converted into The Courage Express is an International Harvester, or IH. IH's were built in Springfield where Jennifer was born and where her maternal grandfather worked for IH for over 40 years, along with his sons, Jennifer's Uncles. If someone "doesn't get" the symbolism of an IH bus, then they have never seen an IH tractor turn the furrow, work the ground, bust the clods, and bring in the harvest. And that is just what the IH Courage Express is going to do for this campaign, which is built on the promise of helping Ohioans prosper and achieve their plans and aspirations.

Please stop by TheCourageExpress.com and help us kick off our bus tour in style. If you're in Ohio, we're looking forward to seeing you in your town or a place near you in the coming weeks."

The Courage Express traveled 6000 miles around Ohio in a three-week period. With EMILY's List long gone, one Washington-based women's organization, the Women's Campaign Fund, had not given up on me. Siobhan "Sam"

Bennett, its new CEO, generously sent its best "Swiss Army Knife," Julie Daniels, now with the Peace Corps in Ukraine, to work on my campaign for more than a month. Julie, working with Mallory Mitchell, my dynamo (former captain of the Ohio State University 50-member cheering squad and now administrative assistant in the office of OSU's president), mapped and scheduled the tour. We began by David, Sandy Theis, other campaign staffers and me sitting down with a map of Ohio spread out on a table in front of us. I knew the state well, having been in every county and having supervised all 88 county boards of elections. I pointed out good towns to make stops in. We also took nominations from our supporters via Internet. Deb Steele, who was our field director, worked with her contacts in the throughout the state. Everyone pitched in. Mallory and Julie set the route. It was an unbelievable feat.

Julie Daniels from the Women's Campaign Fund, lived with me for more than four weeks and helped our scheduler, Mallory Mitchell, develop and execute a three-week statewide tour of Ohio by The Courage Express

Meanwhile, Julie rode with me, as my "body person," making sure I had what I needed. On the day of the Cleveland City Club debate Rick was worried to death about my health riding the bus and gave her extra instructions to look out for me.

The maiden voyage of The Courage Express was to Meigs
County; here with Rick and dogs, Lane and Jake, in the
background during interview on the bus by New Left Media's
Chase Whiteside and filmmaker John Wellington Ennis

Our first trip on the Courage Express was to economically
depressed Meigs County, one of my favorite counties. The bus
was not completely lettered then, but it was clearly marked as
"The Courage Express." *New Left Media* reporter Chase
Whiteside and videographer Erick Stoll traveled with us. Our
three dogs, Jake, McGuffey and Lane went with us. Jake, a
Belgian Malenois rescue dog, was clearly the most comfortable,
a statewide campaign veteran already. (He died in July 2011, after
having stood on the banks of the Ohio River and walked
through the waves on the shore of Lake Erie.) A full contingent
of campaign staff accompanied us. As I stood at the dais to give
my speech and watched this staff in action, it hit me that this
was a real Senate campaign—now it looked like one.

Jim Dean, Chair of Democracy for America, traveled a day with us through western Ohio; DFA, founded by his brother, former Vermont Governor and 2004 Presidential candidate Howard Dean, endorsed my candidacy and provided grassroots support; Adam Niswonger driving

We went on to unlikely places like Bluffton College, a remote township in Tuscarawas County where the older people I talked with at the senior center said softly as I left, "Don't forget the seniors." Reporters rode the bumpy bus with us, barely able to write on their steno pads. We traveled to abandoned steel mill compounds that were being repurposed for innovation technologies. The bus traveled through residential neighborhoods for fundraising events, and we strategically parked it on the street in Cleveland near Jacobs Field just before opening day for the Cleveland Indians baseball team (until we were threatened with a ticket by the Cleveland Police). People asked timidly if they were allowed to go on the bus to take a look. We willingly obliged, watching their anticipation as they stepped aboard and their delight that, as one supporter in Akron put it, "Now, I'm part of the bus."

The Courage Express in Cadiz, Ohio (Harrison County), parked
in front of the county courthouse

When we traveled to northeast Ohio, Rick's family farm was our
outpost. Between the farmhouse and his sister's house "next
door," which on a farm means "up the road," we had a place to
park our campaign bus and free places for our campaign staff to
spend the night during our northeastern forays. Rick's parents
were thrilled to be a part of the campaign, and his dad, having
driven a school bus for 30 years, went aboard and said, excitedly,
"That's a great bus!" It was a 1991 bus, built several years after he
stopped driving his bus. No wonder. Rick's sister, Becky, who
never failed to send care packages to Rick's and my kids when
they were in college, seemed to have the preferred place to stay, ·
and Becky and Fred could not have been more hospitable. I
stayed with Rick's parents in the 1860's farmhouse that I had
grown to love, along with loving them over three decades.

The bus broke down just two times, both in Cleveland. Once it
was on a Sunday morning when we were attending African
American church services. Adam had to fix it temporarily with a
garden hose he bought at a home improvement store. It was the
only place open on a Sunday morning.

On the Sunday before the election, with the help of supporter and sister candidate (for the Ohio Senate), Tamela Lee, I went to seven church services in a span of just over five hours. It was a feat I had never imagined possible. I asked her if it would be rude to leave before the end of the service. She had it all worked out ahead of time. By the end of the campaign, I had to sing all the hymns in a lower octave; because I had given so many speeches I had no singing voice left. It took over a year to be able to sing as I used to.

One of the last rides I took on the bus, Rick was with me. I sat with my back up against his side. He put his arm around me. I wanted to take it all in and remember how special this time was. I knew that it was unlikely we would be using the bus in a general election campaign, because Lee Fisher had poured almost another $1 million dollars into television advertising the last weekend of the campaign. Apparently, the first $300,000 or so that he had spent wasn't doing for him what he expected. I had no money for television, and at the end David and I decided not to spend money for radio.

The Saturday before the election, I had not exactly been invited to speak at a statewide meeting of the Ohio Democratic Party Women's Caucus in Columbus, because to appear and speak, I needed to buy a program ad. I had no motivation to do it and was going to skip it. Janet Carson bought the program ad and exhorted me to appear. Even though my

Very alone on the stage speaking to the Ohio Democratic Party Women's Caucus in Columbus the last weekend before the primary election

Secretary of State campaign had contributed the first $500 to this caucus in 2005, by 2009, its bylaws purpose clause had been changed from supporting women candidates to supporting candidates who support women, now that the party faced a primary election between a man and a woman. The caucus director introduced me without giving any of the typical introductory biographical information. She appeared so stressed out at this event, that I actually felt empathy for her.

I plainly told the large group of women there that my opponent was placing another $1 million dollars of television advertising against me and that, if anyone wanted to help in my campaign, now was the time. I saw shocked faces. I left to board the bus to a standing ovation, and we headed north to Kent and Akron, Ohio, for the final weekend.

I breathed a sigh of relief that this uncomfortable event was over. I didn't know until after the primary, after seeing the type of support the Ohio Democratic Party had given to Maryellen O'Shaughnessy, who was running to succeed me, just how alone I had been in that primary.

The day before the election, my campaign staff and I had traveled on the bus to Cleveland from our outpost at the farm. I was standing in the parking lot of a Dairy Queen where we had stopped with the bus for lunch. When The Courage Express pulled up to nearly any establishment for our traveling campaign office to stop for a break, we could tell that the owners liked it. I was pacing in the parking lot, talking on my Blackberry about the Senate race to a reporter from Politico, a Washington, Internet-based publication on national politics.

The reporter referred to a poll released that day showing that I was 20 points behind Lee Fisher. I said staunchly, "Look, if I lose, it won't be by 20 points. You're not out here. You can't see the reaction to our campaign. The question will be whether we've reached enough people." I was right. I lost by just over 10 points. One of my political consultants, Dane Strother, used to say that the candidate on the ground is the best poll a campaign can have. He was right. I could sense how we were doing in every one of my campaigns based on the reactions of the people I met "on the ground."

A grassroots campaign can be an iconic campaign if it is people-centered and remains that way. So many campaigns today layer polling, focus groups, the call-time chase for dollars to pay for them and targeted mailings and carefully crafted television and radio ads between the voter and the candidate. All of these are important, but they should never supplant the contact between the candidate and the voters.

On primary election day, May 4, 2010, Rick and I went to the "Red Mass" for lawyers and judges at 5:00 p.m. at St. Joseph's Cathedral in downtown Columbus. Then we walked home, changed and went to campaign headquarters to be there when the polls closed at 7:30 p.m. Most of my key women supporters in my campaign came to our headquarters that night. There were dozens more, people from all walks of life. As the polls closed and returns began to be made available, we were trying to track the vote, but the boards of elections were slow to send them to the Secretary of State's office.

Chandra, my assistant, kept several laptops going simultaneously, compiling information from the various county websites. When Cuyahoga County's results started coming in (the television market in which Lee had spent the bulk of his advertising dollars, his home area and where there is the greatest concentration of Democrats in Ohio), we knew it was over. Sandy Theis told me that AP was calling the race. That was it. I would not linger, because little is worse than someone who does not gracefully accept defeat when it is clear.

Rick, David, Sandy and I went into David's office and briefly reviewed what to do to concede. We already had sample statements for each outcome, but we were pretty sure which one we would use. Television cameras were there, and the room was packed with supporters, staffers and volunteers. I saw one reporter with tears in his eyes as I gave my statement. (Later a blogger to whom I'd promised an interview was sobbing as I gave the interview.) I had already called Lee Fisher to concede.

I was touched when even Rob Portman called me and congratulated me on a great campaign. He said that he hoped that someday we would have the chance to work together in public service. John and Kate were there, both having developed a stoicism from what they learned in the first statewide campaign. My mother had tried to fly in from Louisiana, but her flight had been canceled, and she couldn't get another flight in time. It was just as well.

I walked out to the podium, conceded that we did not have enough votes to win and publicly congratulated my opponent. It was important to the many supporters there to talk about what the campaign meant and what the future held. I vowed to continue to work for candidates, to promote diversity in public office—gender, racial, LGBT and more. I said I would be starting an organization to encourage them to run and that I would not stop being involved. I haven't stopped being involved.

In 2010, with what was left of my Senate campaign infrastructure as a base, I formed a political action committee called, "Courage PAC." David assisted me with the launch of a website in 2011 and then readied himself for his next adventure, working for

Democracy International in Bangladesh, as chief of party for democracy building work there.

The purpose of Courage PAC is to encourage citizen advocacy. It uses the slogans, "Every voice matters. Together we're stronger," and quotes Thomas Jefferson with, "One person with courage is a majority." in its masthead. I continued communicating with supporters even after the campaign. It has not been unusual for someone whom I don't know to stop me and say, "I get your emails."

The day after the election, with Jeff's help, we issued a thank you email to my supporters. It included a picture of the bus.

The word, "iconic" is derived from the word, "icon." An icon stands for something, reminding us of a principle or belief we are to remember. I often said our campaign was a "new, old-fashioned campaign," because it combined "netroots" with grassroots to create something that people believed belonged to them. A loss in such a campaign hits some people hard.

Of course, Rick and I were disappointed, but we were also very tired. Rick and I stayed in our condominium den on the top floor and did not come out of the house for two days. We watched as our neighbors held a Cinco de Mayo celebration in the courtyard below us and meekly said, "Oh, that's nice." We were exhausted. We knew that going someplace for rest after a campaign is for us, basically, a waste of money. We would lay exhausted in an expensive hotel room when we would be just as comfortable at home. While resting at home, I began looking at the extensive Facebook sites from the campaign and saw there were scores of messages from supporters. I wrote to console many of them, as they were more upset by the loss than I was. I was grateful that the campaign was over. I had kept my promise and stayed in the race.

Some of the messages really touched me. Some said they had given up on politics until my campaign, but that they had hope after this campaign. That is what an iconic campaign can do—remind people of why they need to be involved and what being involved can do for them, for those they love and for their communities. Getting involved, like many people did, reminded them of how democracy worked, and more importantly, that they mattered. ≈

PART V

✦

GOING GLOBAL

Chapter 28

A Changing Electorate

It was during the Senate campaign that I gained my first real understanding of the immigration debate that has been raging in our country in recent years. That education continued past the end of the campaign as I was approached as Secretary of State by the U.S. Department of Justice to assist in reaching a consent decree to implement the use of bilingual ballots in Cuyahoga County. This was the first time bilingual ballots would be used anywhere in Ohio.

While many Americans proudly claim their heritage as Irish, Italian or Slovak, even though their families have been here for generations, I, personally, can really only say I'm American. With family history that has suggested Cherokee Indian and that has been traced to one of the signers of the Mayflower Compact, Thanksgiving is almost as important a holiday in my family as is Christmas. The only time I spent Thanksgiving away from someone in the family that I grew up with was the year Rick and I were engaged, in 1977. I went to his sister's house that day and was shocked when she was trying a "new" dish, oyster dressing—a staple of all the Thanksgivings of my youth.

In the spring of 2010, I had been endorsed by the state's United Food and Commercial Workers Union locals, who had invited me to a large rally on immigration reform in northern Cincinnati. I was not very familiar with the issues until this time; I just knew that immigration reform did not fall simply along partisan political party lines. Many Democrats did not seem open to immigration reform. Some Republicans did. Many against it believed immigrants were taking away jobs that belonged to Americans. Others saw some contractors' and service companies' indiscriminate use of undocumented workers as depriving contracts for unionized and skilled trade jobs. Others saw immigrants, especially "illegal immigrants" as they called them, as taking benefits that they had no right to or had not paid for (even if social security taxes were taken from their wages). Additionally, there were those who scorned immigrants who have difficulty with the English language, supporting "English as official language" legislation. This refrain of, "they're here in America and they need to learn English" does not seem to "translate" when these same people travel to a foreign country, if they ever do. They lack understanding of the difficulties of learning a new language when the brain thinks in one's native language, calling those unlike them "anti-social" or lazy in their "refusal" to learn a new language.

There were roughly 2000 immigrants at the rally in Cincinnati, with close to two-thirds of Hispanic descent and the rest mainly immigrants from a variety of African countries. There was a good representation of speakers, from national to state (including State Senator Eric Kearney and myself), to local.

It's difficult to describe the impact of seeing so many foreign faces and wondering about their experiences, elsewhere and here in the U.S., and what I could say to a group like this that would be helpful, meaningful. I addressed the group, bidding them good afternoon, "Buenos tardes, mis hermanos y hermanas y los niños," I said. "Estoy con ustedes," I said. In English, what I said was, "Good afternoon, my brothers and sisters and the children. I am with you."

I then reverted to English, speaking forcefully and simply about solidarity, but also about being careful in their acts of strength and solidarity to stay within the law. I remembered the numerous undocumented immigrants who had appeared before me as a judge, who came from behind the black metal jail door in my courtroom, handcuffed, escorted by two deputy sheriffs. I remember these immigrants walking back in after the disposition of a hearing that resulted in incarceration. At the time, I knew that the INS, the Immigration and Naturalization Service, would be taking custody of them at some point from the Franklin County Sheriff, and that they likely would be leaving their families miles behind, deported usually back to Mexico. I could not see agitating a crowd of people to mayhem such as could lead them away from their loved ones.

It is an extraordinary experience to comprehend humanity for the miracle it is—especially to break through the boundaries of race, culture, nationality, religion and experience to see others as simply just—human. I have difficulty describing the faces of the immigrants I saw before me—dark-eyed with black hair and skin darker than mine and of varying hues, entire families, some with bowl-haircut toddlers whose round, dark faces showed delight as they trundled in front of their mothers while clutching small American flags. Mothers and fathers sat quietly together, some looking hopefully at their children. They all seemed to be waiting for words from which they could derive some beneficial meaning. I had been informed that though many of these workers worked hard, they were not always rewarded with pay, depending on the practices of their employers. Undocumented workers do not fall under the protection of the Fair Employment Practices Act, so if they're not paid, they just deal with it. As jaded as it may seem, I've come to believe that some business-oriented politicians tolerate the situation of undocumented workers because their business contributors make more money that way, even though doing so is illegal.

I asked one of UFCW's reps, "How many of these people are undocumented, do you estimate?" She matter-of-factly told me, "About half." It was shocking that they would even attend this

2

rally. After speakers were finished, I found myself surrounded by men and women alike, many African immigrants, who asked about my campaign, for my card and to have their pictures taken with me. I knew being there was highly controversial. Sherrod Brown had not yet committed to supporting the immigration reform bill, but he eventually did. The UFCW had invited me. The UFCW educated me that this problem was real and that immigration problems faced in the U.S. must be addressed. I know this now without hesitation and continue to push for the United States of America to face its past, present and future as a nation of immigrants.

Children born in the United States to undocumented immigrants have rights of citizenship. However, the children who were *not* born in the U.S., but largely grew up in the U.S. and go on to college, find themselves at graduation not being able to work in the U.S., even though living in the U.S. is all they have known. It is easy to say, "Too bad." But when you humanize it, such as it happened to me that day, talking with several college students who faced a very uncertain future, I realized it is an angst-filled, human dilemma that dwarfs any doctrine or reasoning.

Just as the issues of immigration are not easily categorized according to partisan doctrine, they are not isolated to the United States, either. Often people complain about the influx of immigrants into an area of any given country. However, when there is an examination of which jobs these immigrants often occupy, they are often the jobs that the complainers would never desire or take, even if desperate. That doesn't change from generation to generation or among nations or nationalities. When generations proliferate and education takes hold, no longer do the "immigrants" remain the outsiders, especially as other immigration occurs.

As part of my acclimation to the immigration issues facing
Congress, I had the opportunity to talk with Cleveland attorney
José Feliciano and with Miriam Lugo-González, both of whom
work with the Hispanic Roundtable in the Cleveland area. José is
a partner in a large Cleveland law firm that has offices
throughout the U.S. He is well known in the Cleveland
community and is the respected president of the Hispanic
Roundtable. Miriam Lugo is a board member and founder of
LATINA, Inc.; he is an important catalyst to the round table's
activities.

Miriam had let me know about a candidates' night in the Latino
community during the spring of 2010 in the Senate primary. It
was at this candidates' night in western Cleveland that Rick and
I met Jane Portman, Rob Portman's wife. She had driven from
Cincinnati to Cleveland to attend this event. We talked before
the event, especially of our families, and Rick and I were
impressed with how she spoke well on behalf of her husband
and how genuine she was. Even more impressive to us was that
both of them thought it important enough for her to be there,
especially when Rob could not. When Rob called me primary
election night he pointed out how much he appreciated our
kindnesses to Jane. We all had a major interest in common—our
children and the toll the campaign takes on families.

After the primary was over, I had joyfully resumed full duties
with the Secretary of State's office and had reengaged with my
staff on a daily basis. In July of 2011, some of my staff and I were
in Providence, Rhode Island, attending the summer conference
of the National Association of Secretaries of State. Sitting in my
hotel room during a break, the U.S. Attorney for the Northern
District of Ohio, Steve Dettelbach, called me with a question.

Steve indicated that Tom Perez, chief of the civil rights section
of the U.S. Department of Justice, had been overseeing an effort

to gather information on ballot accessibility for Puerto Rican voters in Cuyahoga County. This effort had been underway for approximately three years. The Justice Department attorneys working on that project were ready to move ahead with compliance measures. Steve wanted to know if, as Secretary of State, I would assist with obtaining a consent decree from the Cuyahoga County Board of Elections in lieu of full-blown litigation. The Justice Department wanted the Cuyahoga County Board of Elections to implement bilingual ballots in the English and Spanish languages. I was willing and believed it would be an important achievement for the state and for what had become a model board of elections. Since so much of the rest of the country judged Ohio by how Cuyahoga County performed, if this could be achieved smoothly, without acrimony, it would ease the use of these ballots here and in other areas of the state where they may be needed. Throughout my years of elected public service as both a trial court judge and as Secretary of State I had observed that the state's population was steadily changing. There were greater numbers of immigrants in Ohio from around the globe.

I had to remind myself that Puerto Rican Americans are just that, Americans. They are not immigrants. When they are educated in Puerto Rico, they are educated in Spanish in what are called "American flag" schools. The American flag flies atop schools where the primary language spoken is Spanish. It's not that the children don't learn English, because they do, but it is not their primary language. Many native Spanish speakers from Puerto Rico will tell you that when they move to the mainland, even having learned English, their accents are made fun of or the way they learned it in Puerto Rico is not the way it is spoken on the mainland. An individual's level of adjustment varies with his or her ability to adapt. Anyone who spends time in a foreign country knows that the ability to adapt and thrive in that non-native environment depends on many factors, internal and external.

Talking with children of Somali immigrants as they arrived home from school on Columbus public school buses; they were excited about the visit and the bus, I pinned all the campaign badges I could find on the little girls' hijabs.

The Justice Department had been wise in proceeding under Article 4(e) of the Voting Rights Act, which specifically addresses Americans whose native language is not English (this occurs with some Alaskans and others, beyond Puerto Ricans). Using this section helps ease the acceptance of using bilingual or even multi-lingual ballots and helps more than just the Spanish-speaking Americans who were born in the U.S. Bilingual ballots would be a major milestone for Ohio, and I wanted to help achieve it in a peaceable manner to strengthen tolerance for diversity in Ohio. I see diversity as strength.

I remembered the faces of those whom I had seen at the Cincinnati rally. I also remembered my experiences with the Somali community in Columbus. I had been invited into the home of one of their elders. I was told I was the first elected official to enter the home of a native Somali in their central Ohio community. It was an honor to be invited into the elder's home. Several young people, whom I believed to be his grandchildren led me into a first floor room where he was bedridden. He greeted me warmly, unable to leave the bed.

There were few words spoken between us, except when we looked into each other's eyes. I sensed his blessing, and I believe he sensed my respect for him. His young adult grandchildren were college students. Bright and smiling, they spoke perfect English. These young people talked with me about their college studies and their future. They respectfully and cheerfully bridged the old world and the new. They were impressive. All I did that day was to "show up" and show kindness. It was returned tenfold. This special meeting meant a great deal to all of us.

I remembered the myriad faces of newly naturalized citizens I had addressed as Ohio's Secretary of State in the federal courtroom of Judge Algenon Marbley and at Veterans Memorial Hall with federal Judges Ed Sargus and Gregory Frost. Yes, I would help achieve bilingual ballots in Cuyahoga County.

When negotiations began, Justice Department attorneys from Washington, DC flew to Cleveland. They joined U.S. attorneys from Steve Dettelbach's office around a very large group of tables situated in a rectangle with space in the middle. Jane Platten, the board's director, and Pat McDonald, the board's deputy director, attended each negotiation session, along with one Republican and one Democratic board of elections member. Sandy McNair was there for the Democrats each time. Former judge Jeff Hastings and county Republican chair Rob Frost traded off in attending the negotiations. Two of my office's attorneys, Brian Shinn, by this time General Counsel, and Josh Kimsey, Elections Counsel, and I attended each negotiation session.

During those sessions of which there were at least three, there were so many lawyers around the table that, even as a former judge, I sometimes became exasperated and even bored as the discussions droned on. A delicate consensus began to be reached on some initial points. Much depended on Jane Platten. If Jane said she could do what needed to be done, it could be done. Even before an agreement was reached, she voluntarily began a phase-in of bilingual ballots and began training and using bilingual poll workers in a limited number of precincts for the September 7, 2010 primary election of officers under the county's new charter form of government. This new form of county government had been adopted at the May 4 primary election after the FBI launched a massive investigation into corruption of local officials and related individuals in Cuyahoga County. The ballots and Spanish-speaking poll workers would be utilized in areas targeted to be where they were most needed. For the 2010 general election there would be a wider, targeted implementation, which would continue to full, county-wide implementation in 2011 and beyond. I agreed to use federal dollars I had for the extra expense in implementing the consent decree, and eventually Cuyahoga County would take over that expense, once it could be budgeted.

Because Cuyahoga County is primarily a Democratic County, the resistance on the Democratic side, which came primarily from board member Sandy McNair, was based on not wanting to be forced by a court order to provide what it would have gladly done had it been informed of the extent of the problem. Sandy was disappointed that the Board was not first approached and requested to make changes rather than threatened with litigation. Sandy would have been the last person to accept the board being characterized as having failed in its duties to treat everyone equally. The Republicans were opposed, with not a lot of specified reasons, but seemingly generally to the cost. A board member like Sandy could not be guaranteed to always be a member of the board of elections, so a consent decree assured continuity no matter who served on the board.

What I had learned from nearly four years as Secretary of State in some of the most contentious circumstances is that proactive rather than reactive communication actually aids the effective change and implementation of public policy. Sometimes a policy is never changed or implemented if it is not well communicated. Often, and in many political situations, when the first storm of discontent blows, the best course is abandoned because of the political consequences. This is why having political experience provides strength, even in a situation calling for the best mindset for public service. Anticipating the political blowback and being proactive with communication helps foster real and significant change.

The first news report of the talks was met with a stinging column in the Cleveland Plain Dealer published on August 12, 2010, "The Election Repairmen Are Back." The columnist charged an overreach by the Department of Justice and used the Spanish language in a mocking and derogatory manner. I responded with a letter to the editor that was published on a Sunday, three days later. I knew there was serious work to do on the communications front to make the consent decree happen.

During a weekend before the negotiations, Rick and I were at Lake Chautauqua with our friends, State Rep. Lorraine Fende and Willowick Municipal Judge Larry Allen. Steve Dettelbach called me on my cell phone to talk about upcoming issues related to the planned negotiation. I sat on a brightly colored blue wooden rocker on Lorraine and Larry's cottage porch, squinting at the gentle lake in front of me. An idea came to mind as Steve and I talked. I was back in campaign mode without even thinking.

"Hey, Steve," I said. "How about if my office creates a video about what it would be like to try to vote when you don't know the language? What if we talked about the experiences of Puerto

Rican Americans and what it's like to come to the mainland and try to vote, experiencing a language barrier—the human side of things? My office will create it and disseminate it. Would you have a problem if I do something like that?" I asked. What choice did he really have? The Secretary of State was asking if it was okay to make a video about the lives of people the Justice Department was trying to help, which I could have done anyway.

Steve didn't object. I knew it wasn't really registering with him, because he was focused on the legal side of the equation. I also knew that he trusted me to know what I was doing. When I arrived home Sunday night, I unpacked and stayed home the next morning. If we were going to get a video completed in a reasonably short period of time, it would take my making the actual phone calls to rally the troops we needed in Cleveland.

Grateful for the contact from the Senate campaign, I called José Feliciano and left him a message. Next I tried Miriam Lugo. We connected. She loved the idea and began to mobilize people in the Puerto Rican community in Cleveland. Miriam managed to reach José on his cell phone, who called me back immediately. She connected me with Lydia Caballero, Cesar Castro and several other Latina activists. I wanted to bring Christa, who was now our official office videographer, to Cleveland to shoot a video on the human benefits that would be realized with bilingual ballots. I wanted to educate the greater Cuyahoga County community about what it was like to come to Cleveland and the surrounding suburbs from Puerto Rico and try to assimilate, to manage the language, to shop in a grocery store, to go to school, to read a ballot. I enlisted David Dettman's and Christopher Nance's help. Chris was now director of our Cleveland office that provided business services filings we offered in Columbus, but to the northern Ohio business community onsite at our Cleveland office. In one day, we set up interviews of people in the Puerto Rican community in Cleveland who could talk to us about what it would mean to have bilingual ballots in Cleveland and Cuyahoga County.

Christa, David Dettman, Chris Nance and Emily Puffenberger and I met in Cleveland and began the quest of interviewing as many Puerto Rican Americans in the Cleveland area as we could muster with Miriam's, Lydia's and José's help in twenty-four hours. We went to a Puerto Rican club, closed during the day and interviewed Lydia and a Spanish-speaking woman, Maria Carabarro. Christa traveled to the offices of the Cleveland City Schools and interviewed Natividad Pagan, the Cleveland City Schools' Multilingual/Multi-Cultural Education Executive Director. Christa interviewed José, himself. Chris Nance told me before I saw the video how effective José had been. José talked about his mother's voting experiences, how José's father had to help her vote as long as he was alive and how it was one of her greatest wishes that her children learn English. We interviewed Caesar Castro, a local grocer, who, like Lydia, talked of his experiences of coming to the mainland and the transition from life in Puerto Rico to Cleveland.

Each spoke about how bilingual ballots would help ease the transition for many in the Puerto Rican community in Cleveland, the tenth largest Puerto Rican community in the U.S. They spoke of how many older people would now vote and how it would be easier for many to participate with confidence. Each individual we interviewed was able to add dimension to the experience of a non-English speaker in an English language world. Speakers were able to articulate how, when they tried to speak English, they were often ridiculed. Some were even placed in special education classes because of their language barriers. The human side of things is what I wanted for people to see, understand and share.

Christa at first assembled a video that was very much like a news report. I reviewed it and implored her to make this a persuasive piece. A graduate of broadcast journalism at Otterbein University, she had a difficult time envisioning a video that was anything different than a cut-and-dried, down-the-middle news report. And, having grown up in Marion, Ohio, bilingual cultural issues were "foreign" to her.

"You're asking me to be persuasive?" she said, incredulously.

"Yes," I said, "I *need* for it to be persuasive. It's okay. We're allowed to do that," I said. She was clearly conflicted. David talked with her separately, assuring her that this was necessary and perfectly acceptable.

I told her that bilingual ballots will happen in Cleveland either by a consent decree, or the Justice Department will sue in protracted litigation to get a court order for them, and that the Justice Department, in the end, would win. If the latter happened, the psyche of the greater community would suffer. Cuyahoga County had been through enough when it came to elections.

"I don't want to divide the community," I said, "So we must persuade."

Finally, I sat with her and went frame-by-frame through the digital videos until we had the shots and takes that would work. She augmented it with her usual research, captions, still shots and music, and we had a video that we were able to upload to the office's YouTube account by the following Monday. We had accomplished this in one week. The day we had gone to Cleveland for the shoot, I visited with Joe Frolik, an editor of the Plain Dealer to proactively discuss with him what was about to happen. I mentioned casually that my office would be releasing a video about the matter.

The following week, we released the video to not only the news media but to the several hundred thousand email subscribers from my Senate campaign. I posted on Daily Kos. Other media outlets covered it. The first editorial from the Cleveland Plain Dealer was cautious. Jane Platten had helped that to happen, as she is well-respected by the Plain Dealer for the yeo-woman's work she has done in transforming the board's operations. Subsequent editorials were well-informed and accepting of the need for the ballots. The proactive approach, using a human perspective worked. And it ensured dignity for those who would benefit from the new measures to implement federal law in Cuyahoga County.

Negotiations had proceeded in several sessions. The board of elections members, especially Sandy McNair, worked hard on the language of the consent decree. When we neared the end of negotiations, it was clear that the Republicans on the board would not vote for the consent decree. Brian Shinn, then Chief Elections Counsel was with me when this became clear during the negotiations. I asked Brian if I could carry out in person my statutory duty to break the board's anticipated tie vote. Tie votes were usually communicated by letter after a thorough review of the record. I had been present for all of the negotiations and knew what would be contained in any record of proceedings. My attorneys had been there as well. Brian researched the law and found nothing to prohibit my voting "live." Doing this would facilitate quick adoption in time for the September primary when the ballots would be used for the first time. We communicated this to the Justice Department attorneys.

The board scheduled its next meeting on September 1, 2010. I appeared at the hearing and sat at the round table with the board. Only once before had I done this—when I swore in all four of them. When the tie vote occurred as expected, television cameras were there. I stated my reasons for my vote in siding with the Democrats. I broke the tie in favor of accepting and signing the consent decree for bilingual ballots. I know it killed Sandy to see the board in the position of having to be ordered to do something his passion for equality would have insisted on had he known. He did not stand before the media in the impromptu press conference with Steve Dettelbach after the meeting, and I understood.

Lydia Caballero and Caesar Castro were at the board meeting. They stood with us afterward before the media, and they were proud. So was I. We had achieved something major for Ohio without name-calling, ugliness, protests or strife. People would benefit, and so would the greater community. Later, after the consent decree had been implemented and bilingual ballots and Spanish-speaking poll workers used for the first time under the decree, I was in Cleveland. The time was close to the general election, and we were training community organizers and social service agency staff about the nuances of voter registration and absentee voting. During the training, I met a poll worker from a precinct where bilingual ballots and bilingual poll workers had been used for the first time. She volunteered to me that she had noticed how it had helped voters in the precinct where she worked. It was good news to hear.

After the consent decree had been entered, I somewhat perversely mentioned while speaking at a regional meeting of boards of elections in southern Ohio, that Cuyahoga County now issued ballots in two languages. The stunned and confused looks on some of the faces demonstrated the vast cultural differences among the many regions of Ohio. This diversity is also why Ohio remains a battleground, bellwether state.

Weeks after the consent decree was reached, signed and filed with the northern district federal court without any litigation beyond the filing, I received a call on my cell phone.

"Secretary Brunner, this is Tom Perez, Assistant Attorney General for the Civil Rights Division of the Department of Justice," he said.

"Well, hello, Tom," I said. (I actually handled the salutation in this call better than I did in the one from Caroline Kennedy that I *knew* would be happening.) He personally thanked me for our work on the consent decree in Cuyahoga County. He said they realized I was leaving office and were glad they could get it done while I was still there. I was, too. We talked a bit more and said our good byes.

Being free of a reelection campaign and finished with the Senate campaign, I had been able to take what I had learned from my experiences as a U.S. Senate candidate and use it for good. I considered myself very fortunate.

The Pew Research Center's Pew Hispanic Center estimated in 2008 that if current trends continue, by 2050, Caucasians would not be the majority race in the United States. It is estimated that the Hispanic population will rise as a percentage of U.S. population from 14% in 2005 to 29% in 2050. Only 47% of the population is projected to be Caucasian. It is often difficult for people to understand that, when racially diverse immigrants stay in the U.S., (and I believe we benefit when they do and when they raise and educate their children here,) the numbers of that diverse population will increase as their children have children. Even if no more immigrants were permitted to enter the country, their numbers in racial and national origin diversity will continue grow as their families grow. That is why we must strive to live with tolerance with one other. It is our country, together.

As of 2010, in California, at least 47% of U.S. citizen children had at least one immigrant parent. Even in Ohio, in the heart of the Midwest, that number is at 6%. In Illinois it is 24%. Utah actually is at a higher percentage than Ohio, at 13%. Massachusetts is at 23%. Overall, in the U.S., it is 21%. Immigration law reform is an issue we must deal with. We must recognize human dignity and the sanctity of families, and we must do so with pragmatism and compassion. If we can do this, and I believe we can, we will strengthen the economic and social fabric of our lives as Americans. ≈

Chapter 29

Power and Money

One of the issues about which I was most passionate in the Senate campaign was the issue of financial reform. For me, it was not just about banking, foreclosures, mortgaged-backed securities and the securitization of just about anything that can be securitized. It included the ubiquitous role of financial institutions in supplying campaign cash to lawmakers. It also included the seeming revolving doors between financial institution officers and regulators that set up conditions for the disastrous chain of events culminating in the banking meltdown of September 2008. Americans still suffer from its effects today at every level of society.

Entire books have been and will continue to be written about what happened. It will take years for non-specialized or non-law school or non-economist-trained Americans to understand just what happened to them, and some never will. Election outcomes are likely to fluctuate wildly as long as markets and financial conditions lack stability. Lending to stimulate economic growth will be stalled as the forces of status quo that continue the quest for illusory and unbridled personal gain clash with measures to prevent overall, further financial decline.
In Europe, author Michael Lewis' *Boomerang*[5] effect threatens to play out under the nervous but watchful eyes of the rest of the world. The leaders of the original countries of the EU that came

---

[5] Lewis, Michael. *BOOMERANG Travels in the New Third World*. New York: W. W. Norton & Company. 2011.

526

together as early as 1952,[6] continue to exhort other countries of the now 27-member union to take austerity and growth measures for sufficient economic EU stability, knowing that nearly any EU demise will "boomerang" back to the U.S., and this would harm the economic stability of the world.

If everyday Americans who own homes began to trace the ownership of their mortgages and notes, they would be shocked to see how many security interests in their homes have been sold and traded. It's likely by now that many, if not most, of the original notes they signed, promising to pay their loans (which should be returned to them marked "paid" when they do pay them in full), cannot and will not ever be located. In 2005, when, as a judge, I handled a variety of general division cases, motions in foreclosure cases were routinely filed seeking relief from longstanding requirements like producing a note. I remember thinking at the time, "How do you lose a note?" Today we know. But more importantly, how do you successfully foreclose on property without that note?

Everyday Americans are likely aware of how many mortgage servicers have handled their loans, because they have to know to whom to write the check. But many are writing checks well above what any real amortized payment would be if it actually corresponded to the now reduced value of their homes. In what has been called utter folly and madness, short-term financial schemes at all levels among individuals, banks, governments and nations have promulgated economic and social malaise for Americans and others in the world today. In the United States, many Americans qualified for credit to the point that they now find themselves paying out high sums they barely or cannot afford. Before the crash many were told that they qualified for

---

[6] These countries are Belgium, France, Germany, Italy, Luxembourg and the Netherlands.

far higher loans than they could comfortably sustain, becoming "house poor" for property that never should have been valued that high in the first instance. Yet, mortgage-backed securities needed these loans, some even included in portfolios when they were ineligible to be traded.

When the mortgages on our homes[7] become the stuff of asset-backed securities,[8] each trade of those securities should result in a local government recording of who now holds our mortgages and notes, that is, which has the security interest. Because real estate is finite, longstanding law is that the public deserves notice of who owns property and who claims an interest in it. The financial industry has failed the public, and government has aided and abetted in this failure.

Information about ownership, property interests and liens, which are supposed to be found in the local recorder's office of the county where the real estate is located, is lacking. Recouping the recording fees for these lost transactions, alone, would make a serious dent in local government budget deficits.

Then there is blight. As Secretary of State, I could never get traction from the Governor or any Attorney General (of which there were three AGs in the four years I served) to sue servicers that took ownership of foreclosed properties but let them sit idle to the point that they became a public nuisances. I wanted to bring a civil lawsuit under a theory that these servicers were doing business in Ohio but were not registered with my office or

---

[7] Mortgages are most simply defined as instruments by which we pledge our homes in exchange for loans based on signed notes containing our promise to pay for what it costs to buy our homes.

[8] This type of securitization has been defined as, "The process of taking many individual assets and combining them into a group, or pool, so that investors may buy interests in the pool rather than in the individual assets." See, http://financial-dictionary.thefreedictionary.com/Asset+securitization.

paying taxes in Ohio as they should have been. No other office holder wanted to bring the action, including none of the three Attorneys General with whom I served.

Sadly, for consumers, American and world financial institutions cannot and have not stopped "Jonesing" on what has become deeply systemic. The full effects of the Dodd-Frank reform bill remain to be seen. Regulators will yield much power in the rule-making process all the while being heavily lobbied by financial institutions to ease up and not cause major organizational changes for them. The now accepted financial models that sent us to our ruin in the first place go on and morph into even riskier, "synthetic" schemes that continue to cause loss at many levels. This fairly recent mechanism of modern finance has been integrally intertwined with what financial institutions in other countries are doing (and have been doing) in what is now a global market.[9]

---

[9] By way of example, according to a 1999 seminar description for Malaysian bankers, ". . . asset securitization techniques, while complex, has won a secure place in corporate financing and investment portfolios because it can, paradoxically, offer originators a cheaper source of funding and investors a superior return. Not only does securitization transform illiquid assets into tradable securities, but it also manages to transform risk by means of the separation of good financial assets from a company or financial institution with little loss of revenue. The assets, once separated from the originator, are employed as backing for high-quality securities designed to appeal to investors.

This seminar asks why and when corporations and financial institutions should issue asset-backed securities, and which kind of such instruments make sense to investors.

The scheme, however, involves " . . . legal, accounting, tax and regulatory principles" that are necessary to make the investments safe, reliable and trustworthy.

No serious prosecutions have yet been undertaken for the fraud that "underwrote" many of these schemes, whether it was in the banking, legal or accounting worlds. Ironically, while the American people for the most part point to Wall Street greed, Wall Street in turn points to American consumers' greed, insolence and laziness. Corrupt practices in the scheme of securitizing assets like mortgage loans are so widespread that it appears that more people could be prosecuted for crimes associated with the practices than could attend an Occupy Wall Street demonstration.

Even in the absence of foreclosure, real security is elusive when a house is "under water" with more owed on the mortgage than the house is worth. Homeowners are told that they are ineligible for government relief programs until they have missed payments on their mortgages. To do that, they face wrecking their credit records and/or swift foreclosure actions that could leave them homeless and vulnerable. In ailing neighborhoods of "drowned" and "under water" homes, crime frequently increases. How many Americans suffer anxiety about the safety of their children or their parents but are unable to change their circumstances to rightfully claim some peace of mind? How do we hold accountable those whose greed has harmed them?

The recent Dodd-Frank Wall Street Reform and Consumer Protection Act provides a hope of some safeguards for the future. Still, many of the same financial institutions that desperately whimpered with fear and exhaustion in 2008 (taking advantage of what amounted to corporate welfare at taxpayer expense), have roared back, anxious to stop the Act's fair implementation. Worse, the political influence of their

---

http://giddy.org/abs-ibbm.htm

campaign contributions in 2010 put four of them in the top ten corporations that gave politically from 1989 to 2010, with Morgan Stanley ($19.8M), JP Morgan ($20.3M), Citigroup ($27.5M), and Goldman Sachs ($36.7M), alone, comprising 40% of funds given by the top ten corporate political givers during this period.

By the spring of 2010, I was already aware of the fairly recent changes in practices of the financial industry. Now people's mortgages on their homes were (and still are) being used to securitize the sale of securities that were essentially creatures of fiction, shaped and molded by mathematical formulas crunched and recrunched by young mathematicians who sit in front of computer screens day in and day out.

On April 23, 2010, I had sent a campaign email, called, "Watch them." In it I had committed that I would not take any campaign funds from banks, financial institutions, or their principals that had received "bailout" or TARP (Troubled Asset Relief Program) funds. I said:

April 23, 2010

. . . last week, Goldman Sachs, a $10 billion beneficiary of TARP money was accused of securities fraud by the Securities and Exchange Commission for selling a mortgage investment that was secretly intended to fail. That's when I said to myself again, "Watch them." Only this time it wasn't the banks and finance firms. It was the candidates and members of Congress--especially the ones who'd taken money from the firms they were now vowing to regulate.

Please click here to read more.

As you prepare to vote in the May 4th election, watch them. Ask yourself, who asks for and takes money from the banks they vow to regulate? I don't--and I won't.

I kept watching even after I lost the primary election. I believed what had happened to the American people was so terribly wrong, and I still do. Now it's reverberating around the world in various forms as the European Union struggles to maintain the Eurozone and its financial viability with a single currency.

On a regular basis, the National Association of Secretaries of State (NASS) sent updates about federal legislation. Long after losing the 2010 primary election for the U.S. Senate, in the fall of 2010, I received an update from Leslie Reynolds, its executive director about a bill providing for the interstate recognition of notarizations, opposed by NASS:

> From: "Reynolds, Leslie"
> Date: September 30, 2010 5:15:59 PM EDT
> To: Secretaries of State, NASS Members
> Subject: NASS Business Services Alert: Interstate Recognition of Notarizations Act passes Congress and headed to the White House
>
> Good Afternoon:
>
> We just learned that H.R. 3808, Interstate Recognition of Notarizations Act, which passed the House under a suspension of the rules in April 2010, was passed by the Senate on September 27, 2010.
>
> On Monday, September 27, 2010 Senator Casey (PA), on the Senate floor, asked that the Judiciary Committee be discharged from further consideration of H.R. 3808 and Senate move forward with immediate consideration of the bill. Sen. Casey asked for unanimous consent that the bill

pass with no other action or debate. The Senate passed the bill without amendment by unanimous consent. The bill has now been cleared for the White House.

I regret that this was not caught sooner. We have been communicating with Senate Judiciary staff since last spring about this bill. We followed up on a regular basis, most recently during the August recess. We were told every time we checked that the bill was NOT on their radar screen. NASS has a position in opposition to this bill, as does the Uniform Law Commission.

Thank you.

Leslie Reynolds
Executive Director
National Association of Secretaries of State
444 N. Capitol Street, N.W.
Washington, DC 20001
www.nass.org

Less than two weeks after I lost the May 4, 2010 primary election for the U.S. Senate in Ohio, on May 17, 2010, Dustin Zacks of the Ice Legal law firm in Florida had taken the deposition[10] of Beth Cottrell, then an employee of Chase Bank in Columbus, Ohio, ("Cottrell Deposition"). In that deposition she described a practice that had become known as "robosigning." Many of Chase's foreclosure documents were being notarized in Franklin County, Ohio, where Chase Home Finance maintained a significant operation.

---

[10] http://4closurefraud.org/2010/05/27/full-deposition-of-beth-cottrell-chase-home-finance-robo-signer-extraordinaire/

Investopedia[11] defines a "robosigner" as:

> An employee of a mortgage servicing company that signs
> foreclosure documents without reviewing them. Rather than
> actually reviewing the individual details of each case,
> robosigners assume the paperwork to be correct and sign it
> automatically, like robots.

* * *

In the third and fourth quarters of 2010, a robosigning
scandal emerged in the United States involving GMAC
Mortgage and a number of major U.S banks. Banks had to
halt thousands of foreclosures in numerous states when it
became known that the paperwork was illegitimate because
the signers had not actually reviewed it. While some
robosigners were middle managers, others were temporary
workers with virtually no understanding of the work they
were doing.

My brother, Dan, an attorney and expert in electronic discovery,
had been working with other attorneys from around the country
on foreclosure defense issues, one of which involved this
practice known as "robosigning." He had forwarded the
deposition of Beth Cottrell to me, pointing out that there
appeared to be violations of common notary practices and laws
found not just in Ohio, but around the country.

One of my responsibilities as Secretary of State was to issue
licenses to notaries public so that they could serve as impartial
officials of "integrity appointed by state government . . . to serve
the public as an impartial witness in . . . fraud-deterrent acts
relating to the signing of important documents," as described by

---

[11] http://www.investopedia.com/terms/r/robo-signer.asp#axzz21a3toQsF

the National Notary Association. Notaries are to have no interest in the transactions about which documents are being signed. They screen signers who are signing documents such as property deeds, wills and powers of attorney in order to ascertain their true identity, their willingness to sign freely without duress or intimidation and their understanding of the general import of the documents they are signing. Often, notary publics are required to put signers under oath to obtain their declaration under penalty of perjury that the information contained in one or more documents is true and correct. As described by the National Notary Association:

> As official representatives of the state, Notaries Public certify the proper execution of many of the life-changing documents of private citizens — whether those diverse transactions convey real estate, grant powers of attorney, establish a prenuptial agreement, or perform the multitude of other activities that enable our civil society to function.

> In this modern era when business transactions between complete strangers are the norm rather than the exception, Notaries engender a trust that the critical signed documents we rely on are authentic. Such trust enables the sensitive documents of commerce and law to be exchanged between strangers with full confidence in their reliability.[12]

I asked my legal staff to review the deposition of Beth Cottrell. I had already done so and was concerned. My staff confirmed that the deposition highlighted a troubling scenario. At Chase, alone, 18,000 foreclosure-related documents a month were being sworn and notarized by eight people. It was admitted that notaries were filling in substantive, informational numbers on

---

[12]

http://www.nationalnotary.org/resources_for_notaries/what_is_a_notary/index.html

the documents and then notarizing those same documents.
Oaths were not being administered as required by law.
Documents were being signed in bulk and notarized in bulk,
with notarization being made separate from their signing. This
scenario didn't pass legal muster, yet it was being used in a
process to take people's homes from them. It was unimaginable
that consumers would be permitted to undertake equivalent
types of shortcuts regarding any aspect of their loans. Their
creditors should be required to exercise the same care.

On August 11, 2010, while working with Steve Dettlebach, U.S.
District Attorney for the Northern District of Ohio, on the
consent decree for bilingual ballots in Cuyahoga County, I
discussed with him what I had in my possession, asked him if he
was interested in seeing the deposition and hand carried the two
volumes of depositions to the first negotiation held regarding
bilingual ballots in Cleveland.[13] Then I waited.

I knew that digging into this would be for the U.S. Department
of Justice like trying to hold one of the largest dragons in the
world by the tail. Still, Steve had said he wanted me to send it,
and I did.

At a later negotiation session in Cleveland regarding bilingual
ballots, I supplied deposition transcripts about the Mortgage
Electronic Recording System's (MERS') practices that avoided
local recording of real estate property interests and liens and
other practices of MERS in the foreclosure process as detailed in
the deposition. Each letter accompanying the particular
deposition transcripts included a request for investigation and
criminal prosecution.

---

[13] http://www.sos.state.oh.us/SOS/Upload/news/DettelbachLtr8-11-
10.pdf

♯536

The MERS system allowed for the interests in mortgages and notes regarding Americans' homes to be recorded figuratively "in the air" in an artificial entity apparently created for this purpose. MERS was to keep track of who had an interest in which transaction and thereby piece of real estate (of which there were millions when it came to Americans' homes) so that the traded interests in the real property (as contained in these securitized assets) did not have to "hit the ground" for recording in the various states as they were traded at computer speed. Steve expressed interest in the MERS deposition as well, and I personally brought a second envelope with another deposition when I returned to Cleveland for more bilingual ballot negotiation work.

At the same time, Rich Cordray, Ohio's Attorney General, was apparently looking at this "robosigning" practice. The day before I revealed I had made these criminal referrals, on September 30, 2010, he announced he had filed suit on behalf of the state against GMAC/Ally Financial in October. He was asking the court to prevent GMAC Mortgage LLC from completing foreclosure sales in the state based on faulty affidavits. Some news outlets chalked it up to his being in a tight race for reelection. I knew the suit was one that needed to be filed. Rich's lawsuit claimed that GMAC and its employees committed fraud on Ohio consumers and Ohio courts by signing and filing at least hundreds and potentially thousands of false affidavits in foreclosure cases. Like me, he used depositions from Florida and Maine of Ally's employee who had executed the affidavits without personal knowledge or verifying the content.

Not having heard from Steve Dettlebach by the end of September 2010 on what the U.S. Justice Department would be doing, if anything, about the criminal referral I had made, I called Steve to ask if I was permitted to publicly reveal the referral. He called me back and assured me it was fine to speak of the referral.

The next day, my office released the fact of the referral, and I published an op-ed piece in the Huffington Post, saying:

> As Secretary of State of Ohio, I license Ohio's notaries. My state's notary laws, like those of many states, don't give me the tools to address the notary problems found in the changing circumstances in mortgage financing. In Ohio, even though I grant notary commissions, I don't have the power to investigate or prosecute when there is suspected wrongdoing. That's why I asked the Department of Justice to review and investigate.

> The seal, date and signature of a notary public are there to bolster the reliability and integrity of a document, especially one that allows a court to order the taking of someone's home. In the situations I have brought to the DOJ's attention, something is clearly amiss.

The day before, Chase announced it was suspending foreclosures in 27 states across America, including Ohio.[14] Less than two weeks later, on October 13, 2010, Attorney Generals from all 50 states announced[15] that they were establishing a "bi-partisan multistate group" to investigate the foreclosure practices of Chase, other servicers and their foreclosure law firms, including Bank of America. In early October 2010, Bank of America stated that it would halt judicial foreclosures while it reviewed its policies and procedures.

---

[14] http://www.nytimes.com/2010/09/30/business/30mortgage.html
[15] http://www.forbes.com/2010/10/13/foreclosure-investigation-freeze-housing-markets-mortgage.html

On October 18, 2010, Bank of America issued a press release reporting that it had completed its review of judicial foreclosures and while it had identified no problems, it would resubmit 102,000 affidavits in judicial foreclosure cases that had not yet gone to judgment.

I did not see the communiqué from Leslie Reynolds at NASS until a day or two after I had announced our referral to the Justice Department. Considering the epic "underwater" battle that was starting to surface, it raised my suspicion. I sent a copy of the memo to my brother, Dan, who was working on litigation and communicated regularly with others also involved in fighting fraudulent and abusive practices of mortgage lenders and servicers in real estate lending and foreclosure.

The summary of the legislation read:

> H.R.3808
> Title: Interstate Recognition of Notarizations Act of 2009
> Sponsor: Rep Aderholt, Robert B. [AL-4]
> (introduced 10/14/2009)   Cosponsors (3)
> Latest Major Action: 9/30/2010 Presented to President.

> SUMMARY AS OF:
> 4/27/2010--Passed House without amendment.

> Interstate Recognition of Notarizations Act of 2010 -
> Requires each federal and state court to recognize any lawful notarization occurring in or affecting interstate commerce which is made by a notary public licensed or commissioned under the laws of a state other than the state where the court is located.

> Requires such a notarization to: (1) use a seal of office as symbol of the notary public's authority; or (2) have the seal information, in the case of an electronic record, securely attached to, or logically associated with, the electronic record so as to render the record tamper-resistant.

The law would basically have attempted to abrogate any state laws on notarization and recording where they would otherwise control. This essentially meant that no state could prevent a notarized document from being honored for a transaction, even if the notarization did not meet that state's requirements and even if, as with real estate, the only place an interest in real estate could be recorded was in that state. By the time I received word from my brother, who consulted with some of his colleagues about what he and they thought the import of this legislation was, I had had a chance to talk with Rick, whom I and many others consider an expert on business and real estate law and litigation.

I questioned Rick as we shuffled through the first leaves of the fall while walking our dogs on that Saturday morning. "Is there anything such as electronic notarization of legal documents?" I asked. He pondered as we walked, opened the gate to the dog park and said, "I don't think so. The whole purpose of notarization is that you have to personally appear before a notary."

"That's what I thought, too," I said. "Do you think there's a chance some states could be authorizing electronic notarization of documents?" I asked.

"I don't think so," he said, "because of the requirement to personally appear."

But still, something was nagging me. There are those moments in life when you know you could do something or just let it go, like handing a dollar to a beggar on the street. You don't always do it, but there just might be the one time, when it makes more of a difference than you know. This was one of those times.

My brother's information was that this bill was very bad for consumers and that the President should veto it. It concerned me that it made it through the Senate so unusually quickly. Leslie Reynolds' memo was dated September 30, 2010, the day Rich Cordray announced his GMAC lawsuit and the day before I announced the criminal referral of Chase, but my referral had been made August 11, 2010. Enough time had passed that, if the Justice Department had begun to act on it, telephone calls and initial inquiries may have been made.

I knew that the actions two state officials had taken in Ohio had sent reverberations throughout the mortgage foreclosure Internet sites. With Congress out of session, the President could exercise what is known as a "pocket veto," figuratively putting the bill in his pocket and not signing it, and that would effectively veto the legislation. The consensus among the foreclosure defense bar and related consultants seemed to be that banks were ramming this legislation through the Congress without the import of it being discussed and that it would accelerate and even legitimize the "robosigning" process.

By the time I had figured this out, it was Sunday evening. The next day, on Monday, I called Leslie Reynolds at NASS and asked her if she knew whether any states permitted electronic notarization of documents. She referred me to the website of the National Notary Association.

Sure enough, three states permitted electronic notarization: Minnesota, Nevada and Arizona. My mind was racing. I could envision banks moving their foreclosure "robosigning" operations to these states. Other states would, by the provisions of HR 3808, be required by federal law to accept electronically notarized documents as valid. Foreclosures could fly through the courts.

Both Rick and I understood that some state was likely to challenge the validity of this new federal law, because states controlled their own real property. It would be a question involving whether real property that formed the basis or collateral for intellectual property such as derivatives and bonds, traded not just between states but internationally, could actually be a subject of federal interstate commerce. For the courts to decide a thorny questions like that would take time. Meanwhile, foreclosures would fly through the process with the click of a computer key. The bottom line, the bill was bad for consumers.

I talked late in the day on that Monday with my former Senate campaign manager, David Dettman, about sending an email to our still huge email list from the Senate campaign and asking our subscribers to contact the President and ask him to veto the bill. David thought it was a great idea, but he thought that we first needed to find out if the President had already signed the bill.

The next morning I called Leslie Reynolds again and asked her what the bill's status was. I could hear the clicking of the keys on her computer keyboard as she checked her legislative reporting service. "Nope," she said, "he hasn't signed it yet. It's still on his desk."

"Great!," I said, telling her that I thought the bill was a problem. When I arrived at the office, I called Campbell Spencer, who was still working at the White House. I was able to reach her and alert her to the potential problems I saw with the bill. She thanked me for the call and said she would pass it on. I worked on the draft of the email and sent it to David. Then, David sent me a test email to ask people to call or email the White House to tell the President to veto the bill. We adjusted text as we needed to, going back and forth by telephone until we were satisfied with it.

Finally, we agreed it was ready to go. I told him to push the button to send the email. We disconnected from the call. Sitting alone in my state office, I lowered my head, my forehead touching my desk and cried. I knew we were doing something big and something good and that we had to do it. But I was nervous. We were going out on a very long limb.

I then let my brother know that the email had been sent. He had alerted foreclosure websites around the country to be ready and forwarded my email to them. Later that day, from our campaign email analytics alone, we knew that more than 4000 people had gone to the White House website to leave a message urging the President to veto the bill. I knew other people who had called. Thanks to the help of my brother the message went viral.

Two days later I was in Mansfield, Ohio, speaking to several hundred women who worked in corrections from around Ohio. It was a great event. The women were positive and upbeat, and I had real appreciation from my days as a judge for just how tough their jobs could be. As I was leaving the large Amish-style restaurant where the event was held, I walked into the parking lot and talked with Dean Evans, my local field representative for the area. He looked at his smart phone and said, "Jennifer, do you realize that the President just vetoed H.R 3808?"

The sun was shining. The landscape was bright. It was a good day. Dean was proud; I was ecstatic. I could have chosen to do nothing, but something told me this was one of those times when it was just worth a try.

Toward the end of my term, my schedulers received a call from Elizabeth Warren, who was later to become a candidate herself for the U.S. Senate from Massachusetts. She had been the crafter of the concept for the legislation that created the Consumer Financial Protection Bureau, which President Obama had signed into law in July 2010. She asked for a meeting with me. When it occurred, it was just the two of us for forty minutes in my office.

She began the meeting with a statement that she was stopping by to thank me for alerting the President to the need to veto HR 3808. Apparently, my telephone call to Campbell Spencer had made it to someone on Elizabeth Warren's staff, who looked at it, saw what they had missed previously and alerted Elizabeth to the problems with the bill. I had read in blogs that it was Elizabeth Warren who had convinced the President that this bill should not become law. Then she said to me, "One person really can make a difference."

Her next meeting was with Richard Cordray. He now holds the job in the agency that in one person's mind, that of Elizabeth Warren, was a concept that became a reality. One person really can make a difference.

It was later revealed that the bill passed when Pennsylvania Senator Bob Casey, at the request of Majority Leader Harry Reid, asked that the Judiciary Committee be discharged from further consideration of H.R. 3808 with unanimous Senate consent (which he received) on immediate consideration of the bill with no other action or debate. I don't think for a minute Senator Casey had a real understanding of the import of what it was he had been asked to do. Rep. Aderholt, who had introduced the bill and had apparently tried for passage of the measure in other sessions, didn't seem to grasp what the bill would have done under the current circumstances—assist a greedy financial industry that wanted to convert financial instruments not much better than toilet paper to documents good enough to take people's homes from them.

HR 3808 would have sped up the foreclosure process to get rid of the bad loans as quickly as possible. To me it was apparent that the banks and many in the financial industry were working, regardless of the human cost, to get rid of the bad loans as if they were a clog in a toilet—just get rid of it, plunge it, and flush it away to keep the water flowing into the tank and the money flowing freely. I saw no statement from Senator Reid on the bill.

Excessive money in politics at a minimum buys access. At a maximum it buys opportunities to quietly slip what looks to most like innocuous legislation into law, with few questions asked. Can I connect the dots in this legislative scenario with absolute certainty? No, and it's not worth the effort. We stopped what could have been a real setback for thousands of consumers, and that's all that matters. ≈

Chapter 30

Reflections Past and Forward

"Forgiveness is the fragrance that the violet sheds on the heel that has crushed it."

Mark Twain
(American Humorist, Writer and Lecturer. 1835-1910)

Using Mark Twain's analogy, politics could use more forgiveness. It might not smell so bad then, and perhaps more people would aspire to public service as the noble calling it can be. As I sit with Rick in 2012 on a train traveling from Budapest to Vienna, having completed a second stint of democracy work in Serbia for the U.S. government, I have much to reflect on. To put it simply, I have been blessed.

Photo taken by USAID staff in Belgrade, Serbia in February 2012 during my work on National Center for State Courts' "Judicial Reform and Government Accountability" project

Thinking back to the call I received about what a boring job Secretary of State of Ohio was supposed to be, or to the difficulties of running for the U.S. Senate in a contentious primary, I can't help but think that I wouldn't change a thing. I can say unequivocally, the "coolest" thing I have ever done in my life was presiding over the Ohio Electoral College for the election of the nation's first African American president.

Patrick Gallaway and others worked with students at the Columbus College of Art and Design to create certificates that were not only the largest certificates submitted to the joint session of Congress and the National Archives, but also elegant and beautiful. We had six of them prepared and signed. As they lay side-by-side on the table in the Ohio Senate chambers and as each of Ohio's twenty delegates somberly signed their names to

Presiding over the Ohio Electoral College ceremony in the Ohio Senate chambers with Ohio State Highway Patrol color guard; David Farrell and Brian Shinn (L. to R.) standing in front of podium

them, the design of the watermarks of the various symbols of the state could be seen to flow from one certificate to the next. Joan Brown-Campbell, director of the department of religion at Chautauqua Institution in New York and mother of former and first (and only) woman mayor of Cleveland, Jane Campbell, was our keynote speaker. Joan had marched with the Rev. Dr. Martin

Luther King, Jr. for civil and voting rights for African American citizens before his untimely death. He would have been her age had he lived. NBC national network news needed video feed of an electoral college proceeding. It picked Ohio's, as all electoral colleges around the country were meeting as required at noon, on the same day, at the same time.

As the last elector began to sign the documents, I looked to Brian Shinn for the cue to step down from the President's dais and to be the final signer of each certificate, certifying it for history and the future. As I signed each one, I savored the moment. Rick, Kate and nearly all of my top staff were there. The Ohio government channel filmed it. It was done. The major test of the success of my four years in office had culminated on that day, not so much as to who was elected, but that all who had wanted access to the ballot box had it, and this was the result when the people spoke. It mattered to the world.

Much is said about the role of government. Multidimensional problems call for multidimensional solutions. Some believe government should play no role, except to feed tax revenue to support businesses that are supposed to create jobs and that enough jobs and money will come from it to solve society's problems. But what about children, the infirmed or the elderly? What about equality and non-discrimination? Does the free market guarantee that? These values can only be supplied by intention. It takes a government to disturb the unchecked forces of the market to create the incentive and the intention. If government is "us," then it exists to execute such intention in a civilized fashion, a democratic way, representing our mores and our values. Some believe that government's role should be expansive, that is, in its truest sense, "liberal," (but not always "progressive"). I believe government growth is best checked according to its equitable and proportional effect on our collective pocketbooks and in the privacy of our bedrooms.

"The Courage Express," now repurposed for a community initiative of WBNS 10TV in Columbus, registering college voters in 2010 on the campus of Columbus State Community College

The reality is that whether it's government, business, education, charitable organizations, friends or family, recognizing that "we are all in this together" is a key element to moving the fulcrum to a point that interests are balanced and democracy works. When we strengthen the rights and opportunities available to each individual, we honor a core principle of any democracy where one person, one vote, is the creed. When any and all of these organizations work together, we better address the ever-changing nature of the relationships between them and in turn the needs of human advancement. It is not to say that a simple formula, never to be pondered again, will suffice.

The call is that the institutions of society become more fully humanistic in their approaches. Money or greed has been all too often excused as being part and parcel with the "free market." In this century, that mutated concept is failing us badly. Faith in the better facets of the human condition helps to relinquish the fear of "have not" so that more can "have." It's like the Christian parable of the miracle of the bread and fish to feed the masses. According to one interpretation of that miracle, the people of that time did not leave their homes for the day without taking sufficient food and provisions with them. Jesus attracted a crowd wherever he went, so many impromptu onlookers stayed and listened to his message. As he preached, it was Jesus' message that so moved those in the crowd that they shared among each other to make sure each had enough.

Each individual at one point or another is more prepared at some times than at others to deal with life's hardships and challenges. When we're not, we need the support of others. No one is static. Situations change. Hard work, as much as I preach and support it, is not and cannot be the sole basis upon which to realize security and comfort. Our work, like the human condition, is and must include interaction with others. It must remain open and flexible to account for change. Our ability to adapt to change is, in fact, a major wonder of human resiliency.

If we dedicate ourselves to individual and collective betterment, we will gasp upon discovering the unmatched progress that occurs when empowered humans work together for a common purpose in service to one another. The result is, again, truly greater than the sum of its parts.

To put it in words more oriented toward a Horatio Alger point of view, when we work together to ensure opportunities that offer a "hand up" more than a "hand out," the dignity of each individual is strengthened. A world filled with more self-actualized people is more likely to flourish, if, of course, you believe in the innate goodness of the human condition. This "common ground" upon which all can stand allows us to step together, supporting one another into the journey, taking each individual at the point where they are while helping them to see where they can be.

I have been asked whether or not I'll run for office again. Old school politicos would say I've irreparably blown my chances by writing and publishing this book. If what they said mattered to me, you would not be reading these words. My life is good. I returned to the law firm I started in 1988. In that milieu I have the freedom and flexibility to not only enjoy being an attorney again, but also to create art, write, continue my work on protecting voting rights, walk my dogs, ride a scooter named "Libby" with Rick, take my nephews to soccer games, see our young granddaughter, spend more time with my adult children and work overseas to help other democracies grow and flourish in the global effort to alleviate human suffering.

In a democracy, the emphasis is on the institution—that it be kept strong enough to pass wholesale from one group of people to another in a peaceable manner. I like to think I've helped strengthen that institution, and no matter where I am or what I do, I will continue to fight for that. I'm grateful for the experiences I've had, and I don't want to be the only one to have them. I'm sure I won't be. I have been blessed to be in the place and time I was, to be able work with so many amazing people, each of whom answered their call that brought us together to do our collective parts.

Alexander Claud Cockburn, an Irish American writer, believed strongly in the power of the written word to motivate people and in acting now to change our society. John Nichols, writing for *The Nation,* said this of his passing on July 21, 2012:

Alex chose as the title and the underlying theme of his finest collection of essays, *The Golden Age Is In Us* (Verso), a line from the anthropologist Claude Levi-Strauss. In Tristes Tropiques Levi-Strauss wrote:

> If men have always been concerned with only one task—how to create a society fit to live in—the forces which inspired our distant ancestors are also present in us. Nothing is settled; everything can still be altered. What was done but turned out wrong, can be done again. The Golden Age, which blind superstition had placed behind [or ahead of] us, is in us.

Alex taught me, he taught us all, that those were not blandly optimistic words. They are demanding. They suggest that we have fewer excuses than we thought, that this is the place, that now is the time and that there is truth in the maxim that says we are the people we've been waiting for.

If others are inspired to step up by the words they have read here, then I, and they, have achieved something, and this, like public service, is its own reward. ✿

BIOGRAPHY
OF AUTHOR

Jennifer Brunner is an attorney, author, commentator, government affairs strategist and crisis specialist who counsels clients on effectively making their case before government and in the public forum. She is the founding partner of the Columbus, Ohio USA law firm of Brunner Quinn,

Jennifer Brunner

since 1988. She served in elective office as Ohio's first woman Secretary of State from 2007-2011 and as a state trial court judge from 2000-2005. Since leaving office she has consulted as an expert internationally on political finance and public outreach and provided political commentary for local to international media outlets.

Brunner's work while in office in improving Ohio's elections received national recognition, including the nation's most prestigious award for elected public servants, the bipartisan John F. Kennedy Profile in Courage Award, for what Caroline Kennedy called, "her dauntless commitment to the enfranchisement of every Ohio voter." Before serving as Ohio's 52nd Secretary of State, Jennifer Brunner was elected twice judge of the Franklin County Common Pleas Court where she received state, national and international recognition for her work in starting the county's first adult felony drug court with a specific focus on poverty. In 2010, Brunner ran for the U.S. Senate from Ohio.

Since leaving public office Brunner formed and chaired an Ohio voting rights coalition, Fair Elections Ohio, responsible for protecting early voting in the 2012 Presidential election through a statewide election referendum. Brunner is the author of *Cupcakes and Courage,* a book about her state and national political experiences advocating individual political empowerment. She is a mother of three adult children and a grandmother. She and her husband, Rick, also an attorney, have been married since 1978.